Yuto Tsukuda

It's been one whole year since the serialization of *Food Wars!* began, and boy was that year really busy and fulfilling. They say busy times are the best of times, and they'd be right. I'd love to stay busy for the rest of my life.

Shun Saeki

Look, it's a "Western Lowland Gorilla!" (*in Erina's voice*) I saw it at the Ueno Zoo. Apparently, there are Eastern Lowland Gorillas too.

D0925683

About the authors

Yuto Tsukuda won the 34th Jump Juniketsu Newcomers' Manga Award for his one-shot story *Kiba ni Naru*. He made his *Weekly Shonen Jump* debut in 2010 with the series *Shonen Shikku*. His follow-up series, *Food Wars!: Shokugeki no Soma*, is his first English-language release.

Shun Saeki made his *Jump NEXT!* debut in 2011 with the one-shot story *Kimi to Watashi no Renai Soudan*. *Food Wars!: Shokugeki no Soma* is his first *Shonen Jump* series.

Food Wars!
SHOKUGEKI NO SOMA

Volume 6
Shonen Jump Manga Edition
Story by Yuto Tsukuda, Art by Shun Saeki
Contributor Yuki Morisaki

Translation: Adrienne Beck
Touch-Up Art & Lettering: NRP Studios
Design: Izumi Evers
Editor: Jennifer LeBlanc

Printed in Italy

Published by VIZ Media, LLC
P.O. Box 77010
San Francisco, CA 94107

10 9 8 7 6 5
First printing, June 2015
Fifth printing, April 2022

ratings.viz.com RATED T+ OLDER TEEN

PARENTAL ADVISORY
FOOD WARS! is rated T+ for Older Teen and is recommended for ages 16 and up. This volume contains sexual situations/humor.

VIZ MEDIA
viz.com

SHONEN JUMP

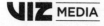

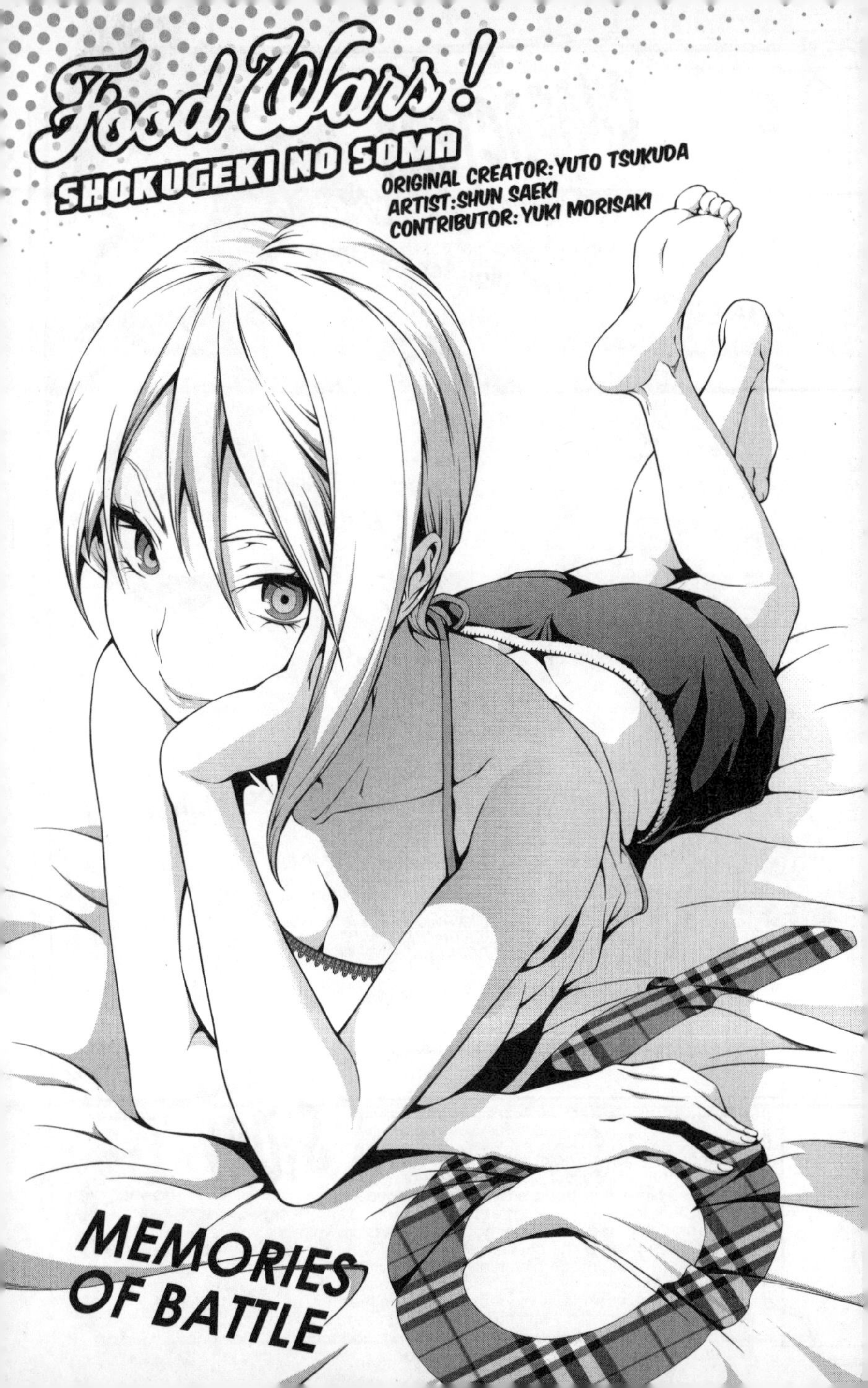
Food Wars!
SHOKUGEKI NO SOMA
ORIGINAL CREATOR: YUTO TSUKUDA
ARTIST: SHUN SAEKI
CONTRIBUTOR: YUKI MORISAKI
MEMORIES OF BATTLE

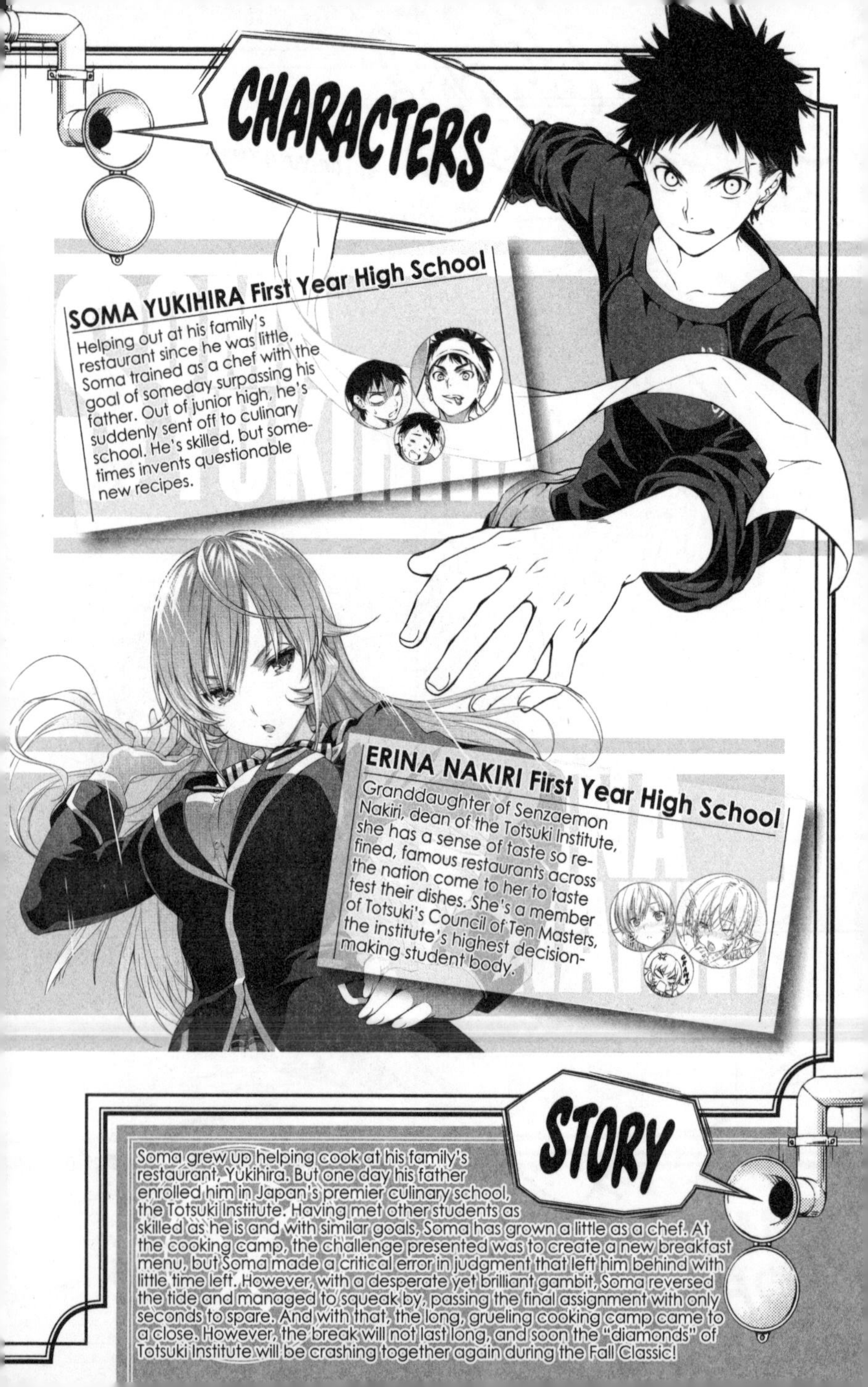
CHARACTERS
SOMA YUKIHIRA First Year High School
Helping out at his family's restaurant since he was little, Soma trained as a chef with the goal of someday surpassing his father. Out of junior high, he's suddenly sent off to culinary school. He's skilled, but sometimes invents questionable new recipes.
ERINA NAKIRI First Year High School
Granddaughter of Senzaemon Nakiri, dean of the Totsuki Institute, she has a sense of taste so refined, famous restaurants across the nation come to her to taste test their dishes. She's a member of Totsuki's Council of Ten Masters, the institute's highest decision-making student body.

STORY

Soma grew up helping cook at his family's restaurant, Yukihira. But one day his father enrolled him in Japan's premier culinary school, the Totsuki Institute. Having met other students as skilled as he is and with similar goals, Soma has grown a little as a chef. At the cooking camp, the challenge presented was to create a new breakfast menu, but Soma made a critical error in judgment that left him behind with little time left. However, with a desperate yet brilliant gambit, Soma reversed the tide and managed to squeak by, passing the final assignment with only seconds to spare. And with that, the long, grueling cooking camp came to a close. However, the break will not last long, and soon the "diamonds" of Totsuki Institute will be crashing together again during the Fall Classic!

Shokugeki no SOMA

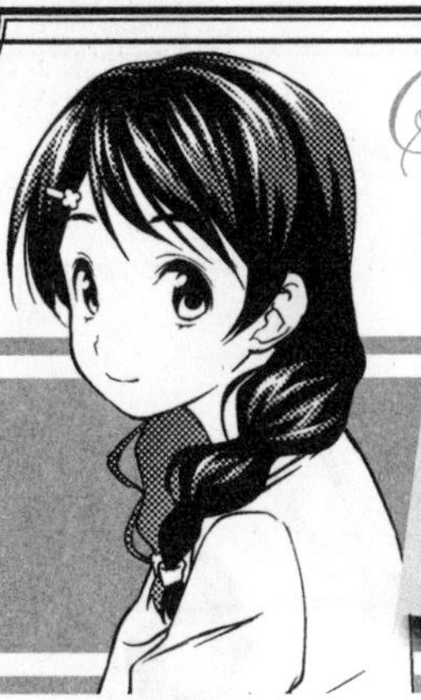

MEGUMI TADOKORO First Year High School

Coming to the big city from the countryside, Megumi made it into the Totsuki Institute at the very bottom of the rankings. Partnered with Soma in their first class, the two became friends. However, he has a tendency to inadvertently yank her around from time to time.

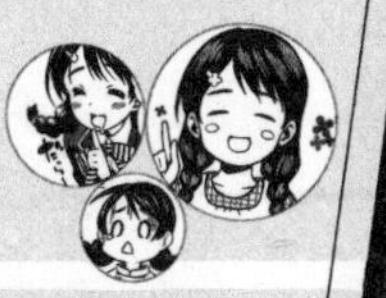

SHUN IBUSAKI
First Year High School

A resident of Polaris Dormitory, he doesn't talk much. With a talent for smoking foods, his dishes are first class.

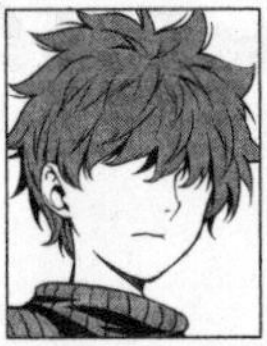

YUKI YOSHINO
First Year High School

A resident of Polaris Dormitory, she raises game animals on campus. Bright and cheerful, she is the energetic one of the Polaris bunch.

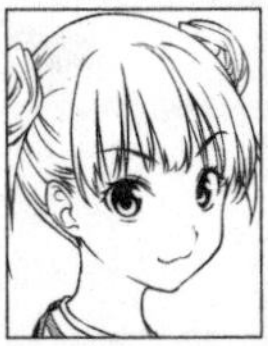

RYOKO SAKAKI
First Year High School

A resident of Polaris Dormitory, she is a kindhearted big-sister figure to the other residents. She specializes in malted and fermented dishes.

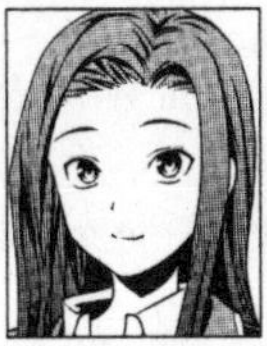

TAKUMI ALDINI
First Year High School

Working at his family's trattoria in Italy from a young age, he transferred into the Totsuki Institute in junior high. Isami is his younger twin brother.

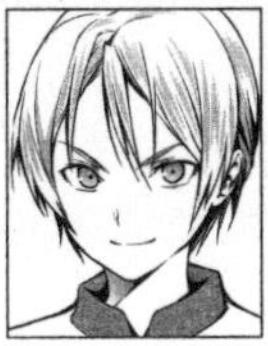

IKUMI MITO
First Year High School

Specializing in meat dishes, she is defeated by Soma in a shokugeki battle and forced to join the Donburi Bowl Society. Her nickname is "Nikumi." (Which she hates.)

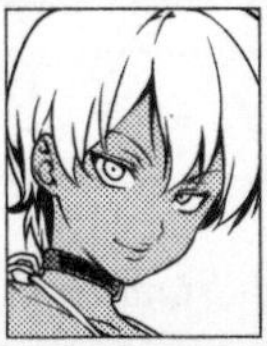

ALICE NAKIRI
First Year High School

Erina's cousin, she has spent much of her life overseas with her parents learning cooking from the scientific perspective through molecular gastronomy.

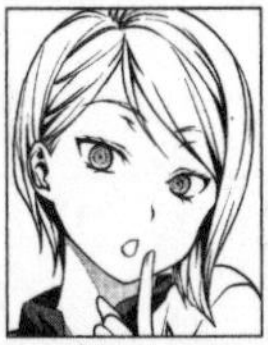

6

Table of Contents

40. Homecoming 7

41. The Man Called "Shura" 27

42. A Wake-Up Kiss 47

43. The Chef Who Wandered the World 67

44. Unexpected Straight Punch 87

45. The Accompanist to Fragrance and Spice... 107

46. Crouching Dragon Ascends 127

47. Memories of Battle 147

48. The Unknown Knowns 167

Side Story—Miss Nikumi's Midsummer Fun 188

40 HOMECOMING

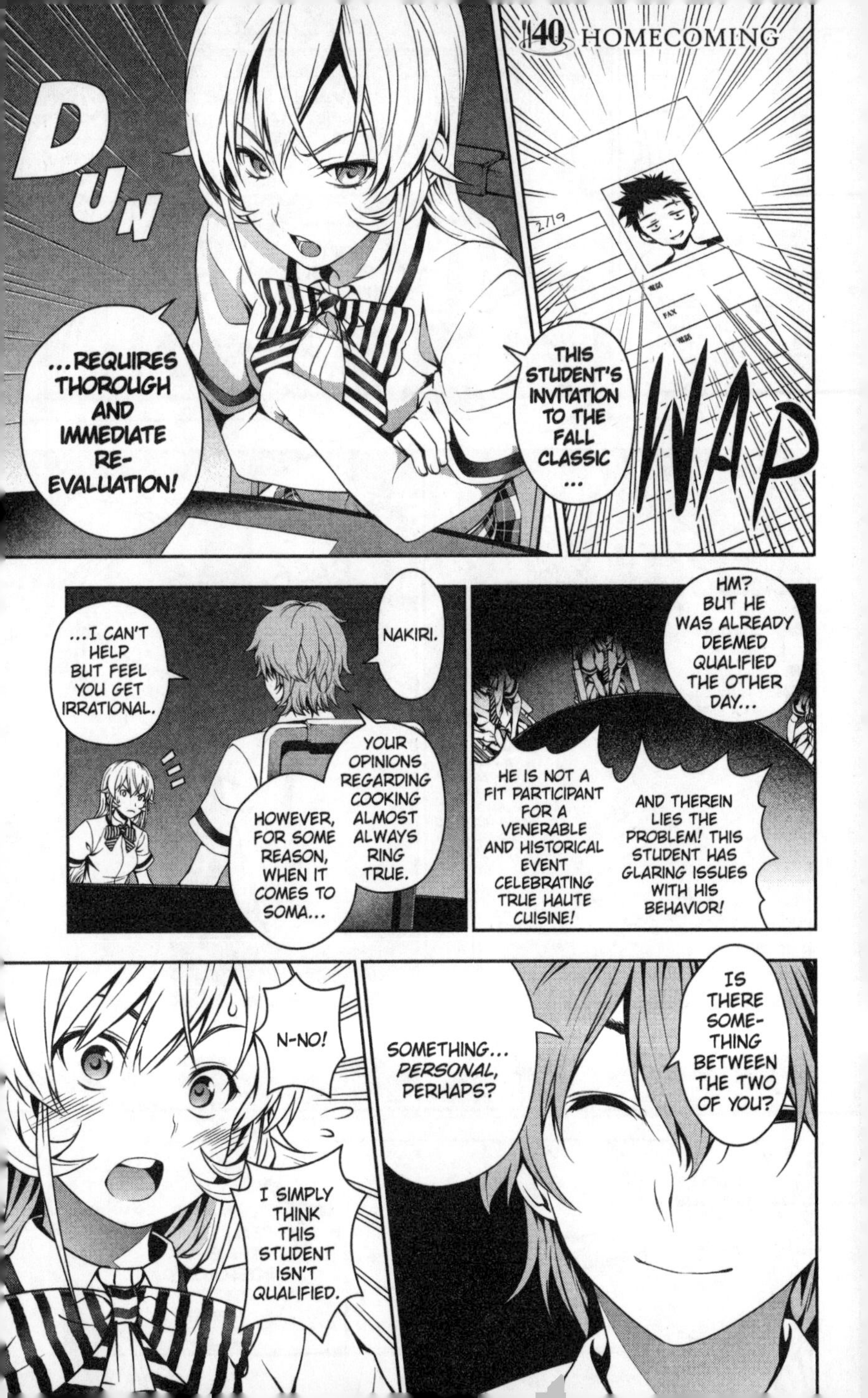

THIS STUDENT'S INVITATION TO THE FALL CLASSIC ...
WAP
DUN
...REQUIRES THOROUGH AND IMMEDIATE RE-EVALUATION!
HM? BUT HE WAS ALREADY DEEMED QUALIFIED THE OTHER DAY...
AND THEREIN LIES THE PROBLEM! THIS STUDENT HAS GLARING ISSUES WITH HIS BEHAVIOR!
HE IS NOT A FIT PARTICIPANT FOR A VENERABLE AND HISTORICAL EVENT CELEBRATING TRUE HAUTE CUISINE!
NAKIRI.
YOUR OPINIONS REGARDING COOKING ALMOST ALWAYS RING TRUE.
HOWEVER, FOR SOME REASON, WHEN IT COMES TO SOMA...
...I CAN'T HELP BUT FEEL YOU GET IRRATIONAL.
IS THERE SOME-THING BETWEEN THE TWO OF YOU?
SOMETHING... *PERSONAL*, PERHAPS?
N-NO!
I SIMPLY THINK THIS STUDENT ISN'T QUALIFIED.

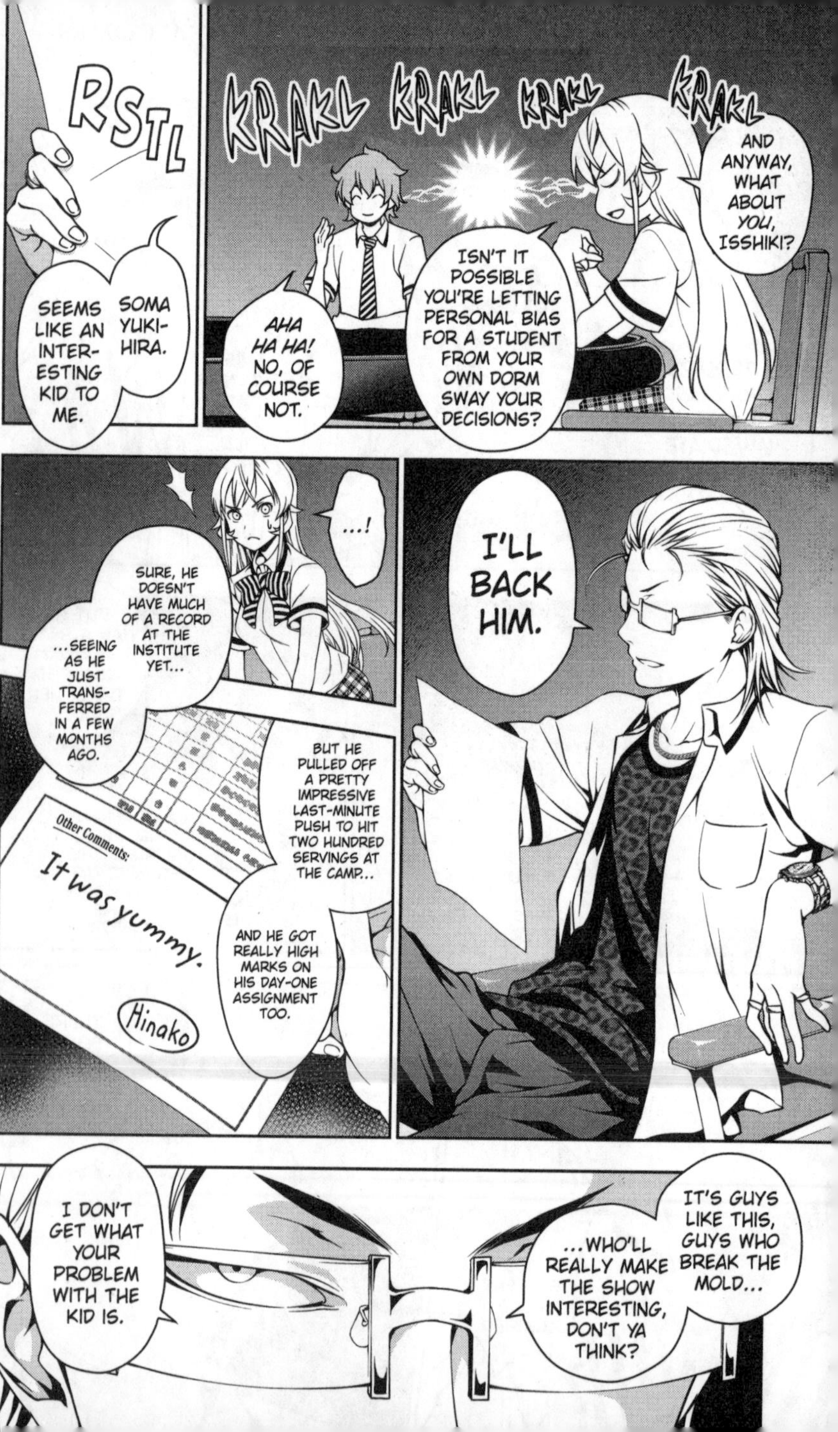
KRAKL KRAKL KRAKL KRAKL
AND ANYWAY, WHAT ABOUT YOU, ISSHIKI?
ISN'T IT POSSIBLE YOU'RE LETTING PERSONAL BIAS FOR A STUDENT FROM YOUR OWN DORM SWAY YOUR DECISIONS?
AHA HA HA! NO, OF COURSE NOT.
RSTL
SOMA YUKIHIRA.
SEEMS LIKE AN INTERESTING KID TO ME.
I'LL BACK HIM.
...!
SURE, HE DOESN'T HAVE MUCH OF A RECORD AT THE INSTITUTE YET...
...SEEING AS HE JUST TRANSFERRED IN A FEW MONTHS AGO.
BUT HE PULLED OFF A PRETTY IMPRESSIVE LAST-MINUTE PUSH TO HIT TWO HUNDRED SERVINGS AT THE CAMP...
AND HE GOT REALLY HIGH MARKS ON HIS DAY-ONE ASSIGNMENT TOO.
Other Comments:
It was yummy.
Hinako
IT'S GUYS LIKE THIS, GUYS WHO BREAK THE MOLD...
...WHO'LL REALLY MAKE THE SHOW INTERESTING, DON'T YA THINK?
I DON'T GET WHAT YOUR PROBLEM WITH THE KID IS.

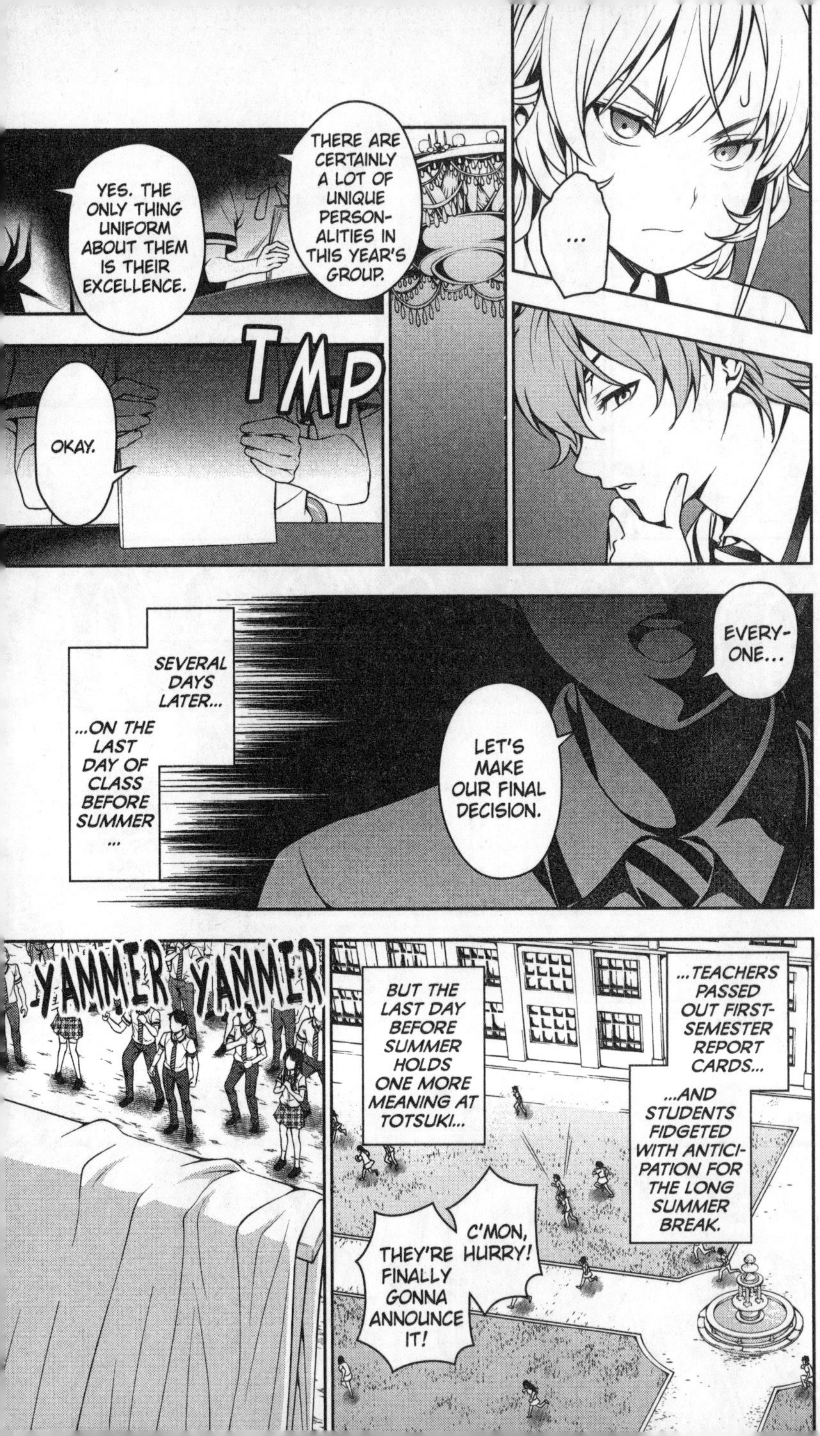
...
THERE ARE CERTAINLY A LOT OF UNIQUE PERSON-ALITIES IN THIS YEAR'S GROUP.
YES. THE ONLY THING UNIFORM ABOUT THEM IS THEIR EXCELLENCE.
TMP
OKAY.
EVERY-ONE...
LET'S MAKE OUR FINAL DECISION.
SEVERAL DAYS LATER...
...ON THE LAST DAY OF CLASS BEFORE SUMMER...
...TEACHERS PASSED OUT FIRST-SEMESTER REPORT CARDS...
...AND STUDENTS FIDGETED WITH ANTICI-PATION FOR THE LONG SUMMER BREAK.
BUT THE LAST DAY BEFORE SUMMER HOLDS ONE MORE MEANING AT TOTSUKI...
C'MON, HURRY!
THEY'RE FINALLY GONNA ANNOUNCE IT!
YAMMER YAMMER

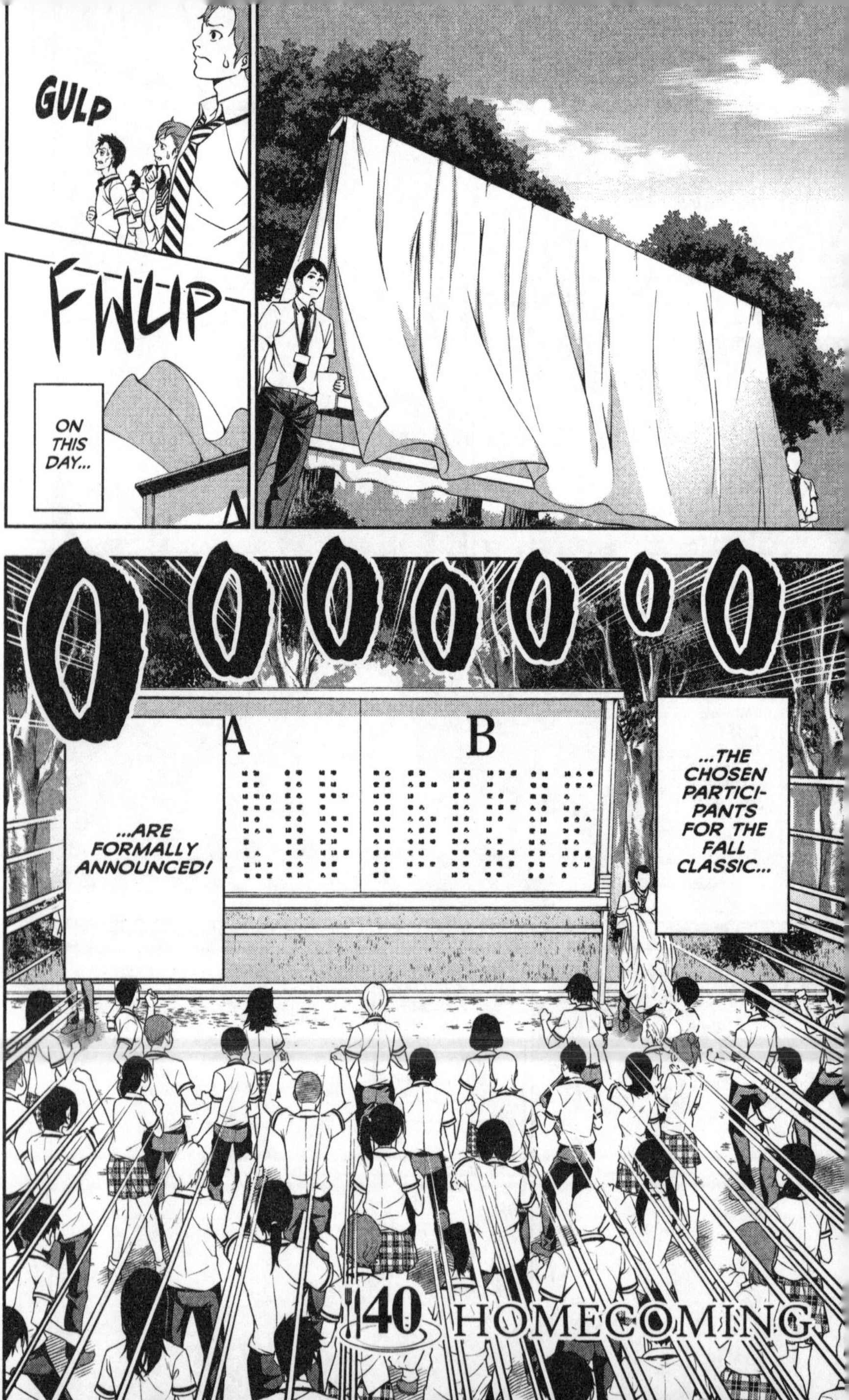
GULP
FWLIP
ON THIS DAY...
OOOOOOO
A
B
...THE CHOSEN PARTICIPANTS FOR THE FALL CLASSIC...
...ARE FORMALLY ANNOUNCED!
40 HOMECOMING

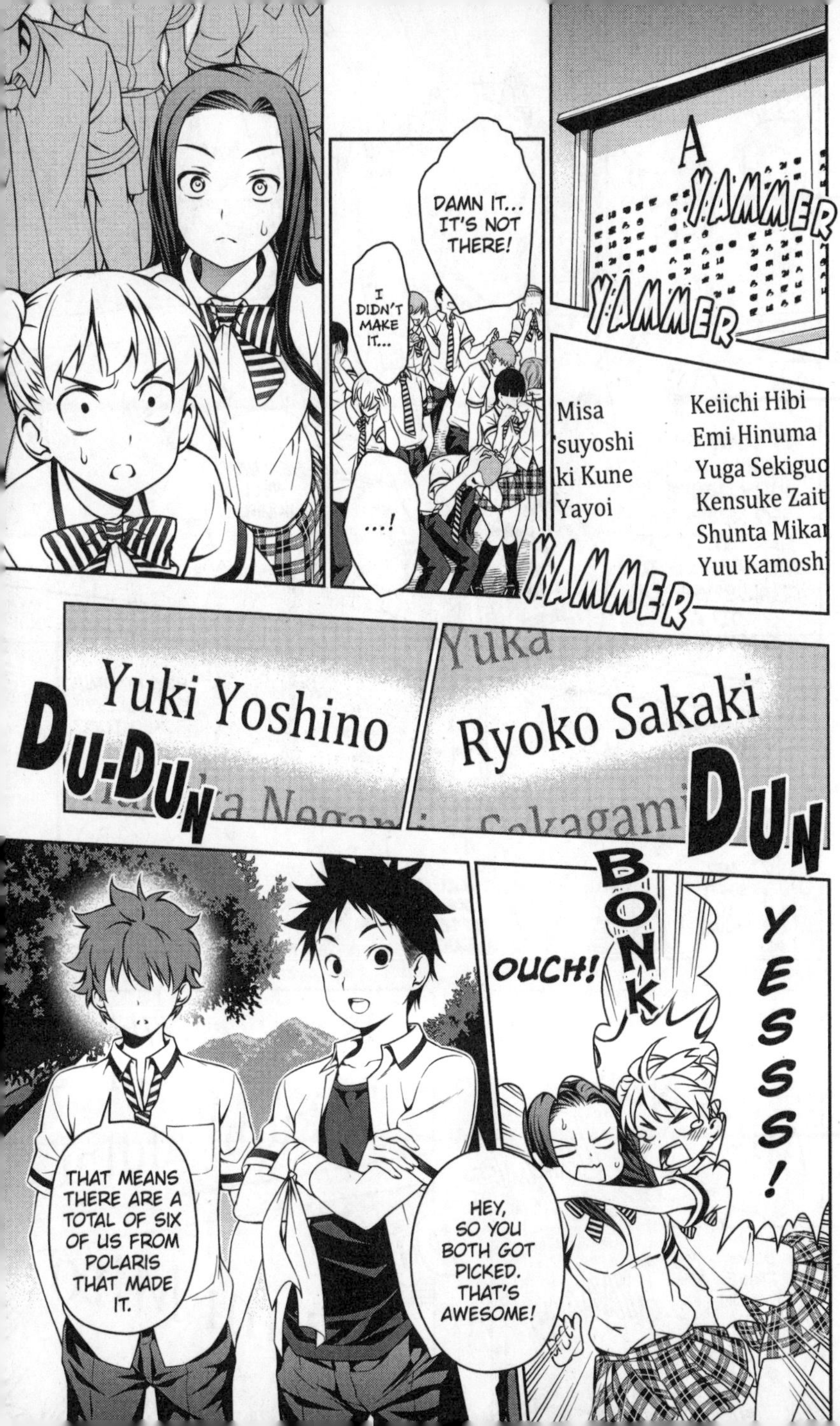
A
YAMMER
YAMMER
Misa
suyoshi
ki Kune
Yayoi
Keiichi Hibi
Emi Hinuma
Yuga Sekiguc
Kensuke Zait
Shunta Mikar
Yuu Kamoshi
YAMMER
DAMN IT... IT'S NOT THERE!
I DIDN'T MAKE IT...
...!
Yuka
Ryoko Sakaki
Sakagami
DUN
Yuki Yoshino
DU-DUN
YESSS!
BONK
OUCH!
HEY, SO YOU BOTH GOT PICKED. THAT'S AWESOME!
THAT MEANS THERE ARE A TOTAL OF SIX OF US FROM POLARIS THAT MADE IT.

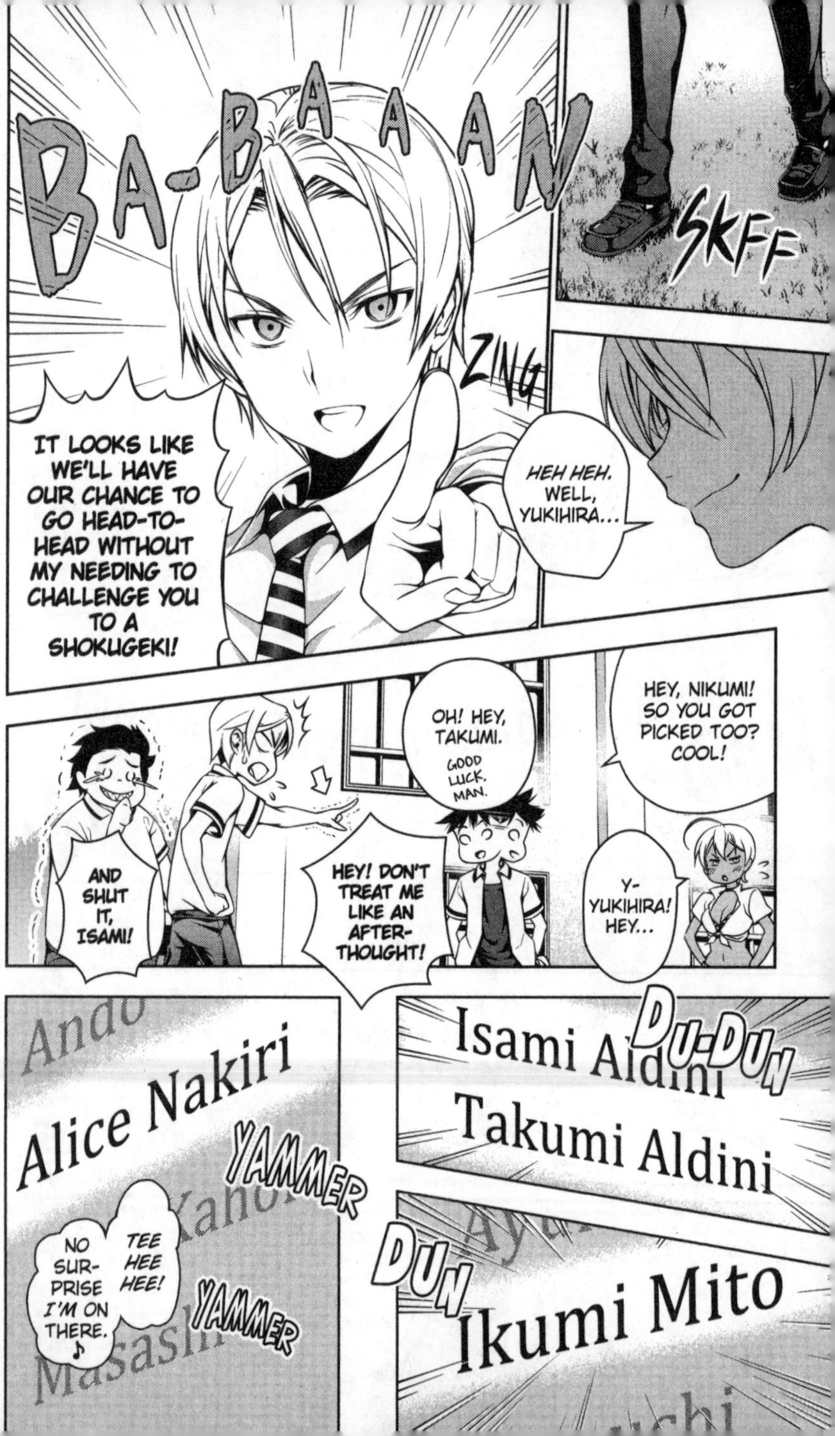
SKFF
HEH HEH. WELL, YUKIHIRA...
BA-BA-A-A-AN
ZING
IT LOOKS LIKE WE'LL HAVE OUR CHANCE TO GO HEAD-TO-HEAD WITHOUT MY NEEDING TO CHALLENGE YOU TO A SHOKUGEKI!
HEY, NIKUMI! SO YOU GOT PICKED TOO? COOL!
OH! HEY, TAKUMI.
GOOD LUCK. MAN.
Y-YUKIHIRA! HEY...
HEY! DON'T TREAT ME LIKE AN AFTER-THOUGHT!
AND SHUT IT, ISAMI!
Isami Aldini
DU-DUN
Takumi Aldini
Ikumi Mito
DUN
Ando
Alice Nakiri
YAMMER
TEE HEE HEE!
NO SUR-PRISE I'M ON THERE. ♪
YAMMER
Masashi

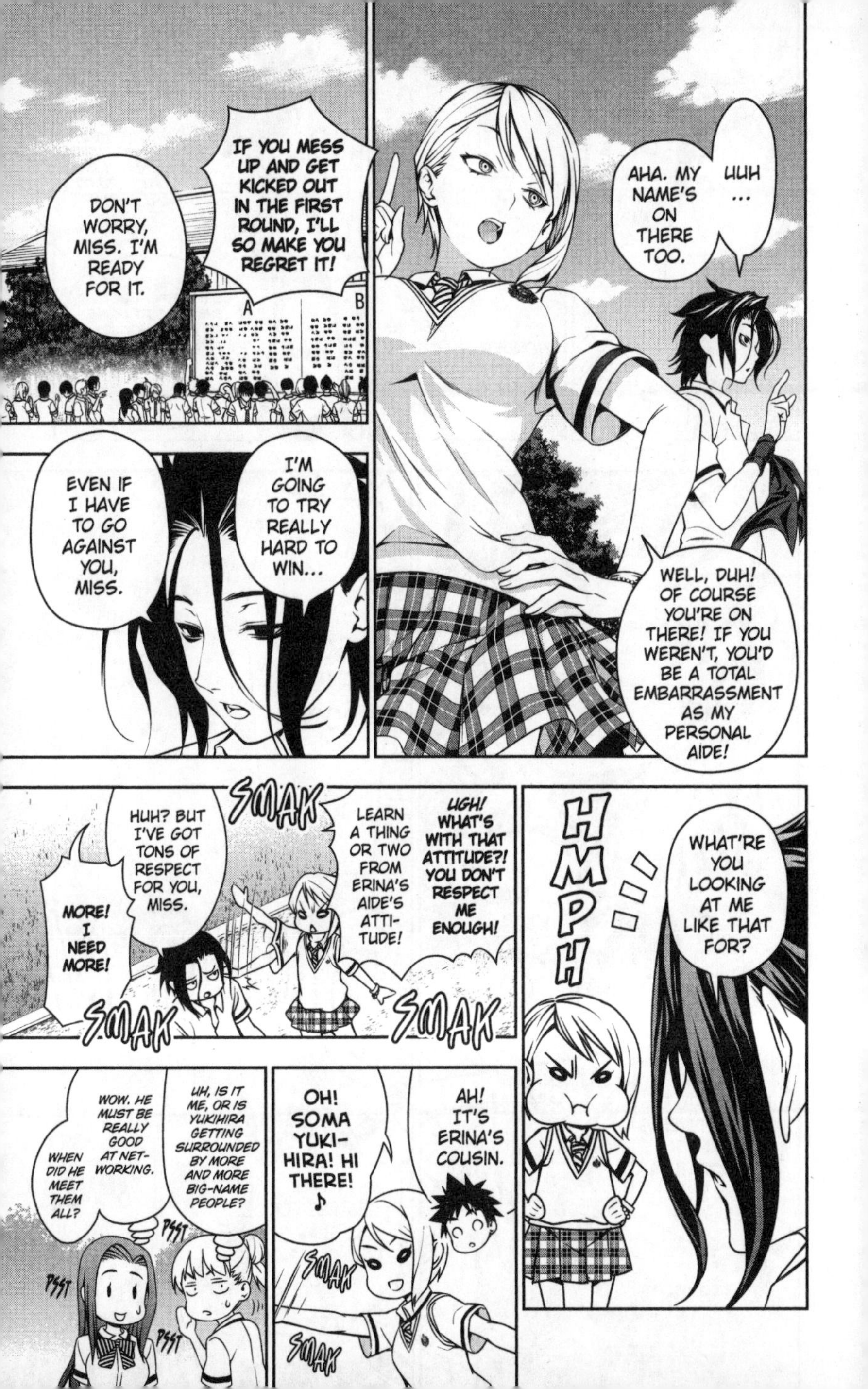
UUH ...
AHA. MY NAME'S ON THERE TOO.
WELL, DUH! OF COURSE YOU'RE ON THERE! IF YOU WEREN'T, YOU'D BE A TOTAL EMBARRASSMENT AS MY PERSONAL AIDE!
IF YOU MESS UP AND GET KICKED OUT IN THE FIRST ROUND, I'LL SO MAKE YOU REGRET IT!
DON'T WORRY, MISS. I'M READY FOR IT.
I'M GOING TO TRY REALLY HARD TO WIN...
EVEN IF I HAVE TO GO AGAINST YOU, MISS.
WHAT'RE YOU LOOKING AT ME LIKE THAT FOR?
HMPH...
UGH! WHAT'S WITH THAT ATTITUDE?! YOU DON'T RESPECT ME ENOUGH!
LEARN A THING OR TWO FROM ERINA'S AIDE'S ATTI-TUDE!
SMAK
HUH? BUT I'VE GOT TONS OF RESPECT FOR YOU, MISS.
MORE! I NEED MORE!
SMAK
SMAK
AH! IT'S ERINA'S COUSIN.
OH! SOMA YUKI-HIRA! HI THERE! ♪
SMAK
SMAK
UH, IS IT ME, OR IS YUKIHIRA GETTING SURROUNDED BY MORE AND MORE BIG-NAME PEOPLE?
WOW. HE MUST BE REALLY GOOD AT NET-WORKING.
WHEN DID HE MEET THEM ALL?
PSST
PSST
PSST

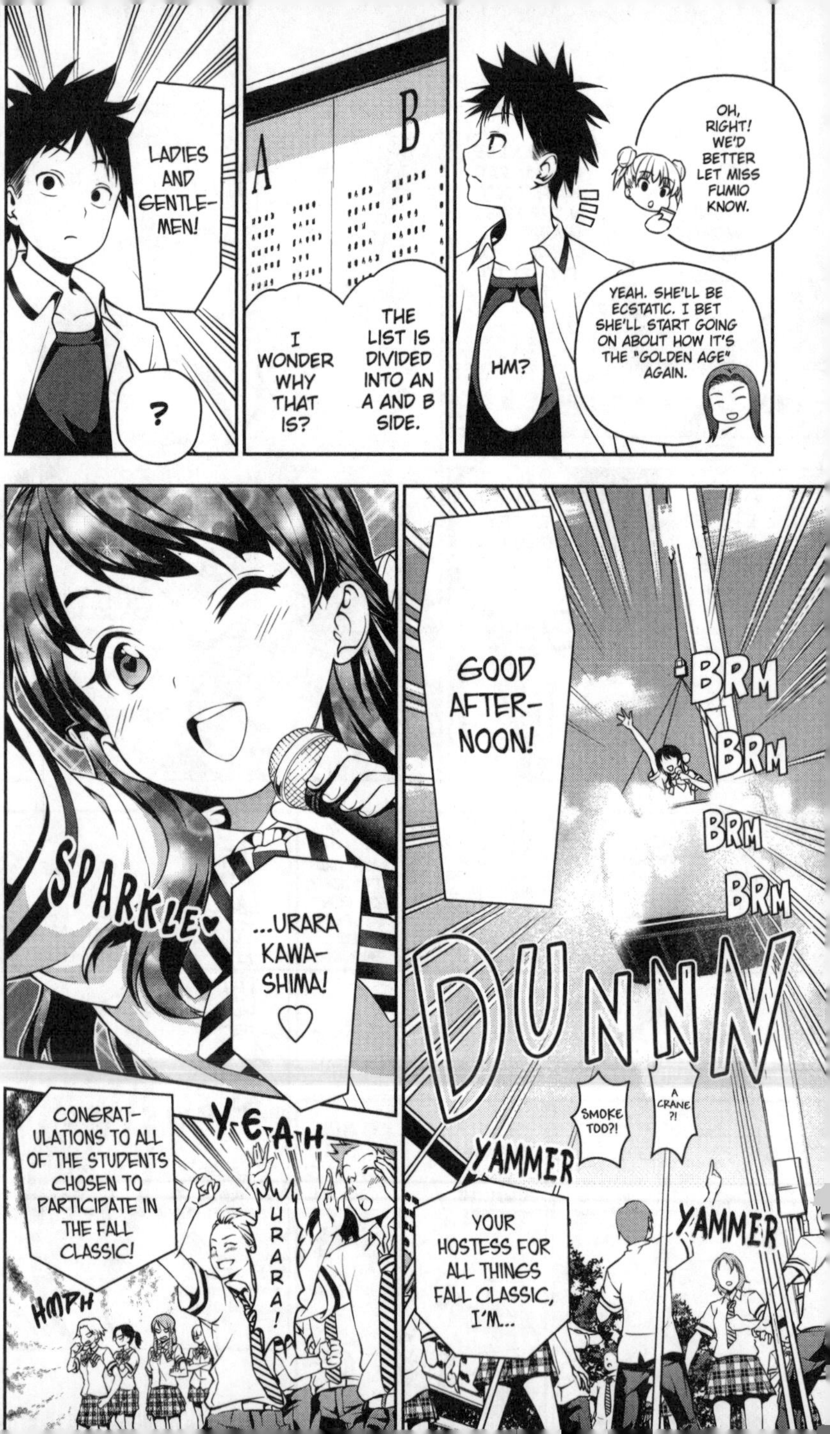
OH, RIGHT! WE'D BETTER LET MISS FUMIO KNOW.
YEAH. SHE'LL BE ECSTATIC. I BET SHE'LL START GOING ON ABOUT HOW IT'S THE "GOLDEN AGE" AGAIN.
HM?
A
B
THE LIST IS DIVIDED INTO AN A AND B SIDE.
I WONDER WHY THAT IS?
LADIES AND GENTLE-MEN!
?
GOOD AFTER-NOON!
BRM
BRM
BRM
BRM
DUNNN
A CRANE ?!
SMOKE TOO?!
YAMMER
YAMMER
YOUR HOSTESS FOR ALL THINGS FALL CLASSIC, I'M...
...URARA KAWA-SHIMA! ♡
SPARKLE♥
CONGRAT-ULATIONS TO ALL OF THE STUDENTS CHOSEN TO PARTICIPATE IN THE FALL CLASSIC!
YEAH
URARA!
HMPH

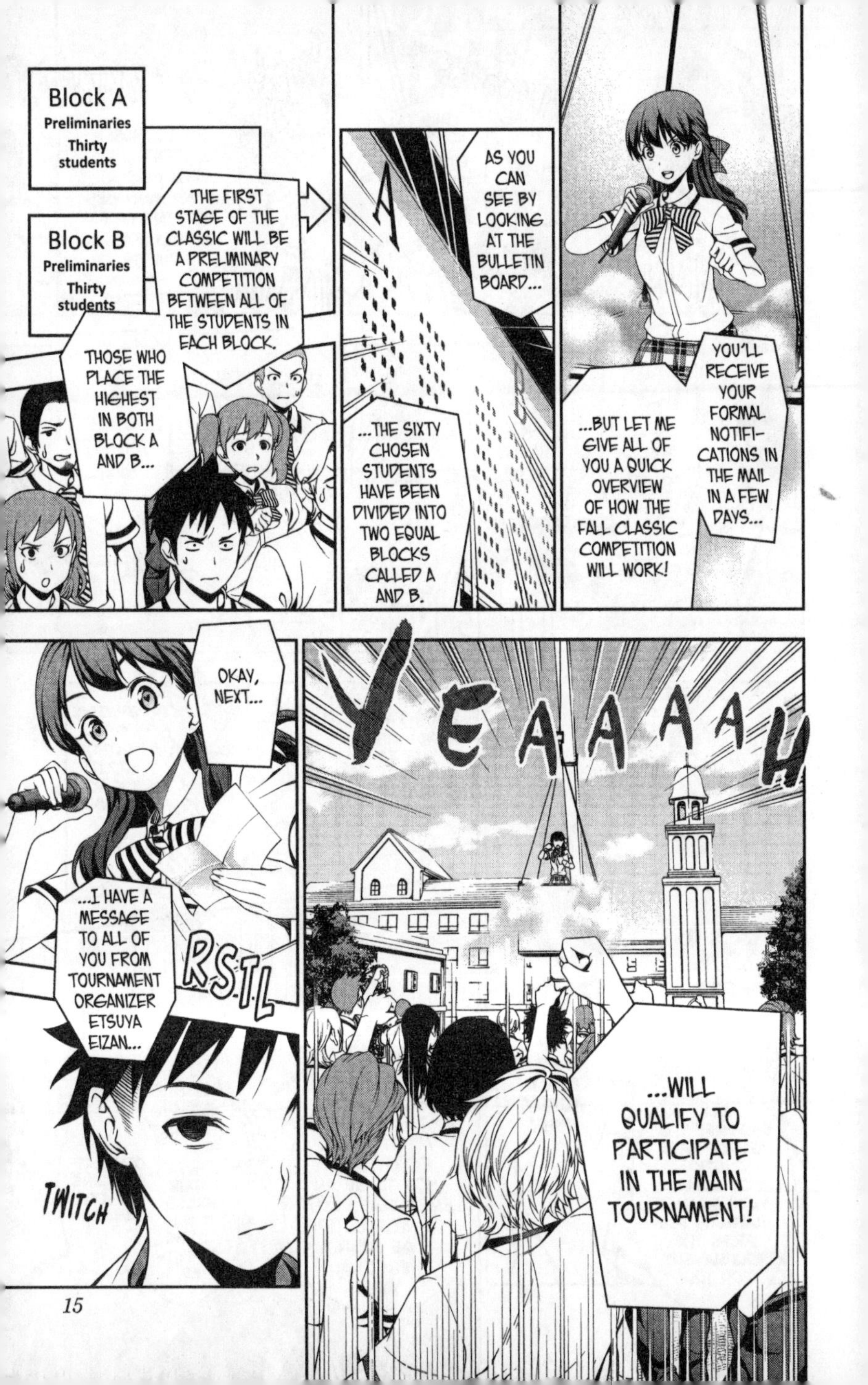
YOU'LL RECEIVE YOUR FORMAL NOTIFI-CATIONS IN THE MAIL IN A FEW DAYS...
...BUT LET ME GIVE ALL OF YOU A QUICK OVERVIEW OF HOW THE FALL CLASSIC COMPETITION WILL WORK!
AS YOU CAN SEE BY LOOKING AT THE BULLETIN BOARD...
...THE SIXTY CHOSEN STUDENTS HAVE BEEN DIVIDED INTO TWO EQUAL BLOCKS CALLED A AND B.
A
B
Block A
Preliminaries
Thirty students
Block B
Preliminaries
Thirty students
THE FIRST STAGE OF THE CLASSIC WILL BE A PRELIMINARY COMPETITION BETWEEN ALL OF THE STUDENTS IN EACH BLOCK.
THOSE WHO PLACE THE HIGHEST IN BOTH BLOCK A AND B...
YEAAAAH
...WILL QUALIFY TO PARTICIPATE IN THE MAIN TOURNAMENT!
OKAY, NEXT...
RSTL
...I HAVE A MESSAGE TO ALL OF YOU FROM TOURNAMENT ORGANIZER ETSUYA EIZAN...
TWITCH

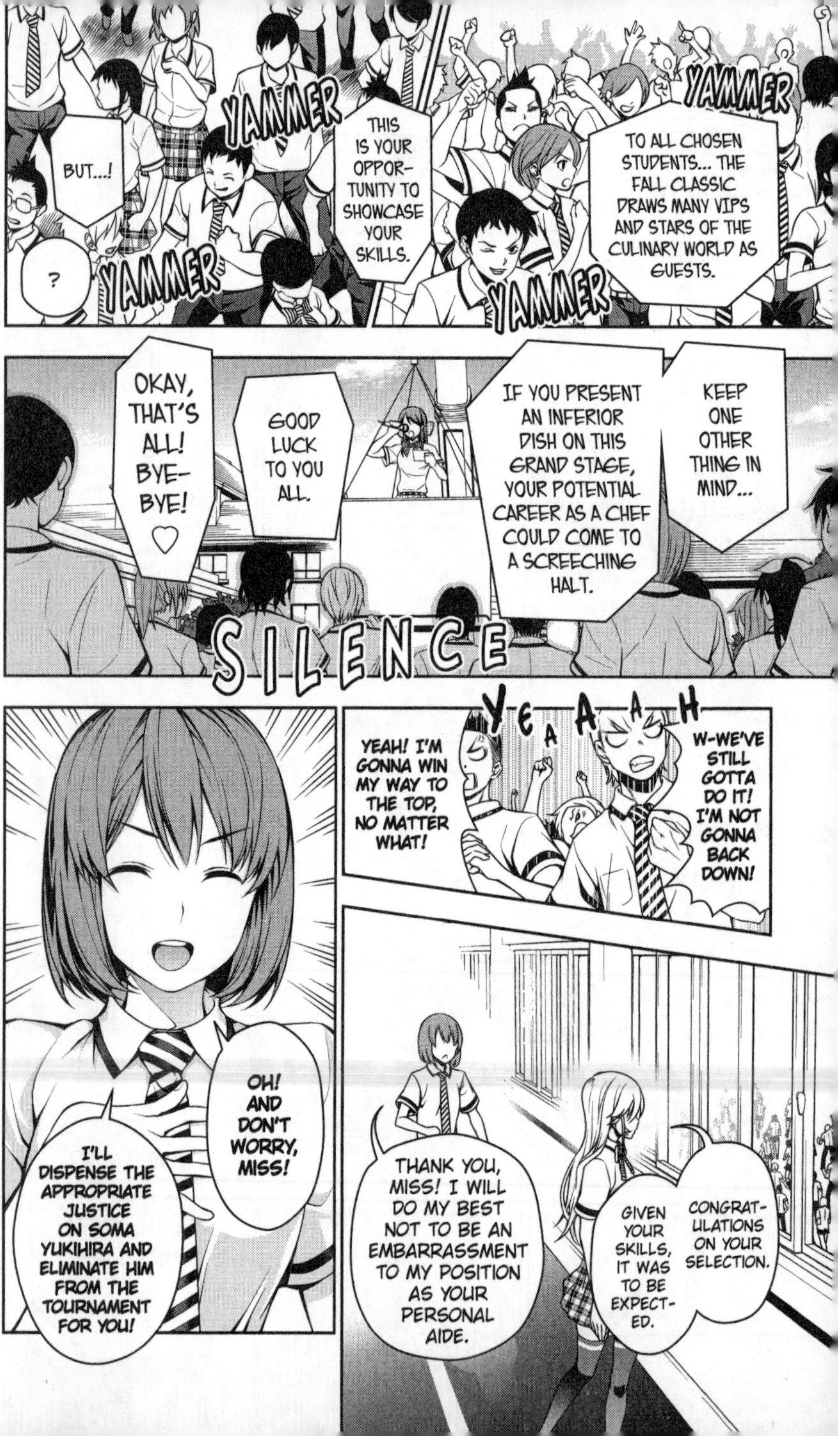
YAMMER
TO ALL CHOSEN STUDENTS... THE FALL CLASSIC DRAWS MANY VIPS AND STARS OF THE CULINARY WORLD AS GUESTS.
YAMMER
THIS IS YOUR OPPOR-TUNITY TO SHOWCASE YOUR SKILLS.
YAMMER
BUT...!
YAMMER
?
KEEP ONE OTHER THING IN MIND...
IF YOU PRESENT AN INFERIOR DISH ON THIS GRAND STAGE, YOUR POTENTIAL CAREER AS A CHEF COULD COME TO A SCREECHING HALT.
GOOD LUCK TO YOU ALL.
OKAY, THAT'S ALL! BYE-BYE! ♡
SILENCE
YEAAAH
W-WE'VE STILL GOTTA DO IT! I'M NOT GONNA BACK DOWN!
YEAH! I'M GONNA WIN MY WAY TO THE TOP, NO MATTER WHAT!
CONGRAT-ULATIONS ON YOUR SELECTION.
GIVEN YOUR SKILLS, IT WAS TO BE EXPECT-ED.
THANK YOU, MISS! I WILL DO MY BEST NOT TO BE AN EMBARRASSMENT TO MY POSITION AS YOUR PERSONAL AIDE.
OH! AND DON'T WORRY, MISS!
I'LL DISPENSE THE APPROPRIATE JUSTICE ON SOMA YUKIHIRA AND ELIMINATE HIM FROM THE TOURNAMENT FOR YOU!

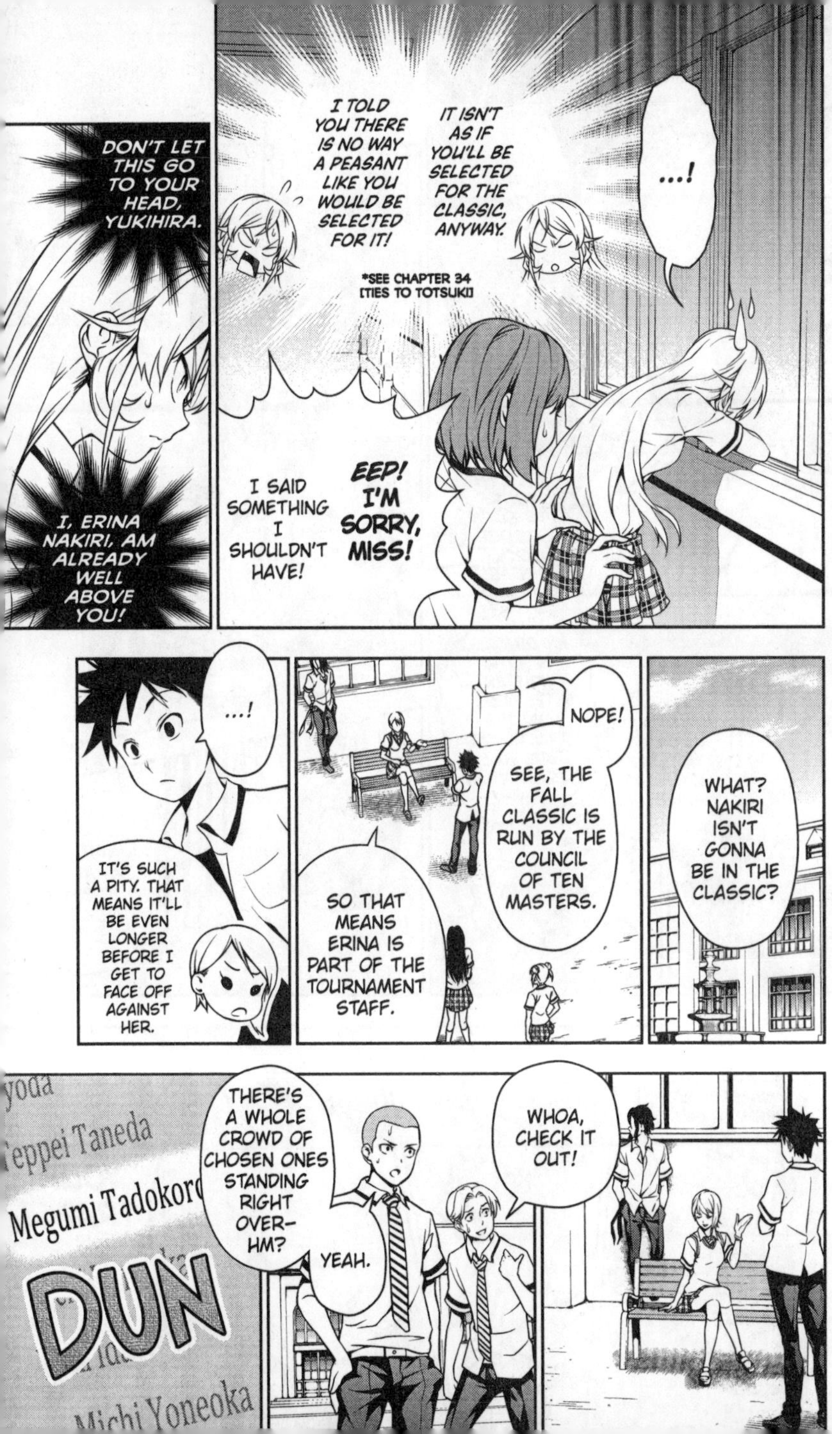
...!
IT ISN'T AS IF YOU'LL BE SELECTED FOR THE CLASSIC, ANYWAY.
I TOLD YOU THERE IS NO WAY A PEASANT LIKE YOU WOULD BE SELECTED FOR IT!
*SEE CHAPTER 34 [TIES TO TOTSUKI]
EEP! I'M SORRY, MISS!
I SAID SOMETHING I SHOULDN'T HAVE!
DON'T LET THIS GO TO YOUR HEAD, YUKIHIRA.
I, ERINA NAKIRI, AM ALREADY WELL ABOVE YOU!
WHAT? NAKIRI ISN'T GONNA BE IN THE CLASSIC?
NOPE!
SEE, THE FALL CLASSIC IS RUN BY THE COUNCIL OF TEN MASTERS.
SO THAT MEANS ERINA IS PART OF THE TOURNAMENT STAFF.
...!
IT'S SUCH A PITY. THAT MEANS IT'LL BE EVEN LONGER BEFORE I GET TO FACE OFF AGAINST HER.
WHOA, CHECK IT OUT!
THERE'S A WHOLE CROWD OF CHOSEN ONES STANDING RIGHT OVER—HM?
YEAH.
Megumi Tadokoro
DUN
Michi Yoneoka

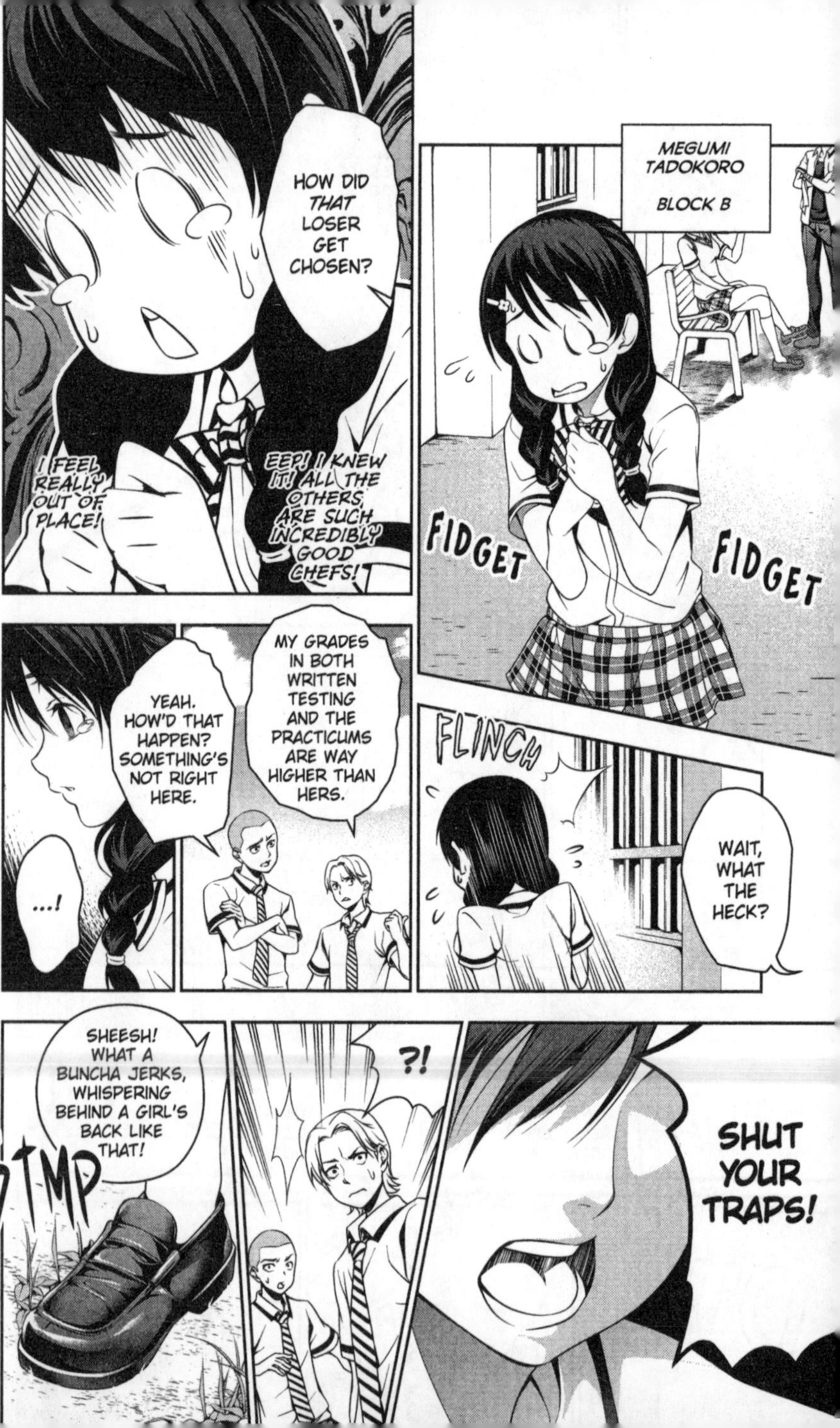
MEGUMI TADOKORO
BLOCK B
FIDGET
FIDGET
HOW DID THAT LOSER GET CHOSEN?
EEP! I KNEW IT! ALL THE OTHERS ARE SUCH INCREDIBLY GOOD CHEFS!
I FEEL REALLY OUT OF PLACE!
FLINCH
WAIT, WHAT THE HECK?
MY GRADES IN BOTH WRITTEN TESTING AND THE PRACTICUMS ARE WAY HIGHER THAN HERS.
YEAH. HOW'D THAT HAPPEN? SOMETHING'S NOT RIGHT HERE.
...!
SHUT YOUR TRAPS!
?!
SHEESH! WHAT A BUNCHA JERKS, WHISPERING BEHIND A GIRL'S BACK LIKE THAT!
STMP

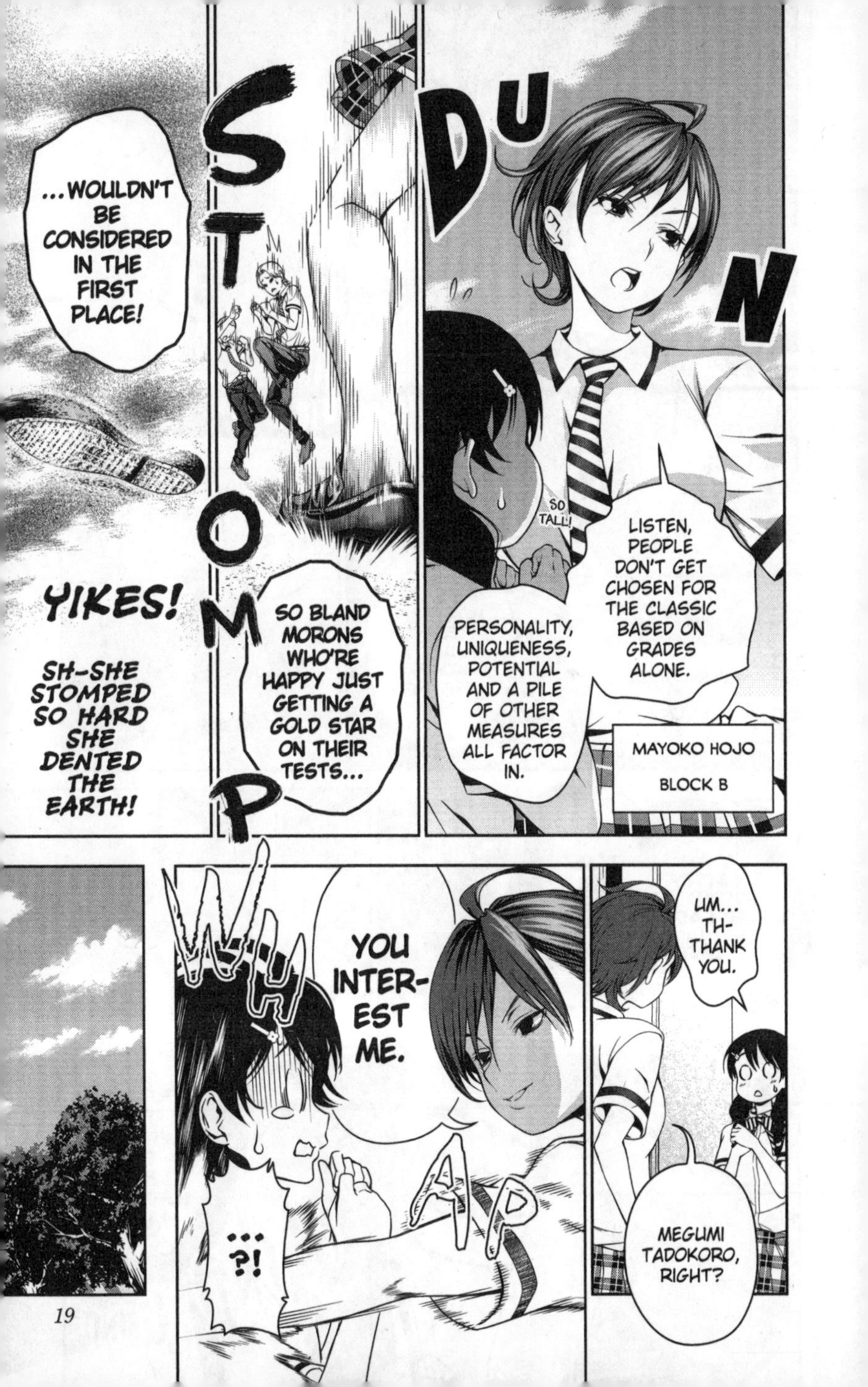
DUN
SO TALL!
LISTEN, PEOPLE DON'T GET CHOSEN FOR THE CLASSIC BASED ON GRADES ALONE.
PERSONALITY, UNIQUENESS, POTENTIAL AND A PILE OF OTHER MEASURES ALL FACTOR IN.
MAYOKO HOJO
BLOCK B
STOMP
SO BLAND MORONS WHO'RE HAPPY JUST GETTING A GOLD STAR ON THEIR TESTS...
...WOULDN'T BE CONSIDERED IN THE FIRST PLACE!
YIKES!
SH-SHE STOMPED SO HARD SHE DENTED THE EARTH!
UM... TH-THANK YOU.
MEGUMI TADOKORO, RIGHT?
WHAP
YOU INTER-EST ME.
...?!

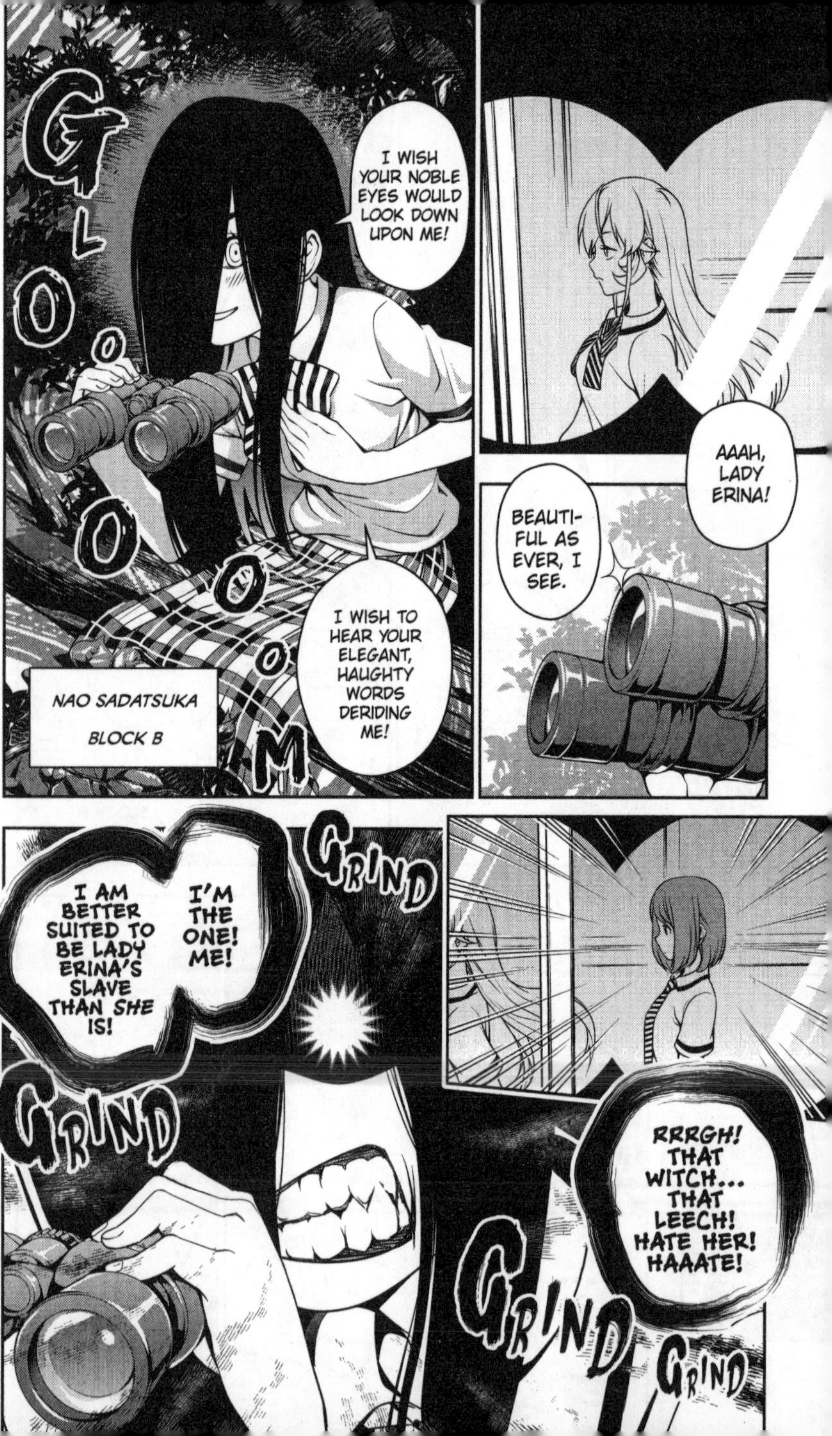
AAAH, LADY ERINA!
BEAUTI-FUL AS EVER, I SEE.
GLOOOOOOM
I WISH YOUR NOBLE EYES WOULD LOOK DOWN UPON ME!
I WISH TO HEAR YOUR ELEGANT, HAUGHTY WORDS DERIDING ME!
NAO SADATSUKA
BLOCK B
GRIND
I'M THE ONE! ME!
I AM BETTER SUITED TO BE LADY ERINA'S SLAVE THAN SHE IS!
RRRGH! THAT WITCH... THAT LEECH! HATE HER! HAAATE!
GRIND
GRIND
GRIND

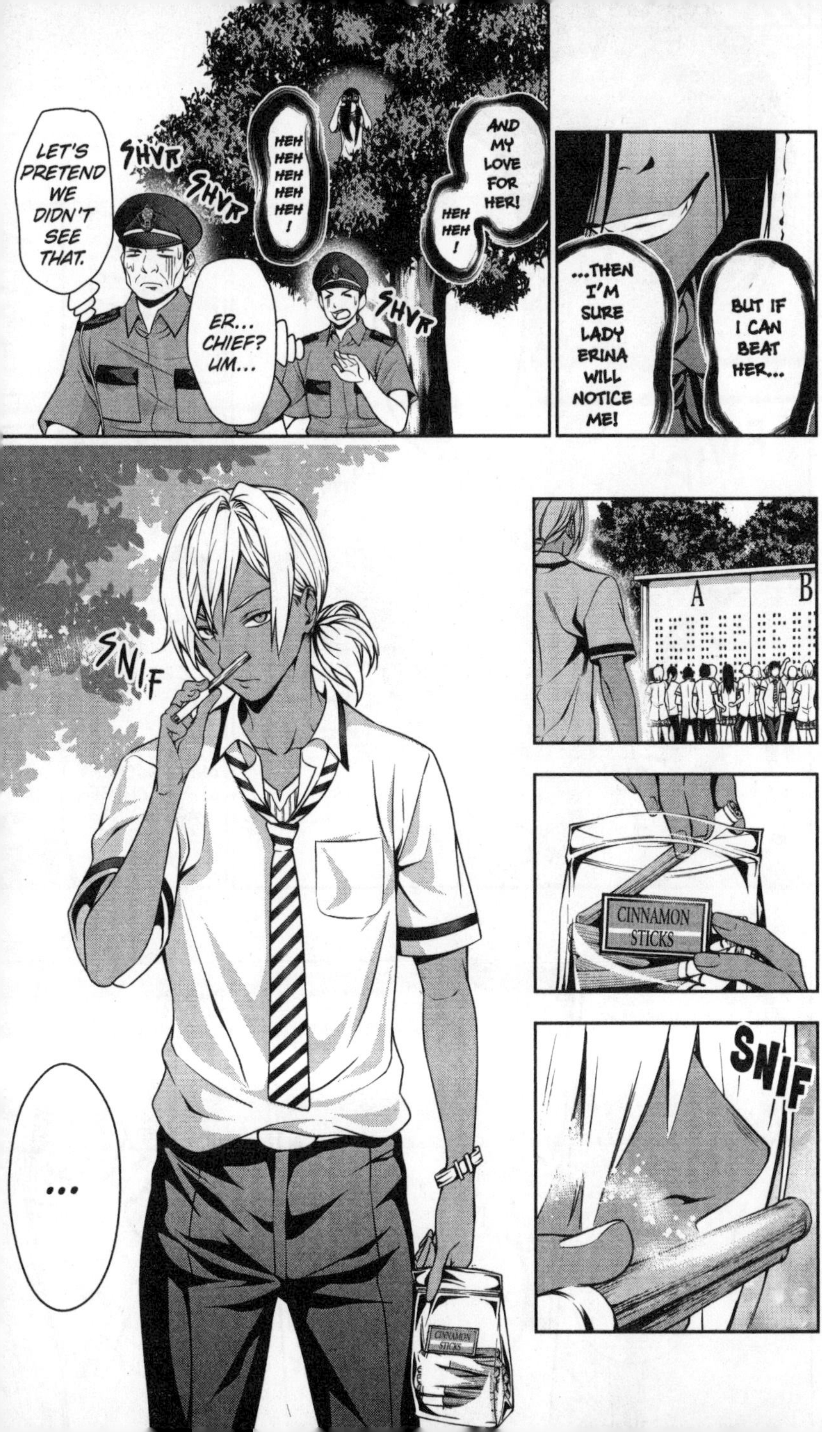
BUT IF I CAN BEAT HER...
...THEN I'M SURE LADY ERINA WILL NOTICE ME!
AND MY LOVE FOR HER!
HEH HEH!
HEH HEH HEH HEH HEH!
SHVR
LET'S PRETEND WE DIDN'T SEE THAT.
SHVR
SHVR
ER... CHIEF? UM...
A
B
CINNAMON STICKS
SNIF
SNIF
...
CINNAMON STICKS

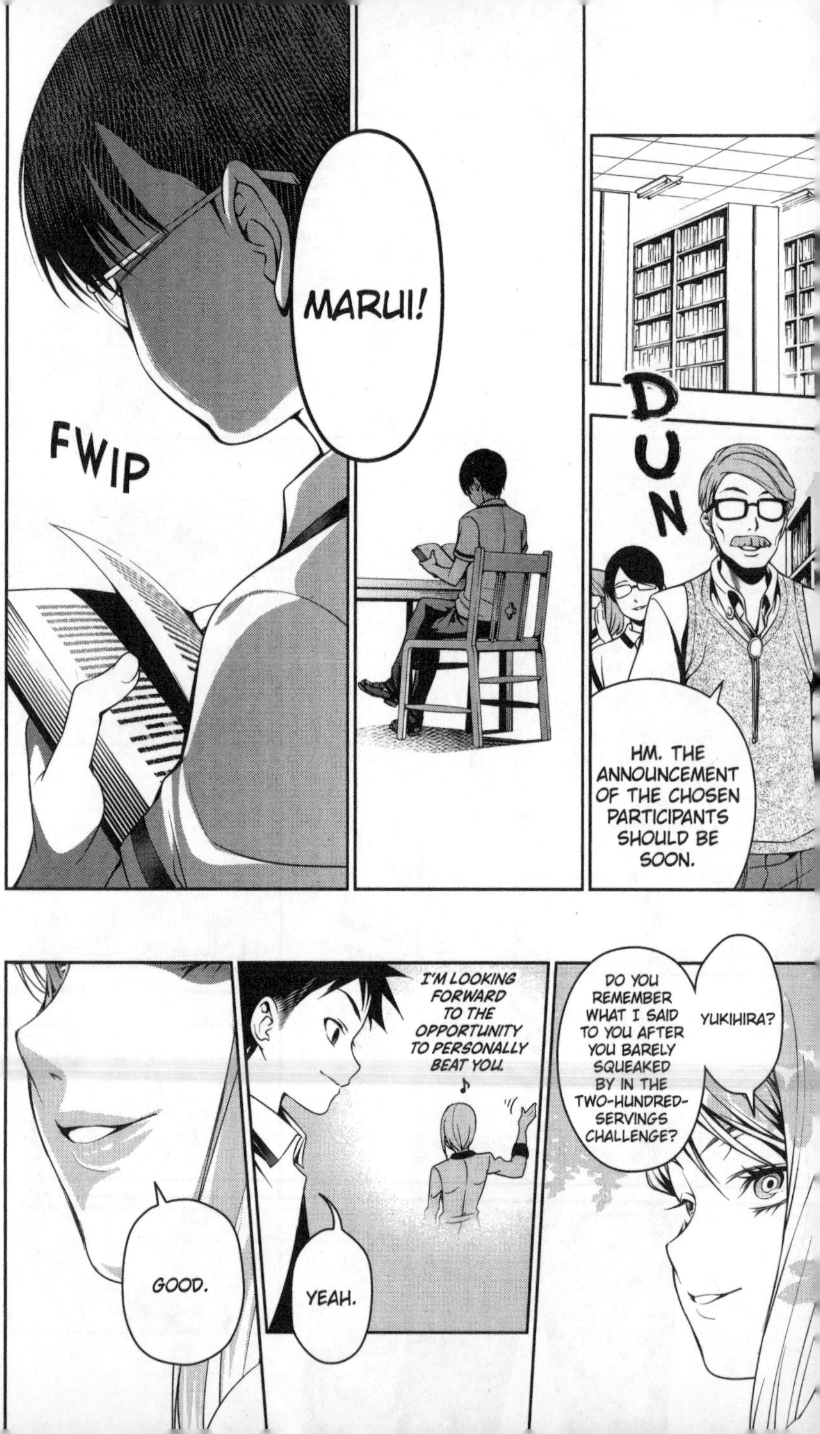
DUN
HM. THE ANNOUNCEMENT OF THE CHOSEN PARTICIPANTS SHOULD BE SOON.
MARUI!
FWIP
YUKIHIRA?
DO YOU REMEMBER WHAT I SAID TO YOU AFTER YOU BARELY SQUEAKED BY IN THE TWO-HUNDRED-SERVINGS CHALLENGE?
I'M LOOKING FORWARD TO THE OPPORTUNITY TO PERSONALLY BEAT YOU. ♪
YEAH.
GOOD.

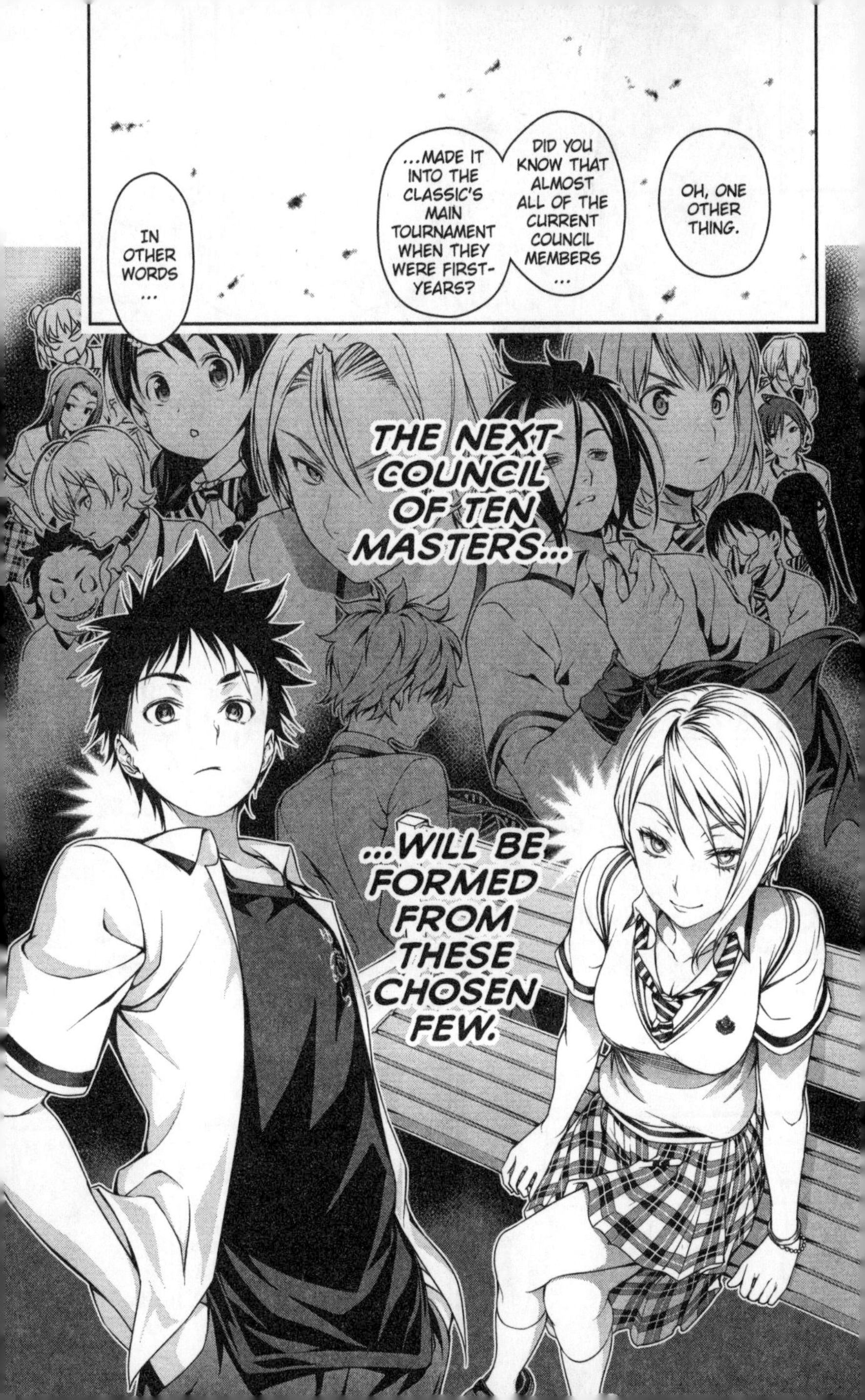
OH, ONE OTHER THING.
DID YOU KNOW THAT ALMOST ALL OF THE CURRENT COUNCIL MEMBERS ...
...MADE IT INTO THE CLASSIC'S MAIN TOURNAMENT WHEN THEY WERE FIRST-YEARS?
IN OTHER WORDS ...
THE NEXT COUNCIL OF TEN MASTERS...
...WILL BE FORMED FROM THESE CHOSEN FEW.

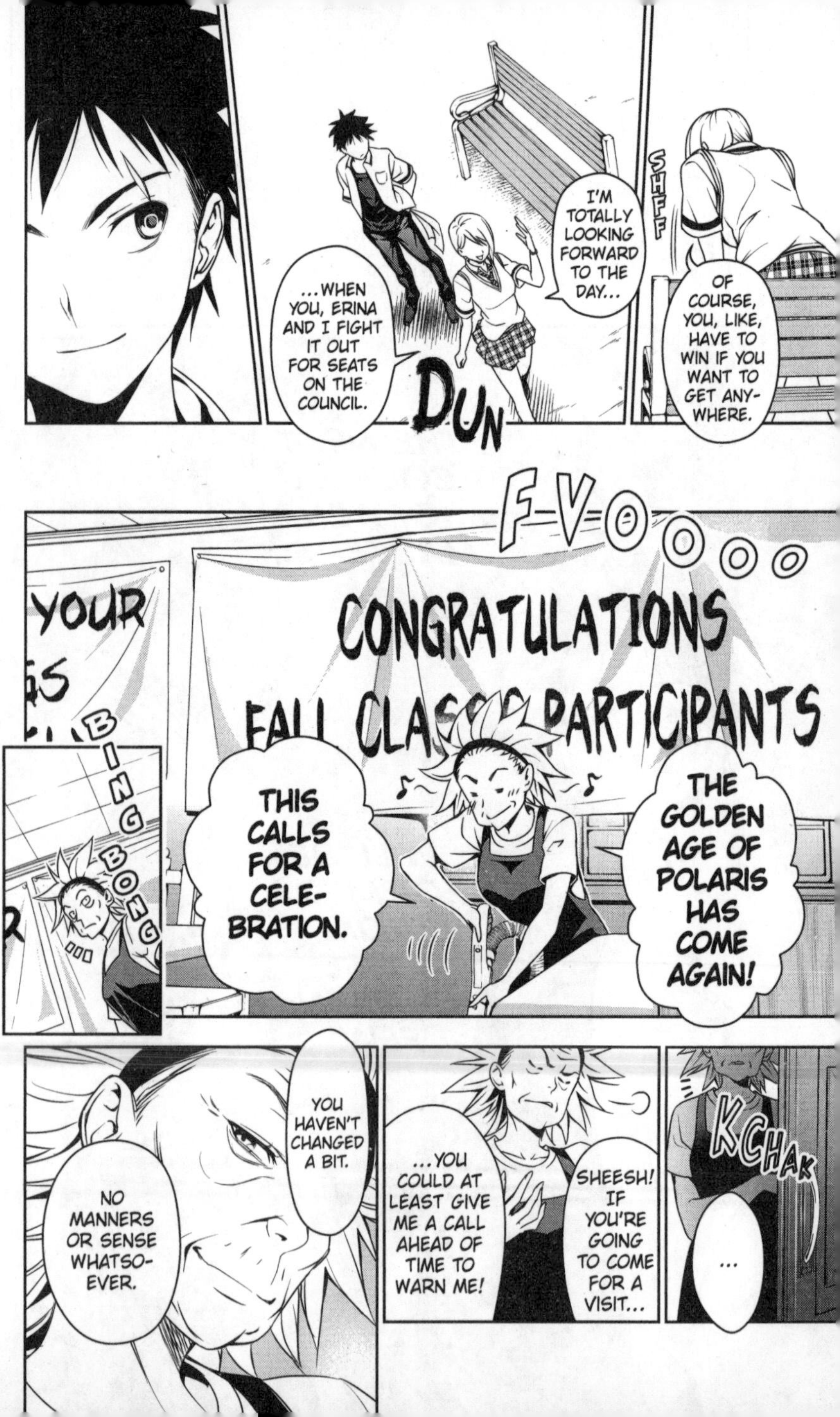
SHFF
OF COURSE, YOU, LIKE, HAVE TO WIN IF YOU WANT TO GET ANYWHERE.
I'M TOTALLY LOOKING FORWARD TO THE DAY...
...WHEN YOU, ERINA AND I FIGHT IT OUT FOR SEATS ON THE COUNCIL.
DUN
FVOOOO
CONGRATULATIONS
FALL CLAS
PARTICIPANTS
THE GOLDEN AGE OF POLARIS HAS COME AGAIN!
THIS CALLS FOR A CELEBRATION.
YOUR
BING BONG
...
KCHAK
...
SHEESH! IF YOU'RE GOING TO COME FOR A VISIT...
...YOU COULD AT LEAST GIVE ME A CALL AHEAD OF TIME TO WARN ME!
YOU HAVEN'T CHANGED A BIT.
NO MANNERS OR SENSE WHATSOEVER.

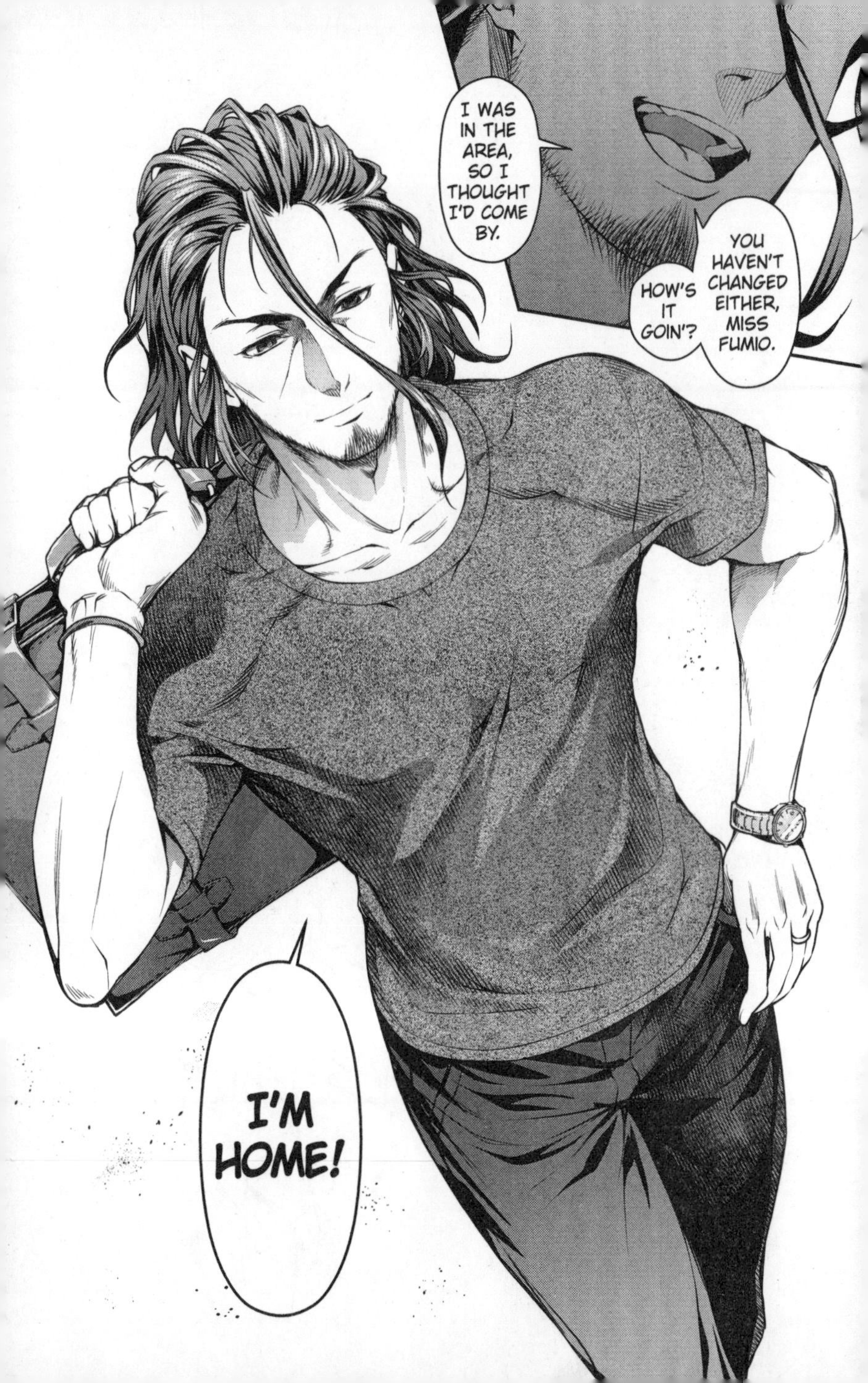
YOU HAVEN'T CHANGED EITHER, MISS FUMIO.
HOW'S IT GOIN'?
I WAS IN THE AREA, SO I THOUGHT I'D COME BY.
I'M HOME!

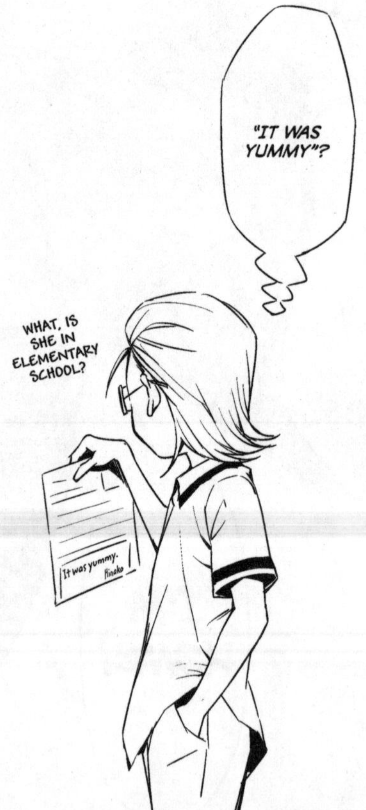
"IT WAS YUMMY"?
WHAT, IS SHE IN ELEMENTARY SCHOOL?
It was yummy.
Hinako

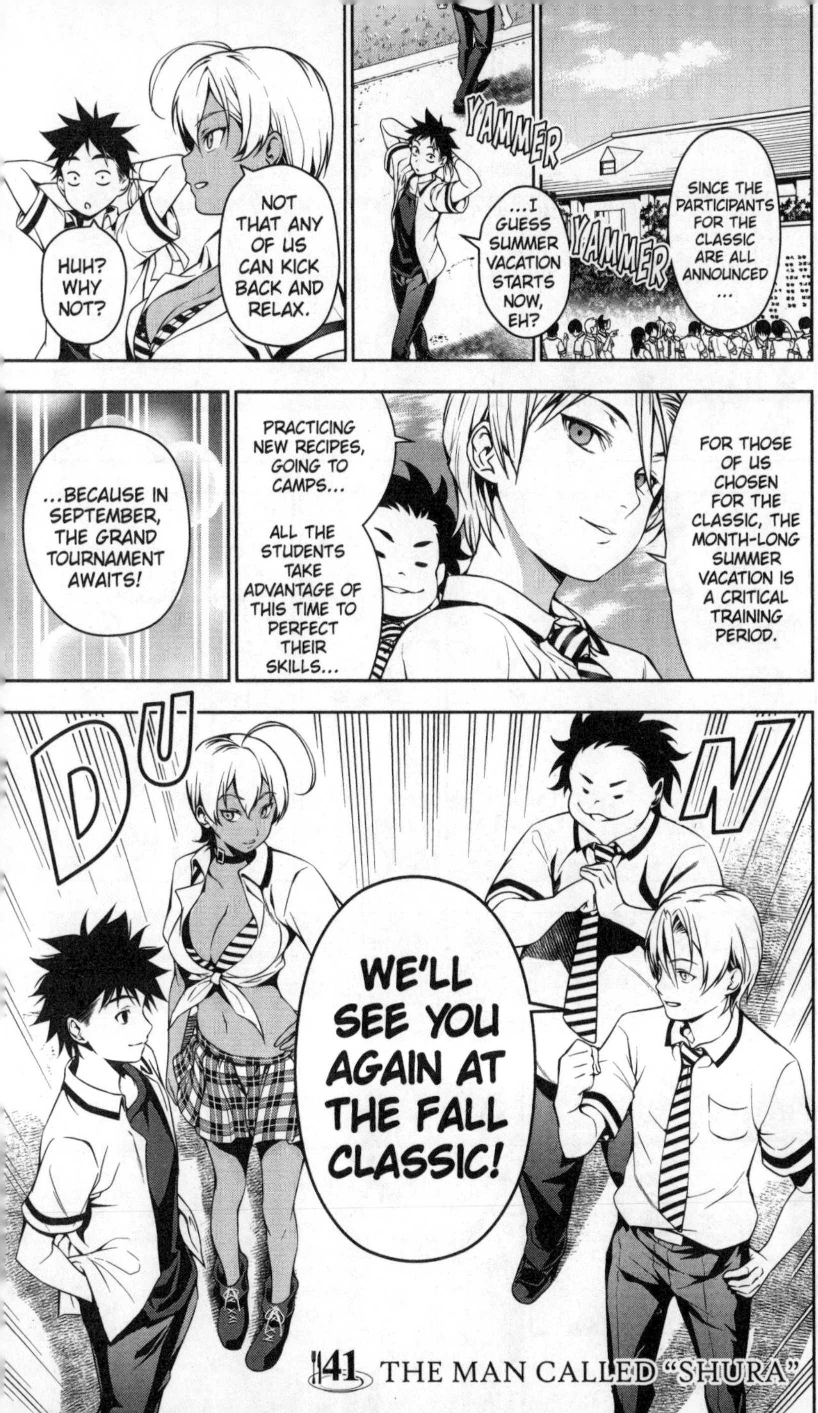
SINCE THE PARTICIPANTS FOR THE CLASSIC ARE ALL ANNOUNCED...
YAMMER
YAMMER
...I GUESS SUMMER VACATION STARTS NOW, EH?
NOT THAT ANY OF US CAN KICK BACK AND RELAX.
HUH? WHY NOT?
FOR THOSE OF US CHOSEN FOR THE CLASSIC, THE MONTH-LONG SUMMER VACATION IS A CRITICAL TRAINING PERIOD.
PRACTICING NEW RECIPES, GOING TO CAMPS...
ALL THE STUDENTS TAKE ADVANTAGE OF THIS TIME TO PERFECT THEIR SKILLS...
...BECAUSE IN SEPTEMBER, THE GRAND TOURNAMENT AWAITS!
DUN
WE'LL SEE YOU AGAIN AT THE FALL CLASSIC!

41 THE MAN CALLED "SHURA"

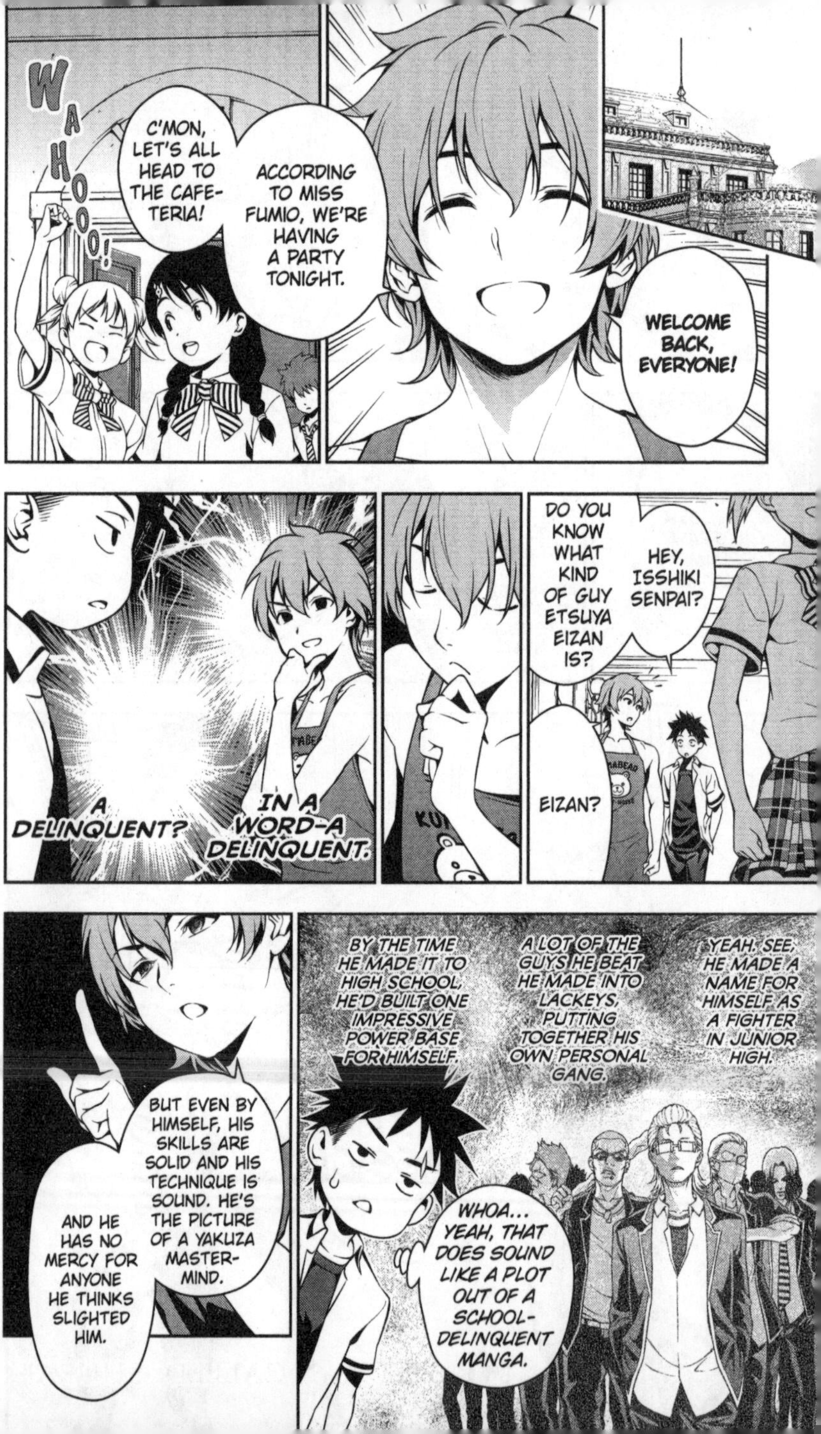
WELCOME BACK, EVERYONE!
ACCORDING TO MISS FUMIO, WE'RE HAVING A PARTY TONIGHT.
C'MON, LET'S ALL HEAD TO THE CAFE-TERIA!
WAHOOO!
HEY, ISSHIKI SENPAI?
DO YOU KNOW WHAT KIND OF GUY ETSUYA EIZAN IS?
EIZAN?
IN A WORD—A DELINQUENT.
A DELINQUENT?
YEAH. SEE, HE MADE A NAME FOR HIMSELF AS A FIGHTER IN JUNIOR HIGH.
A LOT OF THE GUYS HE BEAT HE MADE INTO LACKEYS, PUTTING TOGETHER HIS OWN PERSONAL GANG.
BY THE TIME HE MADE IT TO HIGH SCHOOL, HE'D BUILT ONE IMPRESSIVE POWER BASE FOR HIMSELF.
WHOA... YEAH, THAT DOES SOUND LIKE A PLOT OUT OF A SCHOOL-DELINQUENT MANGA.
BUT EVEN BY HIMSELF, HIS SKILLS ARE SOLID AND HIS TECHNIQUE IS SOUND. HE'S THE PICTURE OF A YAKUZA MASTER-MIND.
AND HE HAS NO MERCY FOR ANYONE HE THINKS SLIGHTED HIM.

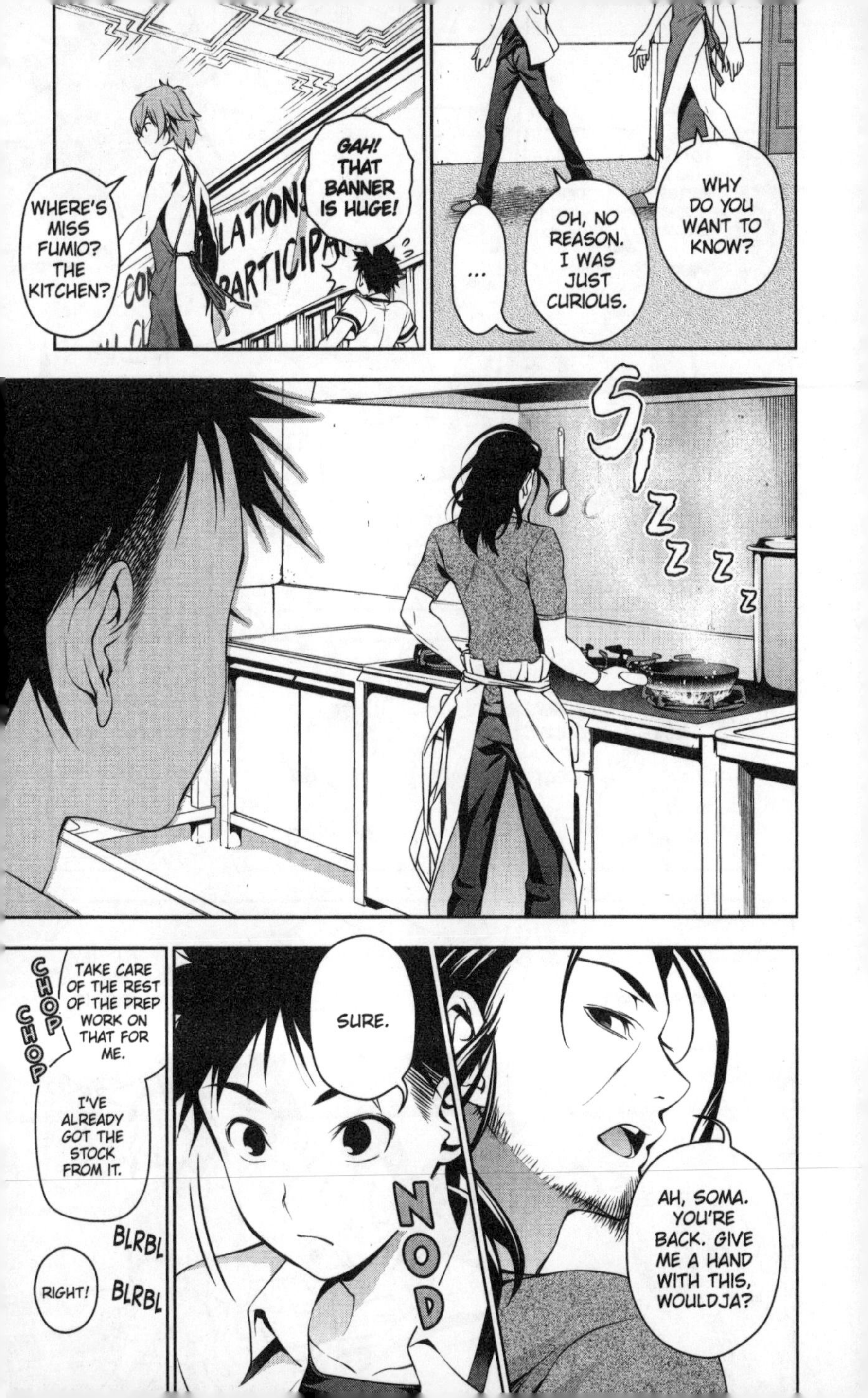
WHY DO YOU WANT TO KNOW?
OH, NO REASON. I WAS JUST CURIOUS.
...
GAH! THAT BANNER IS HUGE!
WHERE'S MISS FUMIO? THE KITCHEN?
SIZZZZZ
AH, SOMA. YOU'RE BACK. GIVE ME A HAND WITH THIS, WOULDJA?
SURE.
NOD
TAKE CARE OF THE REST OF THE PREP WORK ON THAT FOR ME.
CHOP CHOP
I'VE ALREADY GOT THE STOCK FROM IT.
BLRBL BLRBL
RIGHT!

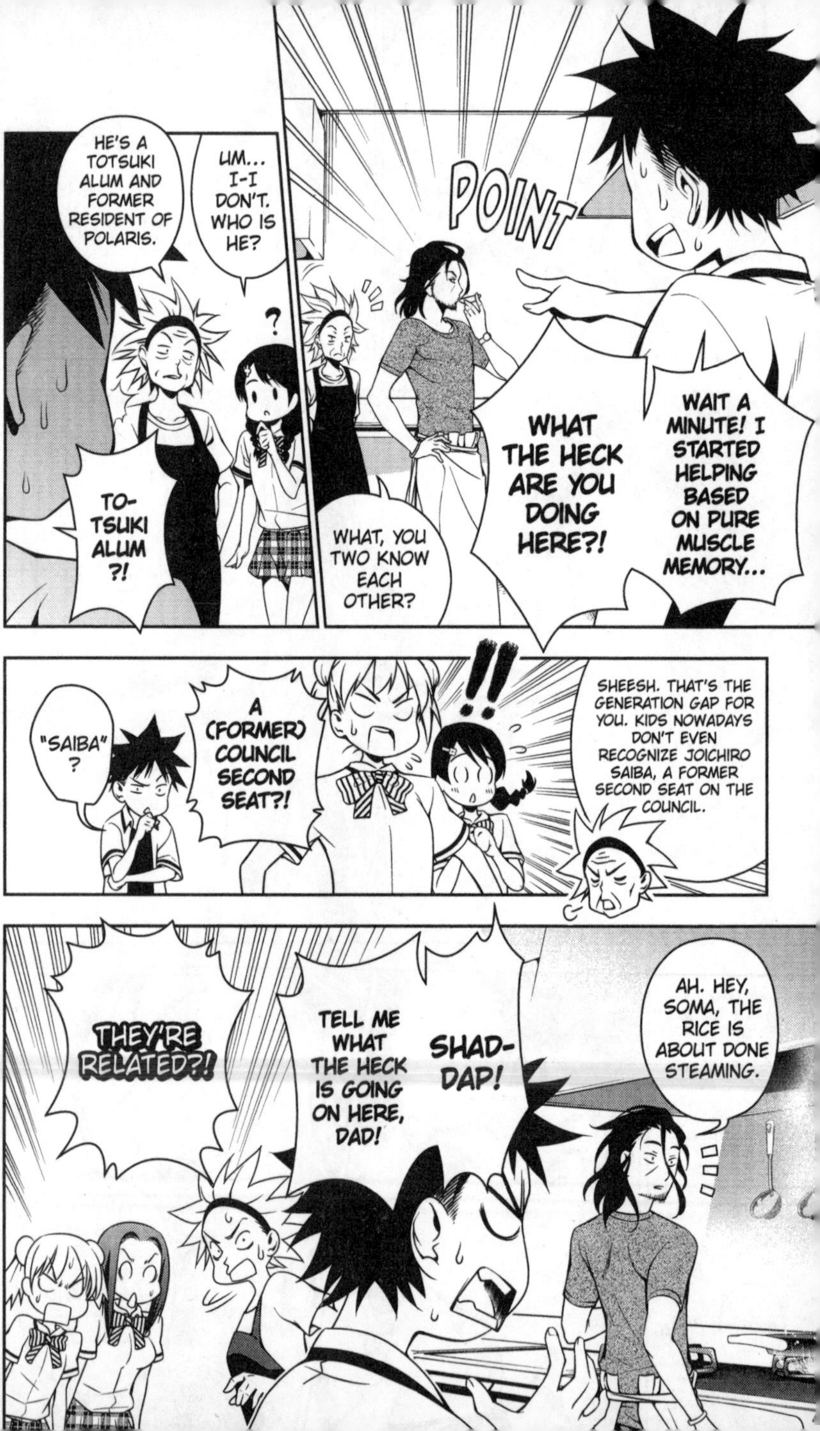
POINT
WAIT A MINUTE! I STARTED HELPING BASED ON PURE MUSCLE MEMORY...
WHAT THE HECK ARE YOU DOING HERE?!
WHAT, YOU TWO KNOW EACH OTHER?
UM... I-I DON'T. WHO IS HE?
HE'S A TOTSUKI ALUM AND FORMER RESIDENT OF POLARIS.
TO-TSUKI ALUM?!
SHEESH. THAT'S THE GENERATION GAP FOR YOU. KIDS NOWADAYS DON'T EVEN RECOGNIZE JOICHIRO SAIBA, A FORMER SECOND SEAT ON THE COUNCIL.
A (FORMER) COUNCIL SECOND SEAT?!
"SAIBA"?
AH. HEY, SOMA, THE RICE IS ABOUT DONE STEAMING.
SHAD-DAP!
TELL ME WHAT THE HECK IS GOING ON HERE, DAD!
THEY'RE RELATED?!

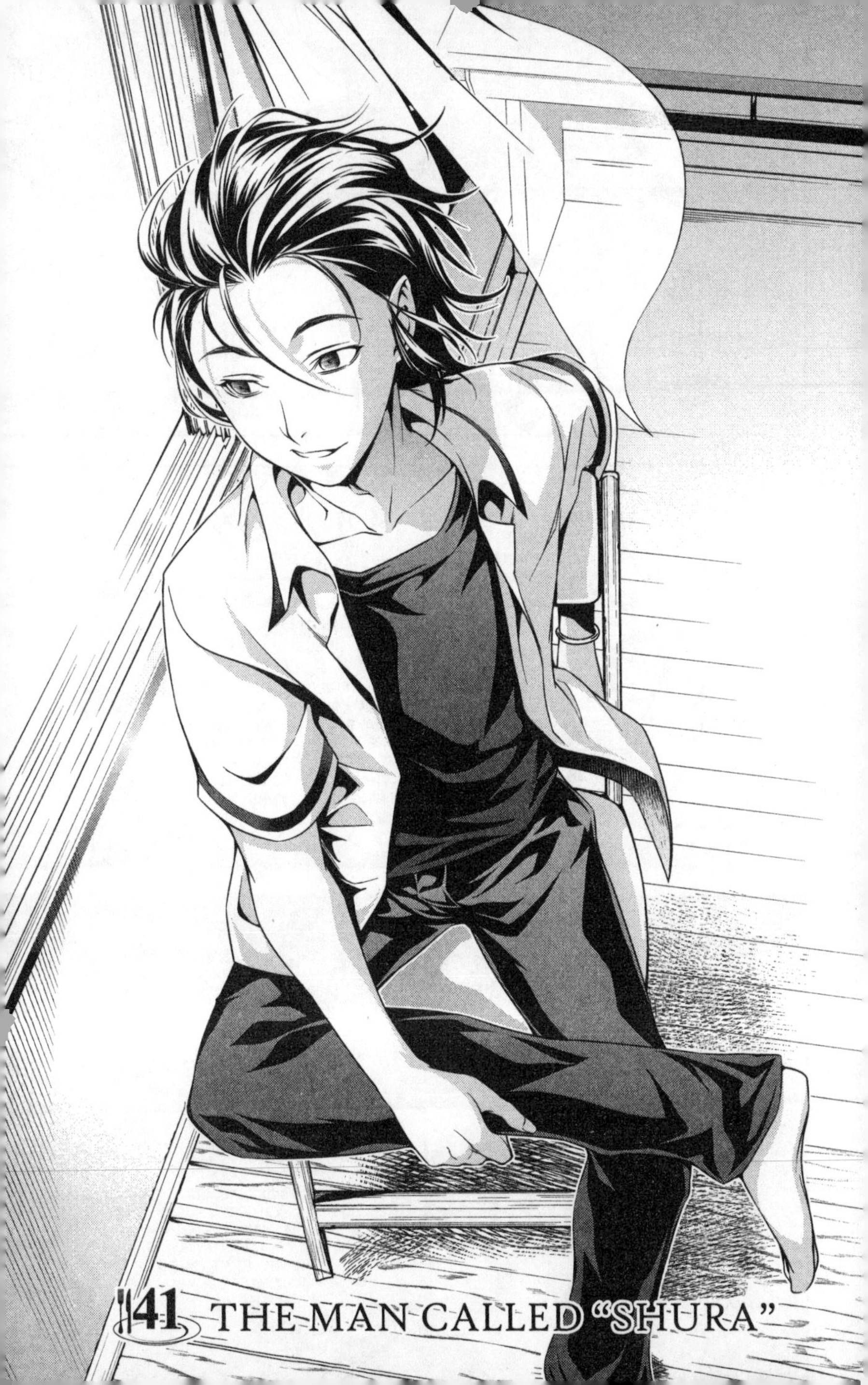

41 THE MAN CALLED "SHURA"

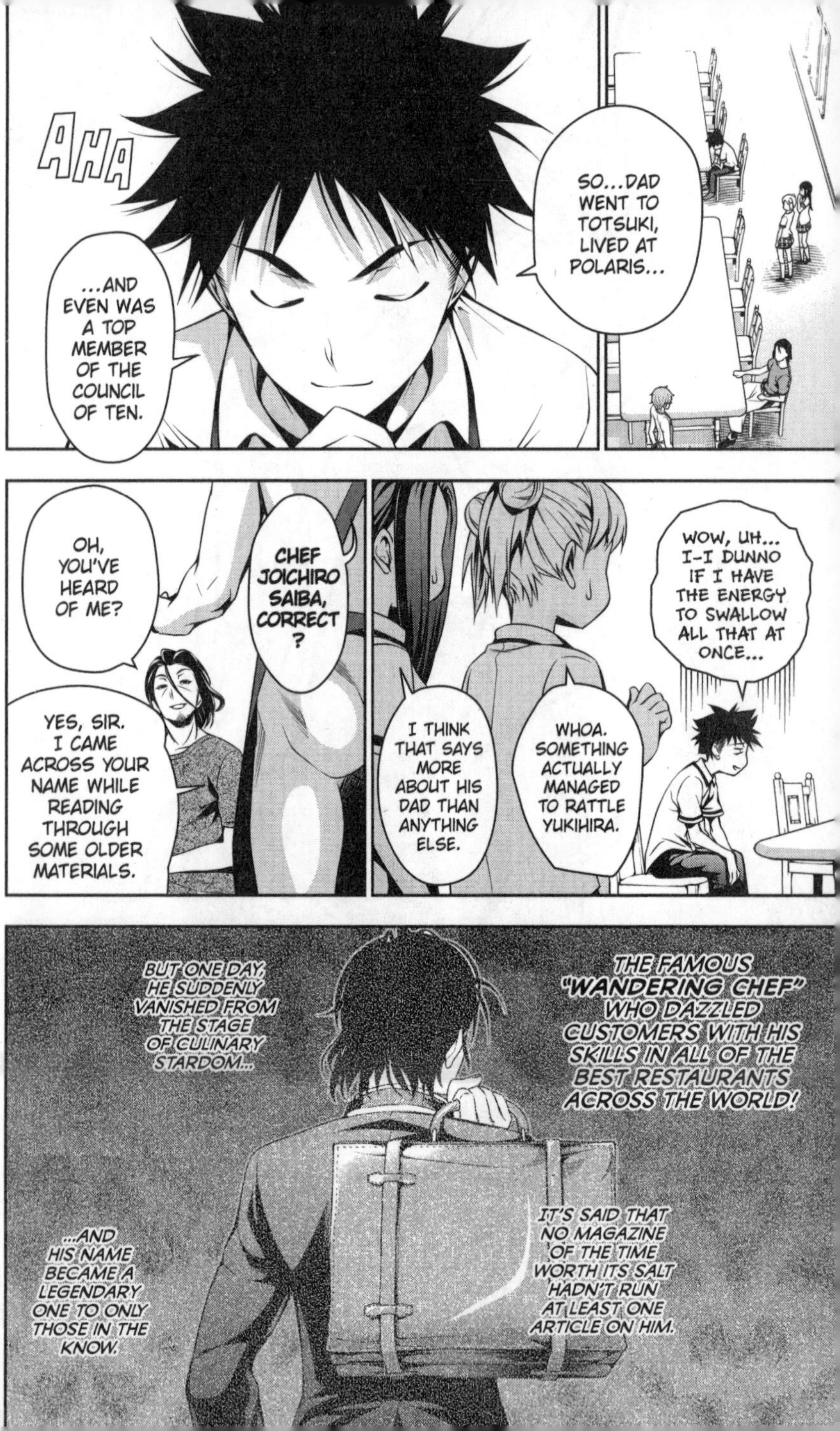
SO...DAD WENT TO TOTSUKI, LIVED AT POLARIS...
AHA
...AND EVEN WAS A TOP MEMBER OF THE COUNCIL OF TEN.
WOW, UH... I-I DUNNO IF I HAVE THE ENERGY TO SWALLOW ALL THAT AT ONCE...
WHOA. SOMETHING ACTUALLY MANAGED TO RATTLE YUKIHIRA.
I THINK THAT SAYS MORE ABOUT HIS DAD THAN ANYTHING ELSE.
CHEF JOICHIRO SAIBA, CORRECT?
OH, YOU'VE HEARD OF ME?
YES, SIR. I CAME ACROSS YOUR NAME WHILE READING THROUGH SOME OLDER MATERIALS.
THE FAMOUS "WANDERING CHEF" WHO DAZZLED CUSTOMERS WITH HIS SKILLS IN ALL OF THE BEST RESTAURANTS ACROSS THE WORLD!
BUT ONE DAY, HE SUDDENLY VANISHED FROM THE STAGE OF CULINARY STARDOM...
IT'S SAID THAT NO MAGAZINE OF THE TIME WORTH ITS SALT HADN'T RUN AT LEAST ONE ARTICLE ON HIM.
...AND HIS NAME BECAME A LEGENDARY ONE TO ONLY THOSE IN THE KNOW.

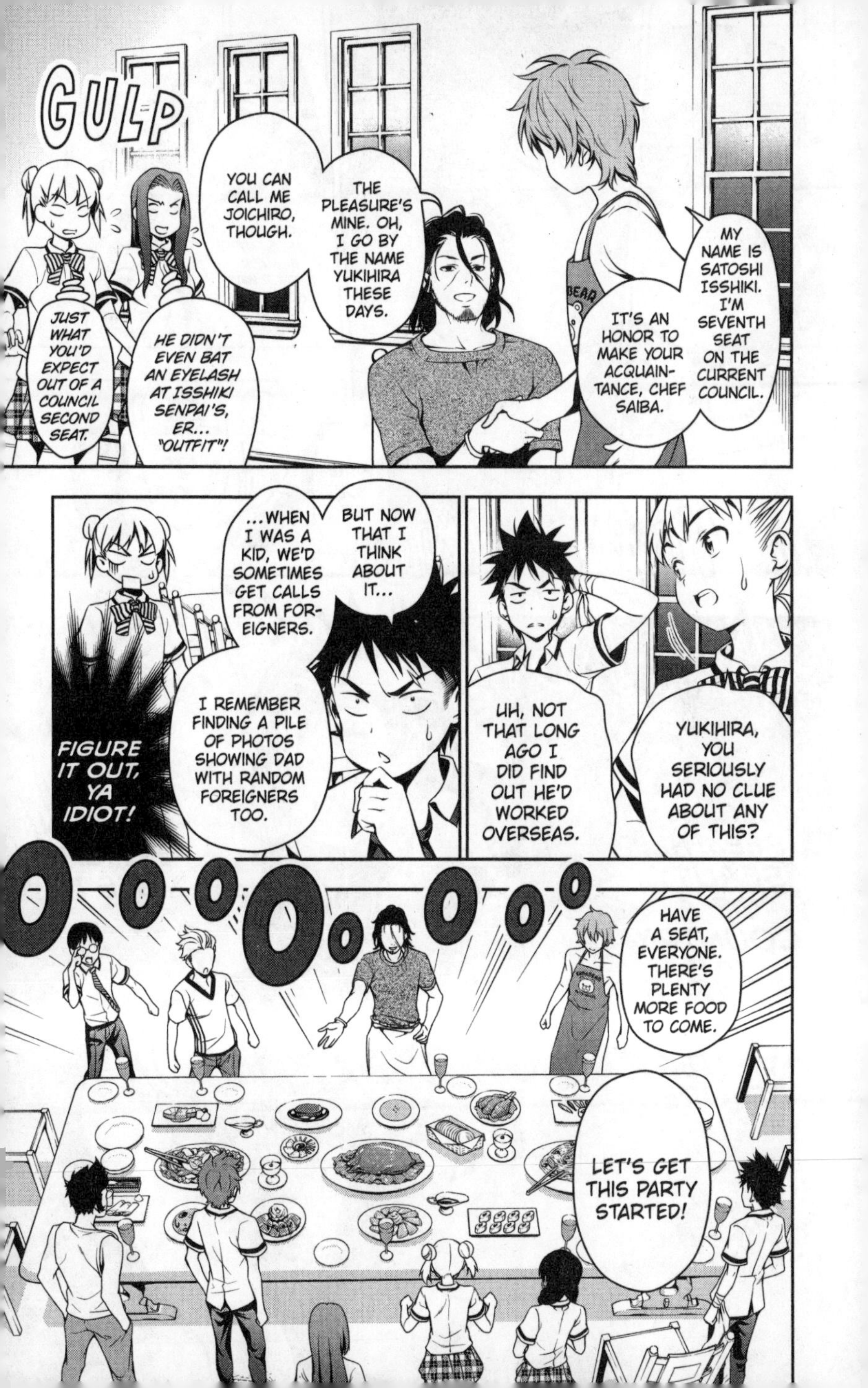
MY NAME IS SATOSHI ISSHIKI. I'M SEVENTH SEAT ON THE CURRENT COUNCIL.
IT'S AN HONOR TO MAKE YOUR ACQUAINTANCE, CHEF SAIBA.
THE PLEASURE'S MINE. OH, I GO BY THE NAME YUKIHIRA THESE DAYS.
YOU CAN CALL ME JOICHIRO, THOUGH.
GULP
HE DIDN'T EVEN BAT AN EYELASH AT ISSHIKI SENPAI'S, ER... "OUTFIT"!
JUST WHAT YOU'D EXPECT OUT OF A COUNCIL SECOND SEAT.
YUKIHIRA, YOU SERIOUSLY HAD NO CLUE ABOUT ANY OF THIS?
UH, NOT THAT LONG AGO I DID FIND OUT HE'D WORKED OVERSEAS.
BUT NOW THAT I THINK ABOUT IT...
...WHEN I WAS A KID, WE'D SOMETIMES GET CALLS FROM FOREIGNERS.
I REMEMBER FINDING A PILE OF PHOTOS SHOWING DAD WITH RANDOM FOREIGNERS TOO.
FIGURE IT OUT, YA IDIOT!
HAVE A SEAT, EVERYONE. THERE'S PLENTY MORE FOOD TO COME.
LET'S GET THIS PARTY STARTED!
OOOOOOOO

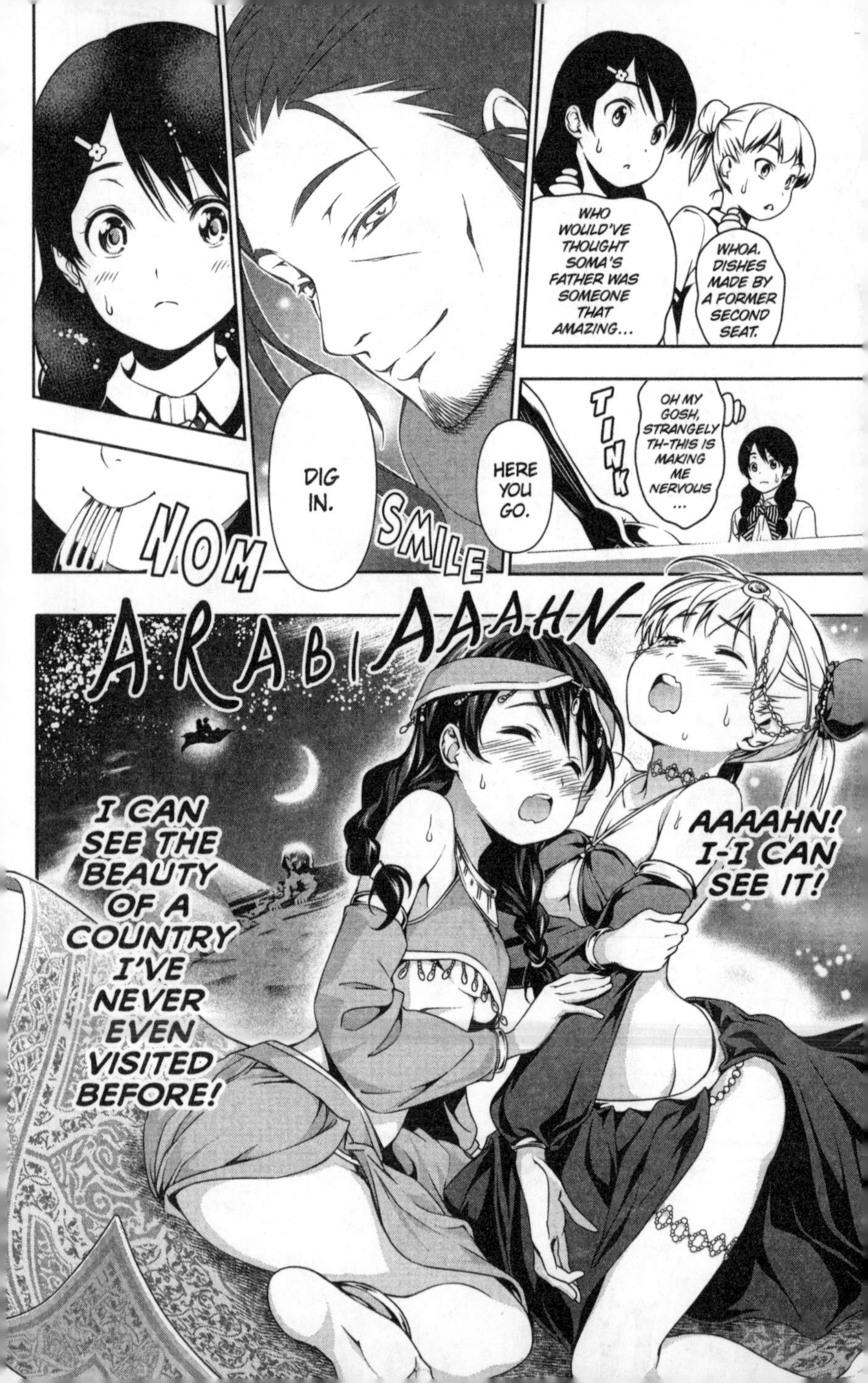
WHOA. DISHES MADE BY A FORMER SECOND SEAT.
WHO WOULD'VE THOUGHT SOMA'S FATHER WAS SOMEONE THAT AMAZING...
TINK
OH MY GOSH, STRANGELY TH-THIS IS MAKING ME NERVOUS...
HERE YOU GO.
SMILE
DIG IN.
NOM
ARABIAAAHN
AAAAHN! I-I CAN SEE IT!
I CAN SEE THE BEAUTY OF A COUNTRY I'VE NEVER EVEN VISITED BEFORE!

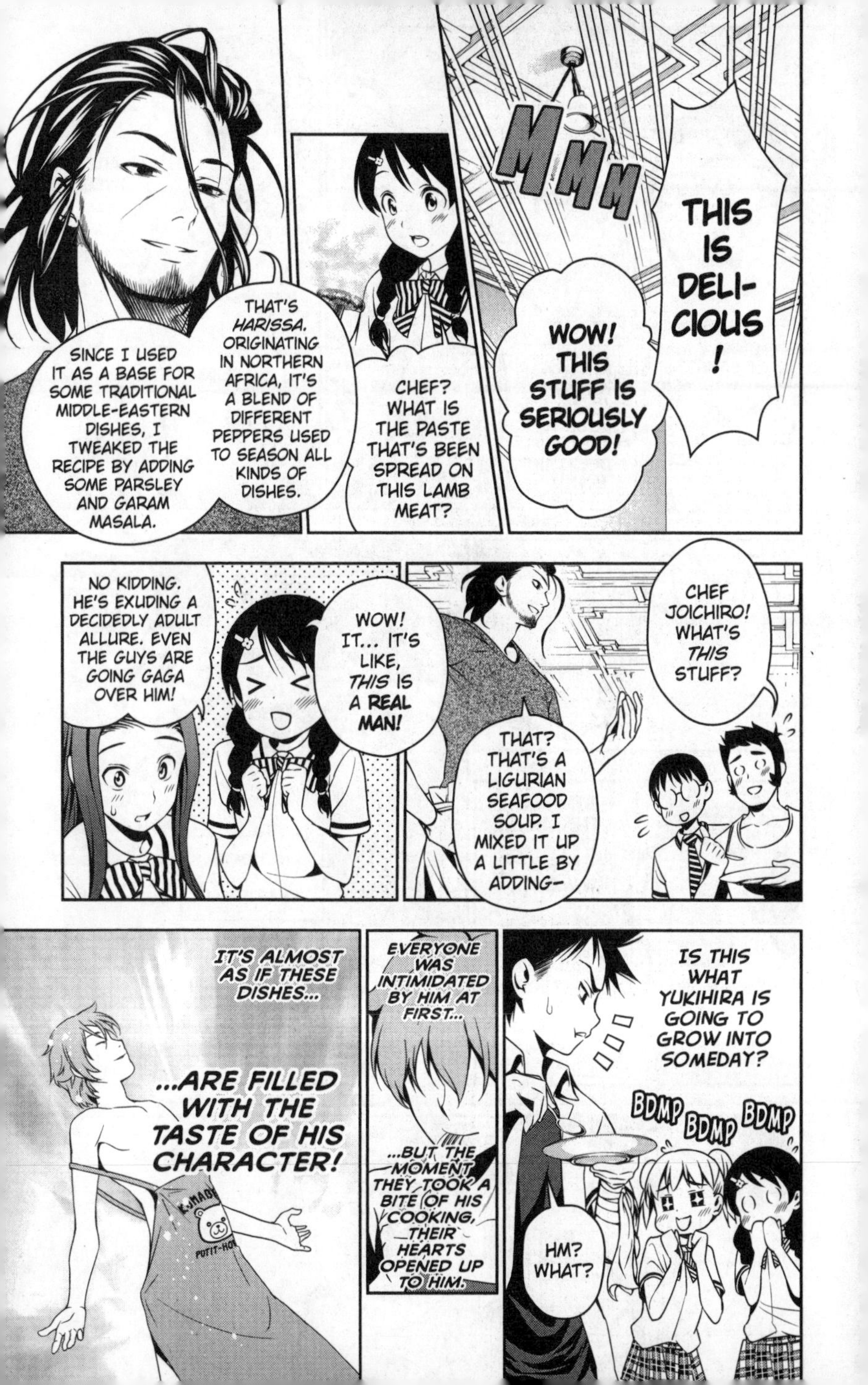
MMM
THIS IS DELI-CIOUS!
WOW! THIS STUFF IS SERIOUSLY GOOD!
CHEF? WHAT IS THE PASTE THAT'S BEEN SPREAD ON THIS LAMB MEAT?
THAT'S *HARISSA*. ORIGINATING IN NORTHERN AFRICA, IT'S A BLEND OF DIFFERENT PEPPERS USED TO SEASON ALL KINDS OF DISHES.
SINCE I USED IT AS A BASE FOR SOME TRADITIONAL MIDDLE-EASTERN DISHES, I TWEAKED THE RECIPE BY ADDING SOME PARSLEY AND GARAM MASALA.
CHEF JOICHIRO! WHAT'S *THIS* STUFF?
THAT? THAT'S A LIGURIAN SEAFOOD SOUP. I MIXED IT UP A LITTLE BY ADDING—
WOW! IT... IT'S LIKE, *THIS* IS A **REAL MAN!**
NO KIDDING. HE'S EXUDING A DECIDEDLY ADULT ALLURE. EVEN THE GUYS ARE GOING GAGA OVER HIM!
IS THIS WHAT YUKIHIRA IS GOING TO GROW INTO SOMEDAY?
BDMP BDMP BDMP
HM? WHAT?
EVERYONE WAS INTIMIDATED BY HIM AT FIRST...
...BUT THE MOMENT THEY TOOK A BITE OF HIS COOKING, THEIR HEARTS OPENED UP TO HIM.
IT'S ALMOST AS IF THESE DISHES...
...ARE FILLED WITH THE TASTE OF HIS CHARACTER!

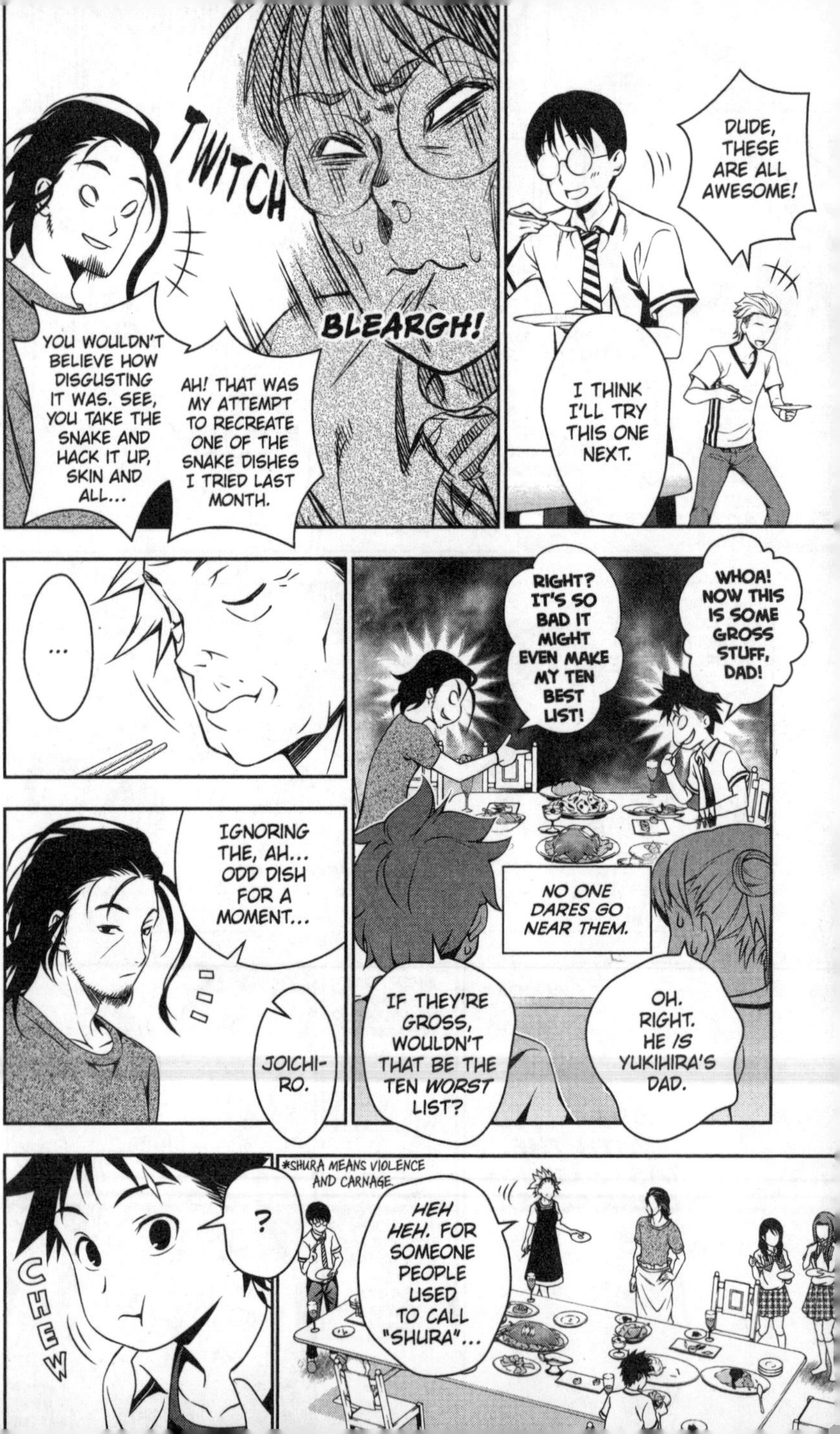
DUDE, THESE ARE ALL AWESOME!
I THINK I'LL TRY THIS ONE NEXT.
TWITCH
BLEARGH!
AH! THAT WAS MY ATTEMPT TO RECREATE ONE OF THE SNAKE DISHES I TRIED LAST MONTH.
YOU WOULDN'T BELIEVE HOW DISGUSTING IT WAS. SEE, YOU TAKE THE SNAKE AND HACK IT UP, SKIN AND ALL...
WHOA! NOW THIS IS SOME GROSS STUFF, DAD!
RIGHT? IT'S SO BAD IT MIGHT EVEN MAKE MY TEN BEST LIST!
NO ONE DARES GO NEAR THEM.
OH. RIGHT. HE *IS* YUKIHIRA'S DAD.
IF THEY'RE GROSS, WOULDN'T THAT BE THE TEN *WORST* LIST?
...
IGNORING THE, AH... ODD DISH FOR A MOMENT...
JOICHI-RO.
*SHURA MEANS VIOLENCE AND CARNAGE.
HEH HEH. FOR SOMEONE PEOPLE USED TO CALL "SHURA"...
?
CHEW

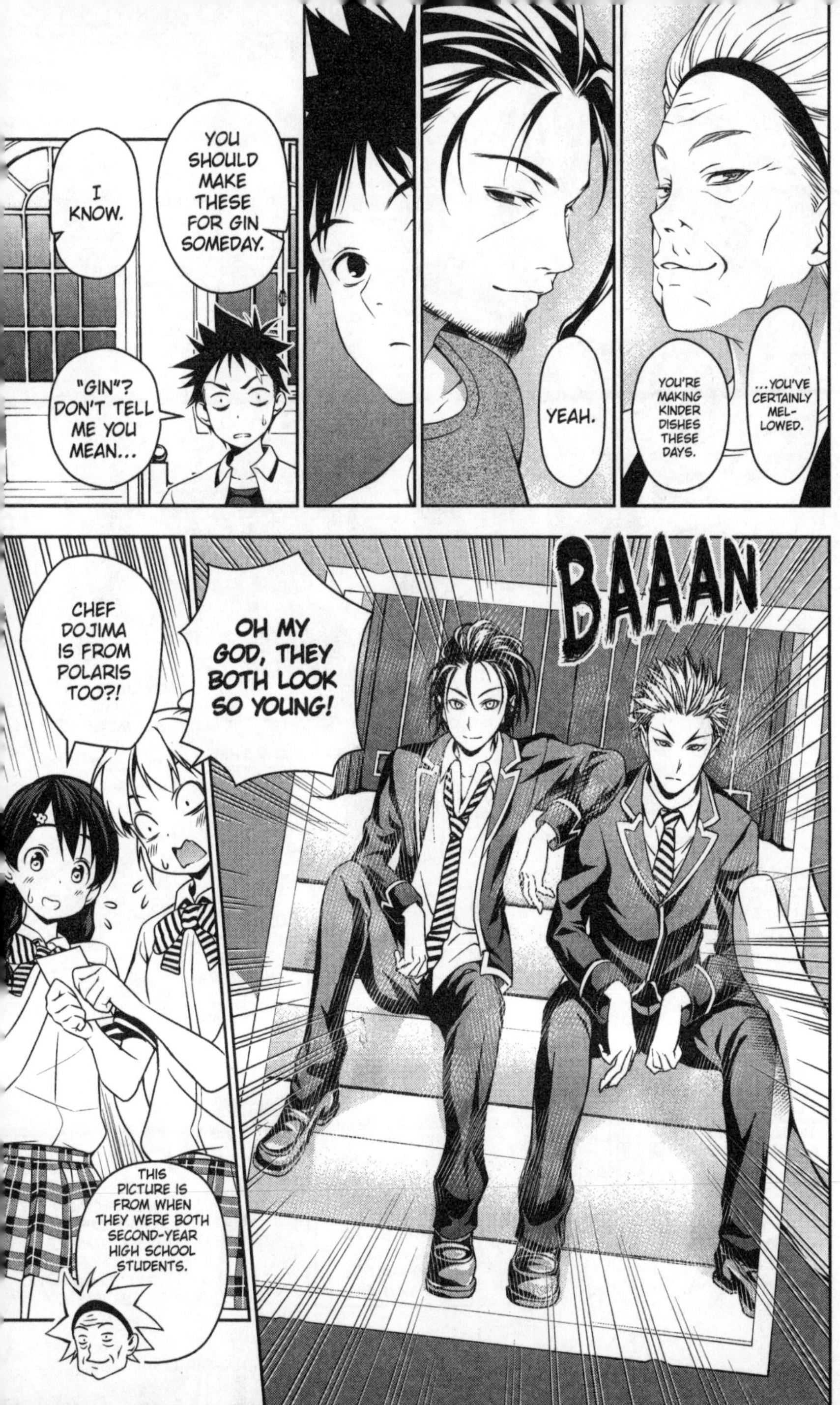
...YOU'VE CERTAINLY MEL-LOWED.
YOU'RE MAKING KINDER DISHES THESE DAYS.
YEAH.
YOU SHOULD MAKE THESE FOR GIN SOMEDAY.
I KNOW.
"GIN"? DON'T TELL ME YOU MEAN...
BAAAN
OH MY GOD, THEY BOTH LOOK SO YOUNG!
CHEF DOJIMA IS FROM POLARIS TOO?!
THIS PICTURE IS FROM WHEN THEY WERE BOTH SECOND-YEAR HIGH SCHOOL STUDENTS.

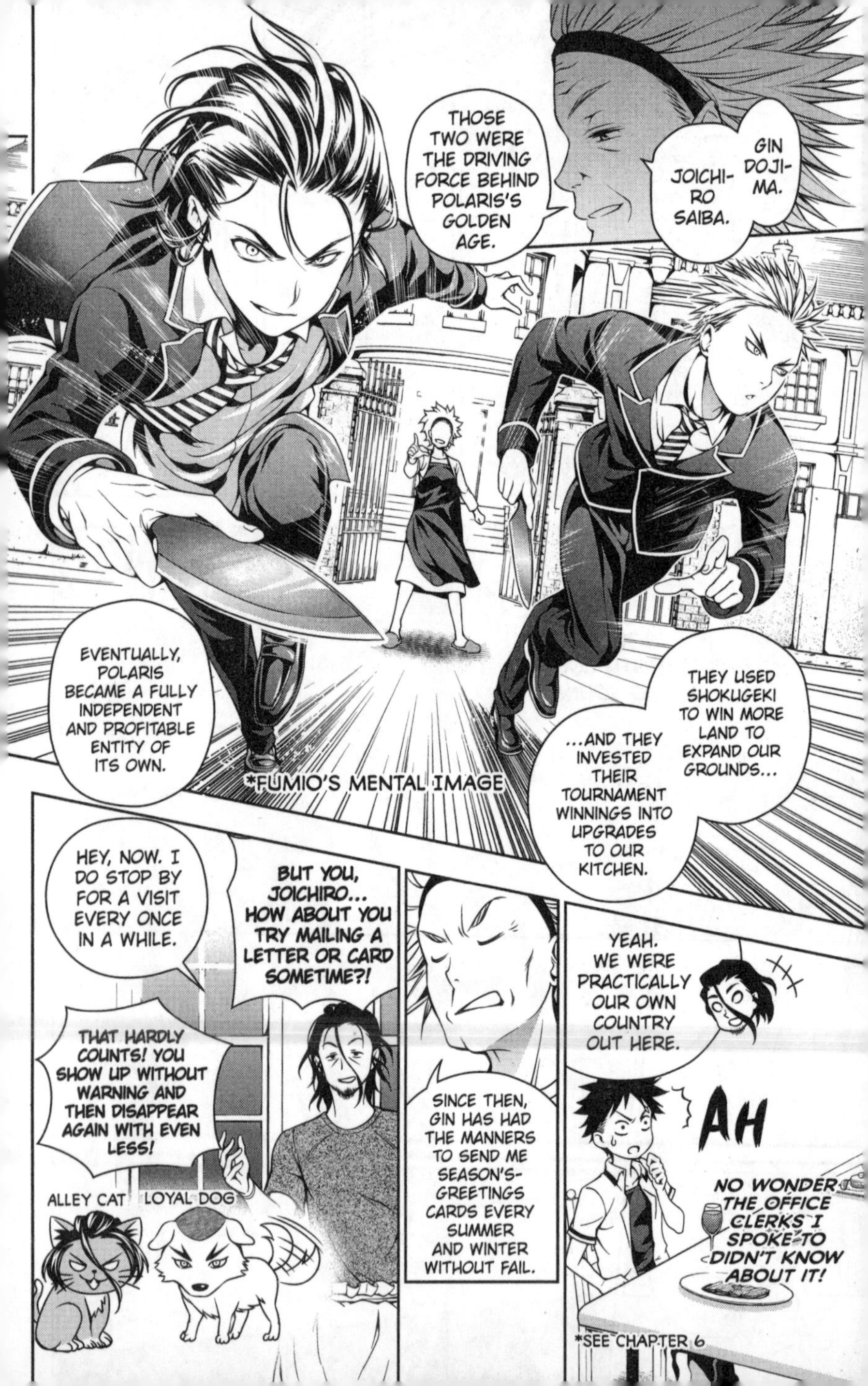
GIN DOJIMA.
JOICHIRO SAIBA.
THOSE TWO WERE THE DRIVING FORCE BEHIND POLARIS'S GOLDEN AGE.
THEY USED SHOKUGEKI TO WIN MORE LAND TO EXPAND OUR GROUNDS...
...AND THEY INVESTED THEIR TOURNAMENT WINNINGS INTO UPGRADES TO OUR KITCHEN.
EVENTUALLY, POLARIS BECAME A FULLY INDEPENDENT AND PROFITABLE ENTITY OF ITS OWN.
*FUMIO'S MENTAL IMAGE
YEAH. WE WERE PRACTICALLY OUR OWN COUNTRY OUT HERE.
AH
NO WONDER THE OFFICE CLERKS I SPOKE TO DIDN'T KNOW ABOUT IT!
*SEE CHAPTER 6
SINCE THEN, GIN HAS HAD THE MANNERS TO SEND ME SEASON'S-GREETINGS CARDS EVERY SUMMER AND WINTER WITHOUT FAIL.
BUT YOU, JOICHIRO... HOW ABOUT YOU TRY MAILING A LETTER OR CARD SOMETIME?!
HEY, NOW. I DO STOP BY FOR A VISIT EVERY ONCE IN A WHILE.
THAT HARDLY COUNTS! YOU SHOW UP WITHOUT WARNING AND THEN DISAPPEAR AGAIN WITH EVEN LESS!
ALLEY CAT
LOYAL DOG

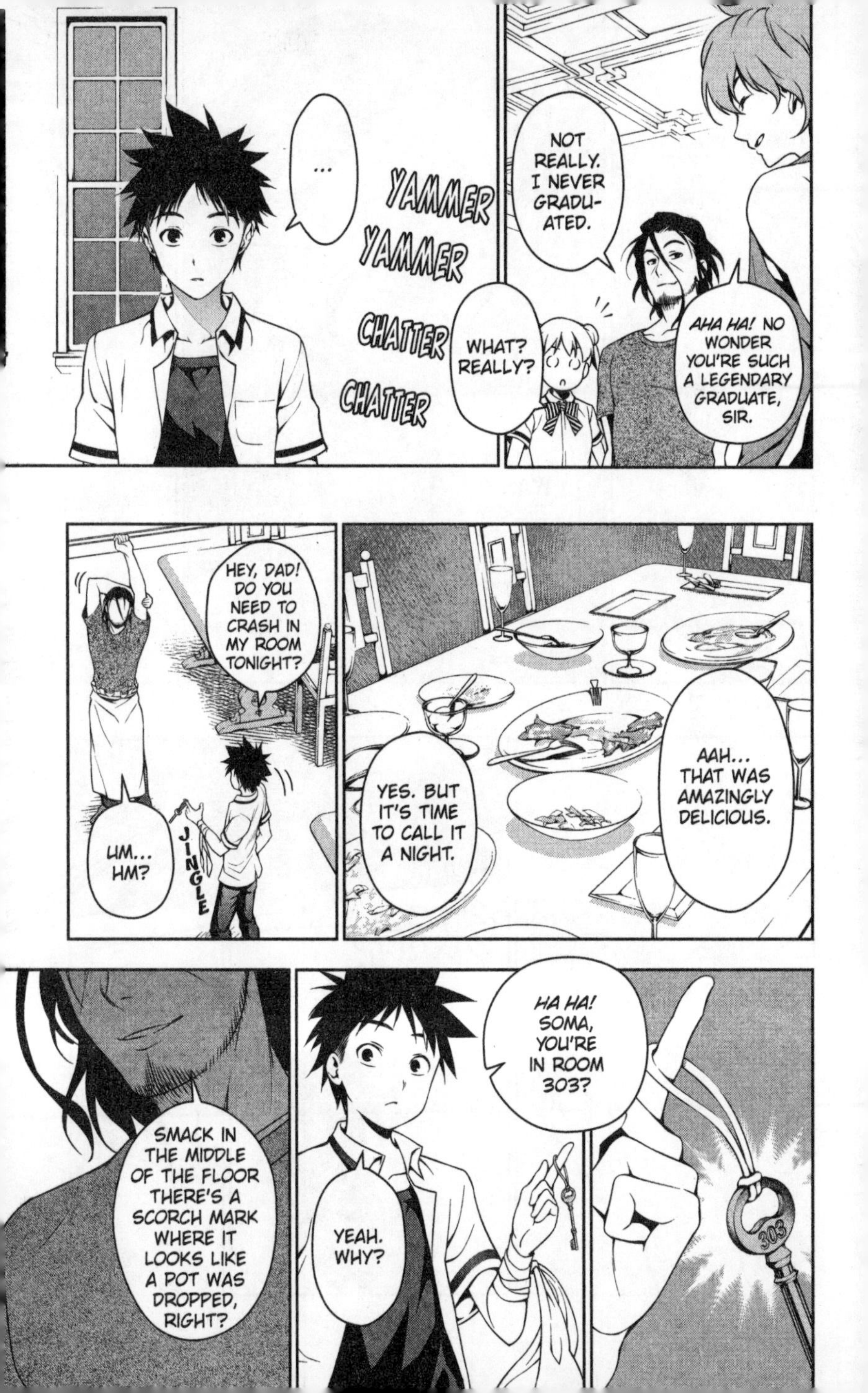
AHA HA! NO WONDER YOU'RE SUCH A LEGENDARY GRADUATE, SIR.
NOT REALLY. I NEVER GRADUATED.
WHAT? REALLY?
...
YAMMER YAMMER
CHATTER CHATTER
AAH... THAT WAS AMAZINGLY DELICIOUS.
YES. BUT IT'S TIME TO CALL IT A NIGHT.
HEY, DAD! DO YOU NEED TO CRASH IN MY ROOM TONIGHT?
UM... HM?
JINGLE
HA HA! SOMA, YOU'RE IN ROOM 303?
YEAH. WHY?
303
SMACK IN THE MIDDLE OF THE FLOOR THERE'S A SCORCH MARK WHERE IT LOOKS LIKE A POT WAS DROPPED, RIGHT?

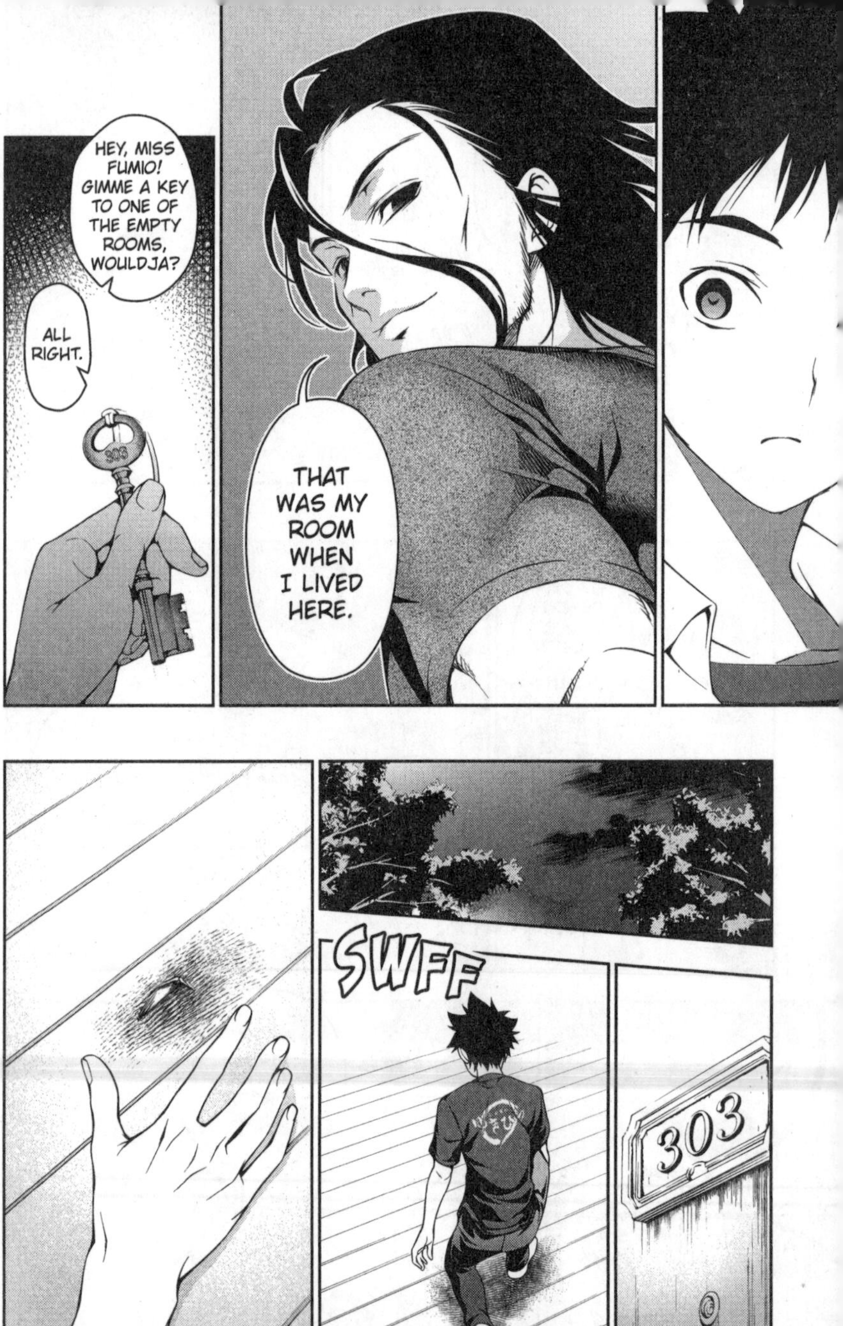
THAT WAS MY ROOM WHEN I LIVED HERE.
HEY, MISS FUMIO! GIMME A KEY TO ONE OF THE EMPTY ROOMS, WOULDJA?
ALL RIGHT.
303
SWFF
303

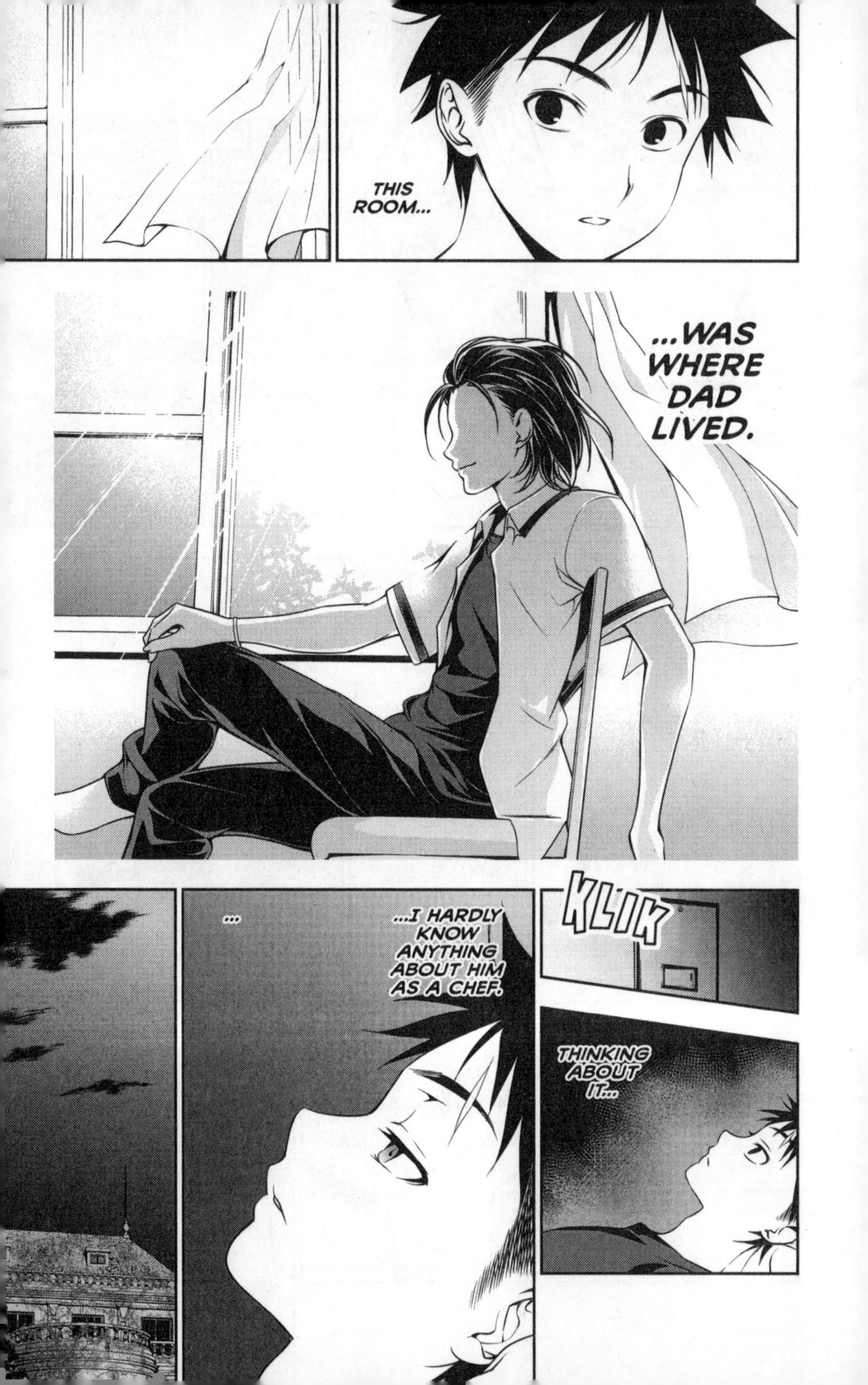
THIS ROOM...
...WAS WHERE DAD LIVED.
KLIK
THINKING ABOUT IT...
...I HARDLY KNOW ANYTHING ABOUT HIM AS A CHEF.
...

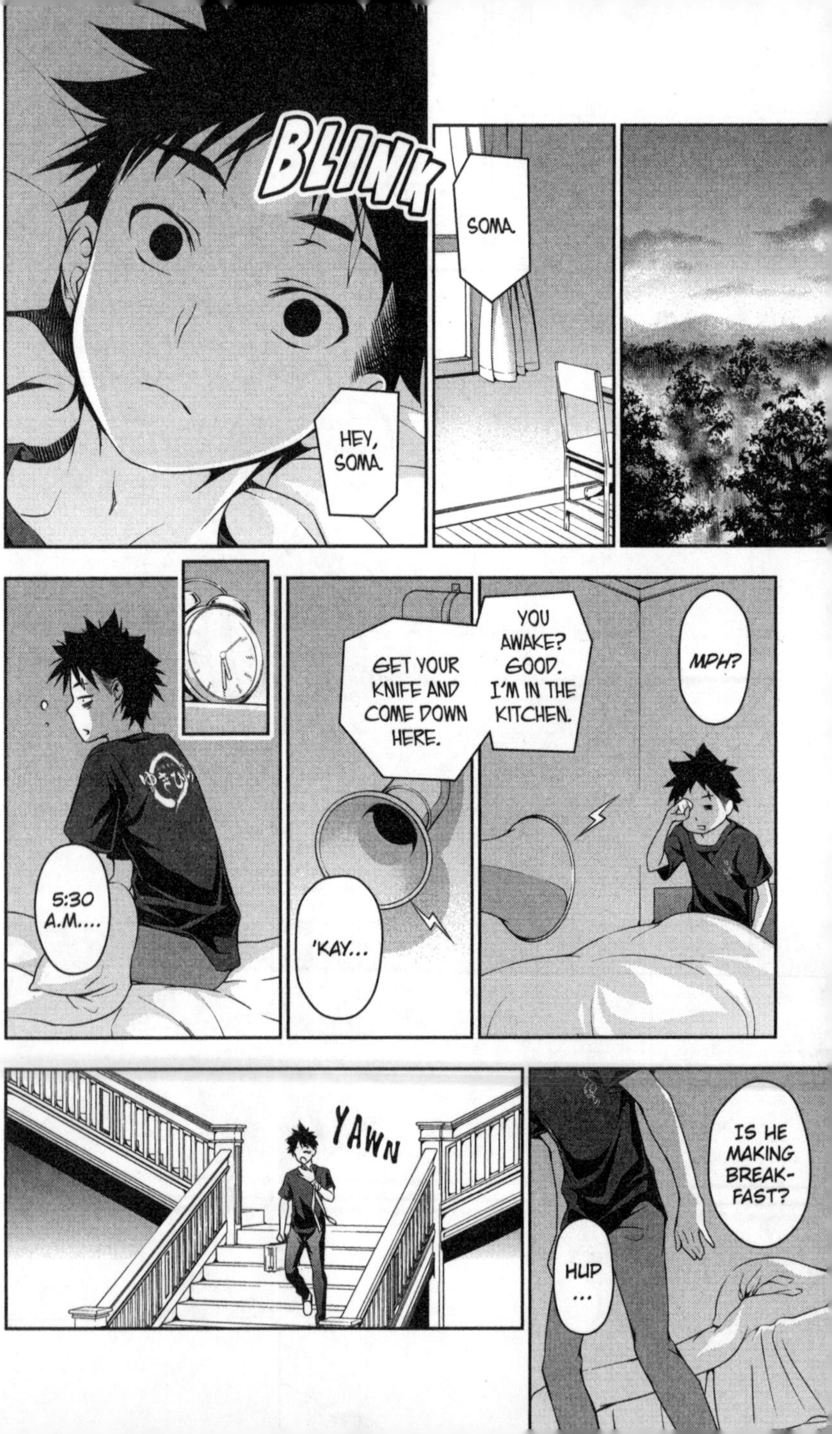
SOMA.
BLINK
HEY, SOMA.
MPH?
YOU AWAKE? GOOD. I'M IN THE KITCHEN.
GET YOUR KNIFE AND COME DOWN HERE.
'KAY...
5:30 A.M....
IS HE MAKING BREAK-FAST?
HUP ...
YAWN

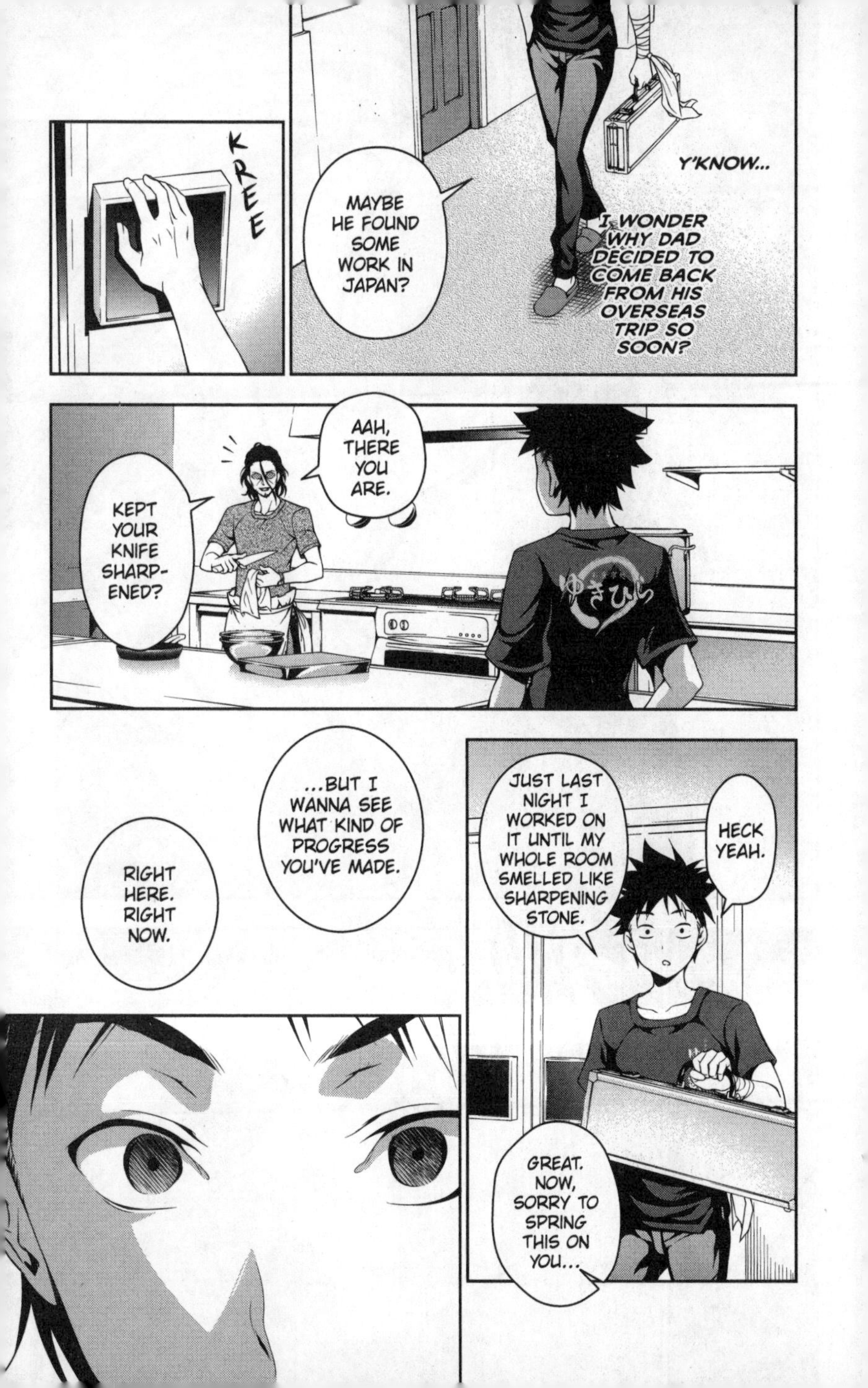
Y'KNOW...
I WONDER WHY DAD DECIDED TO COME BACK FROM HIS OVERSEAS TRIP SO SOON?
MAYBE HE FOUND SOME WORK IN JAPAN?
KREE
AAH, THERE YOU ARE.
KEPT YOUR KNIFE SHARPENED?
HECK YEAH.
JUST LAST NIGHT I WORKED ON IT UNTIL MY WHOLE ROOM SMELLED LIKE SHARPENING STONE.
GREAT. NOW, SORRY TO SPRING THIS ON YOU...
...BUT I WANNA SEE WHAT KIND OF PROGRESS YOU'VE MADE.
RIGHT HERE. RIGHT NOW.

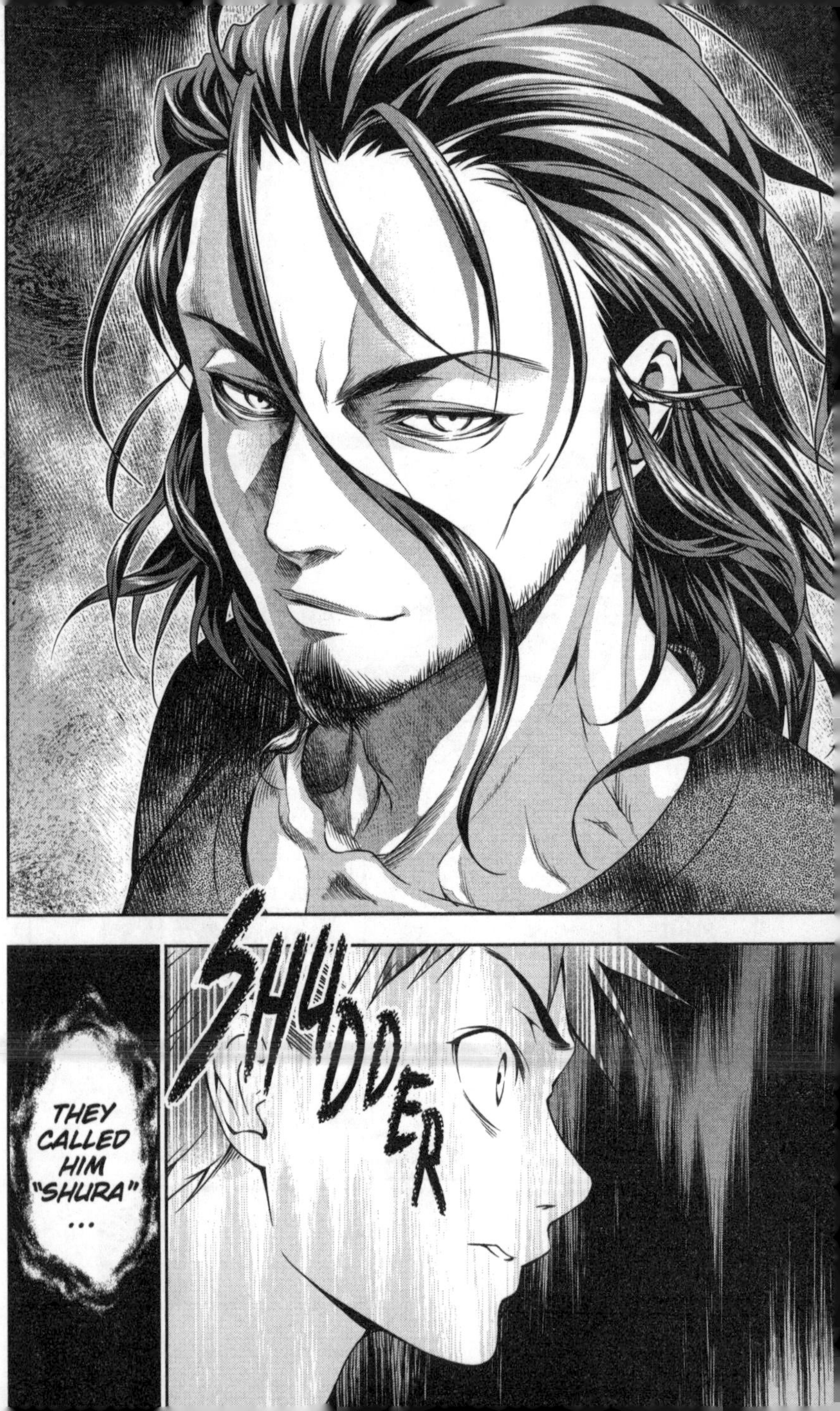
SHUDDER
THEY CALLED HIM "SHURA"...

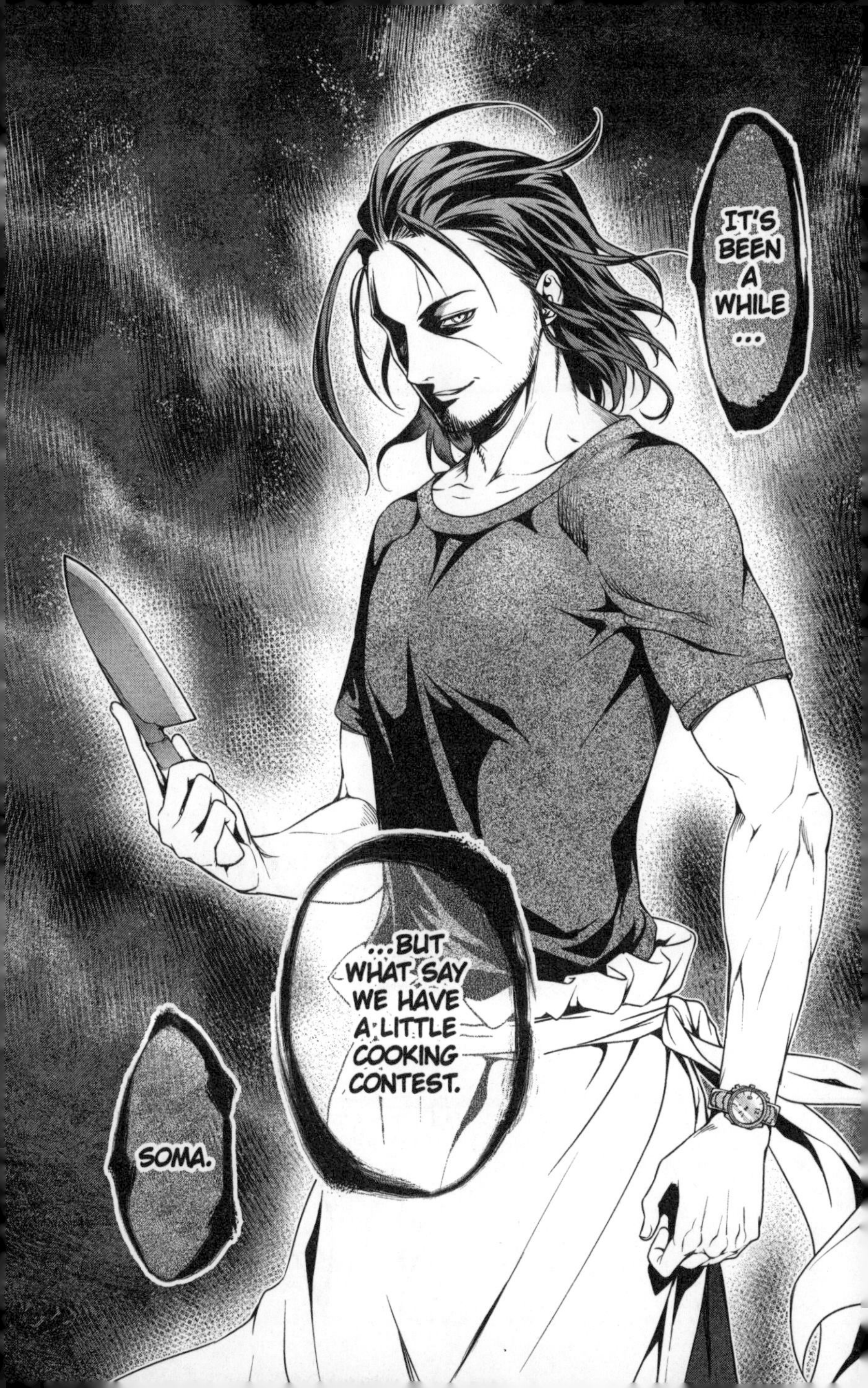
IT'S BEEN A WHILE ...
...BUT WHAT SAY WE HAVE A LITTLE COOKING CONTEST.
SOMA.

THANKS TO MANY PASSIONATE REQUESTS FROM A PORTION OF THE FANBASE, HERE IS A SKETCH OF RYOKO SAKAKI DECKED OUT IN THE "ARABIAAAHN" OUTFIT.

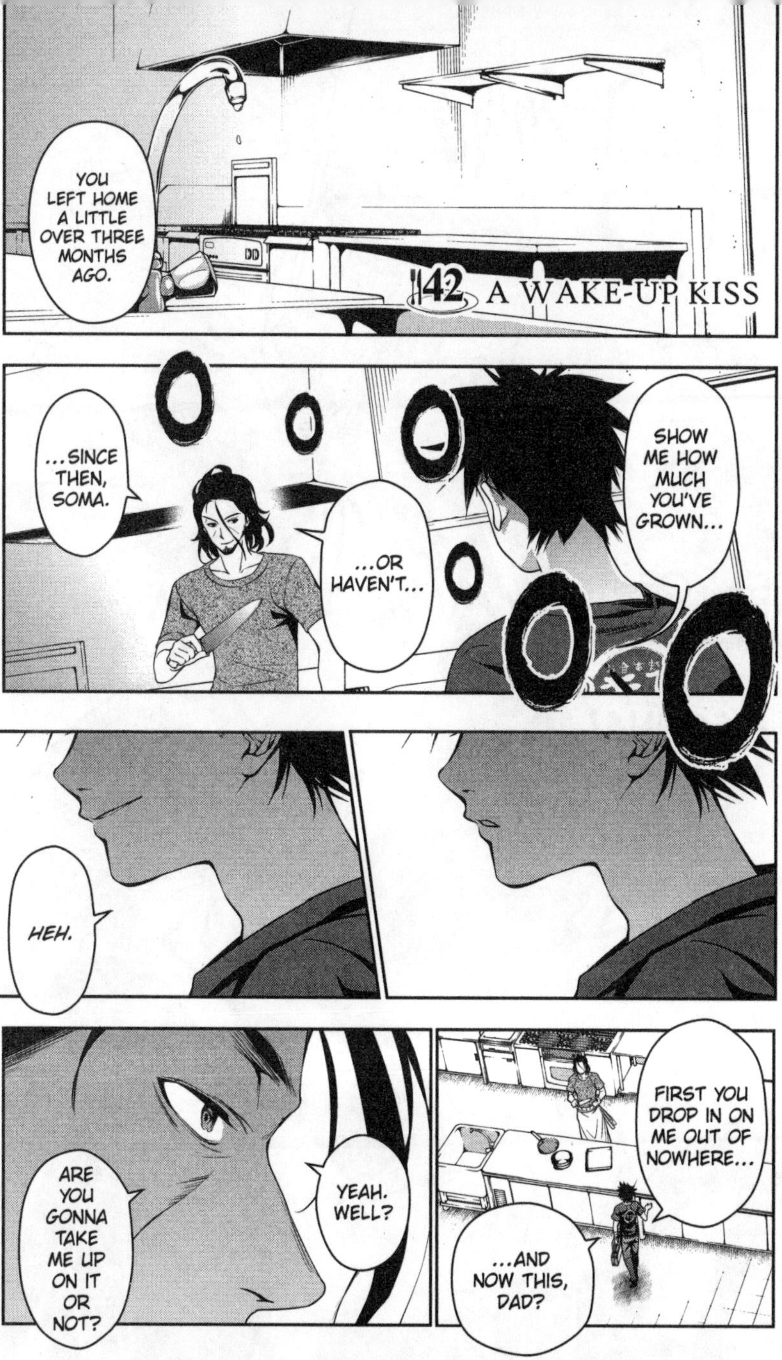
YOU LEFT HOME A LITTLE OVER THREE MONTHS AGO.
42 A WAKE-UP KISS
SHOW ME HOW MUCH YOU'VE GROWN...
...OR HAVEN'T...
...SINCE THEN, SOMA.
HEH.
FIRST YOU DROP IN ON ME OUT OF NOWHERE...
...AND NOW THIS, DAD?
YEAH. WELL?
ARE YOU GONNA TAKE ME UP ON IT OR NOT?

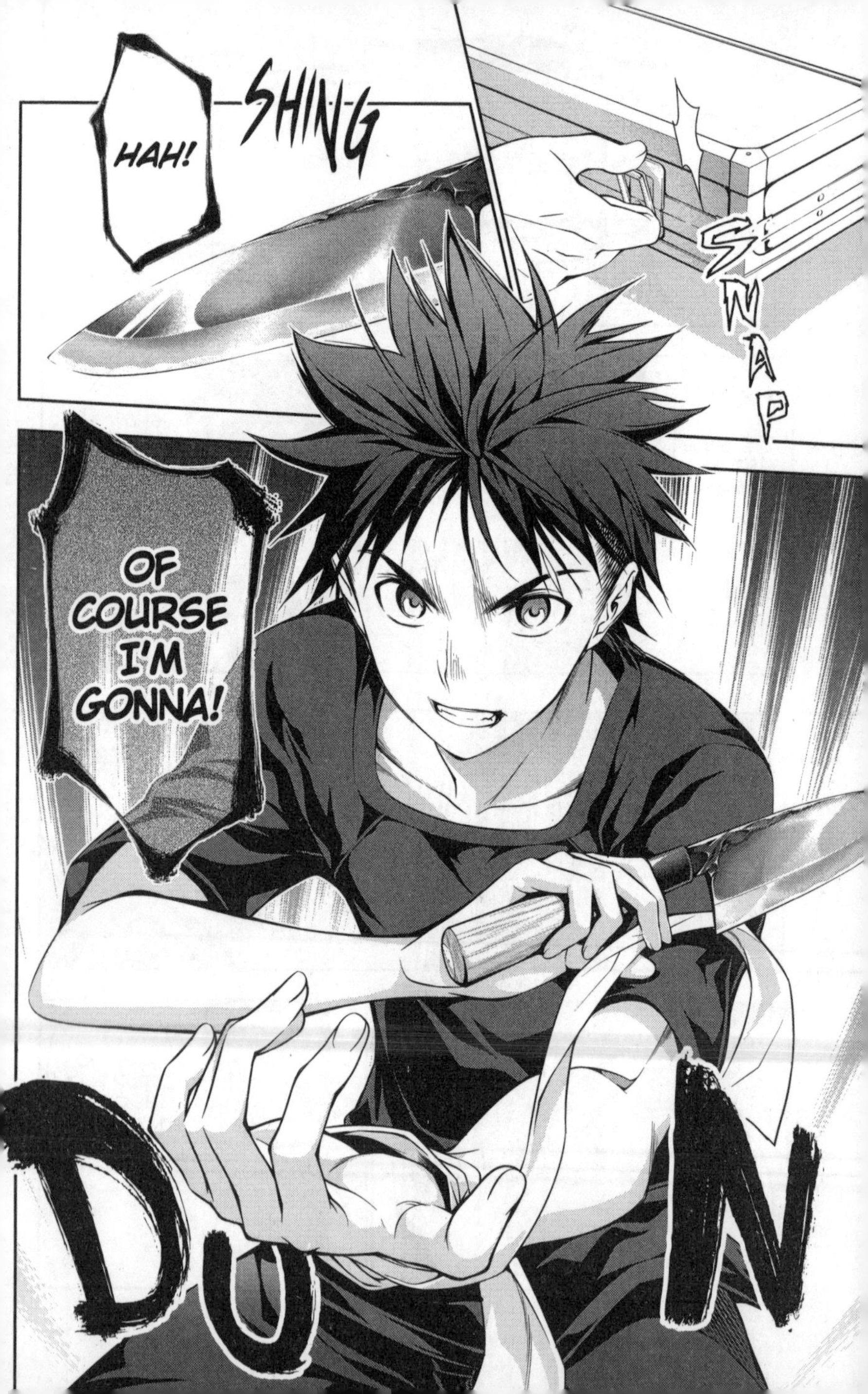
SNAP
SHING
HAH!
OF COURSE I'M GONNA!

42 A WAKE-UP KISS

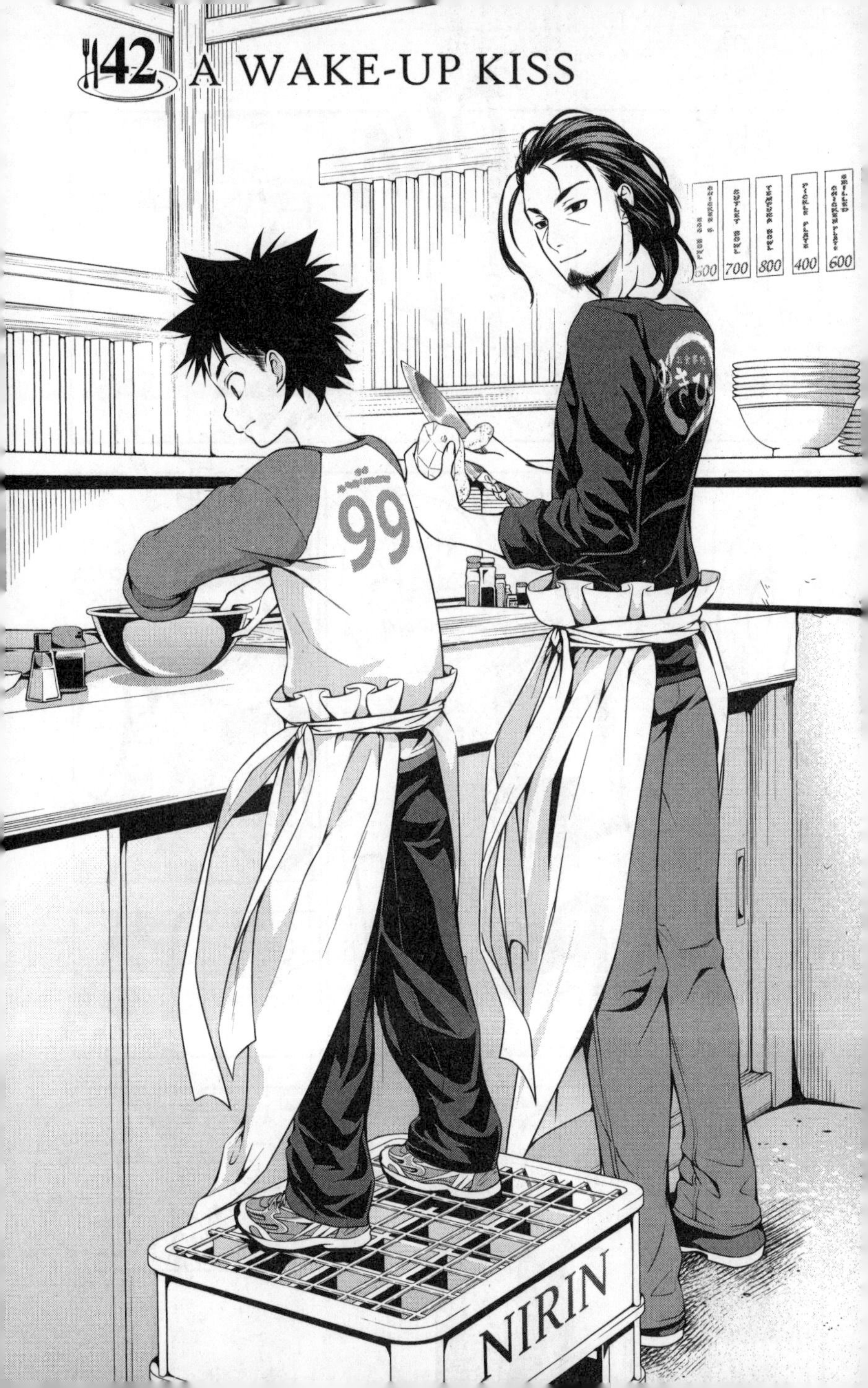
400
600
700
800
400
600
99
NIRIN

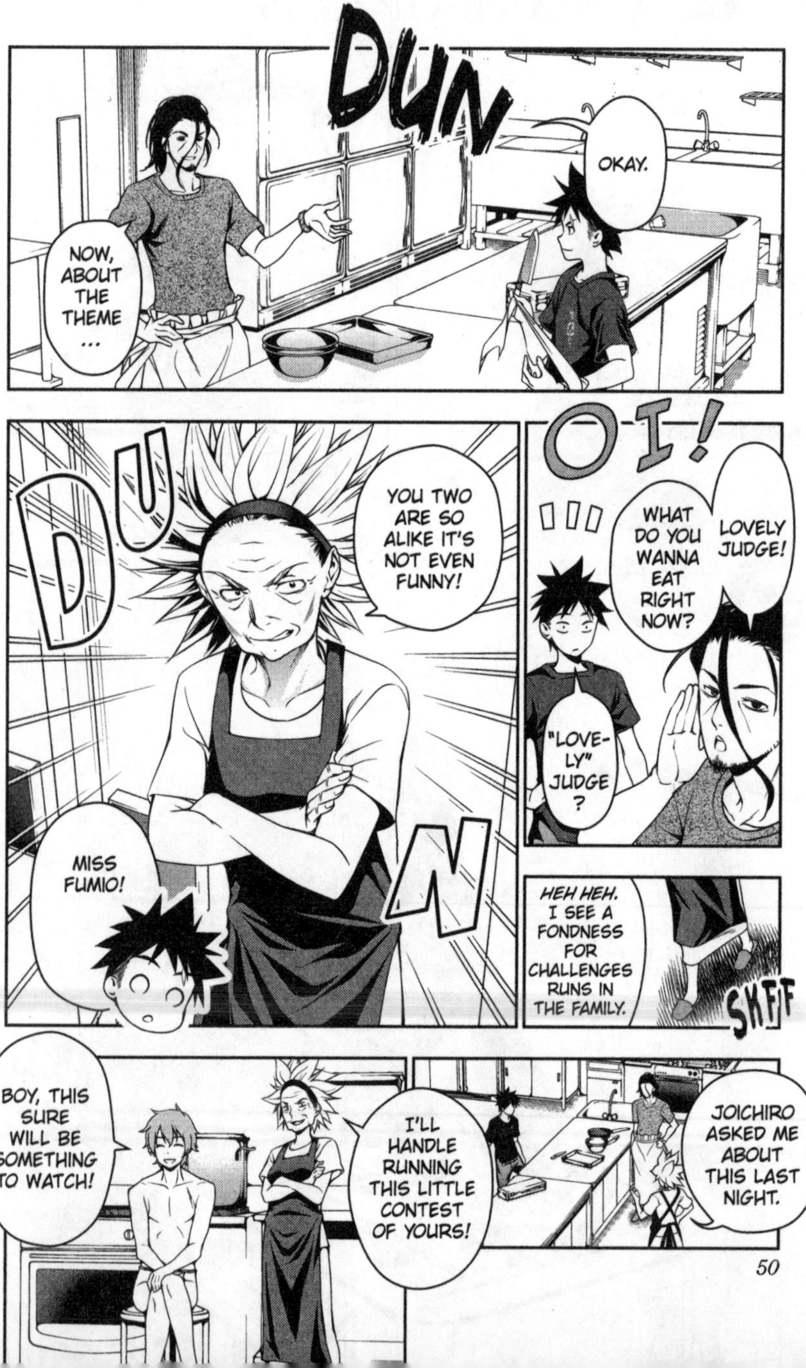
DUN
OKAY.
NOW, ABOUT THE THEME...
OI!
LOVELY JUDGE!
WHAT DO YOU WANNA EAT RIGHT NOW?
...
"LOVE-LY" JUDGE?
HEH HEH. I SEE A FONDNESS FOR CHALLENGES RUNS IN THE FAMILY.
SKFF
DUN
YOU TWO ARE SO ALIKE IT'S NOT EVEN FUNNY!
MISS FUMIO!
JOICHIRO ASKED ME ABOUT THIS LAST NIGHT.
I'LL HANDLE RUNNING THIS LITTLE CONTEST OF YOURS!
BOY, THIS SURE WILL BE SOMETHING TO WATCH!

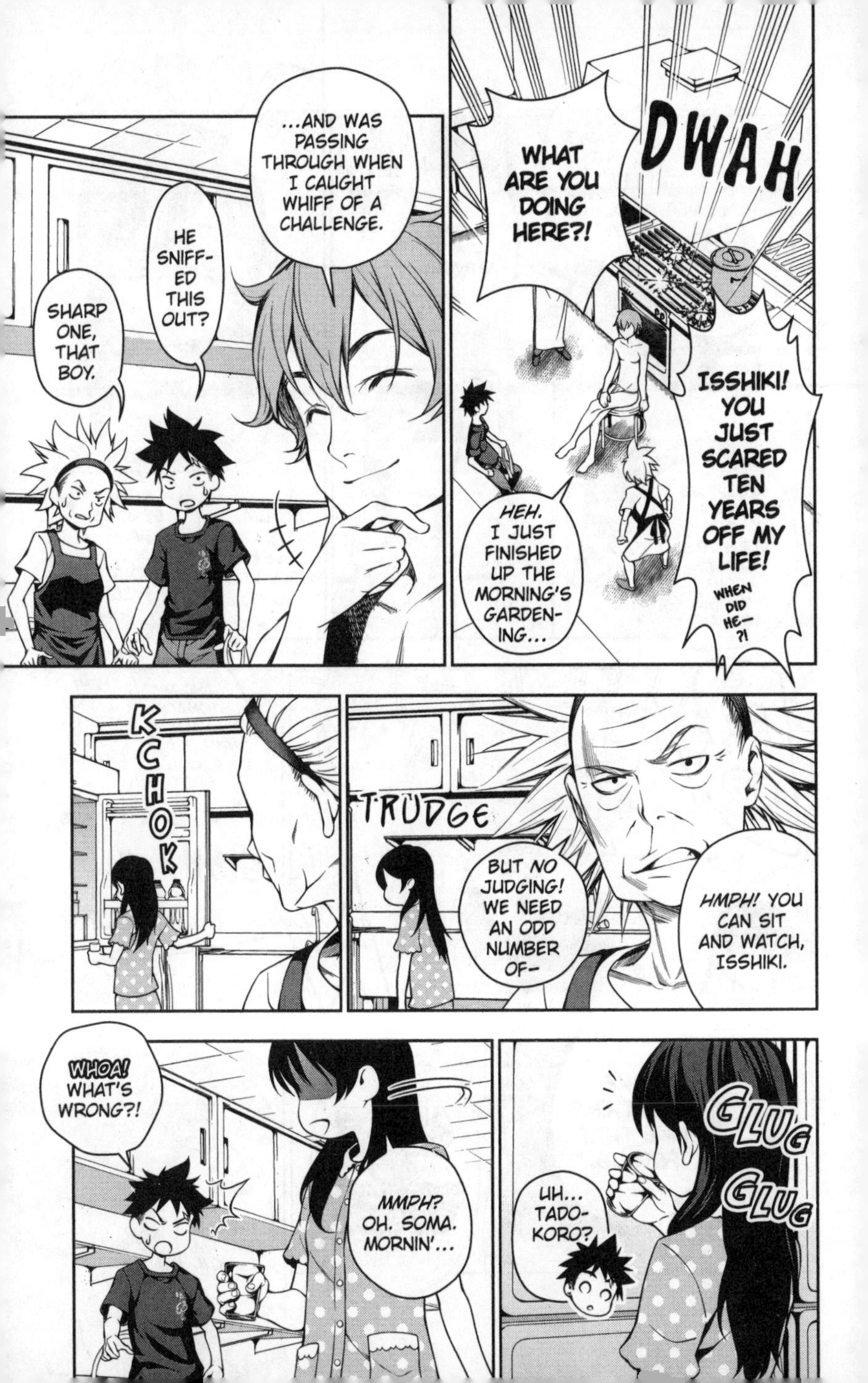
DWAH
WHAT ARE YOU DOING HERE?!
ISSHIKI! YOU JUST SCARED TEN YEARS OFF MY LIFE!
WHEN DID HE—?!
HEH. I JUST FINISHED UP THE MORNING'S GARDEN-ING...
...AND WAS PASSING THROUGH WHEN I CAUGHT WHIFF OF A CHALLENGE.
HE SNIFF-ED THIS OUT?
SHARP ONE, THAT BOY.
HMPH! YOU CAN SIT AND WATCH, ISSHIKI.
BUT NO JUDGING! WE NEED AN ODD NUMBER OF-
TRUDGE
KCHOK
GLUG GLUG
UH... TADO-KORO?
WHOA! WHAT'S WRONG?!
MMPH? OH. SOMA. MORNIN'...

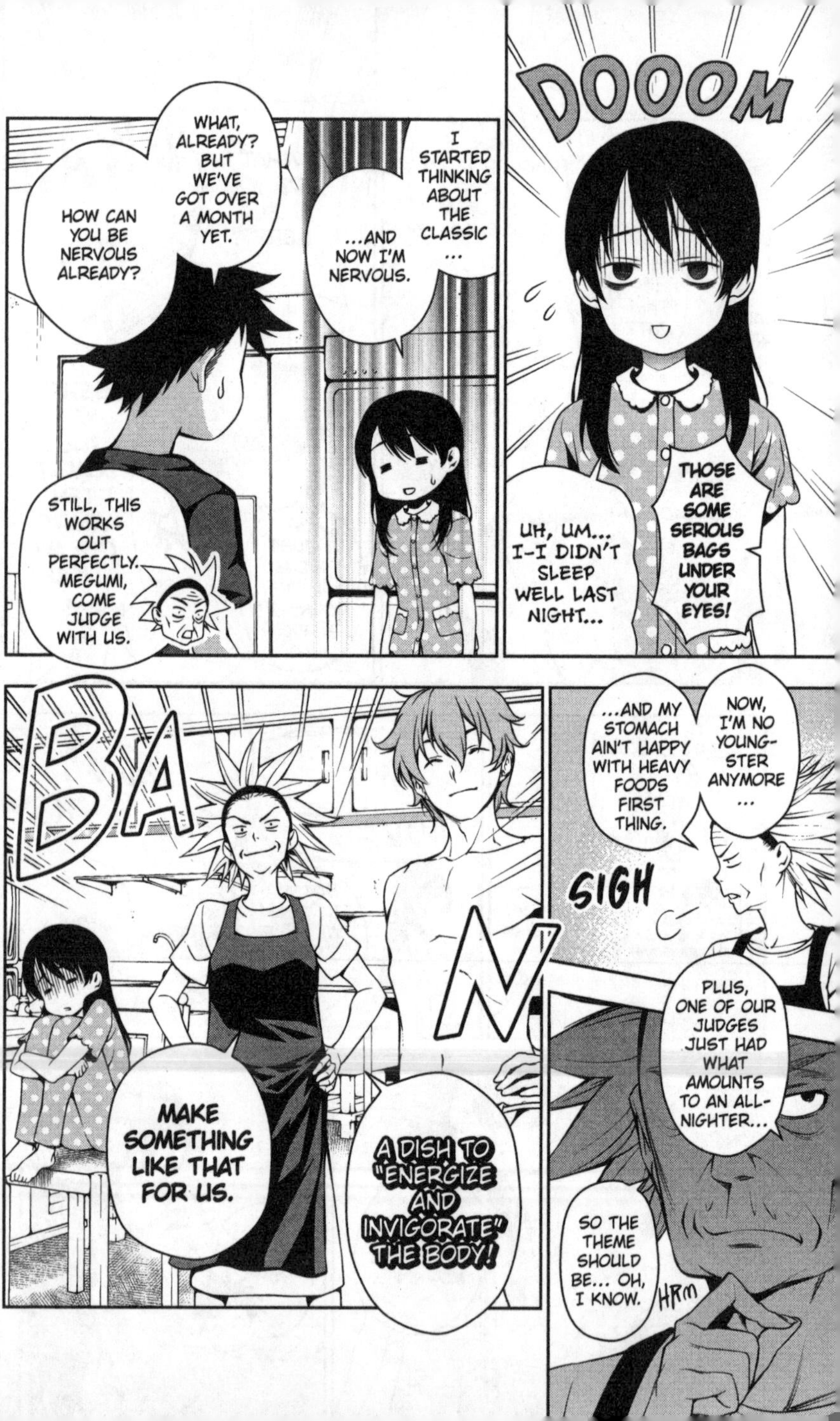
DOOOM
THOSE ARE SOME SERIOUS BAGS UNDER YOUR EYES!
UH, UM... I-I DIDN'T SLEEP WELL LAST NIGHT...
I STARTED THINKING ABOUT THE CLASSIC...
...AND NOW I'M NERVOUS.
WHAT, ALREADY? BUT WE'VE GOT OVER A MONTH YET.
HOW CAN YOU BE NERVOUS ALREADY?
STILL, THIS WORKS OUT PERFECTLY. MEGUMI, COME JUDGE WITH US.
NOW, I'M NO YOUNGSTER ANYMORE...
...AND MY STOMACH AIN'T HAPPY WITH HEAVY FOODS FIRST THING.
SIGH
PLUS, ONE OF OUR JUDGES JUST HAD WHAT AMOUNTS TO AN ALL-NIGHTER...
SO THE THEME SHOULD BE... OH, I KNOW.
HRM
BAN
A DISH TO "ENERGIZE AND INVIGORATE" THE BODY!
MAKE SOMETHING LIKE THAT FOR US.

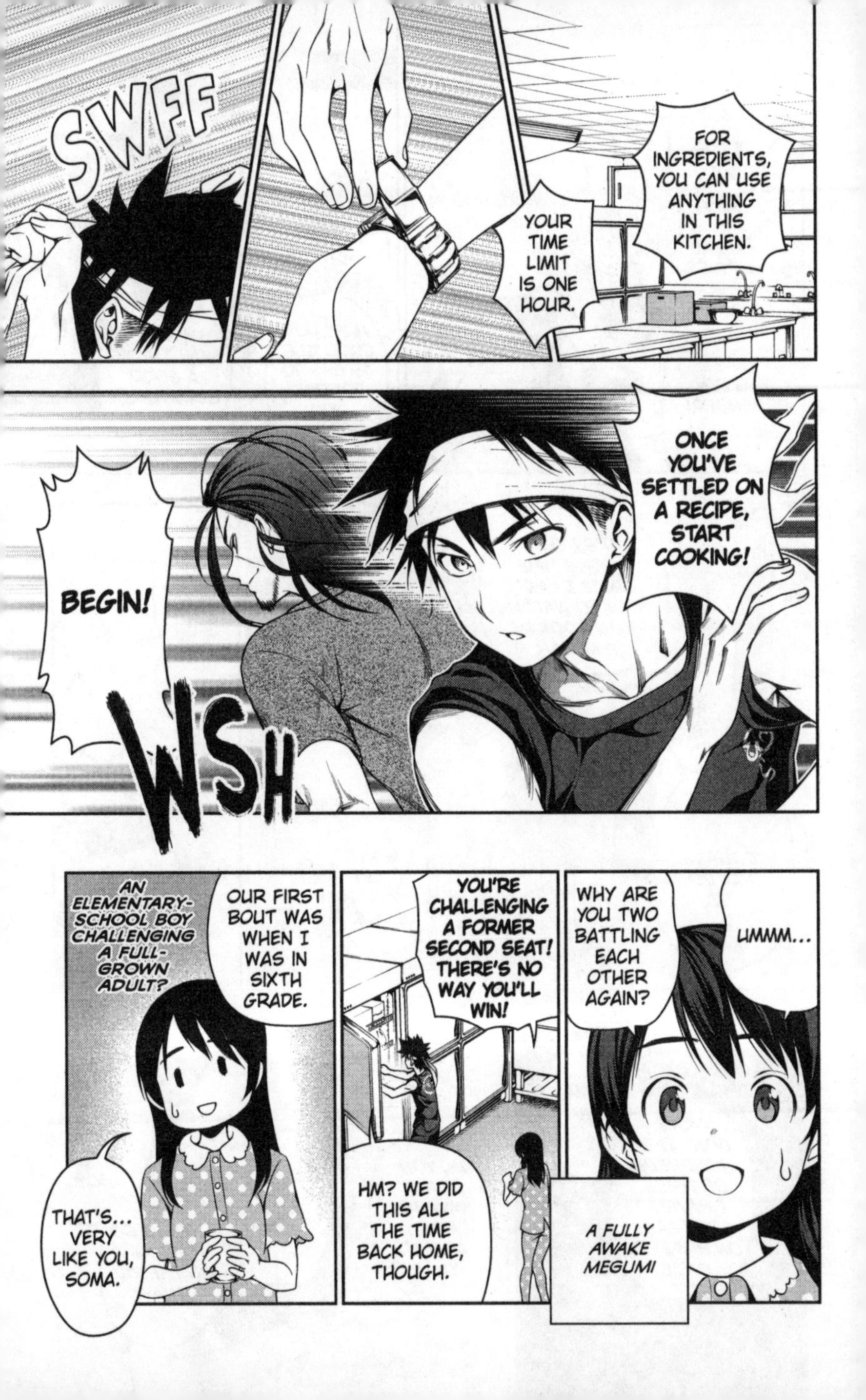
FOR INGREDIENTS, YOU CAN USE ANYTHING IN THIS KITCHEN.
YOUR TIME LIMIT IS ONE HOUR.
SWFF
ONCE YOU'VE SETTLED ON A RECIPE, START COOKING!
BEGIN!
WSH
UMMM...
WHY ARE YOU TWO BATTLING EACH OTHER AGAIN?
A FULLY AWAKE MEGUMI
YOU'RE CHALLENGING A FORMER SECOND SEAT! THERE'S NO WAY YOU'LL WIN!
HM? WE DID THIS ALL THE TIME BACK HOME, THOUGH.
OUR FIRST BOUT WAS WHEN I WAS IN SIXTH GRADE.
AN ELEMENTARY-SCHOOL BOY CHALLENGING A FULL-GROWN ADULT?
THAT'S... VERY LIKE YOU, SOMA.

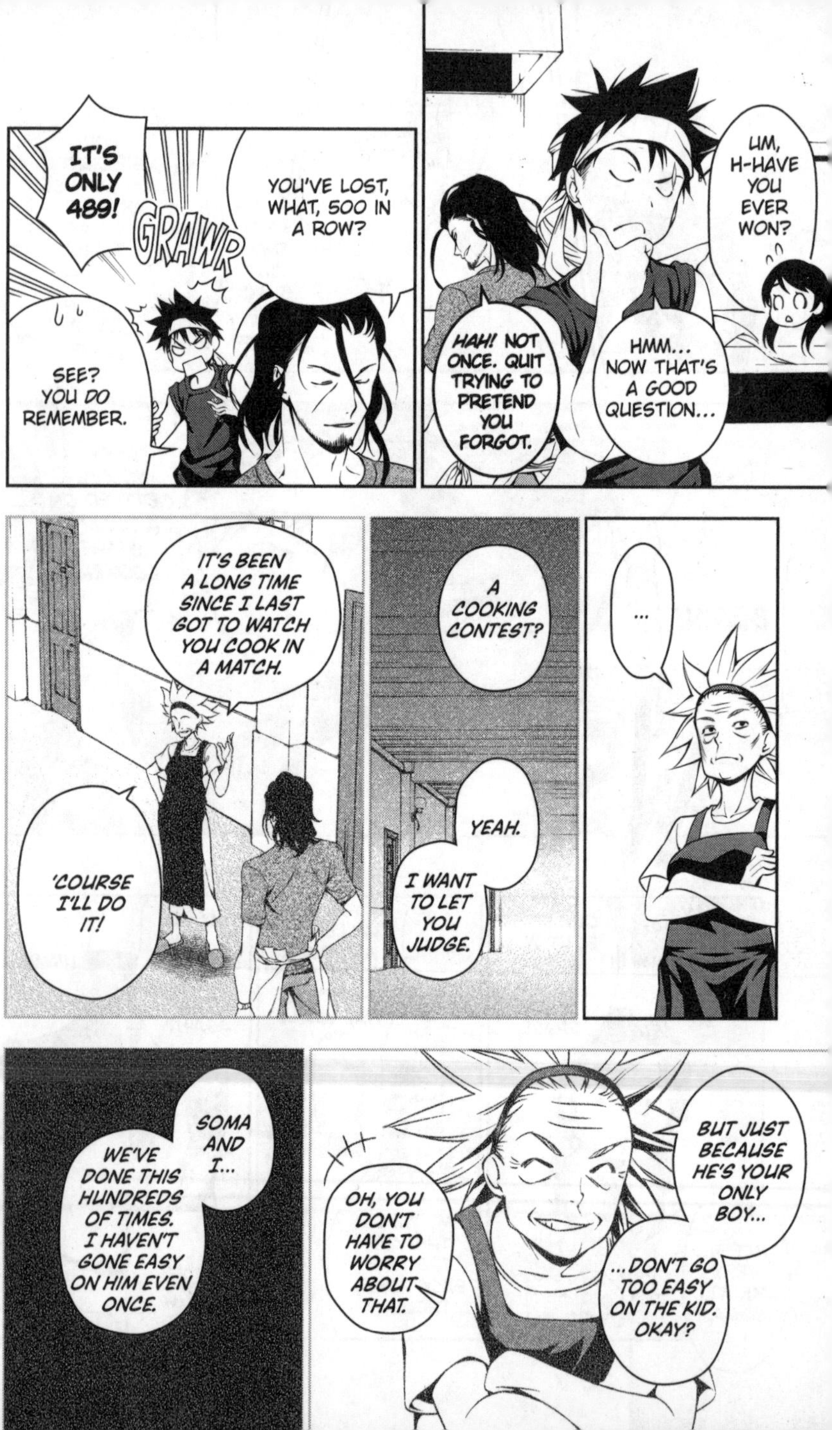
UM, H-HAVE YOU EVER WON?
HMM... NOW THAT'S A GOOD QUESTION...
HAH! NOT ONCE. QUIT TRYING TO PRETEND YOU FORGOT.
YOU'VE LOST, WHAT, 500 IN A ROW?
IT'S ONLY 489!
GRAWR
SEE? YOU DO REMEMBER.
...
A COOKING CONTEST?
YEAH.
I WANT TO LET YOU JUDGE.
IT'S BEEN A LONG TIME SINCE I LAST GOT TO WATCH YOU COOK IN A MATCH.
'COURSE I'LL DO IT!
BUT JUST BECAUSE HE'S YOUR ONLY BOY...
...DON'T GO TOO EASY ON THE KID. OKAY?
OH, YOU DON'T HAVE TO WORRY ABOUT THAT.
SOMA AND I...
WE'VE DONE THIS HUNDREDS OF TIMES. I HAVEN'T GONE EASY ON HIM EVEN ONCE.

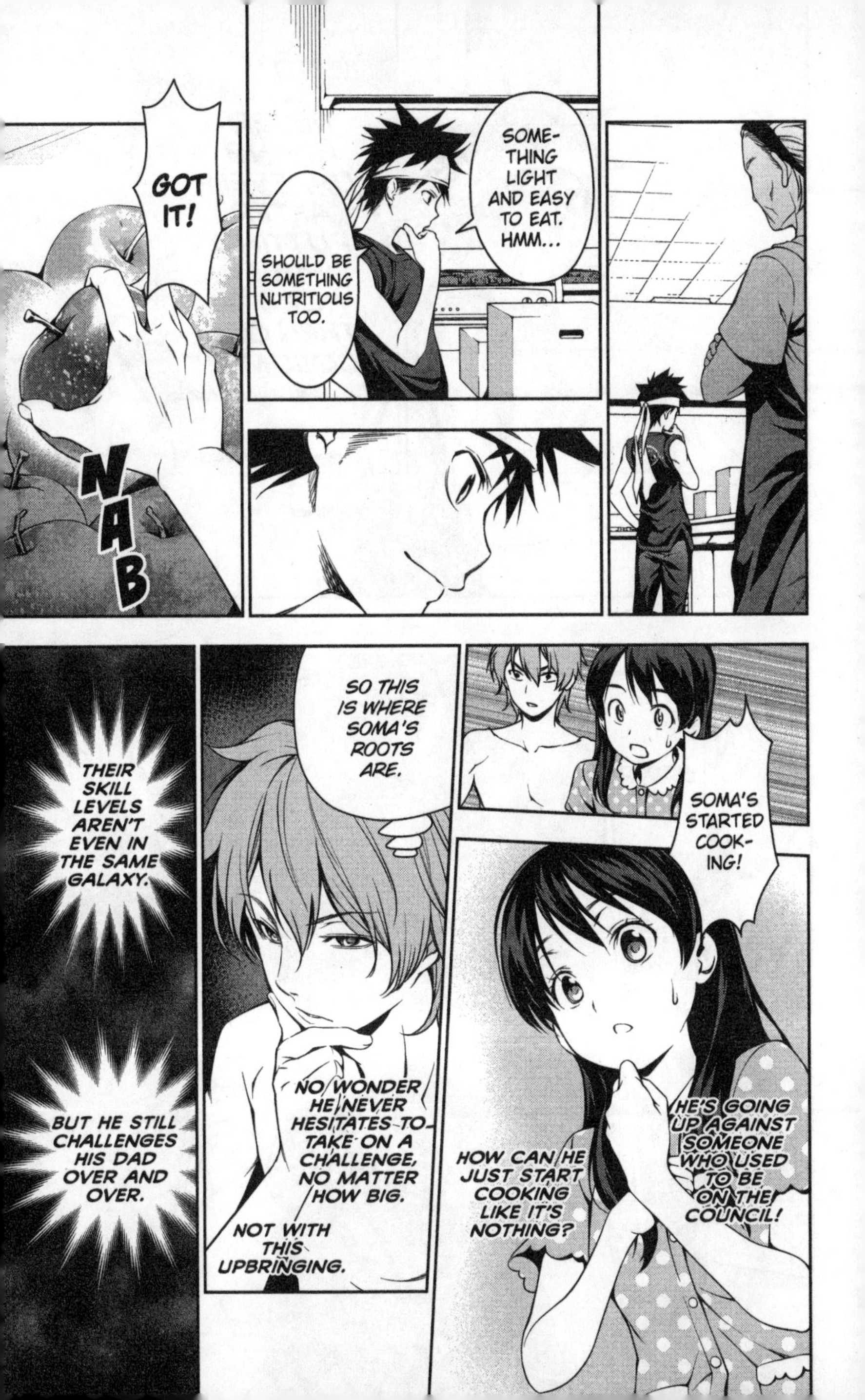
SOME-THING LIGHT AND EASY TO EAT. HMM...
SHOULD BE SOMETHING NUTRITIOUS TOO.
GOT IT!
NAB
SOMA'S STARTED COOK-ING!
HE'S GOING UP AGAINST SOMEONE WHO USED TO BE ON THE COUNCIL!
HOW CAN HE JUST START COOKING LIKE IT'S NOTHING?
SO THIS IS WHERE SOMA'S ROOTS ARE.
NO WONDER HE NEVER HESITATES TO TAKE ON A CHALLENGE, NO MATTER HOW BIG.
NOT WITH THIS UPBRINGING.
THEIR SKILL LEVELS AREN'T EVEN IN THE SAME GALAXY.
BUT HE STILL CHALLENGES HIS DAD OVER AND OVER.

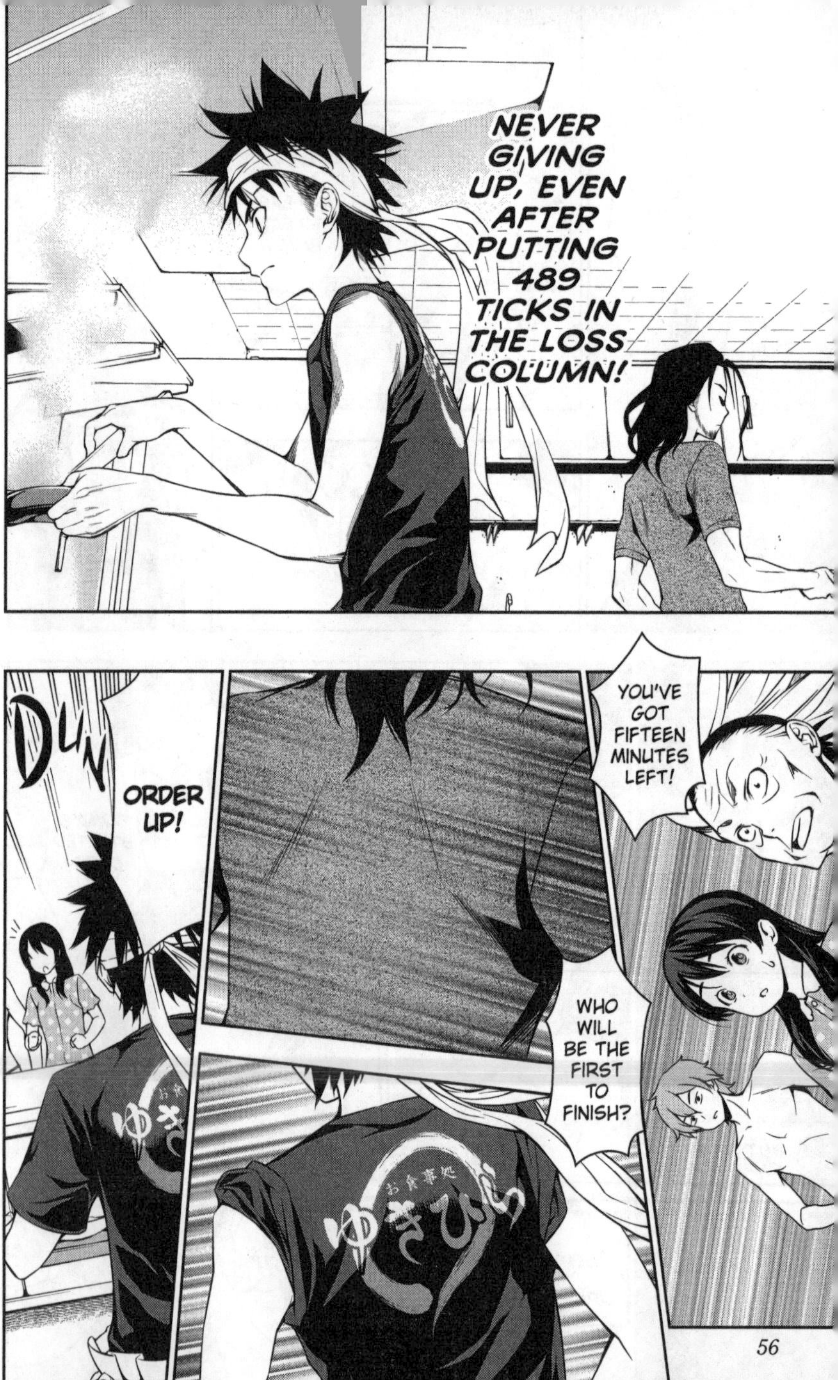
NEVER GIVING UP, EVEN AFTER PUTTING 489 TICKS IN THE LOSS COLUMN!
YOU'VE GOT FIFTEEN MINUTES LEFT!
WHO WILL BE THE FIRST TO FINISH?
お食事処
ゆきひら
DUN
ORDER UP!

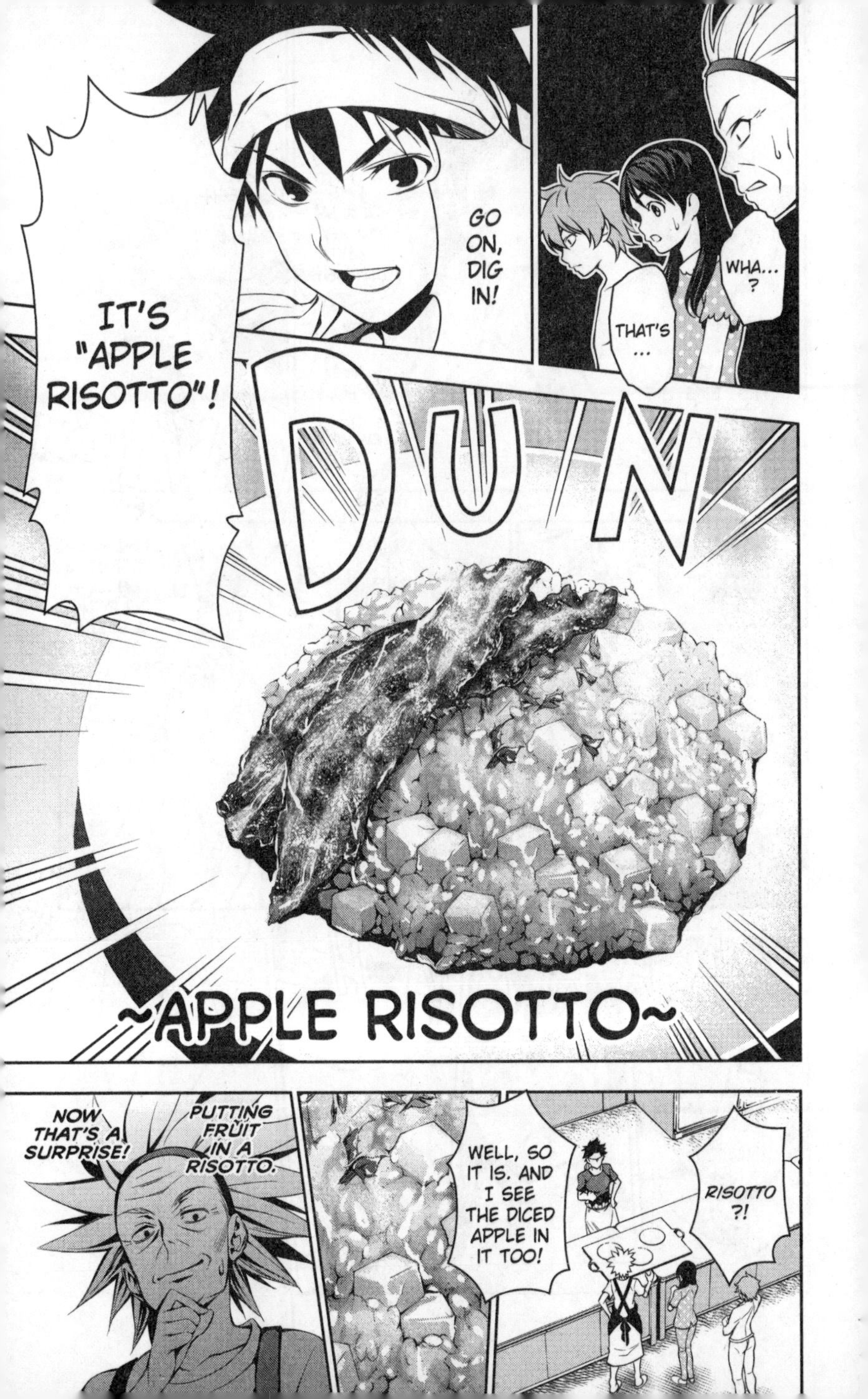
WHA... ?
THAT'S ...
GO ON, DIG IN!
IT'S "APPLE RISOTTO"!
DUN
~APPLE RISOTTO~
RISOTTO ?!
WELL, SO IT IS. AND I SEE THE DICED APPLE IN IT TOO!
PUTTING FRUIT IN A RISOTTO.
NOW THAT'S A SURPRISE!

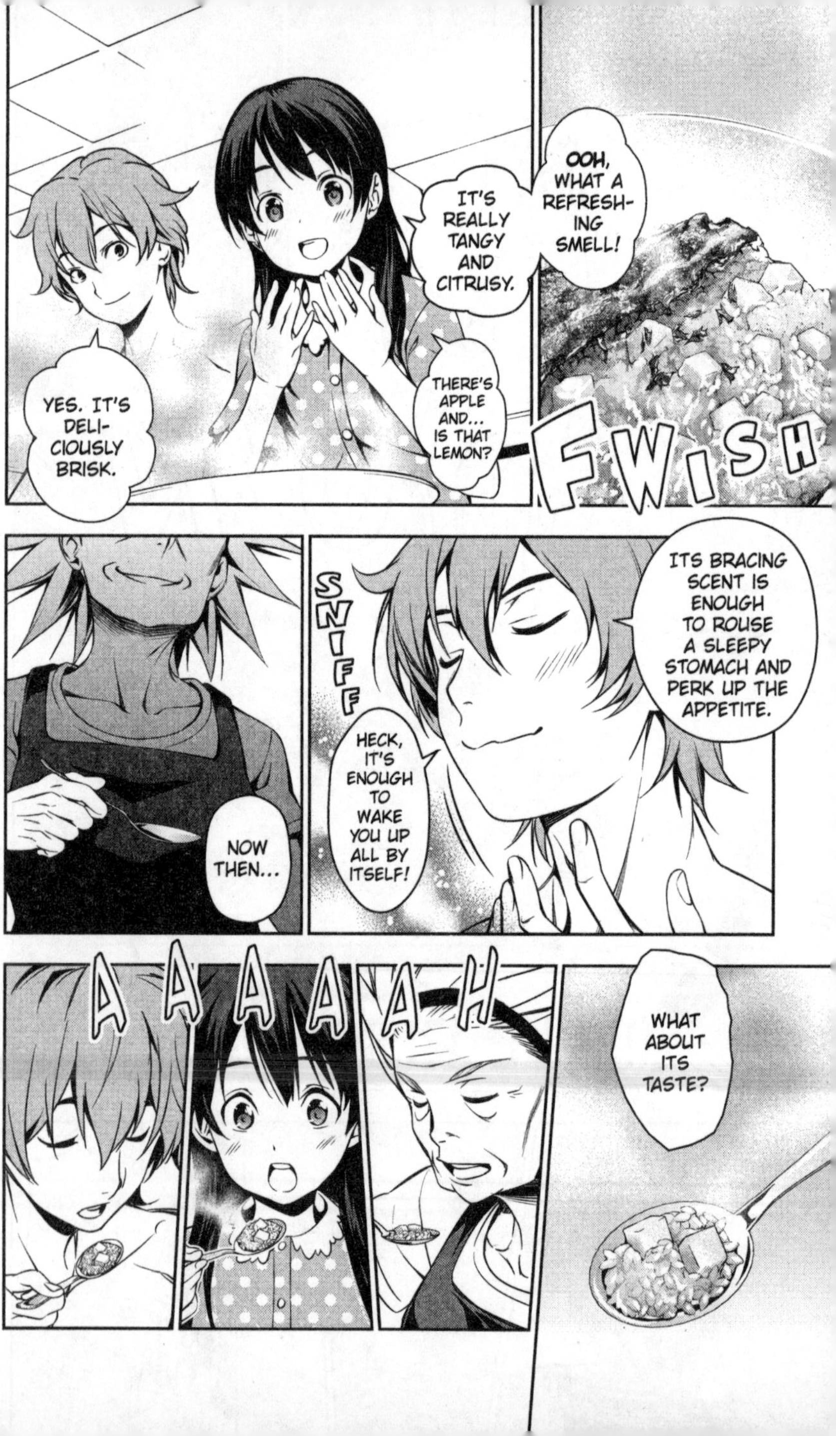
OOH, WHAT A REFRESHING SMELL!
FWISH
IT'S REALLY TANGY AND CITRUSY.
THERE'S APPLE AND... IS THAT LEMON?
YES. IT'S DELICIOUSLY BRISK.
SNIFF
ITS BRACING SCENT IS ENOUGH TO ROUSE A SLEEPY STOMACH AND PERK UP THE APPETITE.
HECK, IT'S ENOUGH TO WAKE YOU UP ALL BY ITSELF!
NOW THEN...
WHAT ABOUT ITS TASTE?
AAAAAH

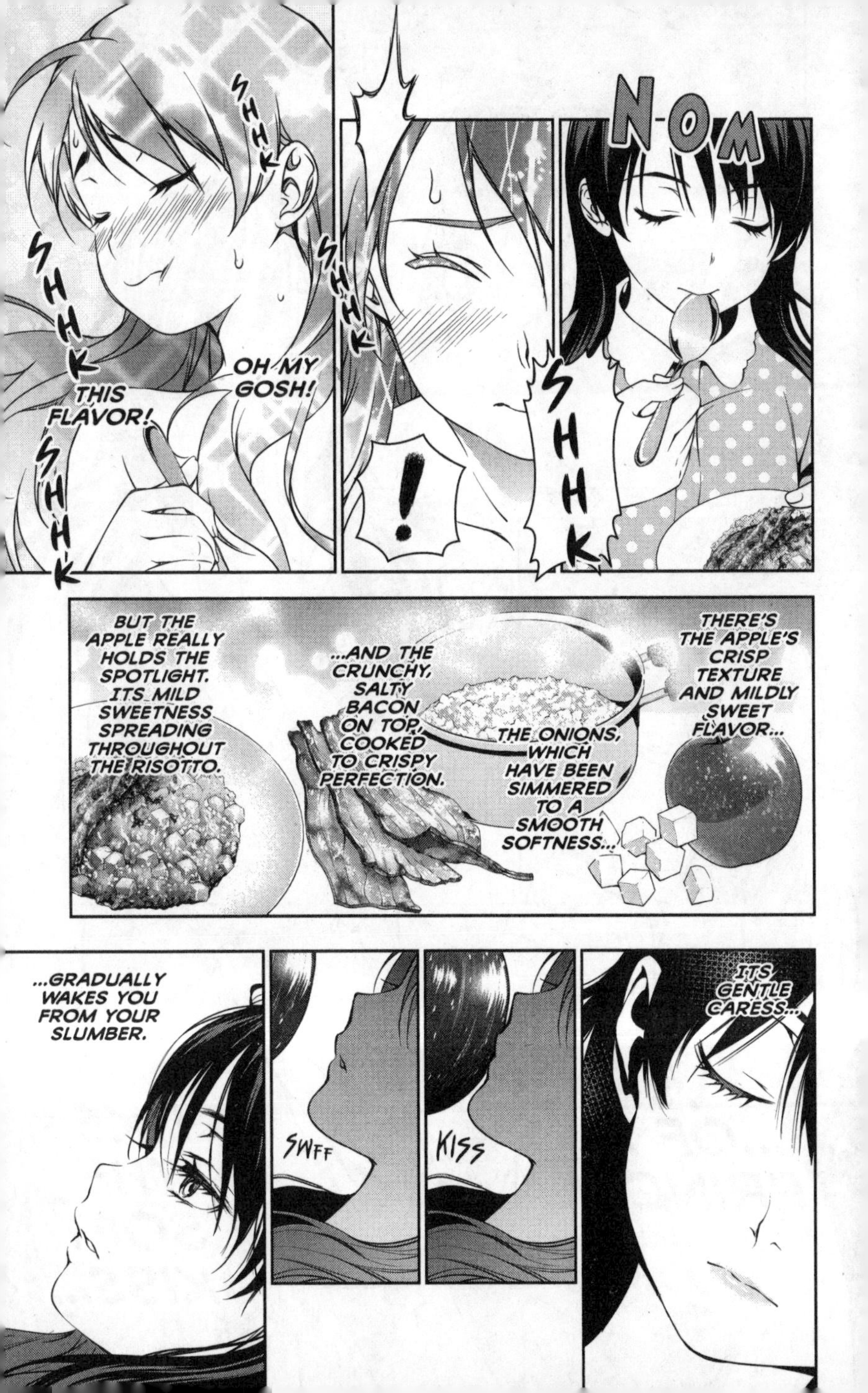
NOM
SHHK
!
SHHHK
SHHHK
OH MY GOSH!
THIS FLAVOR!
SHHHK
SHHHK
THERE'S THE APPLE'S CRISP TEXTURE AND MILDLY SWEET FLAVOR...
THE ONIONS, WHICH HAVE BEEN SIMMERED TO A SMOOTH SOFTNESS...
...AND THE CRUNCHY, SALTY BACON ON TOP, COOKED TO CRISPY PERFECTION.
BUT THE APPLE REALLY HOLDS THE SPOTLIGHT. ITS MILD SWEETNESS SPREADING THROUGHOUT THE RISOTTO.
ITS GENTLE CARESS...
KISS
SWFF
...GRADUALLY WAKES YOU FROM YOUR SLUMBER.

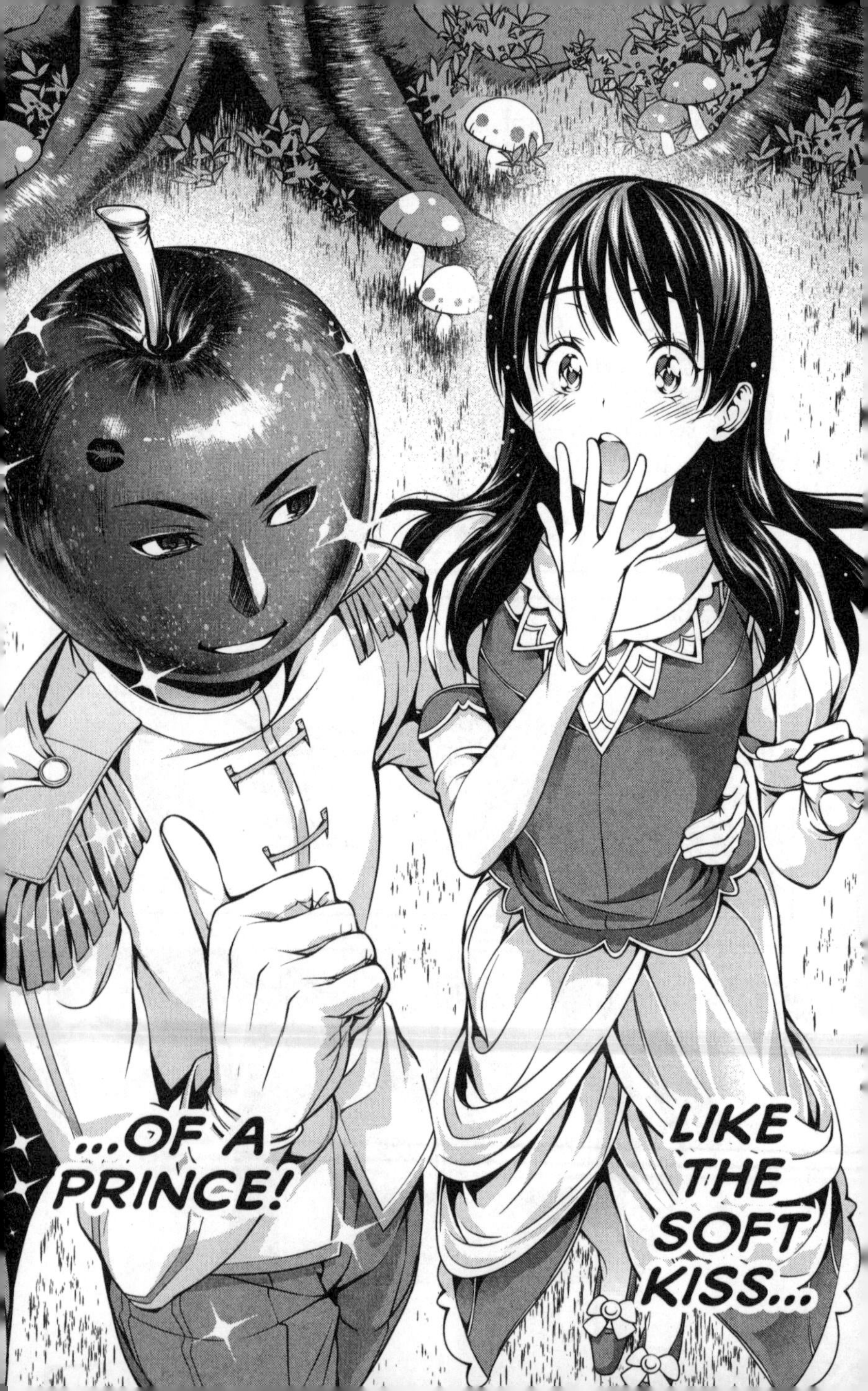
LIKE THE SOFT KISS...
...OF A PRINCE!

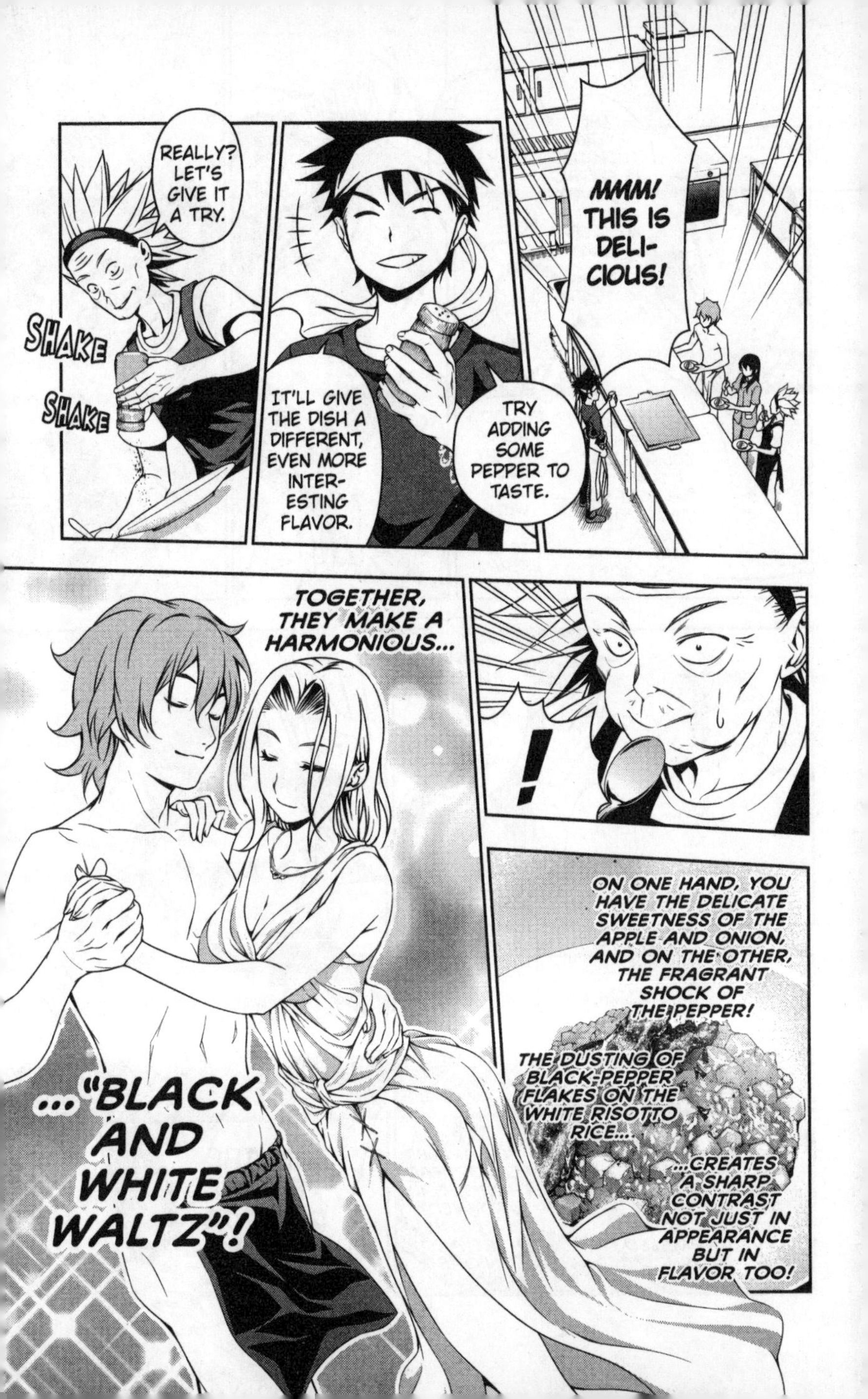
MMM! THIS IS DELI-CIOUS!
TRY ADDING SOME PEPPER TO TASTE.
IT'LL GIVE THE DISH A DIFFERENT, EVEN MORE INTER-ESTING FLAVOR.
REALLY? LET'S GIVE IT A TRY.
SHAKE
SHAKE
!
ON ONE HAND, YOU HAVE THE DELICATE SWEETNESS OF THE APPLE AND ONION, AND ON THE OTHER, THE FRAGRANT SHOCK OF THE PEPPER!
THE DUSTING OF BLACK-PEPPER FLAKES ON THE WHITE RISOTTO RICE...
...CREATES A SHARP CONTRAST NOT JUST IN APPEARANCE BUT IN FLAVOR TOO!
TOGETHER, THEY MAKE A HARMONIOUS...
..."BLACK AND WHITE WALTZ"!

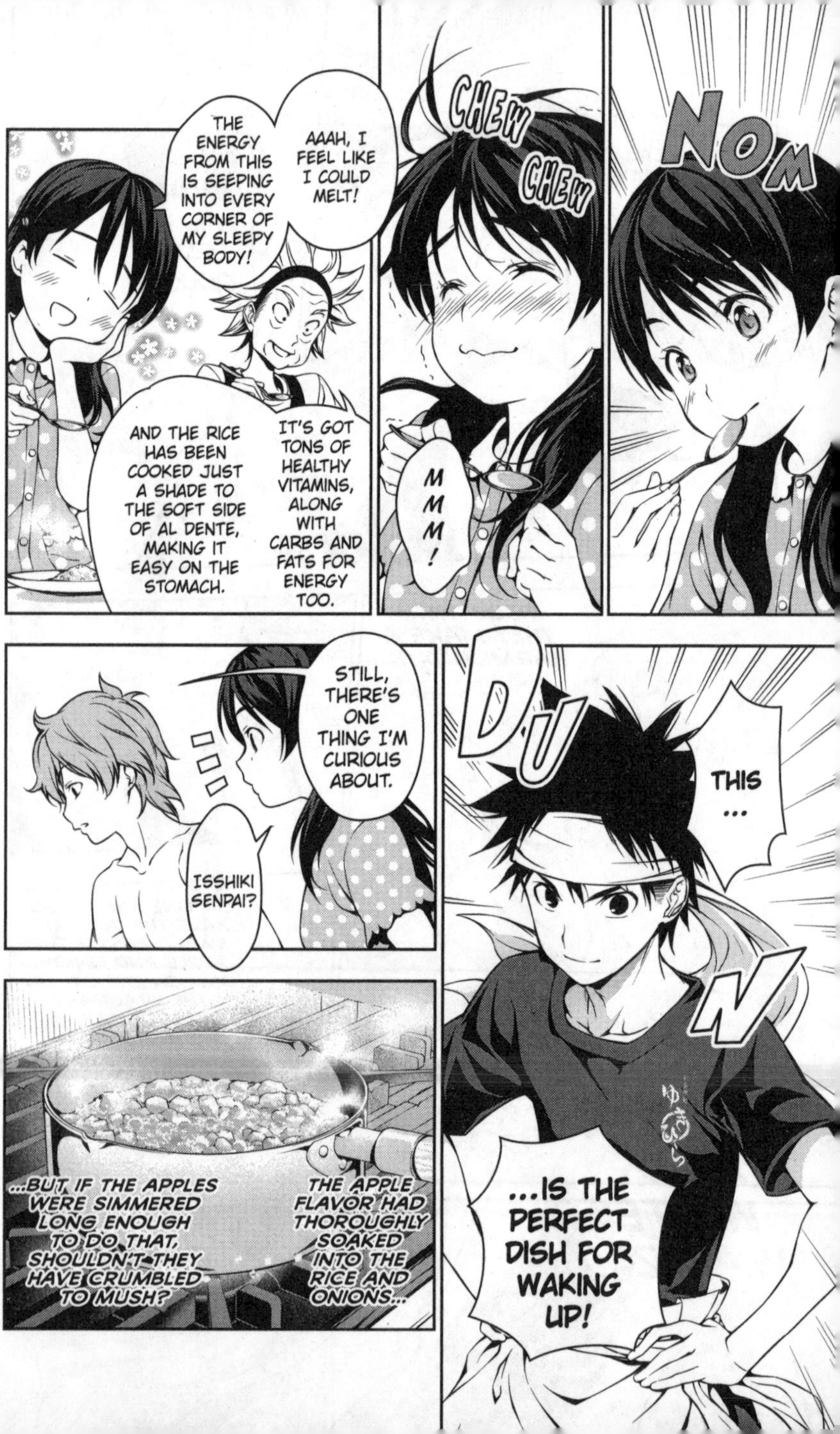
NOM
CHEW CHEW
MMM!
AAAH, I FEEL LIKE I COULD MELT!
THE ENERGY FROM THIS IS SEEPING INTO EVERY CORNER OF MY SLEEPY BODY!
IT'S GOT TONS OF HEALTHY VITAMINS, ALONG WITH CARBS AND FATS FOR ENERGY TOO.
AND THE RICE HAS BEEN COOKED JUST A SHADE TO THE SOFT SIDE OF AL DENTE, MAKING IT EASY ON THE STOMACH.
DUN
THIS ...
...IS THE PERFECT DISH FOR WAKING UP!
STILL, THERE'S ONE THING I'M CURIOUS ABOUT.
ISSHIKI SENPAI?
THE APPLE FLAVOR HAD THOROUGHLY SOAKED INTO THE RICE AND ONIONS...
...BUT IF THE APPLES WERE SIMMERED LONG ENOUGH TO DO THAT, SHOULDN'T THEY HAVE CRUMBLED TO MUSH?

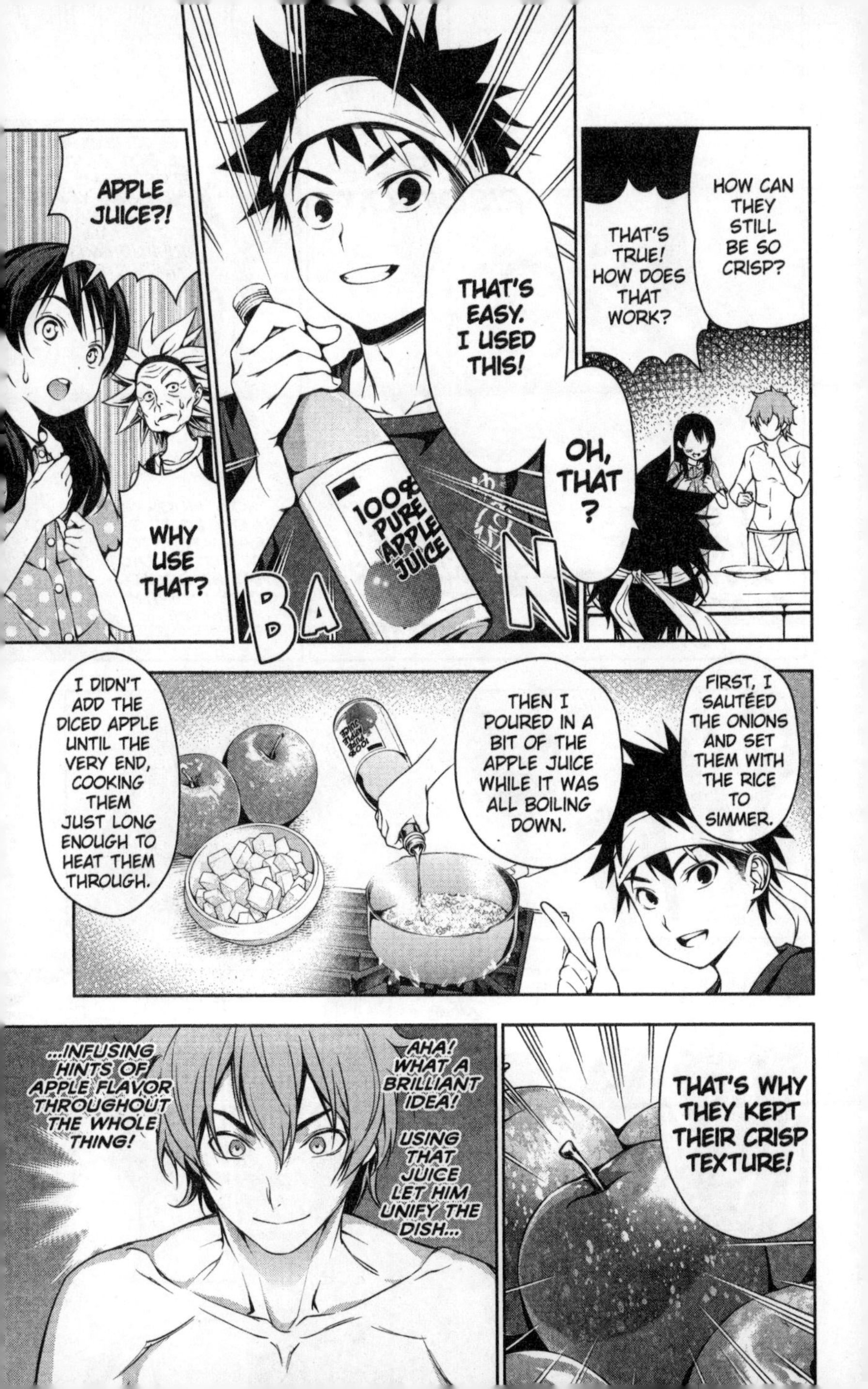
HOW CAN THEY STILL BE SO CRISP?
THAT'S TRUE! HOW DOES THAT WORK?
OH, THAT?
THAT'S EASY. I USED THIS!
100% PURE APPLE JUICE
BAN
APPLE JUICE?!
WHY USE THAT?
FIRST, I SAUTÉED THE ONIONS AND SET THEM WITH THE RICE TO SIMMER.
THEN I POURED IN A BIT OF THE APPLE JUICE WHILE IT WAS ALL BOILING DOWN.
I DIDN'T ADD THE DICED APPLE UNTIL THE VERY END, COOKING THEM JUST LONG ENOUGH TO HEAT THEM THROUGH.
THAT'S WHY THEY KEPT THEIR CRISP TEXTURE!
AHA! WHAT A BRILLIANT IDEA!
USING THAT JUICE LET HIM UNIFY THE DISH...
...INFUSING HINTS OF APPLE FLAVOR THROUGHOUT THE WHOLE THING!

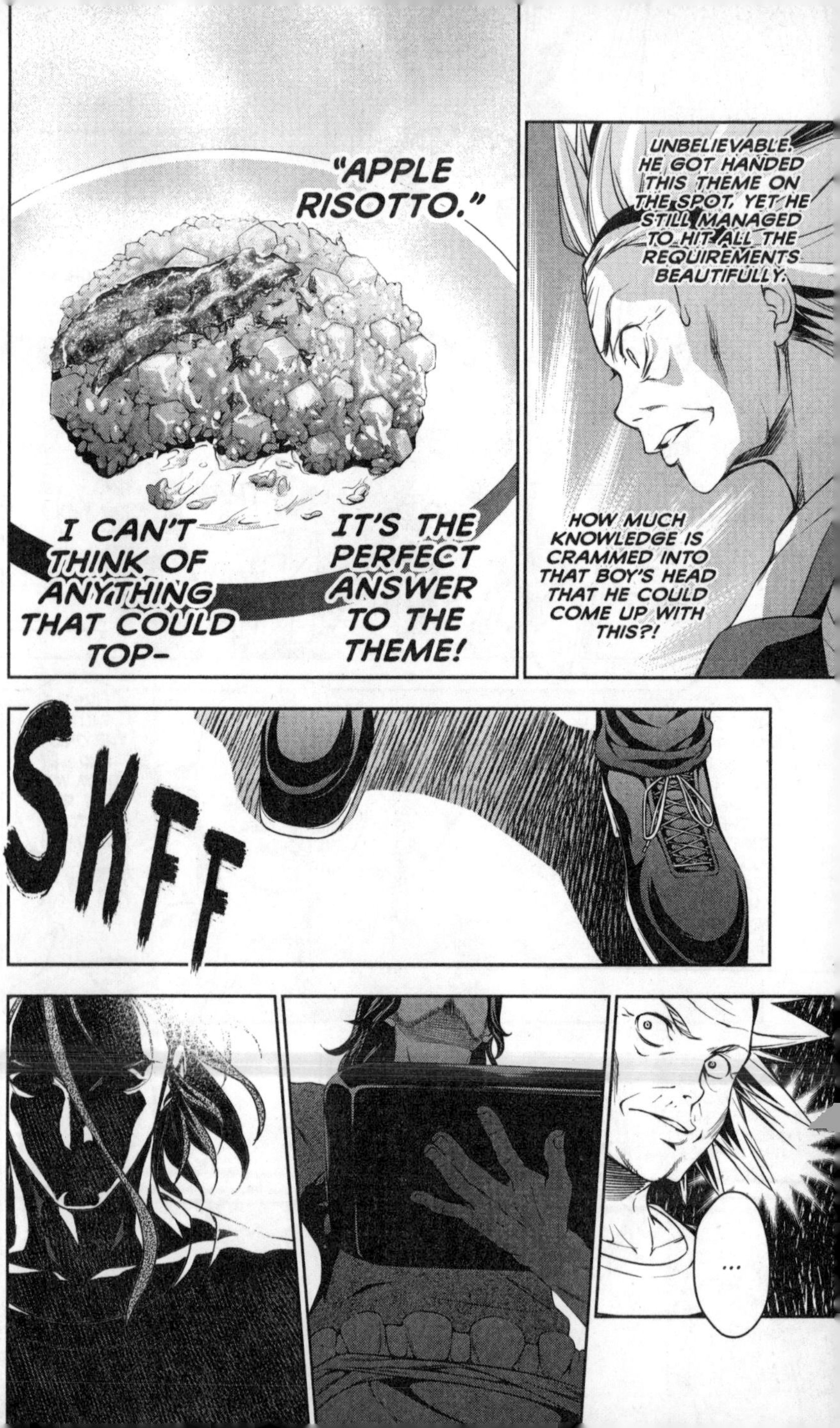
UNBELIEVABLE. HE GOT HANDED THIS THEME ON THE SPOT, YET HE STILL MANAGED TO HIT ALL THE REQUIREMENTS BEAUTIFULLY.
HOW MUCH KNOWLEDGE IS CRAMMED INTO THAT BOY'S HEAD THAT HE COULD COME UP WITH THIS?!
"APPLE RISOTTO."
IT'S THE PERFECT ANSWER TO THE THEME!
I CAN'T THINK OF ANYTHING THAT COULD TOP-
SKFF
...

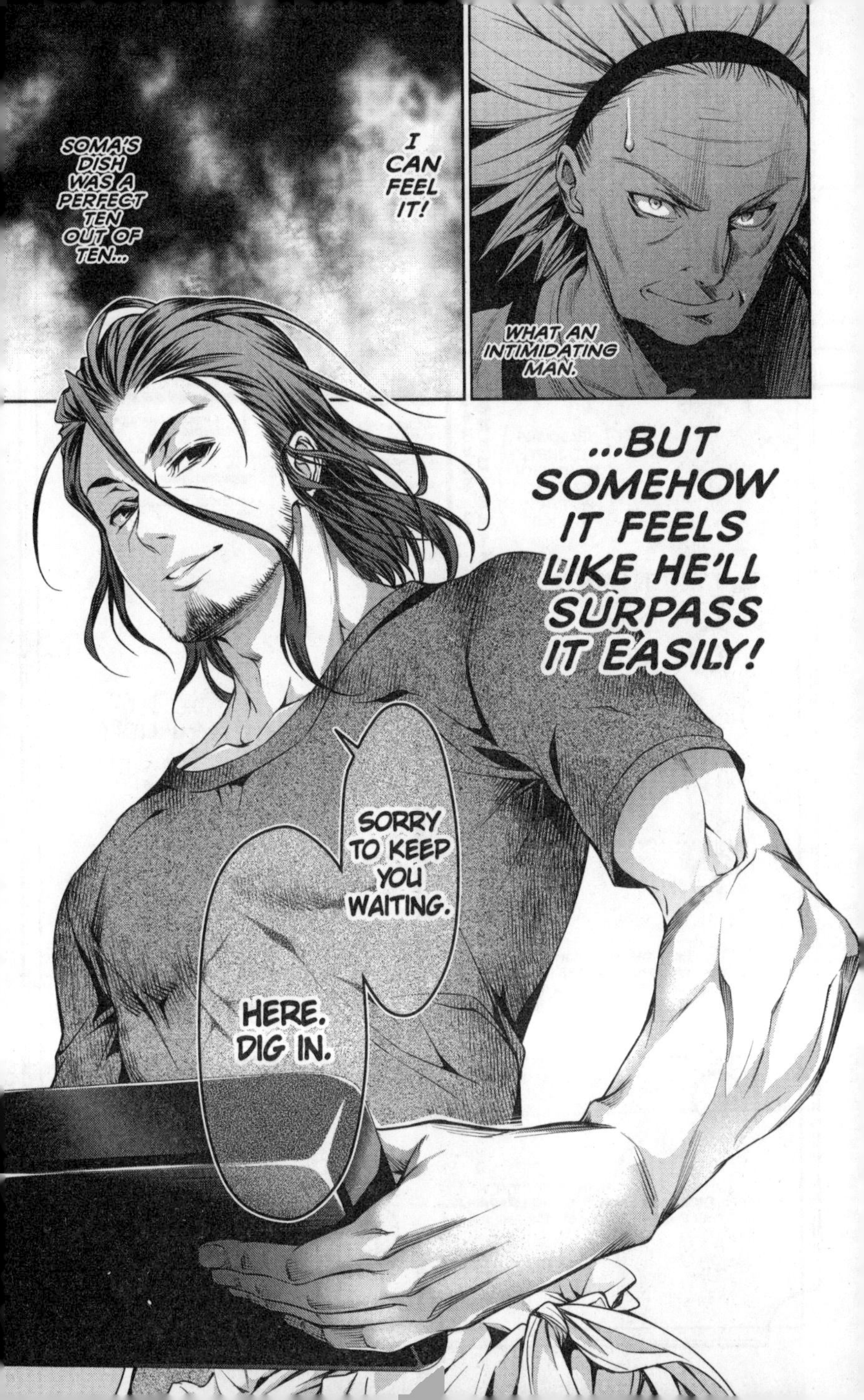
WHAT AN INTIMIDATING MAN.
I CAN FEEL IT!
SOMA'S DISH WAS A PERFECT TEN OUT OF TEN...
...BUT SOMEHOW IT FEELS LIKE HE'LL SURPASS IT EASILY!
SORRY TO KEEP YOU WAITING.
HERE. DIG IN.

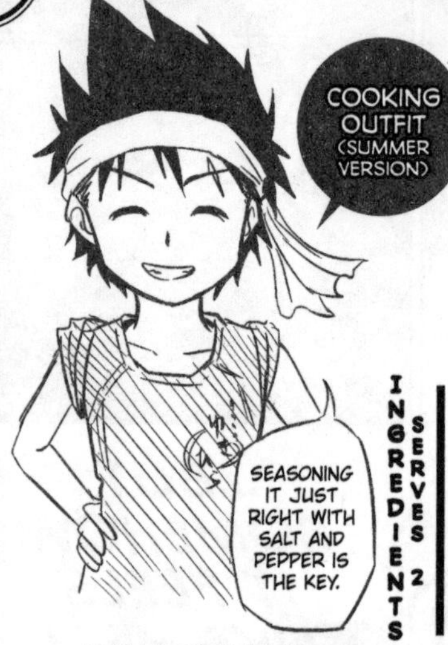
COOKING OUTFIT (SUMMER VERSION)
SEASONING IT JUST RIGHT WITH SALT AND PEPPER IS THE KEY.

PRACTICAL RECIPE #1

VOLUME 6 SPECIAL SUPPLEMENT!

APPLE RISOTTO

ARTIST: YUTO TSUKUDA

INGREDIENTS SERVES 2

- 1/2 APPLE
- 1/2 CUP RICE
- 4 SLICES THICK-CUT BACON
- 1/4 ONION
- 2 TABLESPOONS BUTTER
- 2 TABLESPOONS WHITE WINE

[A]
- 1 CUP EACH OF 100% PURE APPLE JUICE AND WATER
- 1 TEASPOON GRANULATED CONSOMMÉ

- 1 TEASPOON LEMON JUICE
- SALT, PEPPER, POWDERED CHEESE

1) COOK THE BACON IN A FRYING PAN UNTIL CRISPY AND SET TO THE SIDE.

2) PEEL THE APPLE AND DICE IT INTO SMALLISH CUBES. MINCE THE ONION.

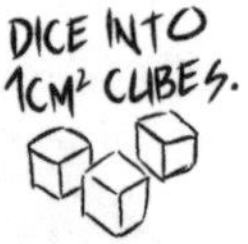
DICE INTO 1CM² CUBES.

3) HEAT THE BUTTER IN A FRYING PAN AND SAUTÉ THE ONIONS. ADD THE RICE AND COOK UNTIL TRANSPARENT.

4) ADD THE WHITE WINE TO (3), AND COOK IT UNTIL THE ALCOHOL BURNS OFF. MIX (A) TOGETHER, AND SLOWLY ADD IT TO THE PAN 1/8 CUP AT A TIME, SIMMERING ON LOW HEAT FIFTEEN MINUTES OR UNTIL ALL THE LIQUID IS ABSORBED. ADD THE DICED APPLE AND LEMON JUICE. SEASON TO TASTE WITH SALT AND PEPPER.

5) PLACE (4) ON A PLATE, AND TOP IT WITH THE BACON FROM (1). SPRINKLE POWDERED CHEESE AND PEPPER ON TOP, AND DONE!

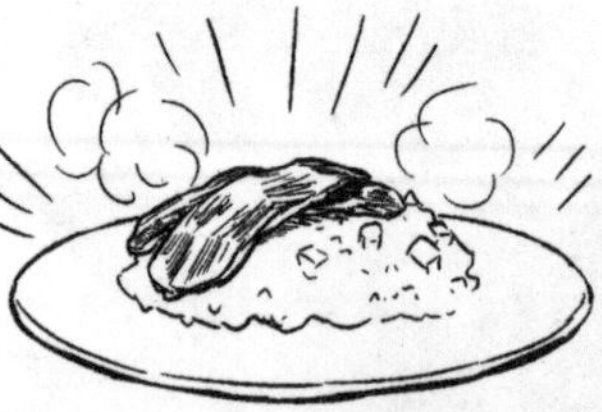

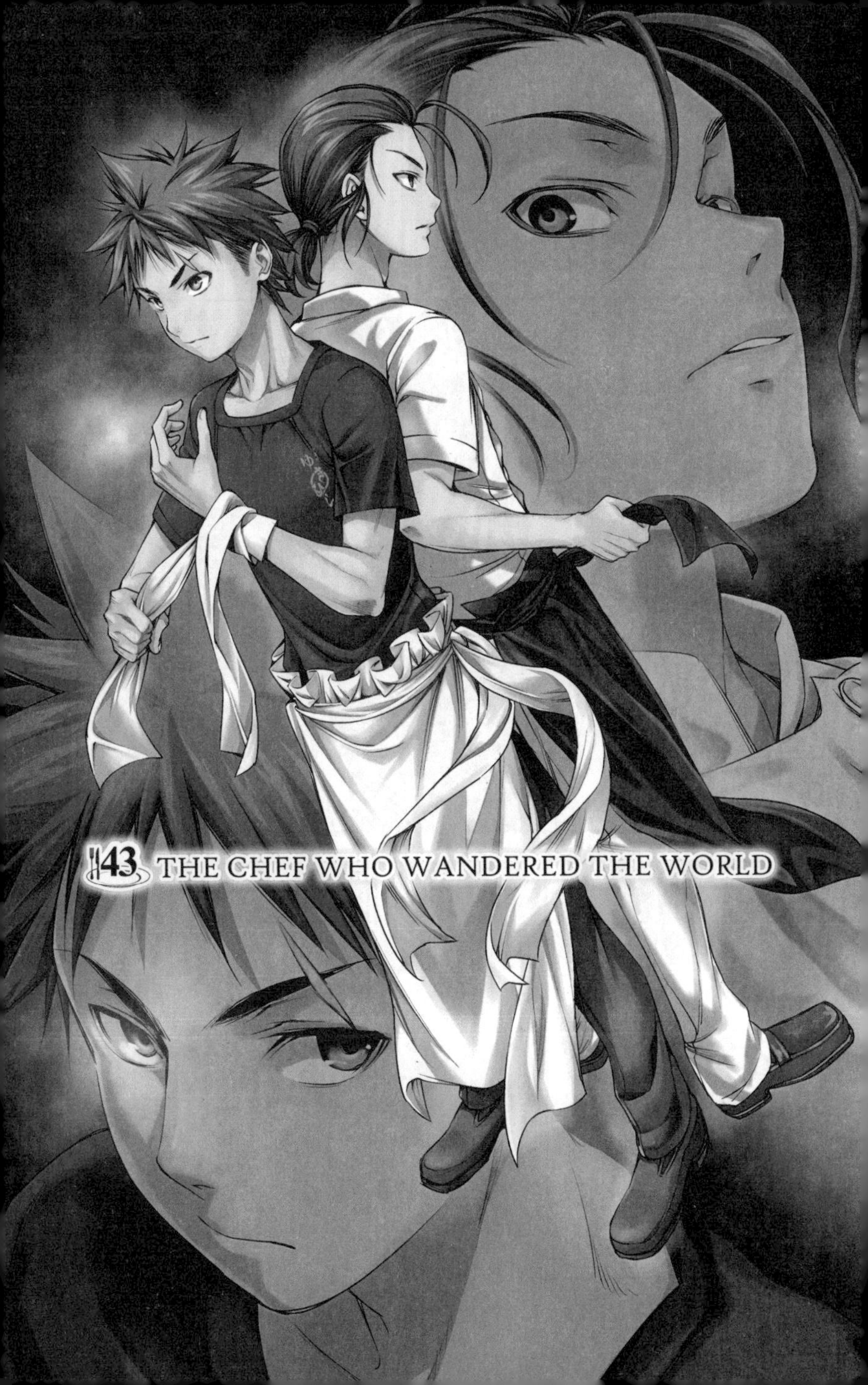
43
THE CHEF WHO WANDERED THE WORLD

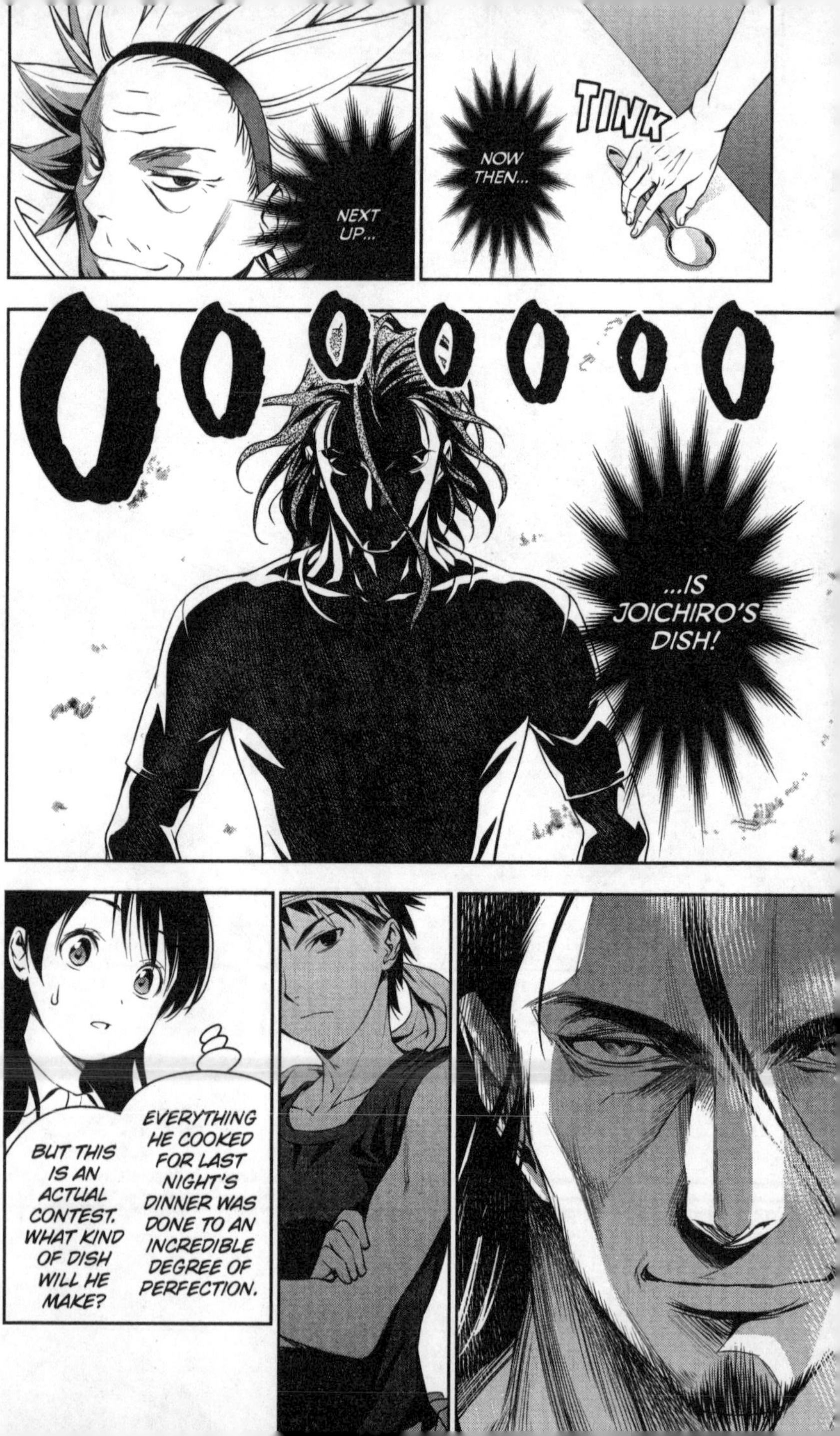
TINK
NOW THEN...
NEXT UP...
OOOOOOO
...IS JOICHIRO'S DISH!
EVERYTHING HE COOKED FOR LAST NIGHT'S DINNER WAS DONE TO AN INCREDIBLE DEGREE OF PERFECTION.
BUT THIS IS AN ACTUAL CONTEST. WHAT KIND OF DISH WILL HE MAKE?

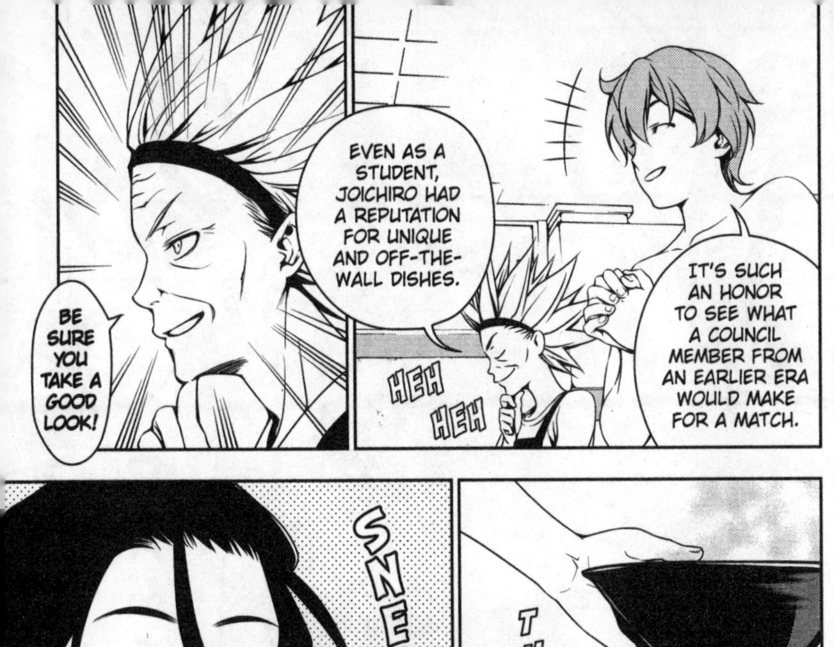
IT'S SUCH AN HONOR TO SEE WHAT A COUNCIL MEMBER FROM AN EARLIER ERA WOULD MAKE FOR A MATCH.
EVEN AS A STUDENT, JOICHIRO HAD A REPUTATION FOR UNIQUE AND OFF-THE-WALL DISHES.
HEH HEH
BE SURE YOU TAKE A GOOD LOOK!
TUNK
ENJOY.
SNERK
IT'S JOICHIRO'S SPECIAL KOTTERI RAMEN.

*KOTTERI IS A TYPE OF RAMEN WITH A HEAVY, RICH BROTH AS OPPOSED TO ASARI RAMEN, WHICH HAS A LIGHT BROTH.

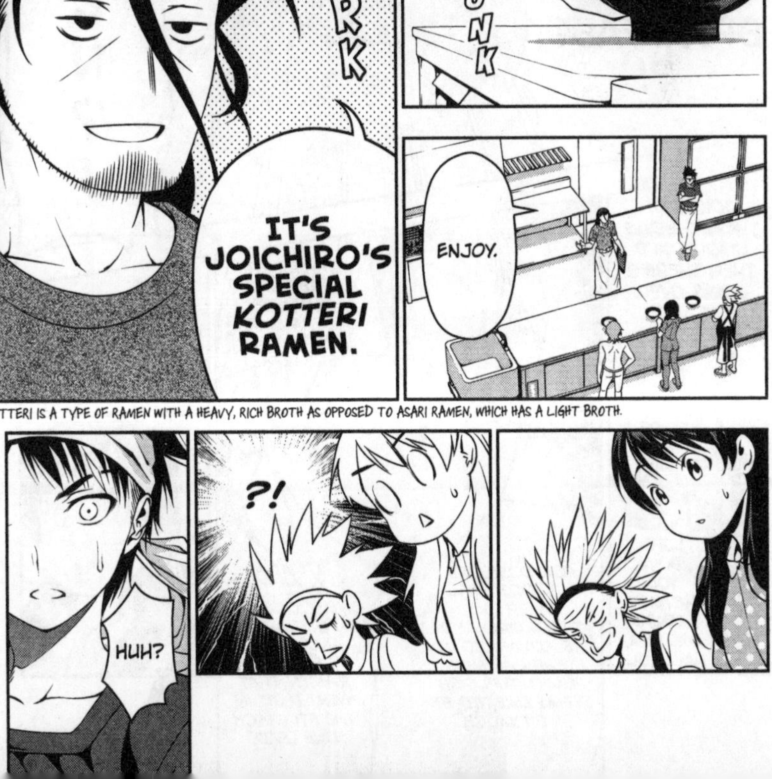
?!
HUH?

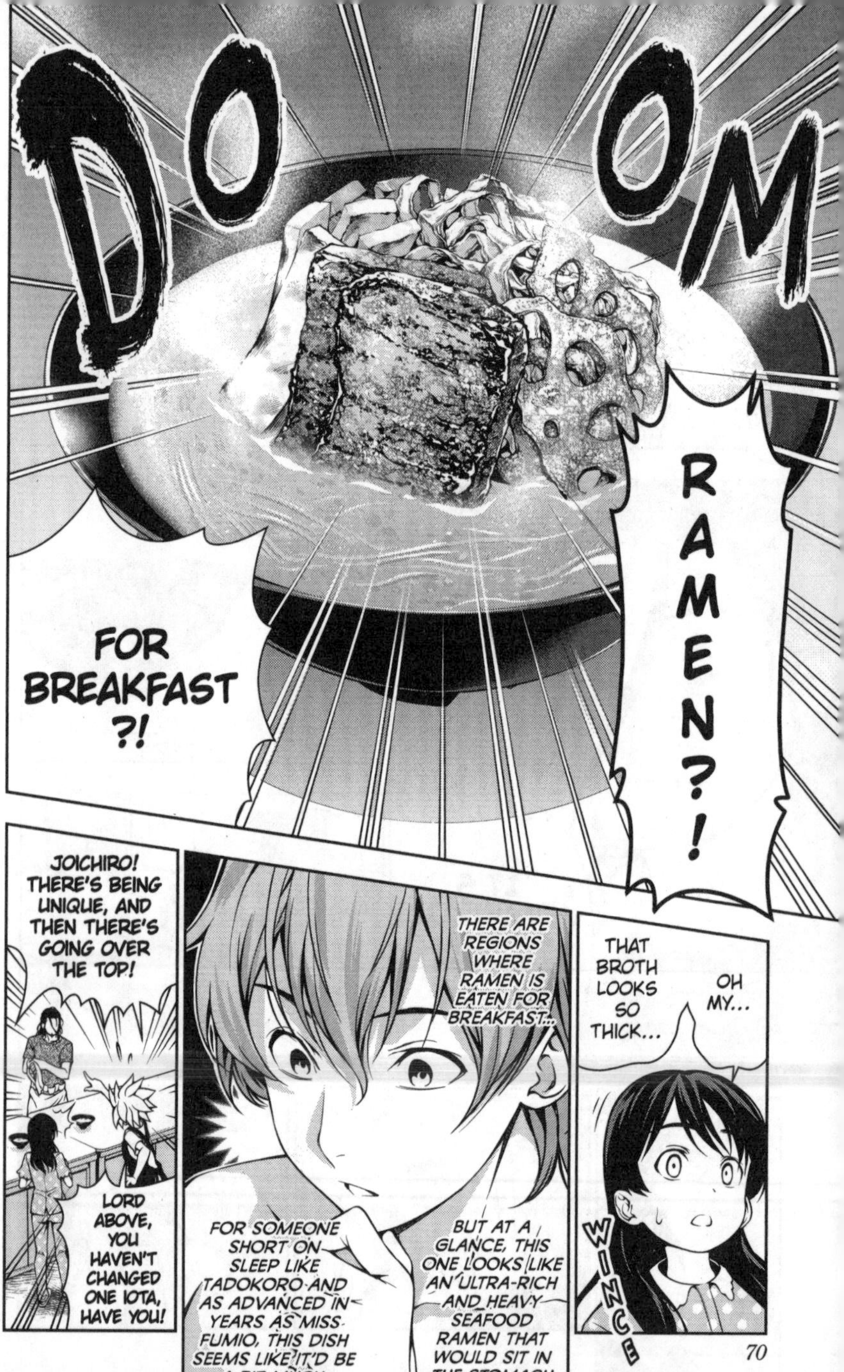
DOOM
RAMEN?!
FOR BREAKFAST?!
OH MY...
THAT BROTH LOOKS SO THICK...
WINCE
THERE ARE REGIONS WHERE RAMEN IS EATEN FOR BREAKFAST...
BUT AT A GLANCE, THIS ONE LOOKS LIKE AN ULTRA-RICH AND HEAVY SEAFOOD RAMEN THAT WOULD SIT IN THE STOMACH LIKE LEAD.
FOR SOMEONE SHORT ON SLEEP LIKE TADOKORO AND AS ADVANCED IN YEARS AS MISS FUMIO, THIS DISH SEEMS LIKE IT'D BE A BIT MUCH.
JOICHIRO! THERE'S BEING UNIQUE, AND THEN THERE'S GOING OVER THE TOP!
LORD ABOVE, YOU HAVEN'T CHANGED ONE IOTA, HAVE YOU!

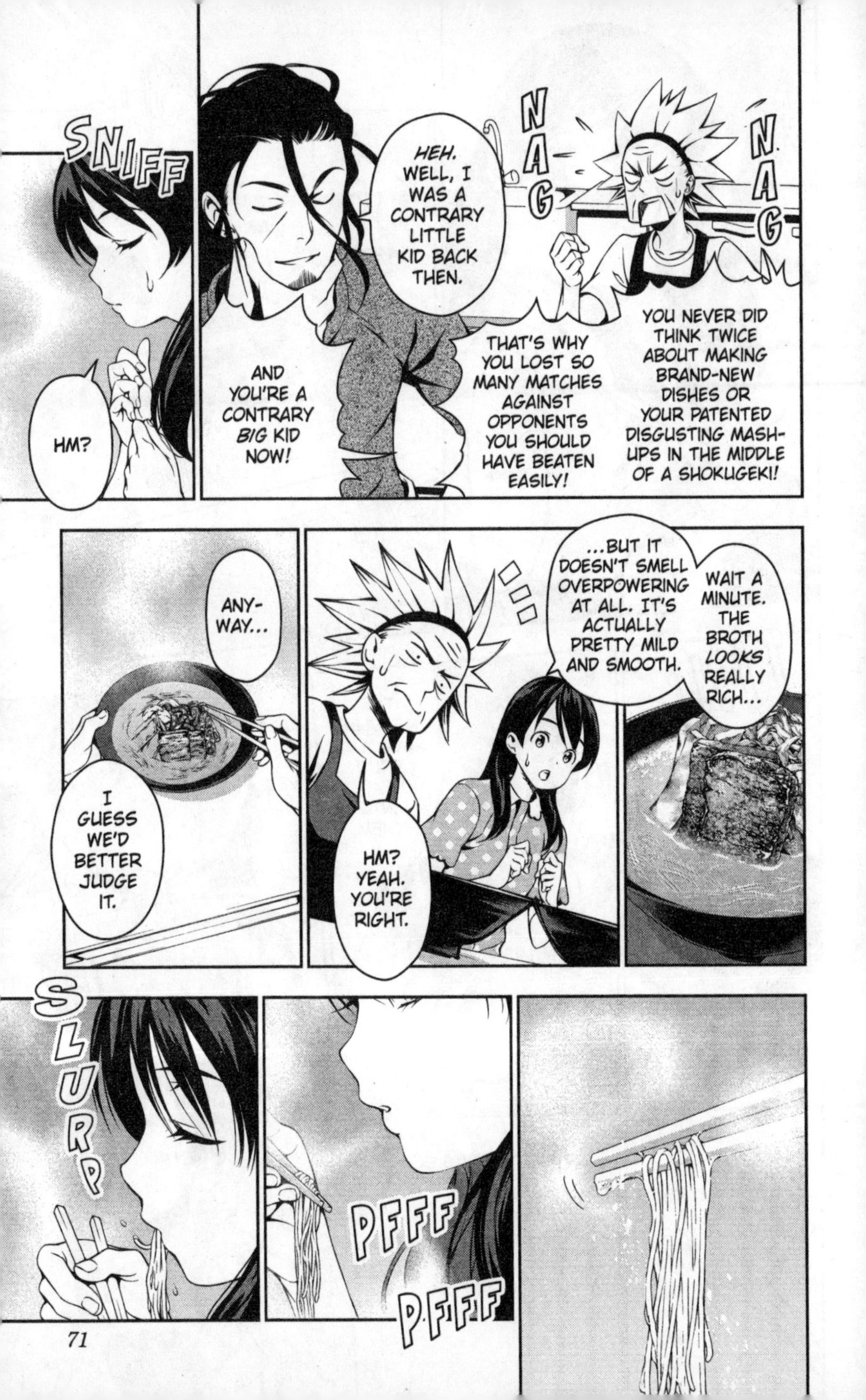
HEH. WELL, I WAS A CONTRARY LITTLE KID BACK THEN.
NAG NAG
YOU NEVER DID THINK TWICE ABOUT MAKING BRAND-NEW DISHES OR YOUR PATENTED DISGUSTING MASH-UPS IN THE MIDDLE OF A SHOKUGEKI!
THAT'S WHY YOU LOST SO MANY MATCHES AGAINST OPPONENTS YOU SHOULD HAVE BEATEN EASILY!
AND YOU'RE A CONTRARY *BIG* KID NOW!
SNIFF
HM?
WAIT A MINUTE. THE BROTH *LOOKS* REALLY RICH...
...BUT IT DOESN'T SMELL OVERPOWERING AT ALL. IT'S ACTUALLY PRETTY MILD AND SMOOTH.
HM? YEAH. YOU'RE RIGHT.
ANY-WAY...
I GUESS WE'D BETTER JUDGE IT.
PFFF
PFFF
SLURP

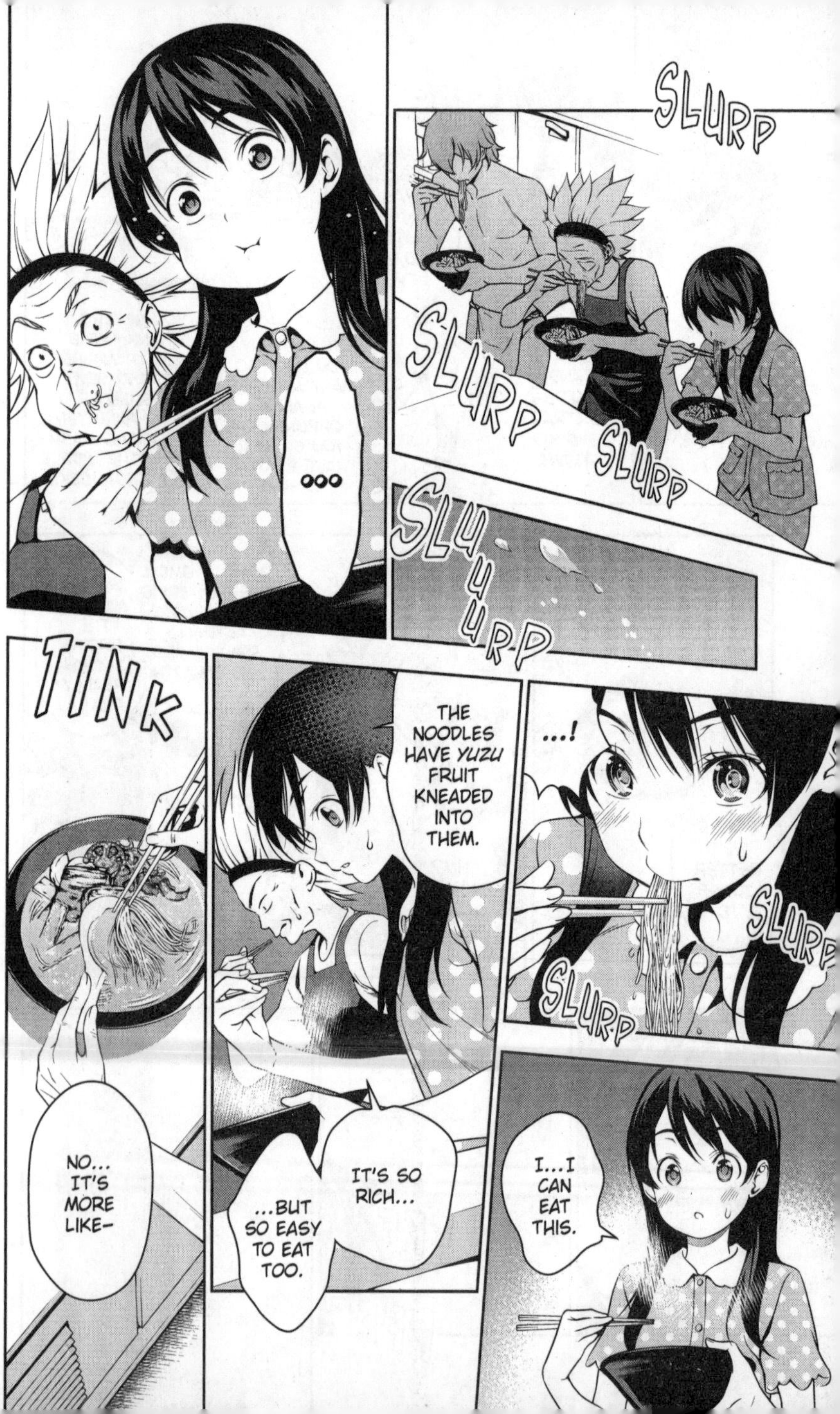
SLURP
SLURP
SLURP
SLUUUURP
...!
SLURP
SLURP
I...I CAN EAT THIS.
THE NOODLES HAVE *YUZU* FRUIT KNEADED INTO THEM.
IT'S SO RICH...
...BUT SO EASY TO EAT TOO.
TINK
NO... IT'S MORE LIKE-

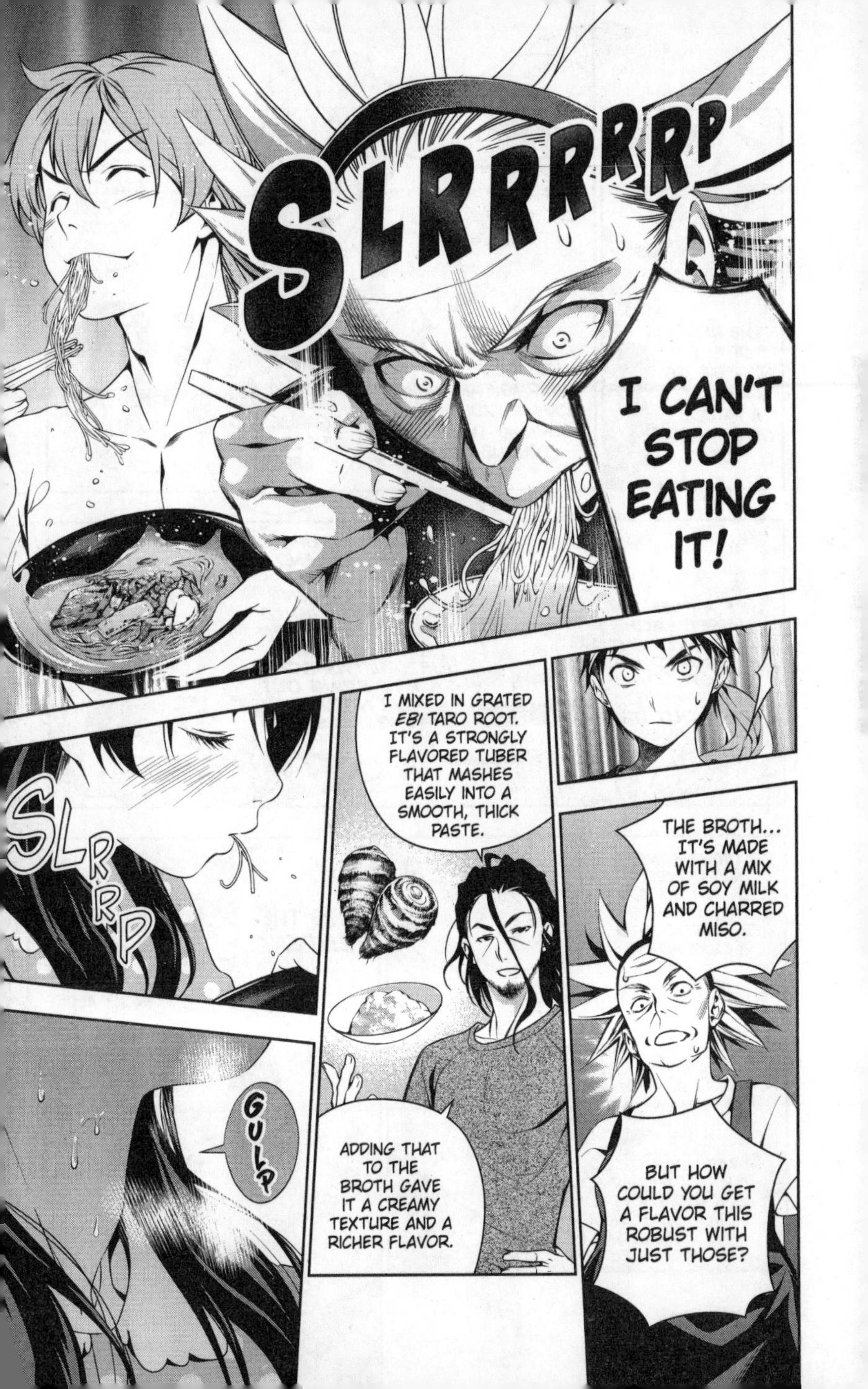
SLRRRRRP
I CAN'T STOP EATING IT!
THE BROTH... IT'S MADE WITH A MIX OF SOY MILK AND CHARRED MISO.
BUT HOW COULD YOU GET A FLAVOR THIS ROBUST WITH JUST THOSE?
I MIXED IN GRATED *EBI* TARO ROOT. IT'S A STRONGLY FLAVORED TUBER THAT MASHES EASILY INTO A SMOOTH, THICK PASTE.
ADDING THAT TO THE BROTH GAVE IT A CREAMY TEXTURE AND A RICHER FLAVOR.
SLRRP
GULP

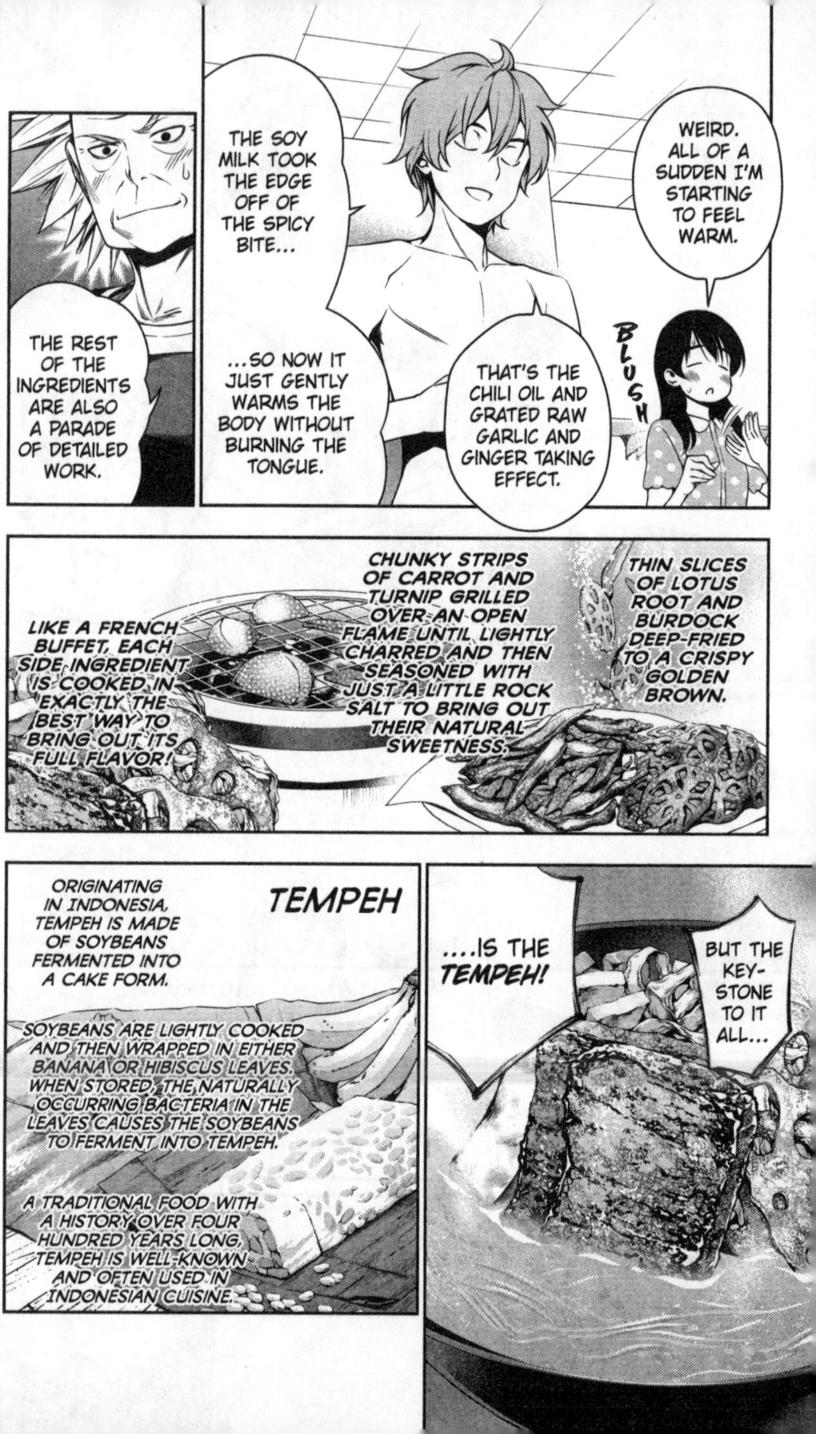
WEIRD. ALL OF A SUDDEN I'M STARTING TO FEEL WARM.
BLUSH
THAT'S THE CHILI OIL AND GRATED RAW GARLIC AND GINGER TAKING EFFECT.
THE SOY MILK TOOK THE EDGE OFF OF THE SPICY BITE...
...SO NOW IT JUST GENTLY WARMS THE BODY WITHOUT BURNING THE TONGUE.
THE REST OF THE INGREDIENTS ARE ALSO A PARADE OF DETAILED WORK.
THIN SLICES OF LOTUS ROOT AND BURDOCK DEEP-FRIED TO A CRISPY GOLDEN BROWN.
CHUNKY STRIPS OF CARROT AND TURNIP GRILLED OVER AN OPEN FLAME UNTIL LIGHTLY CHARRED AND THEN SEASONED WITH JUST A LITTLE ROCK SALT TO BRING OUT THEIR NATURAL SWEETNESS.
LIKE A FRENCH BUFFET, EACH SIDE INGREDIENT IS COOKED IN EXACTLY THE BEST WAY TO BRING OUT ITS FULL FLAVOR!
BUT THE KEY-STONE TO IT ALL...
....IS THE TEMPEH!
TEMPEH
ORIGINATING IN INDONESIA, TEMPEH IS MADE OF SOYBEANS FERMENTED INTO A CAKE FORM.
SOYBEANS ARE LIGHTLY COOKED AND THEN WRAPPED IN EITHER BANANA OR HIBISCUS LEAVES. WHEN STORED, THE NATURALLY OCCURRING BACTERIA IN THE LEAVES CAUSES THE SOYBEANS TO FERMENT INTO TEMPEH.
A TRADITIONAL FOOD WITH A HISTORY OVER FOUR HUNDRED YEARS LONG, TEMPEH IS WELL-KNOWN AND OFTEN USED IN INDONESIAN CUISINE.

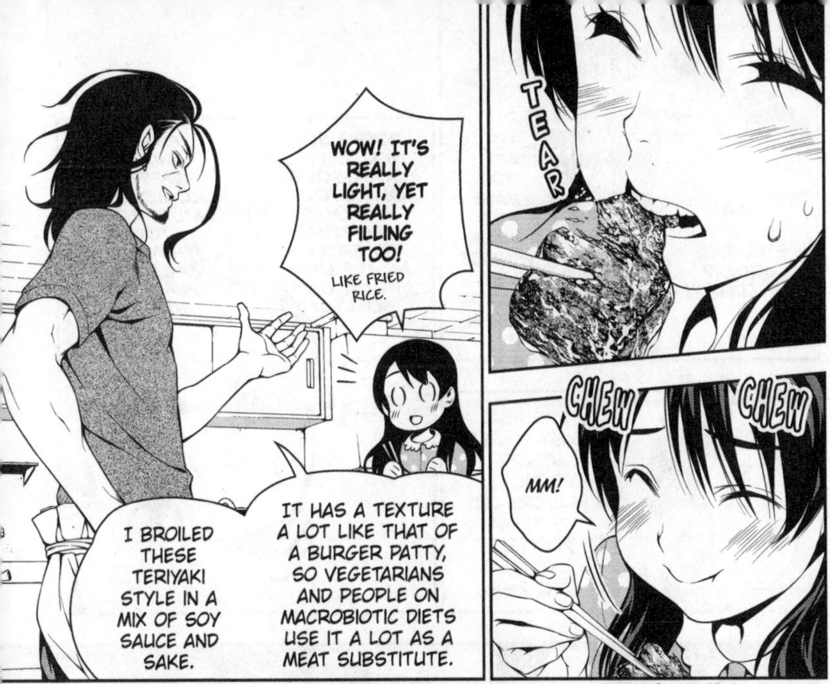
TEAR
CHEW CHEW
MM!
WOW! IT'S REALLY LIGHT, YET REALLY FILLING TOO!
LIKE FRIED RICE.
I BROILED THESE TERIYAKI STYLE IN A MIX OF SOY SAUCE AND SAKE.
IT HAS A TEXTURE A LOT LIKE THAT OF A BURGER PATTY, SO VEGETARIANS AND PEOPLE ON MACROBIOTIC DIETS USE IT A LOT AS A MEAT SUBSTITUTE.

*MACROBIOTIC DIET - A DIET THAT AVOIDS ALL MEAT AND DAIRY PRODUCTS AND FOCUSES ON GRAINS, BEANS AND VEGETABLES.

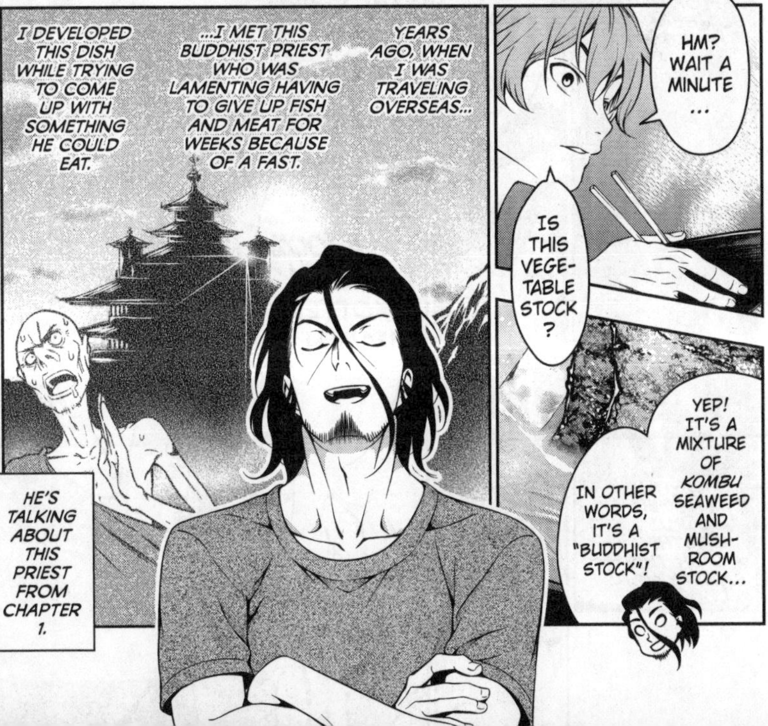
HM? WAIT A MINUTE...
IS THIS VEGE-TABLE STOCK?
YEP! IT'S A MIXTURE OF KOMBU SEAWEED AND MUSH-ROOM STOCK...
IN OTHER WORDS, IT'S A "BUDDHIST STOCK"!
YEARS AGO, WHEN I WAS TRAVELING OVERSEAS...
...I MET THIS BUDDHIST PRIEST WHO WAS LAMENTING HAVING TO GIVE UP FISH AND MEAT FOR WEEKS BECAUSE OF A FAST.
I DEVELOPED THIS DISH WHILE TRYING TO COME UP WITH SOMETHING HE COULD EAT.
HE'S TALKING ABOUT THIS PRIEST FROM CHAPTER 1.

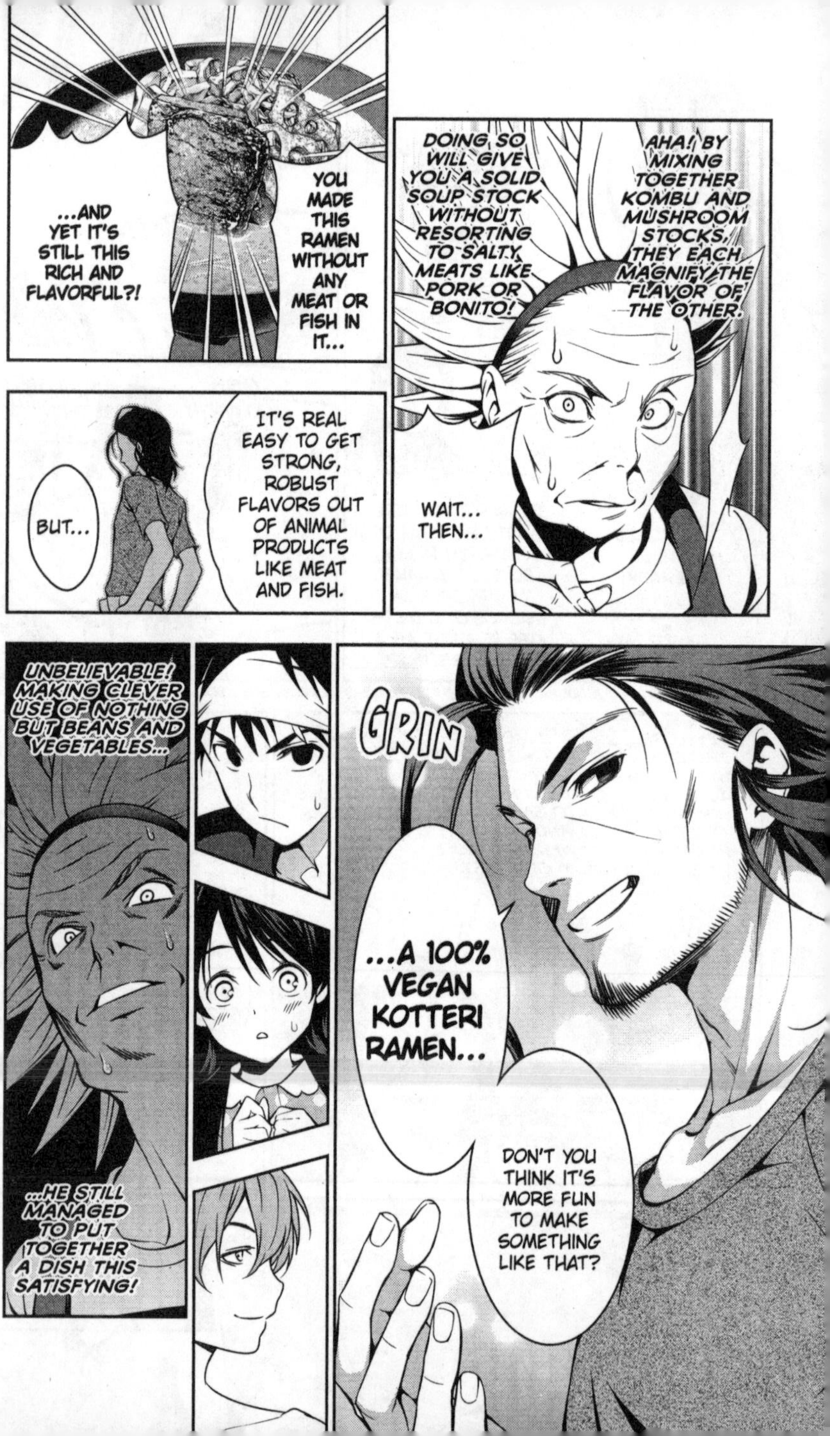
AHA! BY MIXING TOGETHER KOMBU AND MUSHROOM STOCKS, THEY EACH MAGNIFY THE FLAVOR OF THE OTHER.
DOING SO WILL GIVE YOU A SOLID SOUP STOCK WITHOUT RESORTING TO SALTY MEATS LIKE PORK OR BONITO!
WAIT... THEN...
YOU MADE THIS RAMEN WITHOUT ANY MEAT OR FISH IN IT...
...AND YET IT'S STILL THIS RICH AND FLAVORFUL?!
IT'S REAL EASY TO GET STRONG, ROBUST FLAVORS OUT OF ANIMAL PRODUCTS LIKE MEAT AND FISH.
BUT...
GRIN
...A 100% VEGAN KOTTERI RAMEN...
DON'T YOU THINK IT'S MORE FUN TO MAKE SOMETHING LIKE THAT?
UNBELIEVABLE! MAKING CLEVER USE OF NOTHING BUT BEANS AND VEGETABLES...
...HE STILL MANAGED TO PUT TOGETHER A DISH THIS SATISFYING!

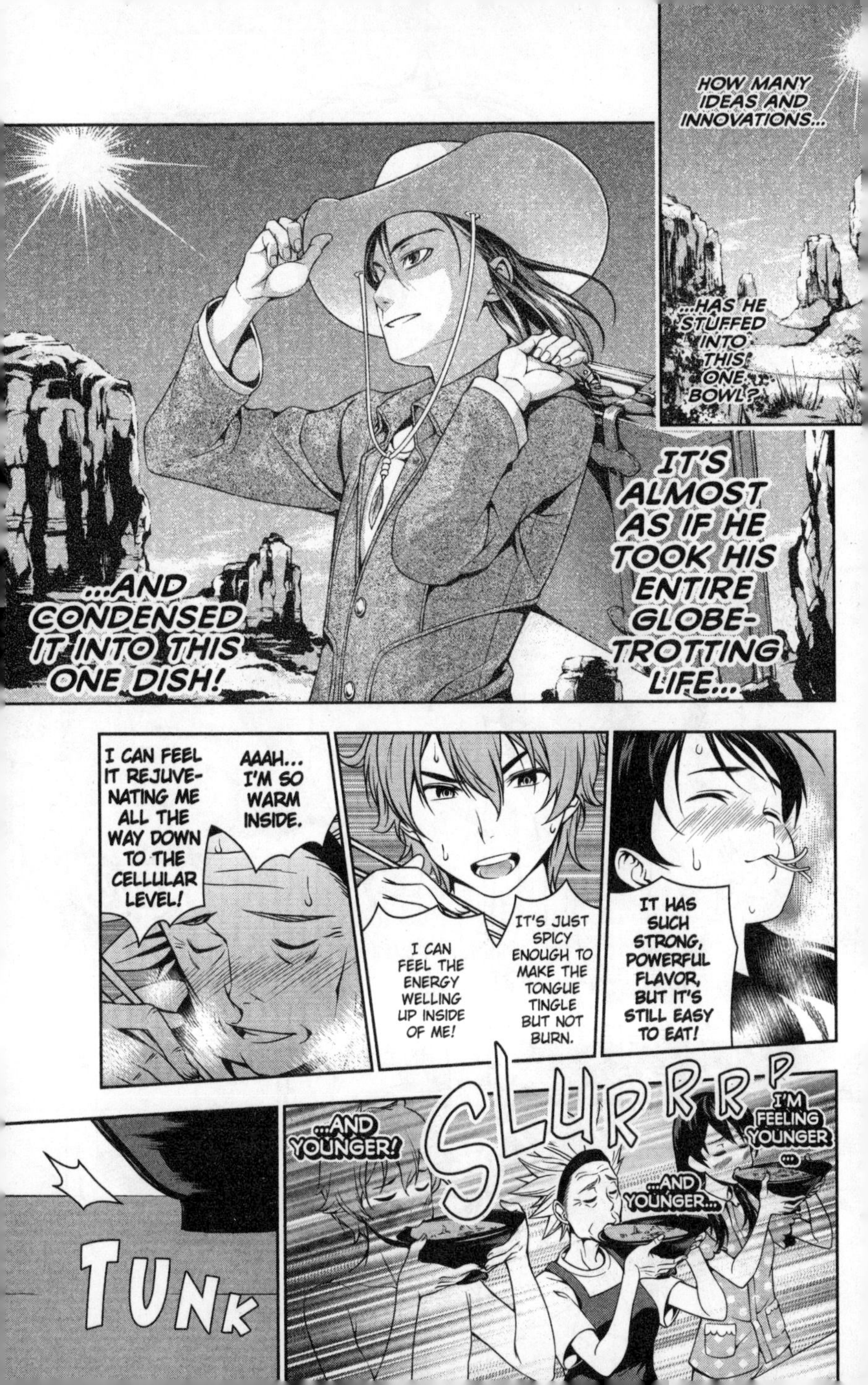
HOW MANY IDEAS AND INNOVATIONS...
...HAS HE STUFFED INTO THIS ONE BOWL?
IT'S ALMOST AS IF HE TOOK HIS ENTIRE GLOBE-TROTTING LIFE...
...AND CONDENSED IT INTO THIS ONE DISH!
IT HAS SUCH STRONG, POWERFUL FLAVOR, BUT IT'S STILL EASY TO EAT!
IT'S JUST SPICY ENOUGH TO MAKE THE TONGUE TINGLE BUT NOT BURN.
I CAN FEEL THE ENERGY WELLING UP INSIDE OF ME!
AAAH... I'M SO WARM INSIDE.
I CAN FEEL IT REJUVENATING ME ALL THE WAY DOWN TO THE CELLULAR LEVEL!
SLURRRP
I'M FEELING YOUNGER...
...AND YOUNGER...
...AND YOUNGER!
TUNK

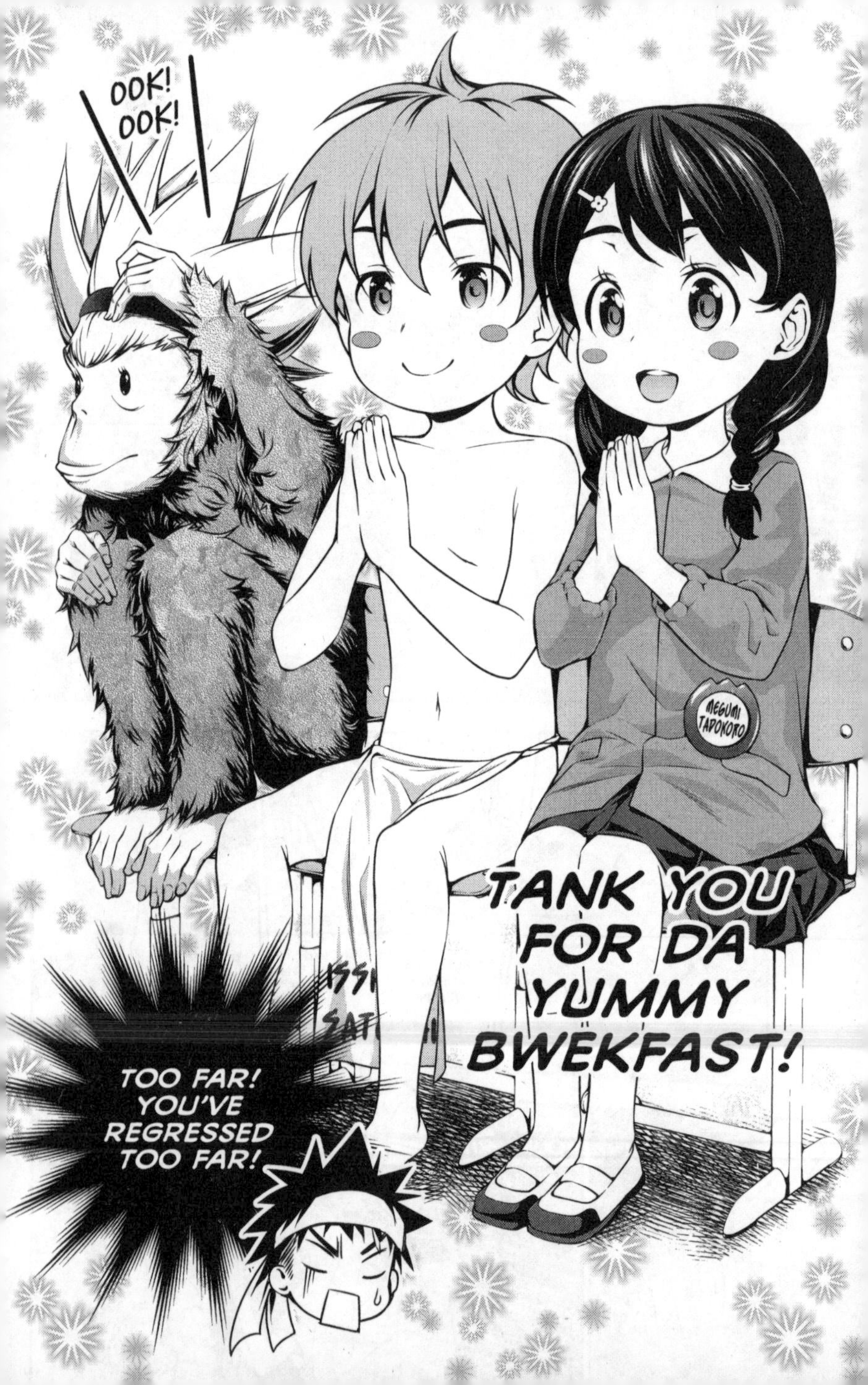
OOK! OOK!
TANK YOU FOR DA YUMMY BWEKFAST!
MEGUMI TADOKORO
TOO FAR! YOU'VE REGRESSED TOO FAR!

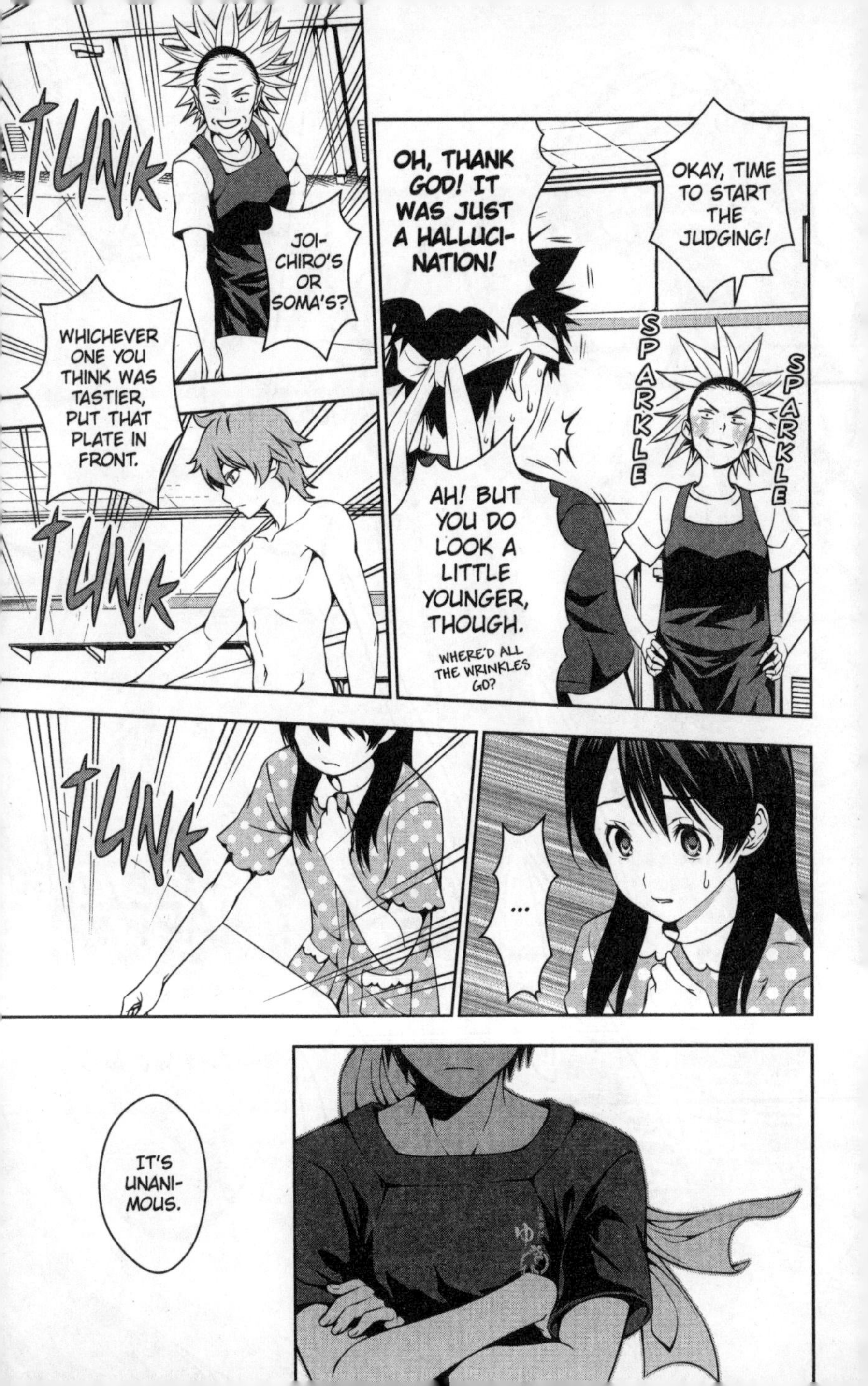
OKAY, TIME TO START THE JUDGING!
SPARKLE
SPARKLE
OH, THANK GOD! IT WAS JUST A HALLUCI-NATION!
AH! BUT YOU DO LOOK A LITTLE YOUNGER, THOUGH.
WHERE'D ALL THE WRINKLES GO?
JOI-CHIRO'S OR SOMA'S?
TUNK
WHICHEVER ONE YOU THINK WAS TASTIER, PUT THAT PLATE IN FRONT.
TUNK
...
TUNK
IT'S UNANI-MOUS.

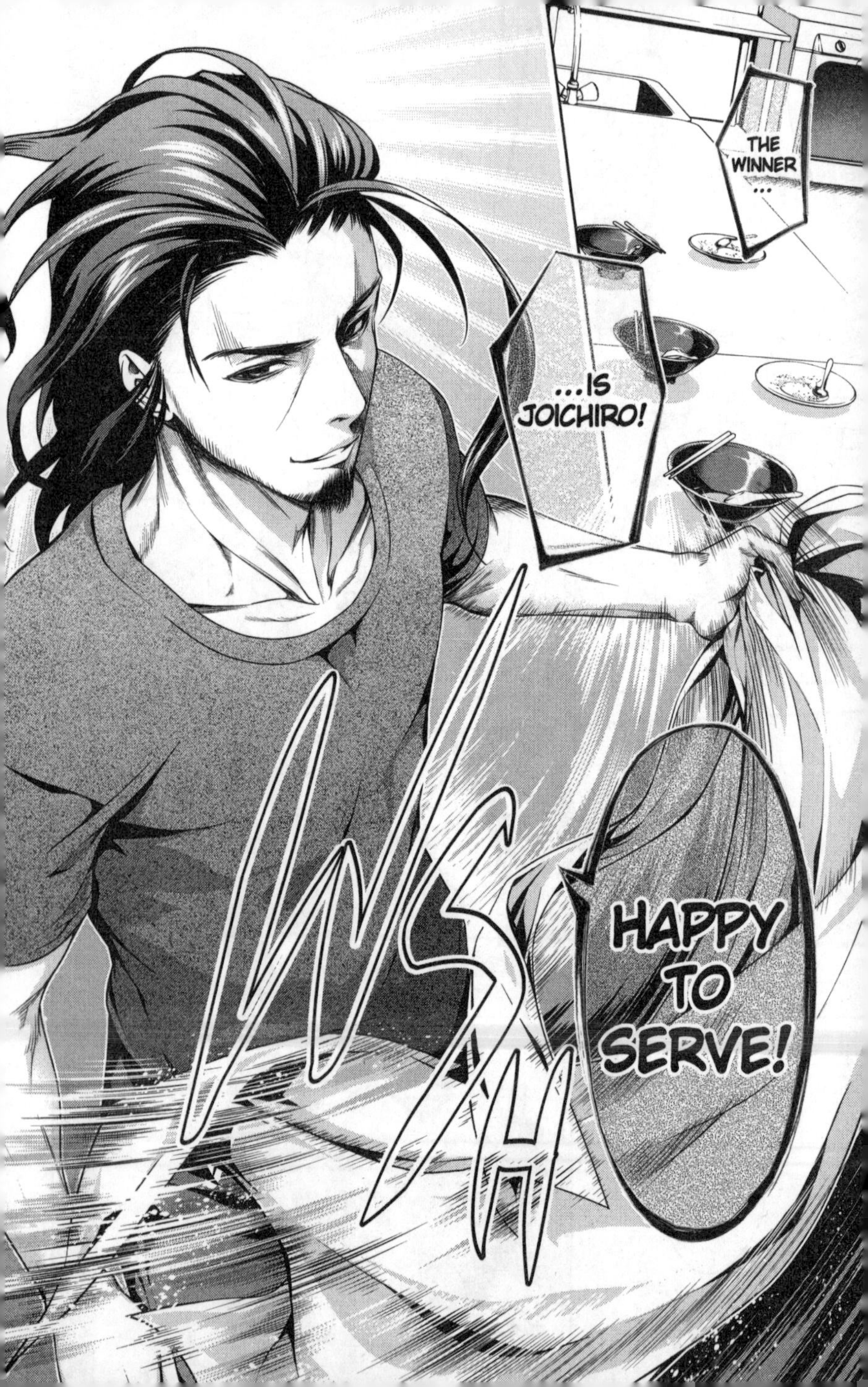
THE WINNER ...
...IS JOICHIRO!
WHSSH
HAPPY TO SERVE!

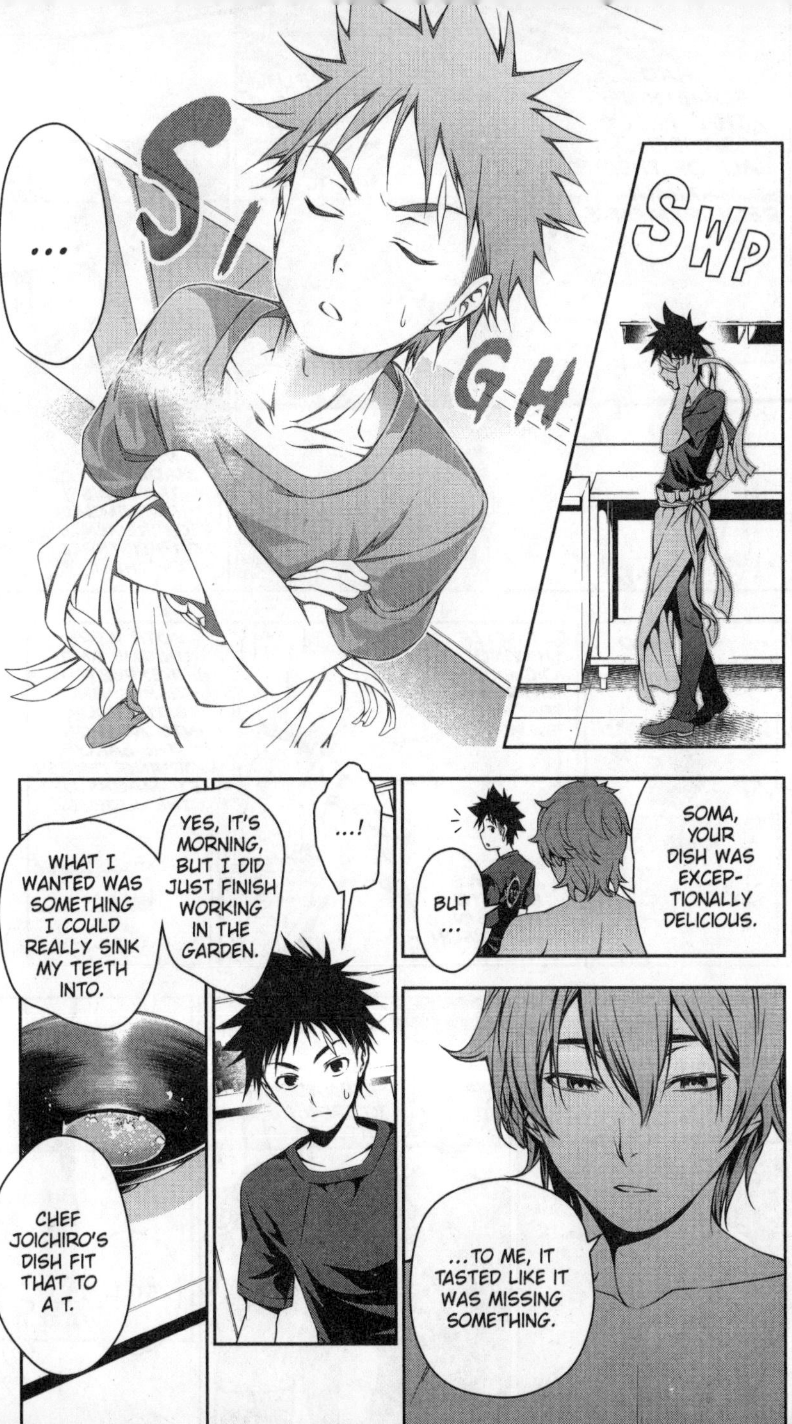
SWP
...
SIGH
SOMA, YOUR DISH WAS EXCEP-TIONALLY DELICIOUS.
BUT ...
...TO ME, IT TASTED LIKE IT WAS MISSING SOMETHING.
...!
YES, IT'S MORNING, BUT I DID JUST FINISH WORKING IN THE GARDEN.
WHAT I WANTED WAS SOMETHING I COULD REALLY SINK MY TEETH INTO.
CHEF JOICHIRO'S DISH FIT THAT TO A T.

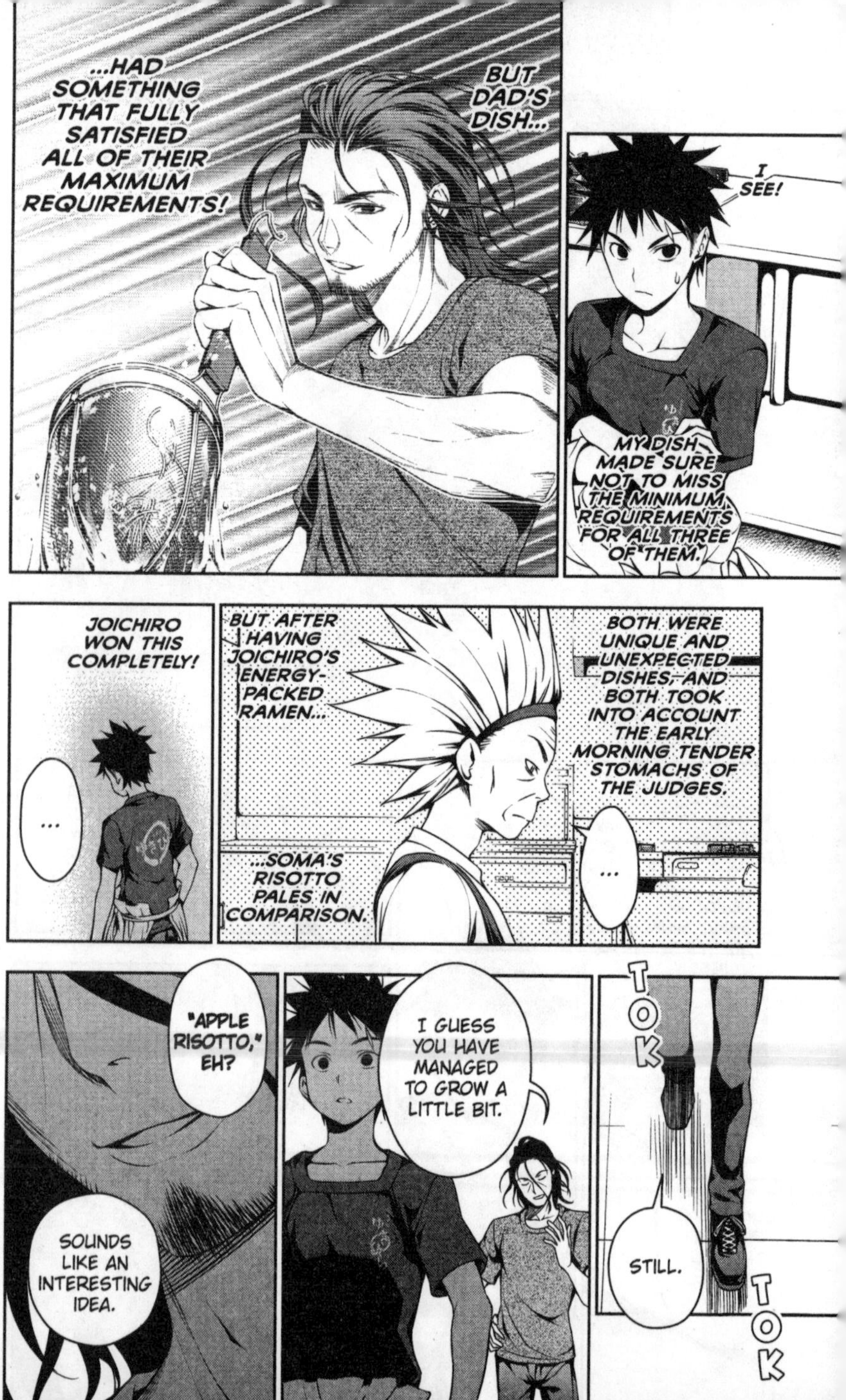
I SEE!
MY DISH MADE SURE NOT TO MISS THE MINIMUM REQUIREMENTS FOR ALL THREE OF THEM.
BUT DAD'S DISH...
...HAD SOMETHING THAT FULLY SATISFIED ALL OF THEIR MAXIMUM REQUIREMENTS!
BOTH WERE UNIQUE AND UNEXPECTED DISHES, AND BOTH TOOK INTO ACCOUNT THE EARLY MORNING TENDER STOMACHS OF THE JUDGES.
...
BUT AFTER HAVING JOICHIRO'S ENERGY-PACKED RAMEN...
...SOMA'S RISOTTO PALES IN COMPARISON.
JOICHIRO WON THIS COMPLETELY!
...
TOK
STILL.
TOK
I GUESS YOU HAVE MANAGED TO GROW A LITTLE BIT.
"APPLE RISOTTO," EH?
SOUNDS LIKE AN INTERESTING IDEA.

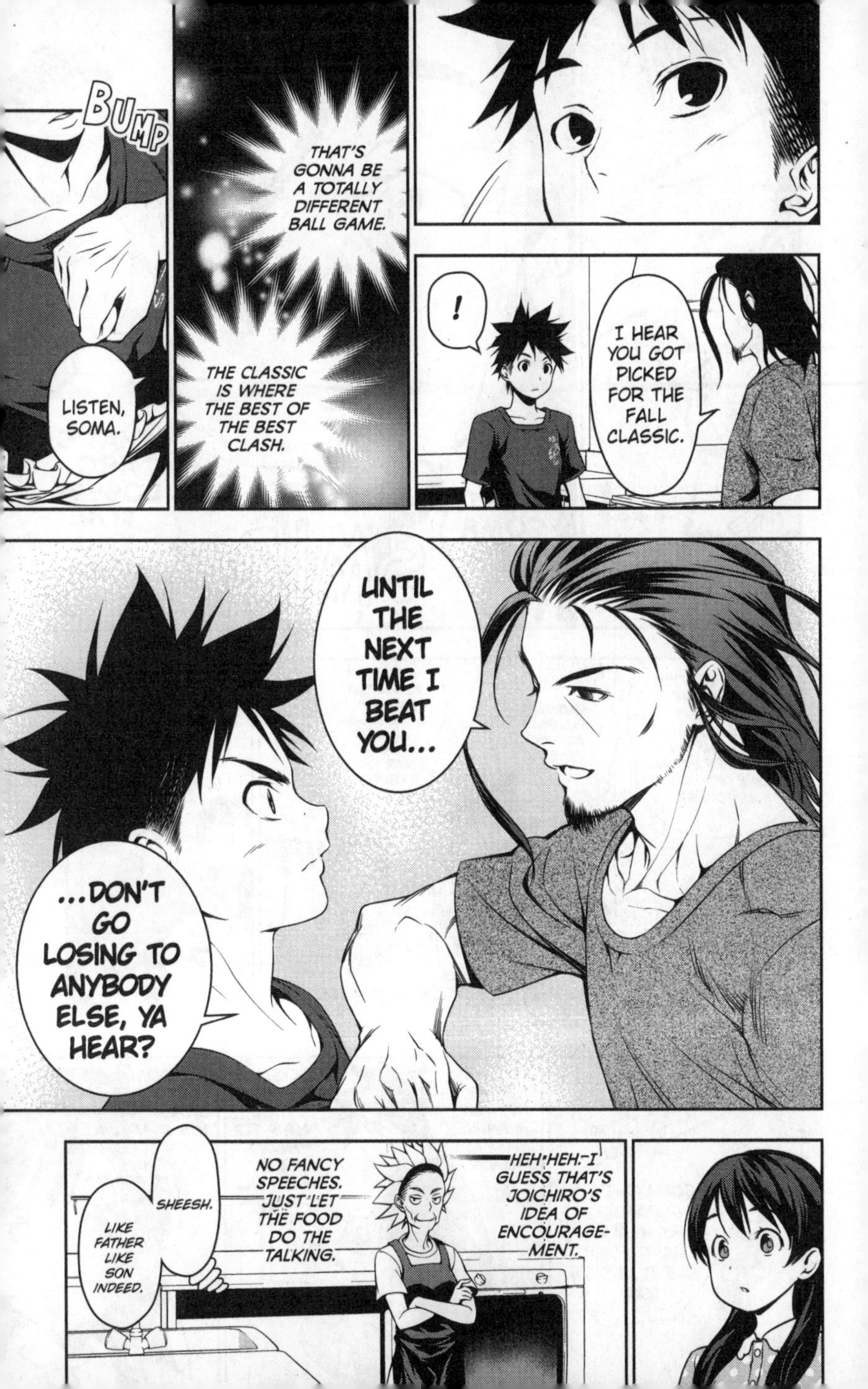
I HEAR YOU GOT PICKED FOR THE FALL CLASSIC.
!
THAT'S GONNA BE A TOTALLY DIFFERENT BALL GAME.
THE CLASSIC IS WHERE THE BEST OF THE BEST CLASH.
BUMP
LISTEN, SOMA.
UNTIL THE NEXT TIME I BEAT YOU...
...DON'T GO LOSING TO ANYBODY ELSE, YA HEAR?
HEH HEH. I GUESS THAT'S JOICHIRO'S IDEA OF ENCOURAGE-MENT.
NO FANCY SPEECHES. JUST LET THE FOOD DO THE TALKING.
SHEESH.
LIKE FATHER LIKE SON INDEED.

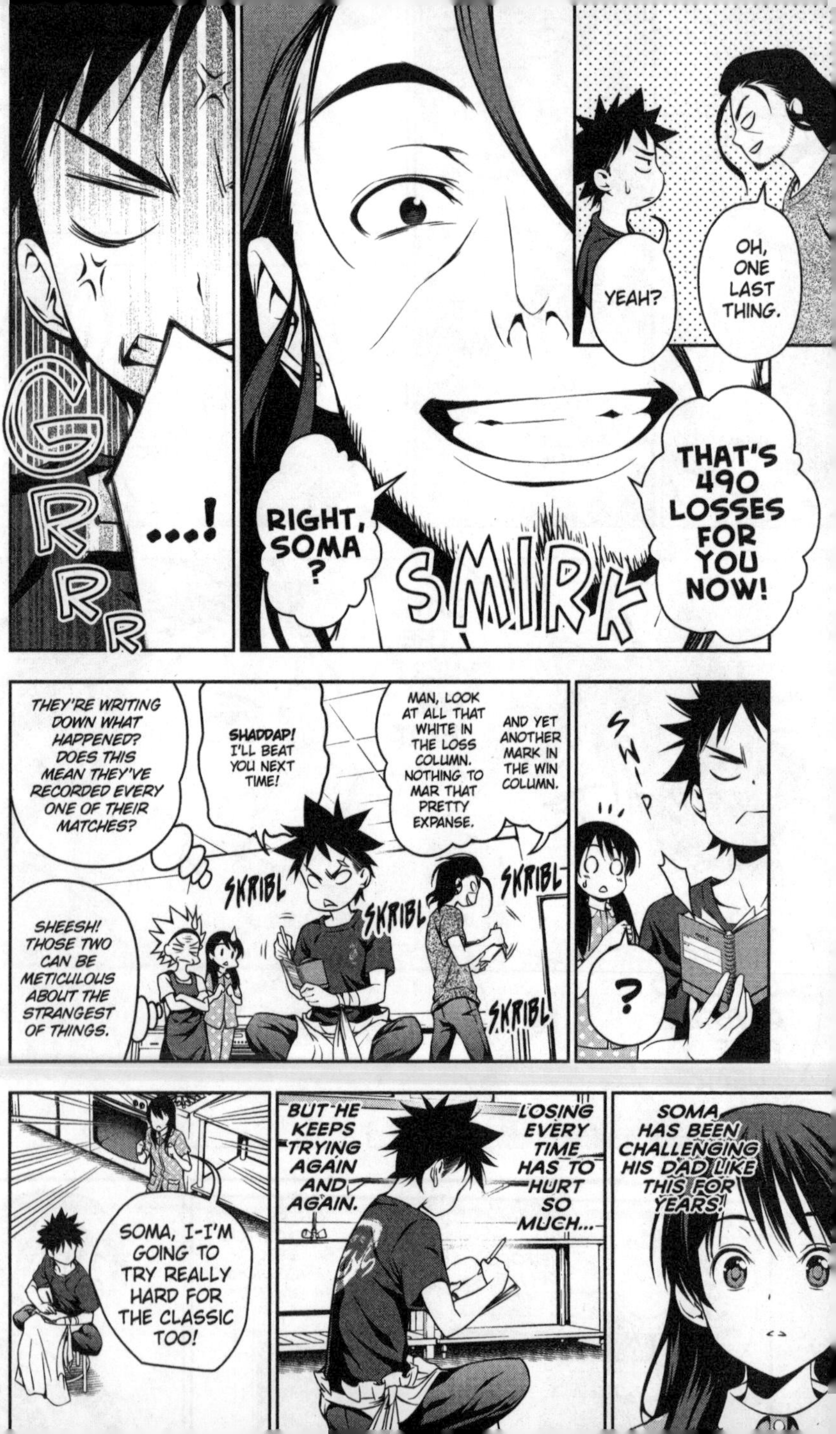
OH, ONE LAST THING.
YEAH?
THAT'S 490 LOSSES FOR YOU NOW!
RIGHT, SOMA?
SMIRK
GRRRR
...!
SWIP
?
AND YET ANOTHER MARK IN THE WIN COLUMN.
MAN, LOOK AT ALL THAT WHITE IN THE LOSS COLUMN. NOTHING TO MAR THAT PRETTY EXPANSE.
SHADDAP! I'LL BEAT YOU NEXT TIME!
THEY'RE WRITING DOWN WHAT HAPPENED? DOES THIS MEAN THEY'VE RECORDED EVERY ONE OF THEIR MATCHES?
SKRIBL
SKRIBL
SKRIBL
SKRIBL
SHEESH! THOSE TWO CAN BE METICULOUS ABOUT THE STRANGEST OF THINGS.
SOMA HAS BEEN CHALLENGING HIS DAD LIKE THIS FOR YEARS!
LOSING EVERY TIME HAS TO HURT SO MUCH...
BUT HE KEEPS TRYING AGAIN AND AGAIN.
SOMA, I-I'M GOING TO TRY REALLY HARD FOR THE CLASSIC TOO!

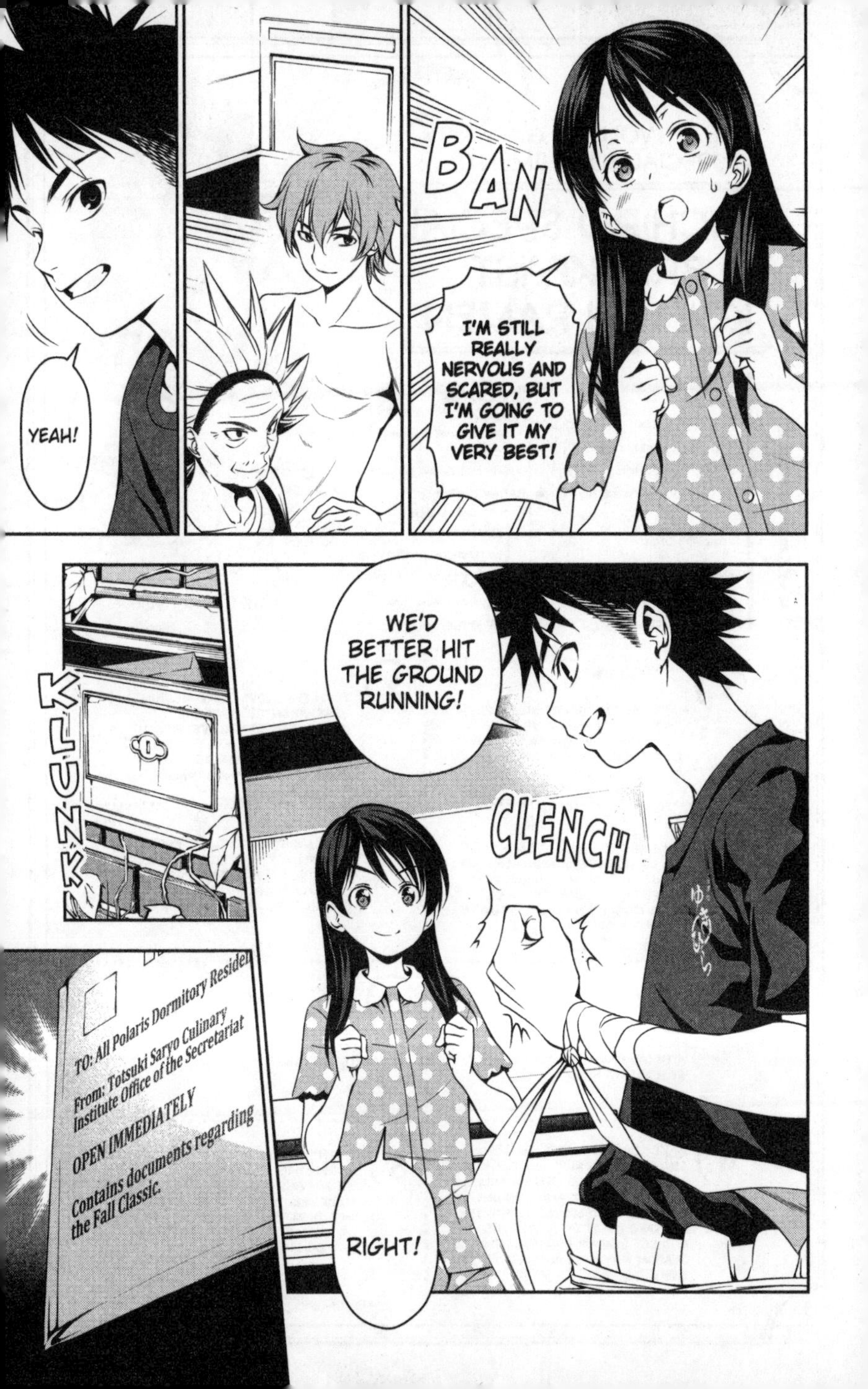
BAN
I'M STILL REALLY NERVOUS AND SCARED, BUT I'M GOING TO GIVE IT MY VERY BEST!
YEAH!
WE'D BETTER HIT THE GROUND RUNNING!
CLENCH
RIGHT!
KLUNK
TO: All Polaris Dormitory Residen
From: Totsuki Saryo Culinary Institute Office of the Secretariat
OPEN IMMEDIATELY
Contains documents regarding the Fall Classic.

PRACTICAL RECIPE #2

VOLUME 6 SPECIAL SUPPLEMENT!

JOICHIRO SPECIAL BREAKFAST KOTTERI RAMEN

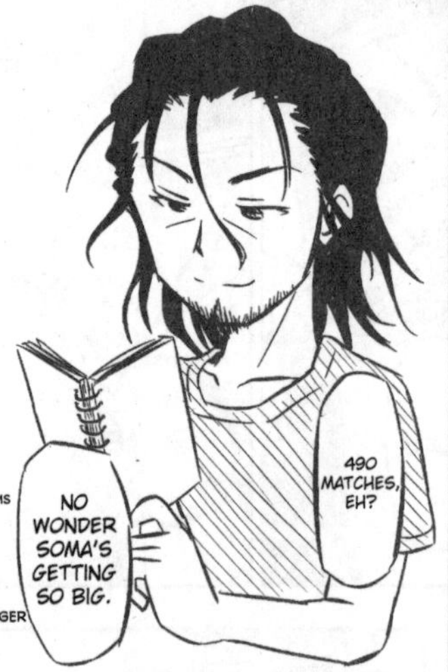
490 MATCHES, EH?
NO WONDER SOMA'S GETTING SO BIG.

ARTIST: YUTO TSUKUDA

INGREDIENTS

SERVES 2

- 2 PACKAGES DRIED RAMEN NOODLES
- 500 CC SOY MILK
- 300 CC "BUDDHIST" STOCK
- 2 TABLESPOONS MISO
- 1/2 TEASPOON EACH GRATED GINGER AND GARLIC
- 50 GRAMS EBI TARO (OR REGULAR POTATO)
- SALT, PEPPER, CHILI OIL, ROCK SALT, SESAME OIL
- LOTUS ROOT, BURDOCK, CARROTS, TURNIP

★ "BUDDHIST" STOCK (MAKES 3 CUPS)
*LEFTOVER BROTH AND MUSHROOMS CAN BE USED IN OTHER SOUPS

- 1 10x10 CM SQUARE OF KOMBU
- 700 CC WATER
- 4 SLICES DRIED SHIITAKE MUSHROOMS

★ TERIYAKI TEMPEH

- 100 GRAMS TEMPEH
- A
  - 1 TABLESPOOON SAKE
  - W1 TEASPOON GRATED GINGER
- 1 TABLESPOON EACH SOY SAUCE AND SESAME OIL
- 2 TABLESPOONS MIRIN
- POTATO STARCH

1. MAKE THE "BUDDHIST" STOCK. PUT THE KOMBU SEAWEED, SHIITAKE MUSHROOMS AND WATER IN A POT. LET SIT FOR THIRTY MINUTES.
2. TURN THE STOVE ON TO MEDIUM HEAT. WHEN THE WATER IS JUST ABOUT TO BOIL, REMOVE THE KOMBU. LET BOIL FOR TWO MINUTES, AND THEN REMOVE FROM THE HEAT AND STRAIN.
3. MAKE THE TOPPINGS. THINLY SLICE THE LOTUS ROOT, LEAVING THE SKIN ON. USE A PEELER TO MAKE THIN STRIPS OF BURDOCK. FRY IN OIL UNTIL CRISPY, AND THEN SPRINKLE WITH ROCK SALT.
4. CUT CARROT INTO STICKS. CHOP THE TURNIP INTO BITE-SIZED PIECES. HEAT THE SESAME OIL IN A FRYING PAN AND SAUTÉ BOTH UNTIL GOLDEN BROWN. SPRINKLE WITH ROCK SALT.
5. MAKE THE TERIYAKI TEMPEH. CUT THE TEMPEH INTO CHUNKS ABOUT FIVE CENTIMETERS WIDE. SPRINKLE WITH (A), AND THEN COAT LIGHTLY WITH POTATO STARCH.
6. HEAT SESAME OIL IN A FRYING PAN AND SAUTÉ UNTIL THOROUGHLY COOKED. ADD SOY SAUCE AND MIRIN, COATING THE TEMPEH WELL.
7. MAKE THE BROTH. PUT THE MISO, GINGER AND GARLIC IN A POT AND SEAR LIGHTLY. ADD THE SOY MILK AND "BUDDHIST" STOCK AND STIR UNTIL THE MISO IS DISSOLVED. GRATE THE EBI TARO (OR POTATO) INTO THE POT AND LET SIMMER FOR FIVE MINUTES. SEASON WITH SALT AND PEPPER TO TASTE.
8. FINISHING TOUCHES. BOIL THE RAMEN NOODLES IN A SEPARATE POT, AND THEN STRAIN AND SHAKE OFF ANY EXTRA MOISTURE. PUT THE COOKED NOODLES IN A BOWL AND POUR (7) IN. TOP WITH (3), (4) AND (6), DRIZZLE WITH CHILI OIL, AND DONE!

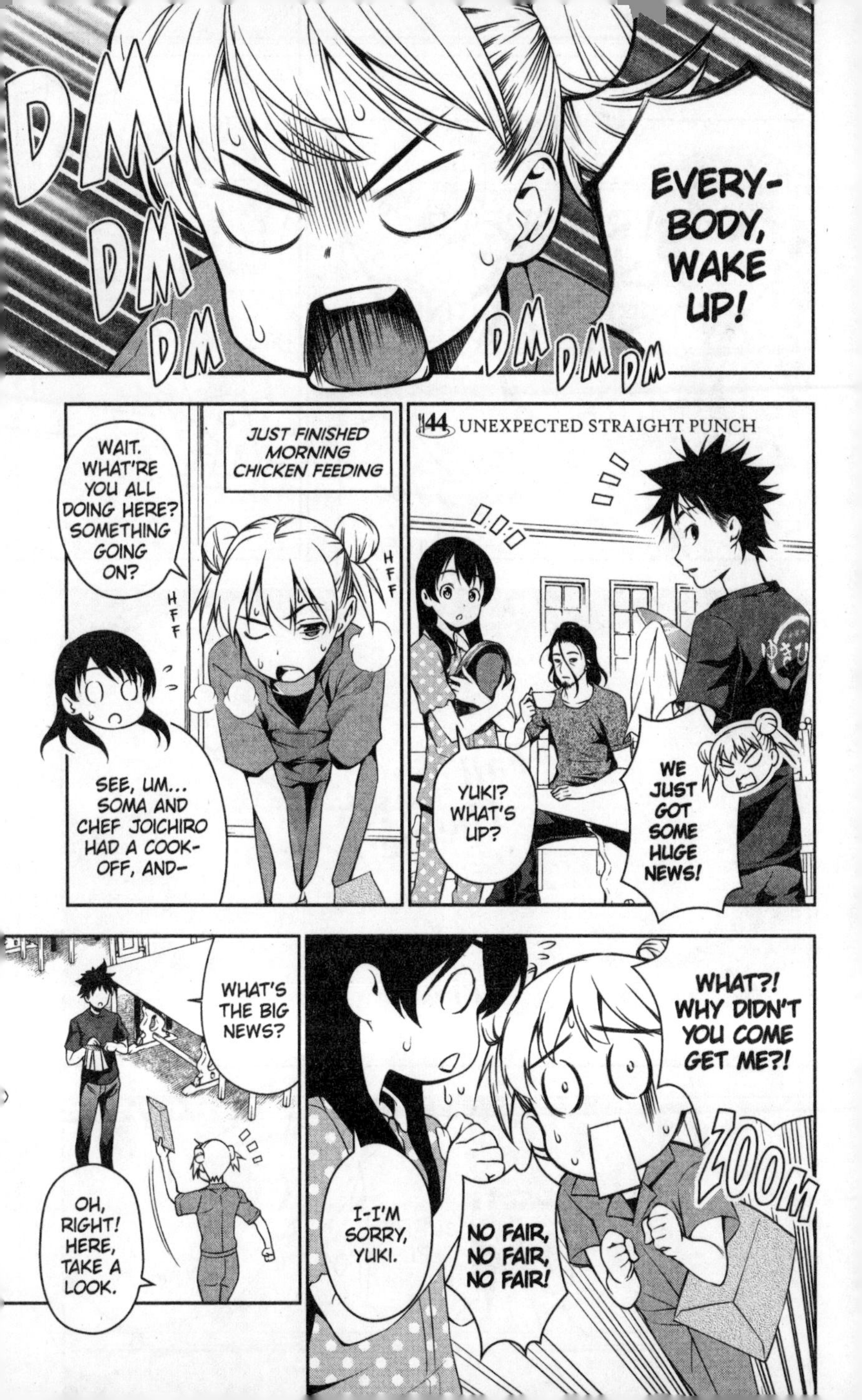
EVERY-BODY, WAKE UP!
DM DM DM DM DM DM DM DM
44 UNEXPECTED STRAIGHT PUNCH
WE JUST GOT SOME HUGE NEWS!
YUKI? WHAT'S UP?
JUST FINISHED MORNING CHICKEN FEEDING
HFF
WAIT. WHAT'RE YOU ALL DOING HERE? SOMETHING GOING ON?
HFF
SEE, UM... SOMA AND CHEF JOICHIRO HAD A COOK-OFF, AND–
WHAT?! WHY DIDN'T YOU COME GET ME?!
ZOOM
NO FAIR, NO FAIR, NO FAIR!
I-I'M SORRY, YUKI.
WHAT'S THE BIG NEWS?
OH, RIGHT! HERE, TAKE A LOOK.

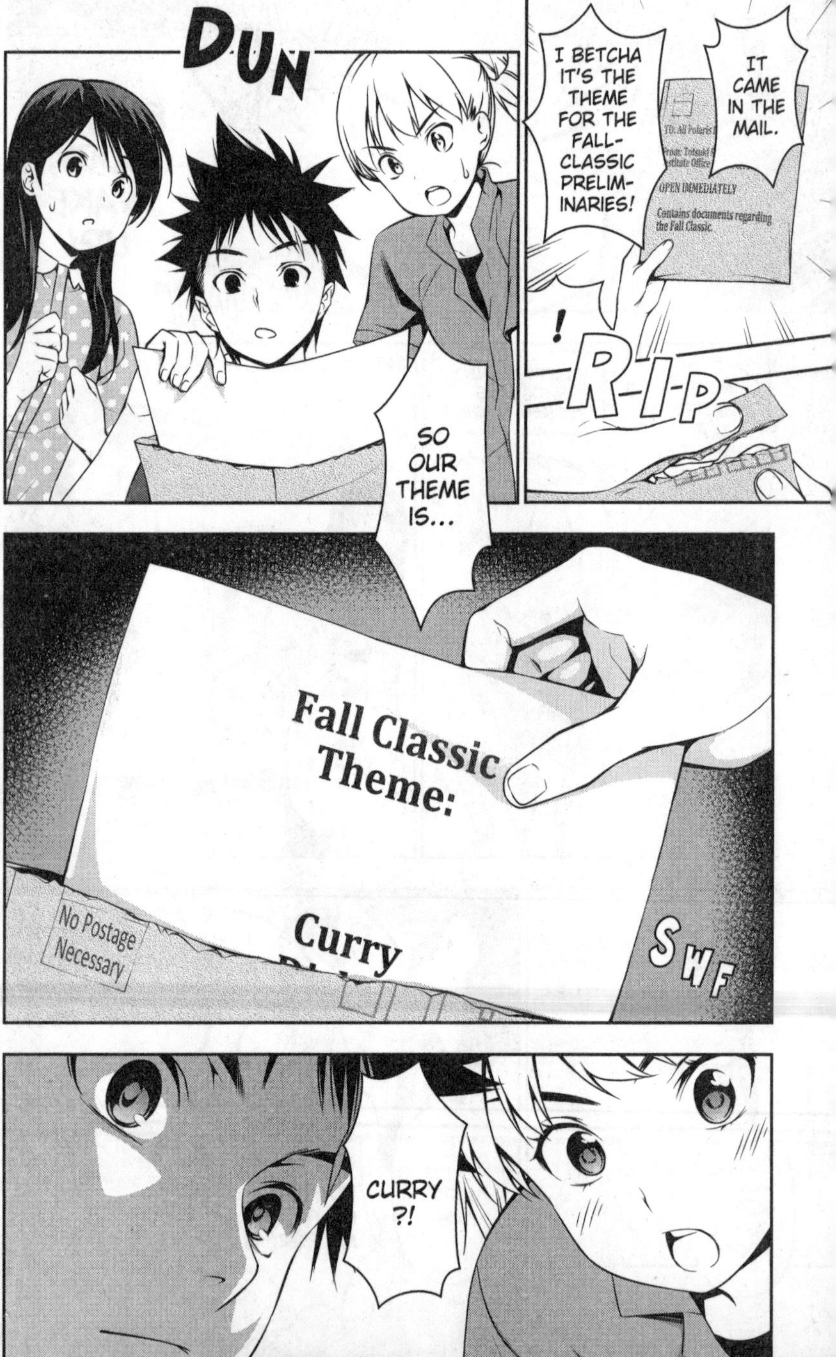
IT CAME IN THE MAIL.
I BETCHA IT'S THE THEME FOR THE FALL-CLASSIC PRELIMINARIES!
OPEN IMMEDIATELY
Contains documents regarding the Fall Classic.
!
RIP
DUN
SO OUR THEME IS...
Fall Classic Theme:
Curry
No Postage Necessary
SWF
CURRY ?!

144 UNEXPECTED STRAIGHT PUNCH

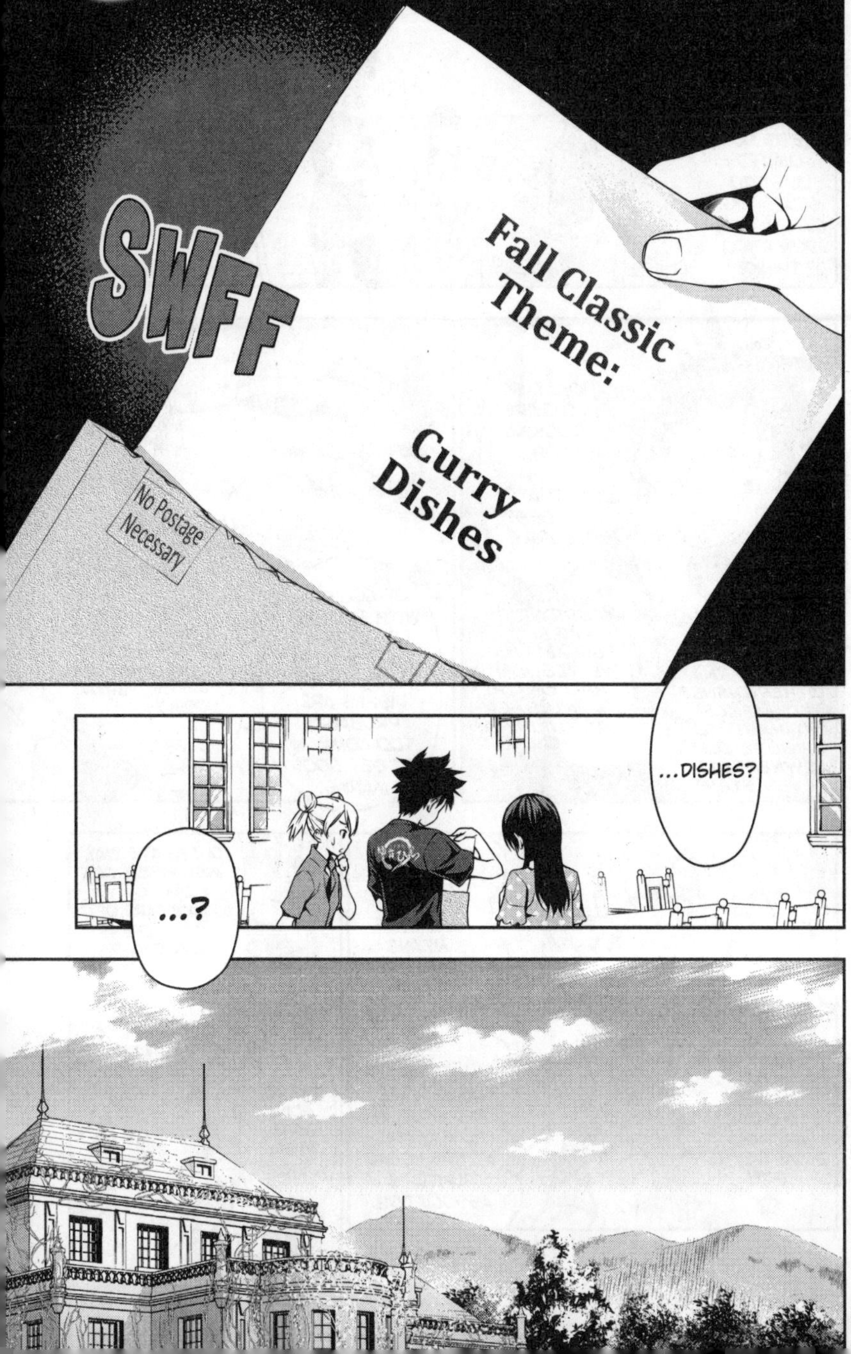
Fall Classic Theme:
Curry Dishes
SWFF
No Postage Necessary
...DISHES?
...?

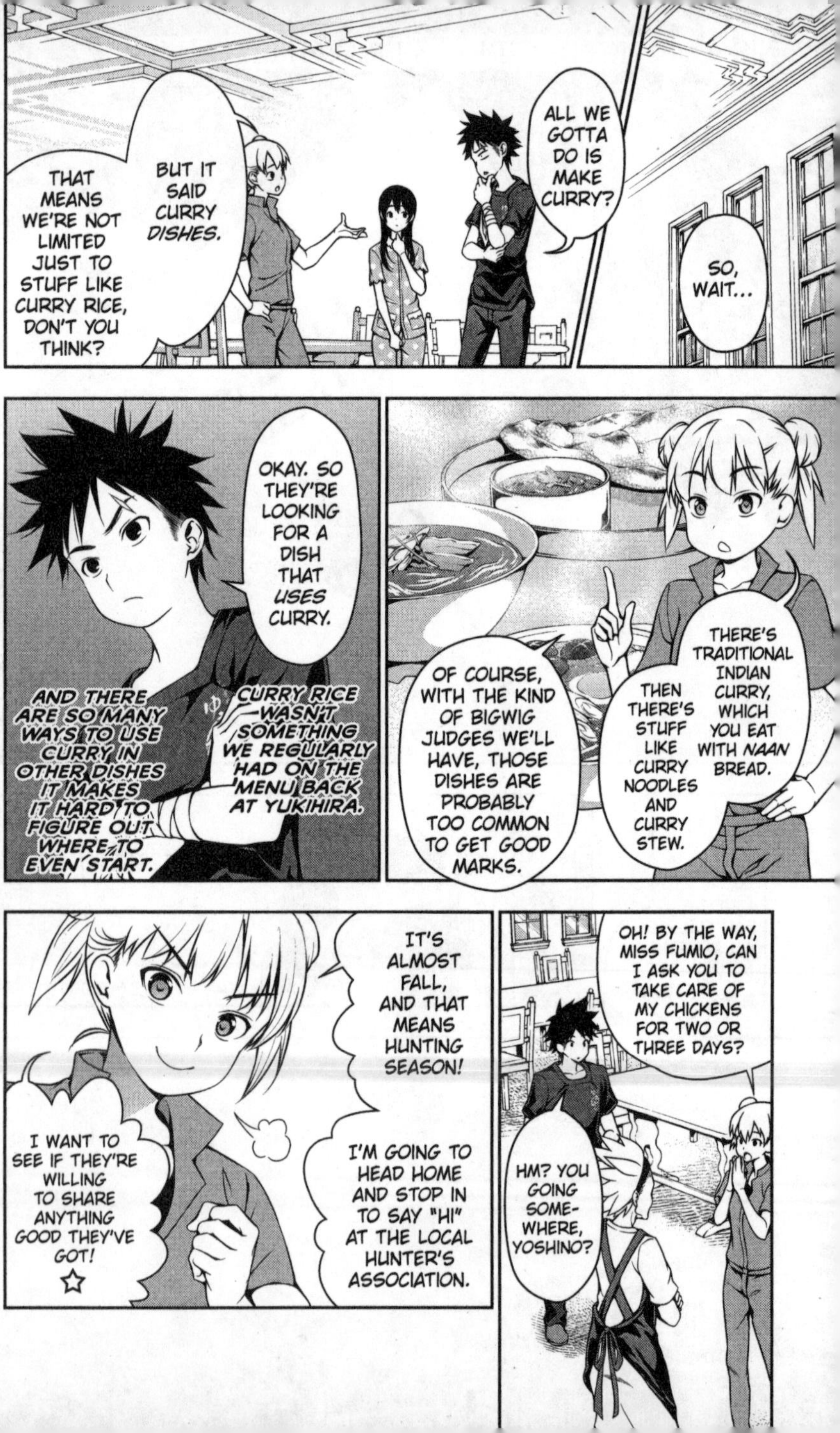
SO, WAIT...
ALL WE GOTTA DO IS MAKE CURRY?
BUT IT SAID CURRY *DISHES.*
THAT MEANS WE'RE NOT LIMITED JUST TO STUFF LIKE CURRY RICE, DON'T YOU THINK?
THERE'S TRADITIONAL INDIAN CURRY, WHICH YOU EAT WITH *NAAN* BREAD.
THEN THERE'S STUFF LIKE CURRY NOODLES AND CURRY STEW.
OF COURSE, WITH THE KIND OF BIGWIG JUDGES WE'LL HAVE, THOSE DISHES ARE PROBABLY TOO COMMON TO GET GOOD MARKS.
OKAY. SO THEY'RE LOOKING FOR A DISH THAT *USES* CURRY.
CURRY RICE WASN'T SOMETHING WE REGULARLY HAD ON THE MENU BACK AT YUKIHIRA.
AND THERE ARE SO MANY WAYS TO USE CURRY IN OTHER DISHES IT MAKES IT HARD TO FIGURE OUT WHERE TO EVEN START.
OH! BY THE WAY, MISS FUMIO, CAN I ASK YOU TO TAKE CARE OF MY CHICKENS FOR TWO OR THREE DAYS?
HM? YOU GOING SOME-WHERE, YOSHINO?
IT'S ALMOST FALL, AND THAT MEANS HUNTING SEASON!
I'M GOING TO HEAD HOME AND STOP IN TO SAY "HI" AT THE LOCAL HUNTER'S ASSOCIATION.
I WANT TO SEE IF THEY'RE WILLING TO SHARE ANYTHING GOOD THEY'VE GOT! ☆

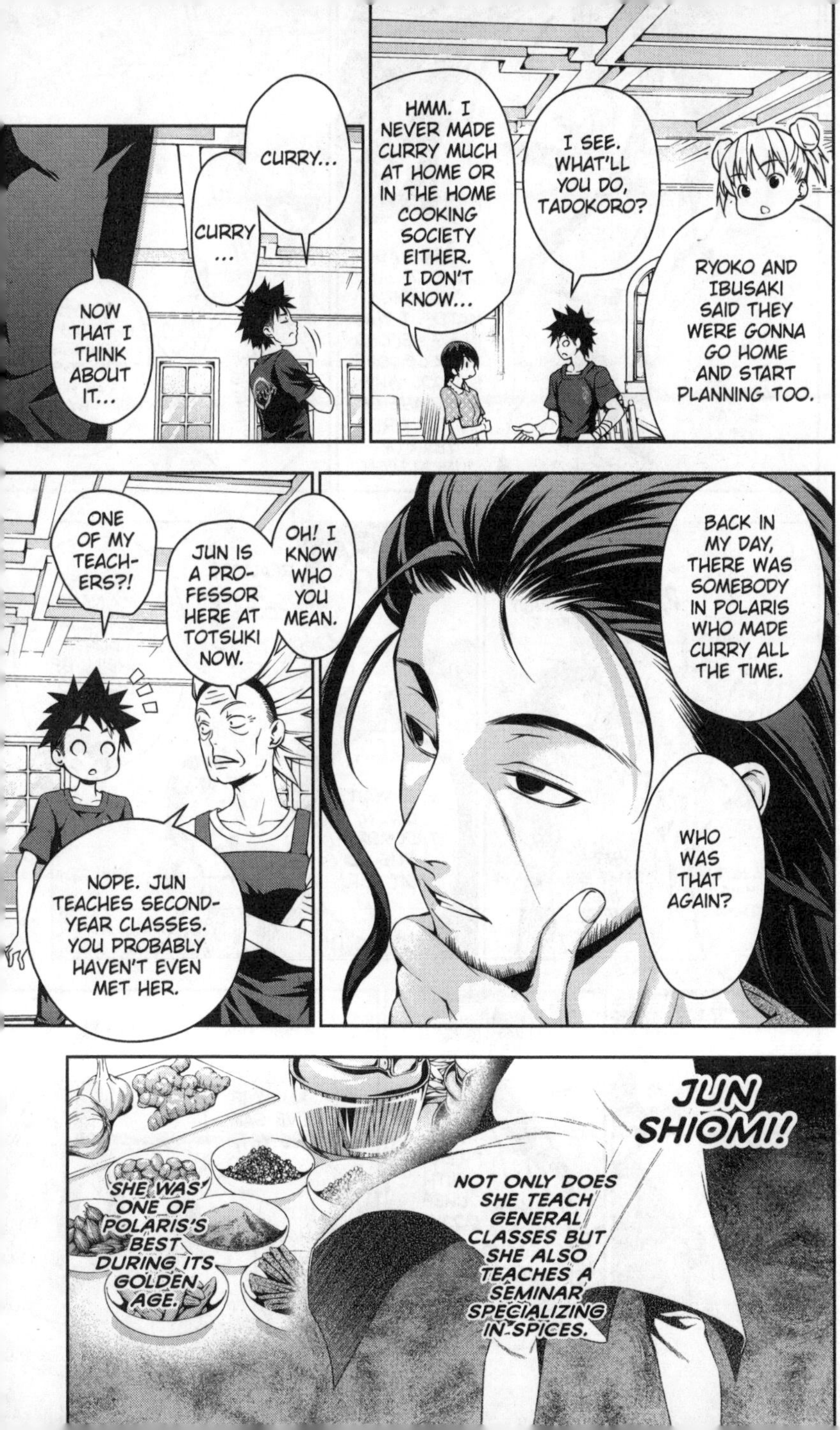
RYOKO AND IBUSAKI SAID THEY WERE GONNA GO HOME AND START PLANNING TOO.
I SEE. WHAT'LL YOU DO, TADOKORO?
HMM. I NEVER MADE CURRY MUCH AT HOME OR IN THE HOME COOKING SOCIETY EITHER. I DON'T KNOW...
CURRY...
CURRY ...
NOW THAT I THINK ABOUT IT...
BACK IN MY DAY, THERE WAS SOMEBODY IN POLARIS WHO MADE CURRY ALL THE TIME.
WHO WAS THAT AGAIN?
OH! I KNOW WHO YOU MEAN.
JUN IS A PRO-FESSOR HERE AT TOTSUKI NOW.
ONE OF MY TEACH-ERS?!
NOPE. JUN TEACHES SECOND-YEAR CLASSES. YOU PROBABLY HAVEN'T EVEN MET HER.
JUN SHIOMI!
NOT ONLY DOES SHE TEACH GENERAL CLASSES BUT SHE ALSO TEACHES A SEMINAR SPECIALIZING IN SPICES.
SHE WAS ONE OF POLARIS'S BEST DURING ITS GOLDEN AGE.

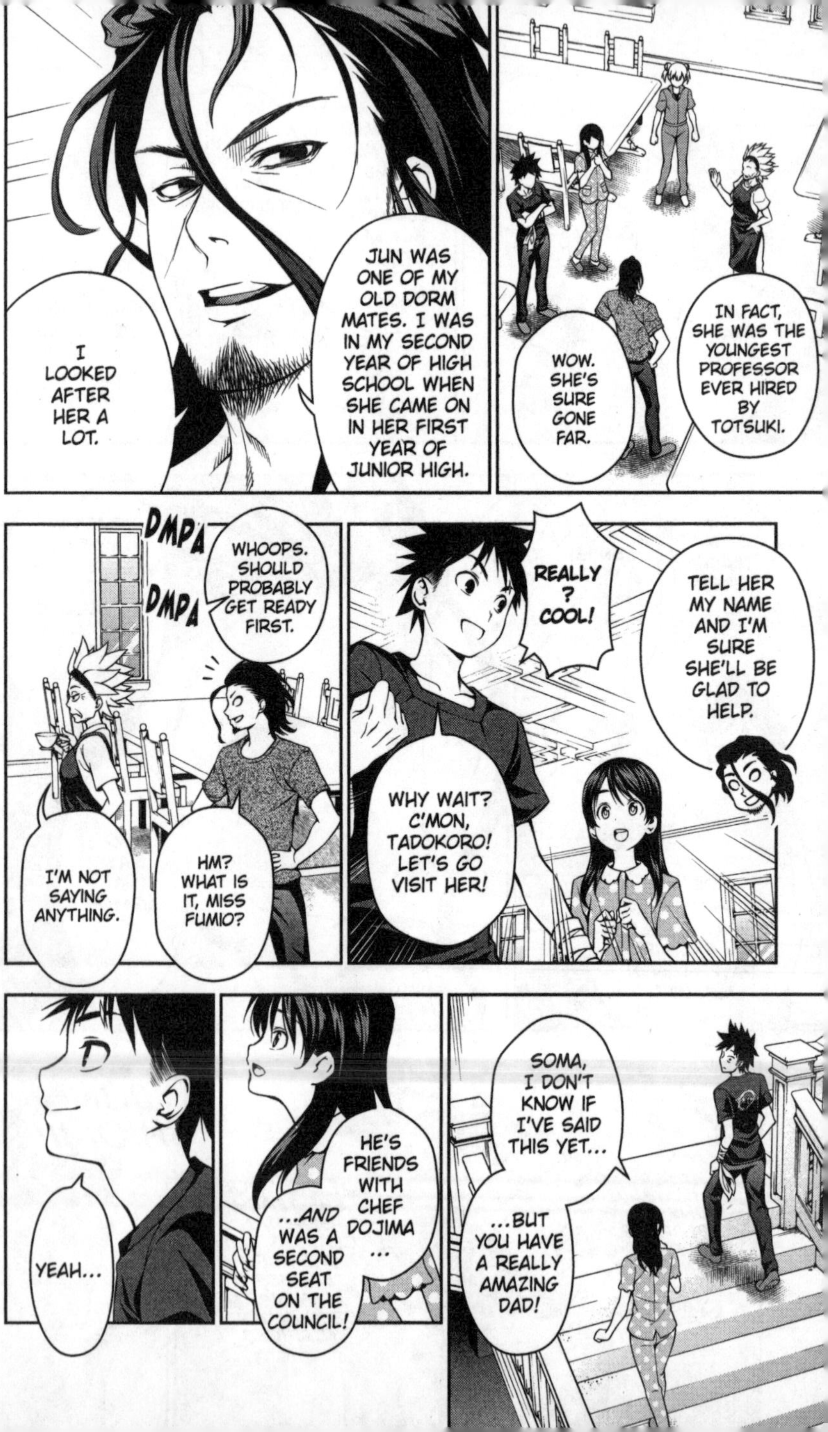
IN FACT, SHE WAS THE YOUNGEST PROFESSOR EVER HIRED BY TOTSUKI.
WOW. SHE'S SURE GONE FAR.
JUN WAS ONE OF MY OLD DORM MATES. I WAS IN MY SECOND YEAR OF HIGH SCHOOL WHEN SHE CAME ON IN HER FIRST YEAR OF JUNIOR HIGH.
I LOOKED AFTER HER A LOT.
TELL HER MY NAME AND I'M SURE SHE'LL BE GLAD TO HELP.
REALLY? COOL!
WHY WAIT? C'MON, TADOKORO! LET'S GO VISIT HER!
WHOOPS. SHOULD PROBABLY GET READY FIRST.
DMPA
DMPA
HM? WHAT IS IT, MISS FUMIO?
I'M NOT SAYING ANYTHING.
SOMA, I DON'T KNOW IF I'VE SAID THIS YET...
...BUT YOU HAVE A REALLY AMAZING DAD!
HE'S FRIENDS WITH CHEF DOJIMA...
...AND WAS A SECOND SEAT ON THE COUNCIL!
YEAH...

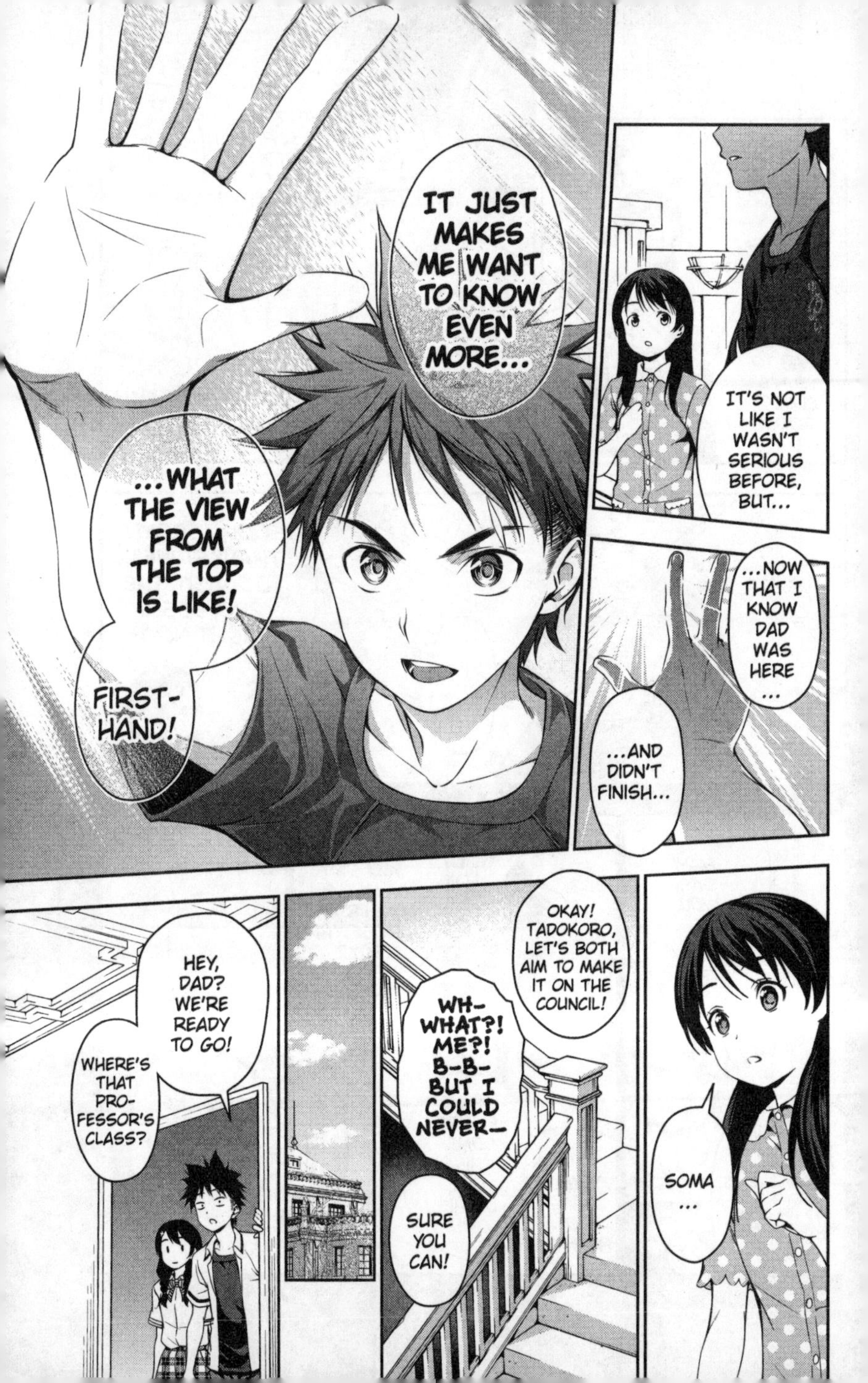
IT'S NOT LIKE I WASN'T SERIOUS BEFORE, BUT...
...NOW THAT I KNOW DAD WAS HERE...
...AND DIDN'T FINISH...
IT JUST MAKES ME WANT TO KNOW EVEN MORE...
...WHAT THE VIEW FROM THE TOP IS LIKE!
FIRST-HAND!
SOMA...
OKAY! TADOKORO, LET'S BOTH AIM TO MAKE IT ON THE COUNCIL!
WH-WHAT?! ME?! B-B-BUT I COULD NEVER—
SURE YOU CAN!
HEY, DAD? WE'RE READY TO GO!
WHERE'S THAT PRO-FESSOR'S CLASS?

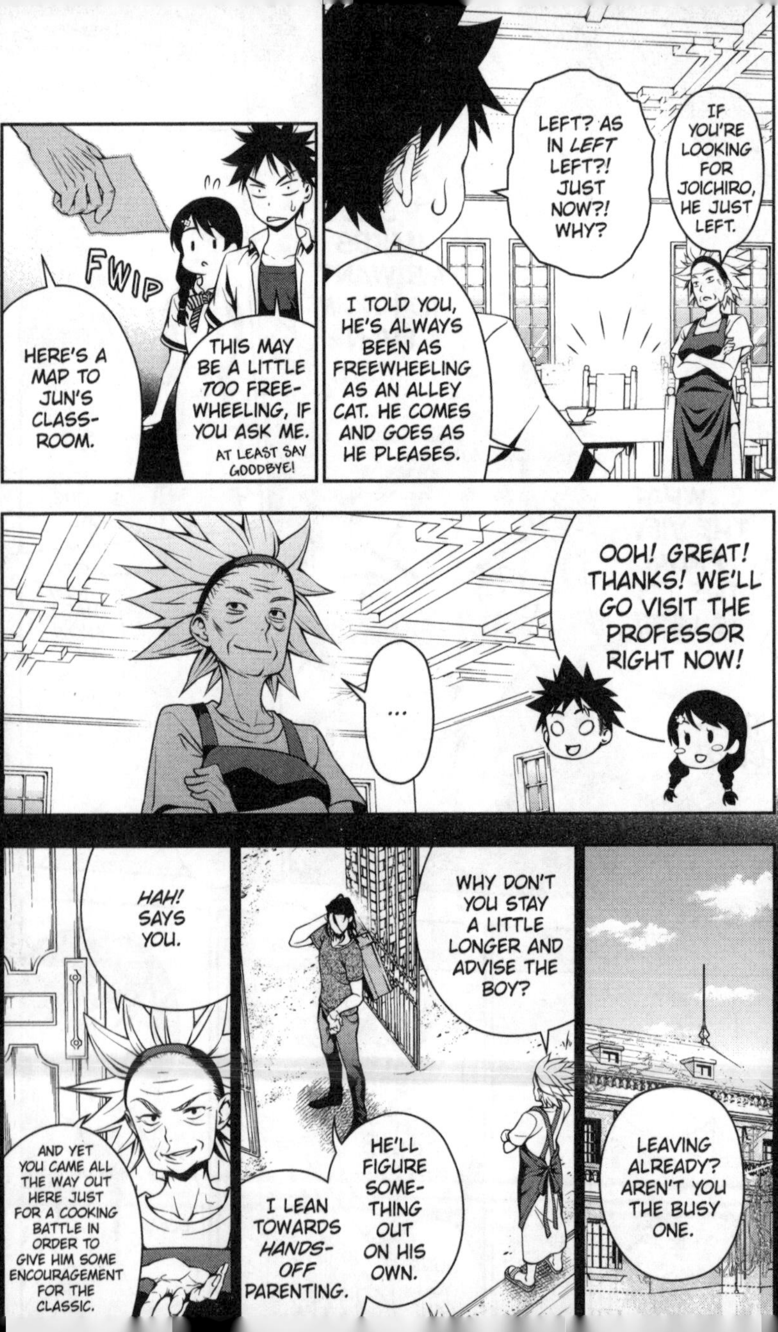

IF YOU'RE LOOKING FOR JOICHIRO, HE JUST LEFT.
LEFT? AS IN *LEFT* LEFT?! JUST NOW?! WHY?
I TOLD YOU, HE'S ALWAYS BEEN AS FREEWHEELING AS AN ALLEY CAT. HE COMES AND GOES AS HE PLEASES.
THIS MAY BE A LITTLE *TOO* FREE-WHEELING, IF YOU ASK ME.
AT LEAST SAY GOODBYE!
FWIP
HERE'S A MAP TO JUN'S CLASS-ROOM.
OOH! GREAT! THANKS! WE'LL GO VISIT THE PROFESSOR RIGHT NOW!
...
LEAVING ALREADY? AREN'T YOU THE BUSY ONE.
WHY DON'T YOU STAY A LITTLE LONGER AND ADVISE THE BOY?
HE'LL FIGURE SOME-THING OUT ON HIS OWN.
I LEAN TOWARDS *HANDS-OFF* PARENTING.
HAH! SAYS YOU.
AND YET YOU CAME ALL THE WAY OUT HERE JUST FOR A COOKING BATTLE IN ORDER TO GIVE HIM SOME ENCOURAGEMENT FOR THE CLASSIC.

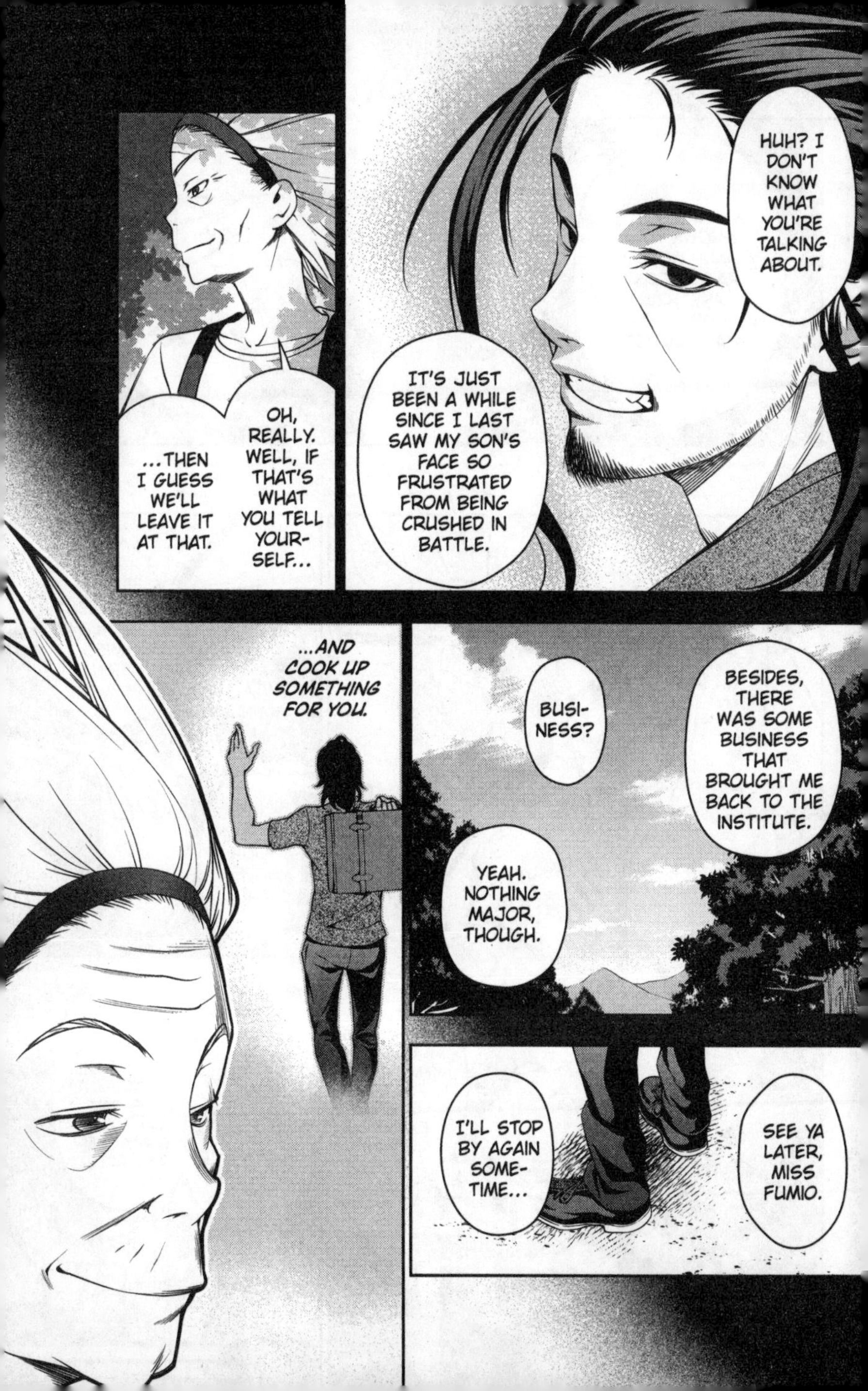
HUH? I DON'T KNOW WHAT YOU'RE TALKING ABOUT.
IT'S JUST BEEN A WHILE SINCE I LAST SAW MY SON'S FACE SO FRUSTRATED FROM BEING CRUSHED IN BATTLE.
OH, REALLY. WELL, IF THAT'S WHAT YOU TELL YOURSELF...
...THEN I GUESS WE'LL LEAVE IT AT THAT.
BESIDES, THERE WAS SOME BUSINESS THAT BROUGHT ME BACK TO THE INSTITUTE.
BUSINESS?
YEAH. NOTHING MAJOR, THOUGH.
SEE YA LATER, MISS FUMIO.
I'LL STOP BY AGAIN SOMETIME...
...AND COOK UP SOMETHING FOR YOU.

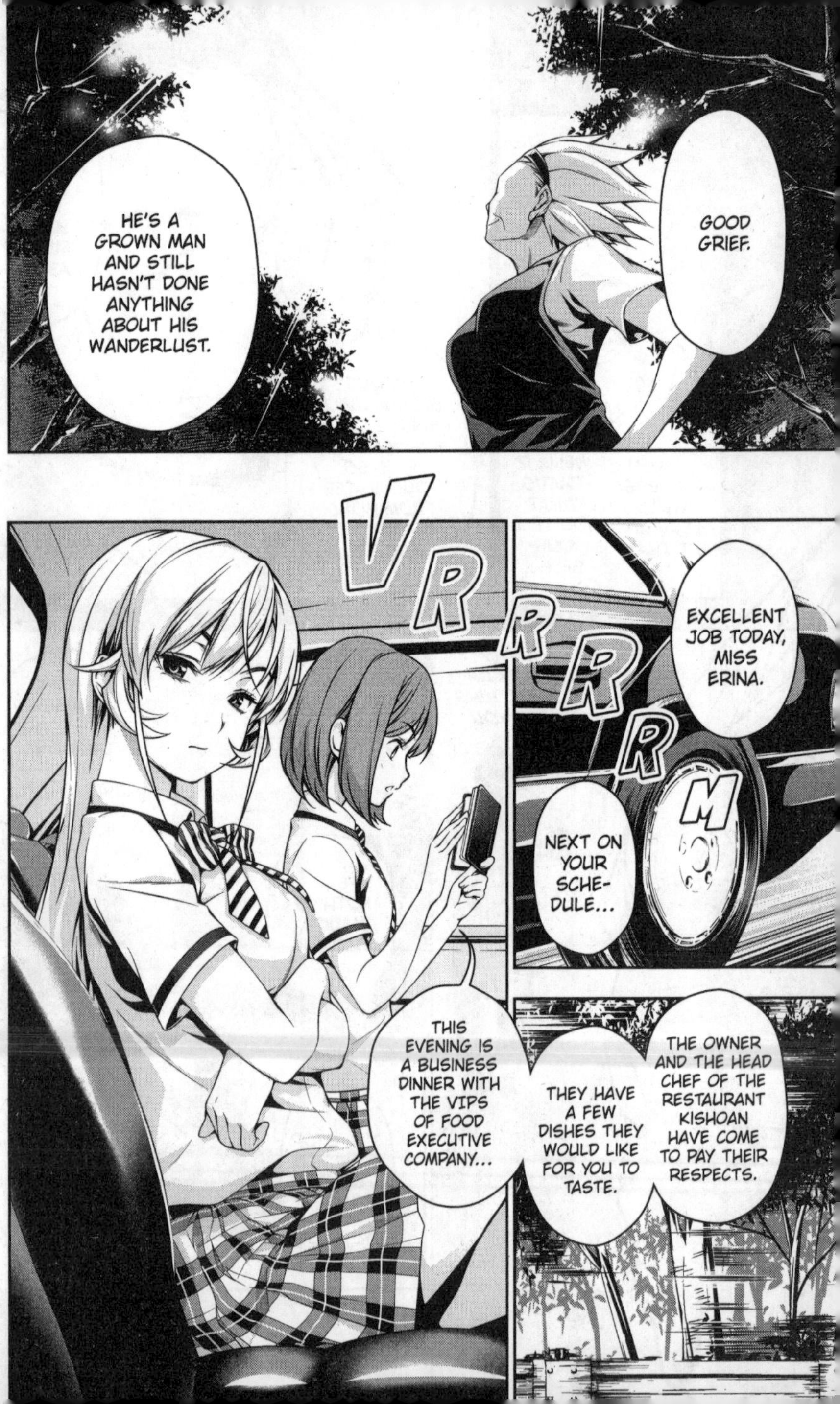
GOOD GRIEF.
HE'S A GROWN MAN AND STILL HASN'T DONE ANYTHING ABOUT HIS WANDERLUST.
VRRRRRM
EXCELLENT JOB TODAY, MISS ERINA.
NEXT ON YOUR SCHEDULE...
THE OWNER AND THE HEAD CHEF OF THE RESTAURANT KISHOAN HAVE COME TO PAY THEIR RESPECTS.
THEY HAVE A FEW DISHES THEY WOULD LIKE FOR YOU TO TASTE.
THIS EVENING IS A BUSINESS DINNER WITH THE VIPS OF FOOD EXECUTIVE COMPANY...

VRRRRM

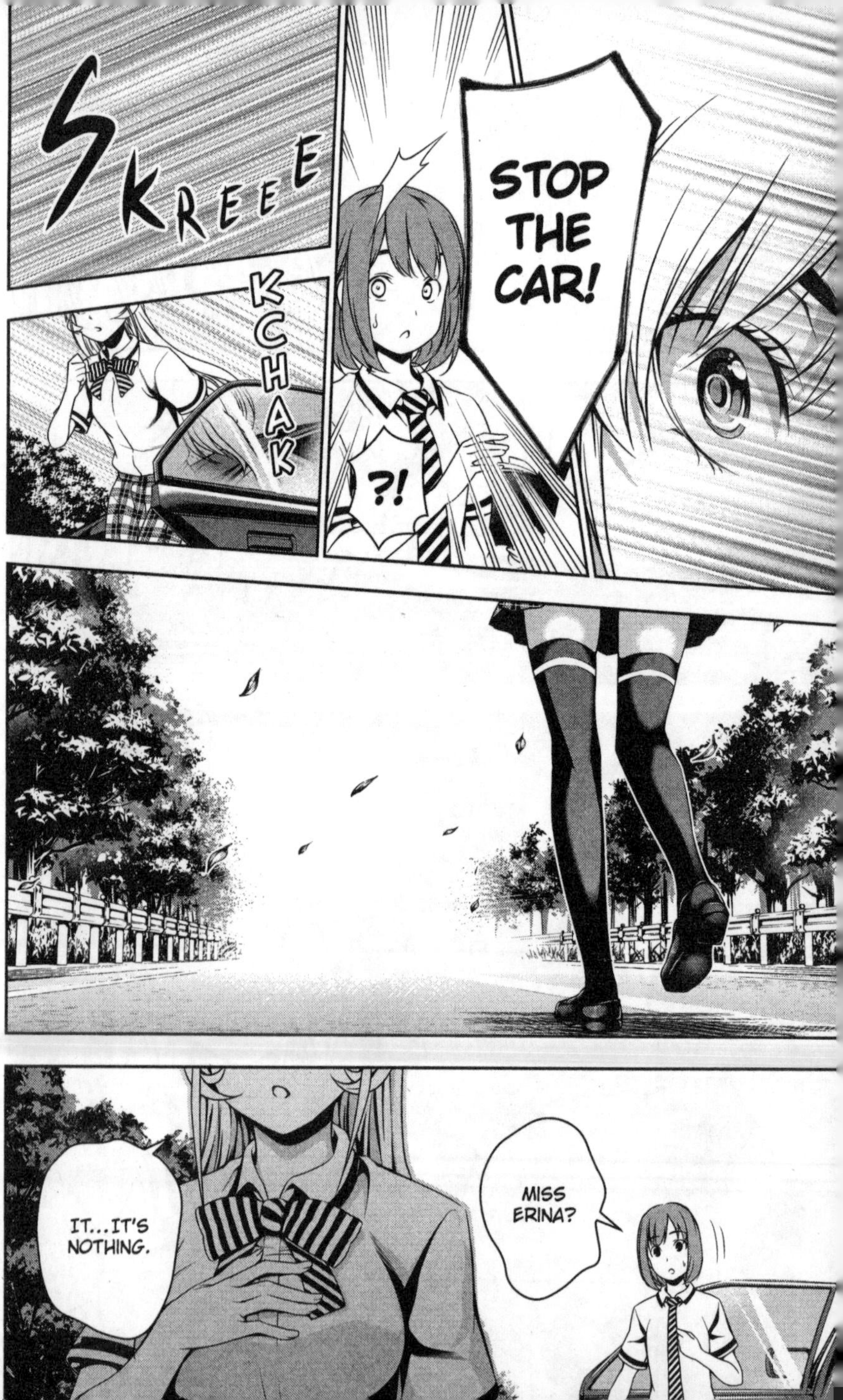
STOP THE CAR!
?!
SKREEE
KCHAK
MISS ERINA?
IT...IT'S NOTHING.

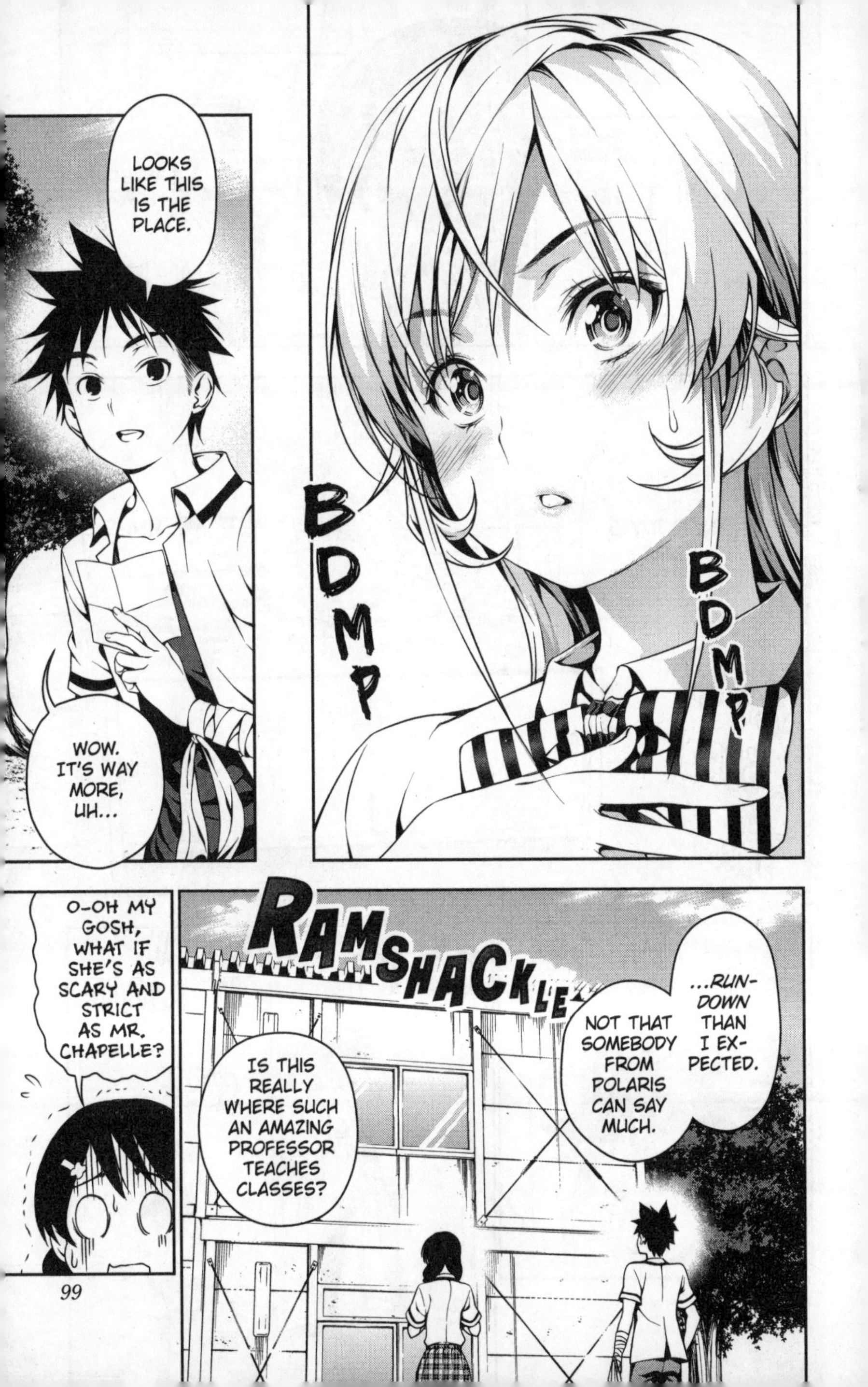
BDMP
BDMP
LOOKS LIKE THIS IS THE PLACE.
WOW. IT'S WAY MORE, UH...
RAMSHACKLE
...RUN-DOWN THAN I EXPECTED.
NOT THAT SOMEBODY FROM POLARIS CAN SAY MUCH.
IS THIS REALLY WHERE SUCH AN AMAZING PROFESSOR TEACHES CLASSES?
O-OH MY GOSH, WHAT IF SHE'S AS SCARY AND STRICT AS MR. CHAPELLE?

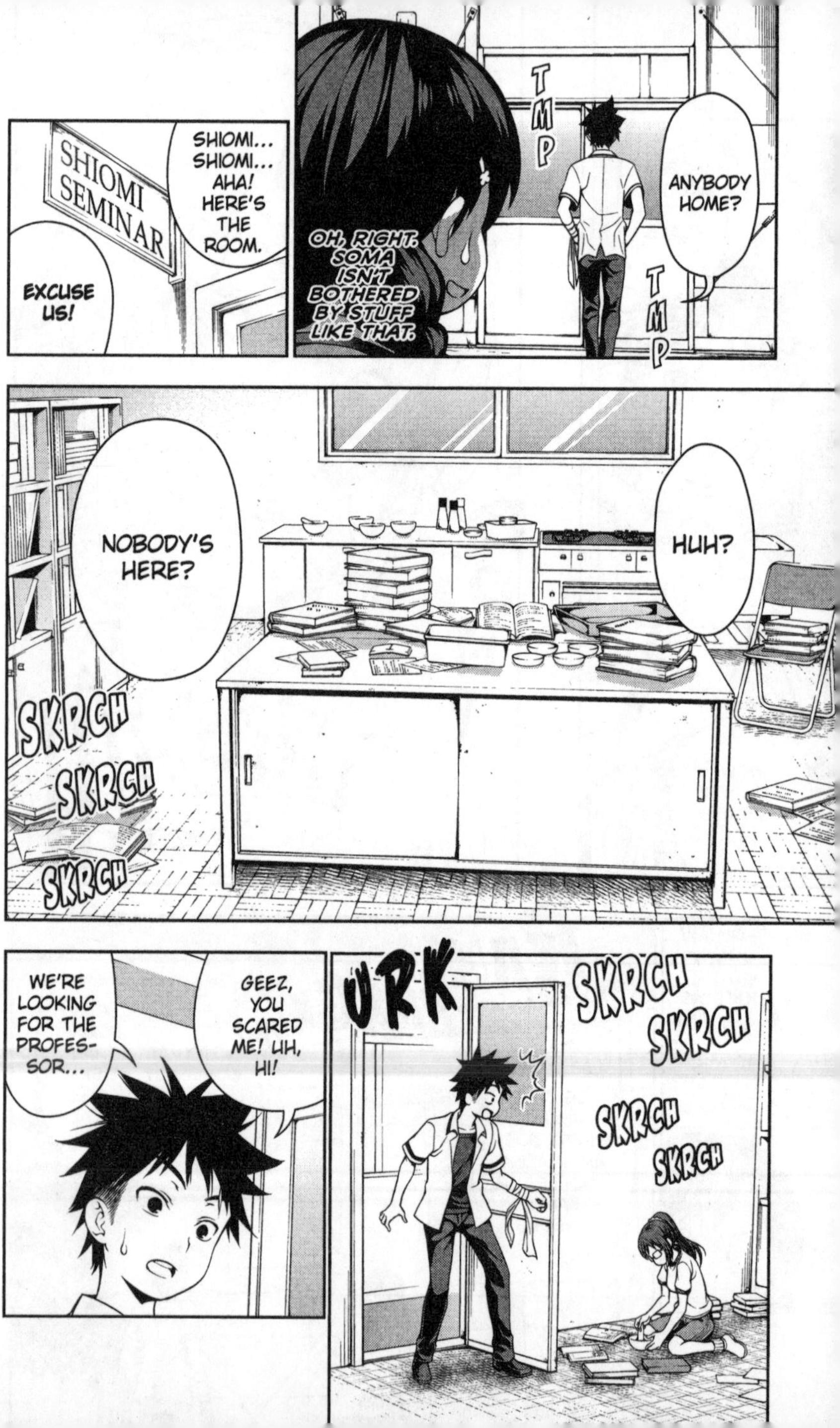
ANYBODY HOME?
TMP
TMP
OH, RIGHT. SOMA ISN'T BOTHERED BY STUFF LIKE THAT.
SHIOMI... SHIOMI... AHA! HERE'S THE ROOM.
SHIOMI SEMINAR
EXCUSE US!
HUH?
NOBODY'S HERE?
SKRCH
SKRCH
SKRCH
SKRCH
SKRCH
URK
SKRCH
SKRCH
GEEZ, YOU SCARED ME! UH, HI!
WE'RE LOOKING FOR THE PROFES-SOR...

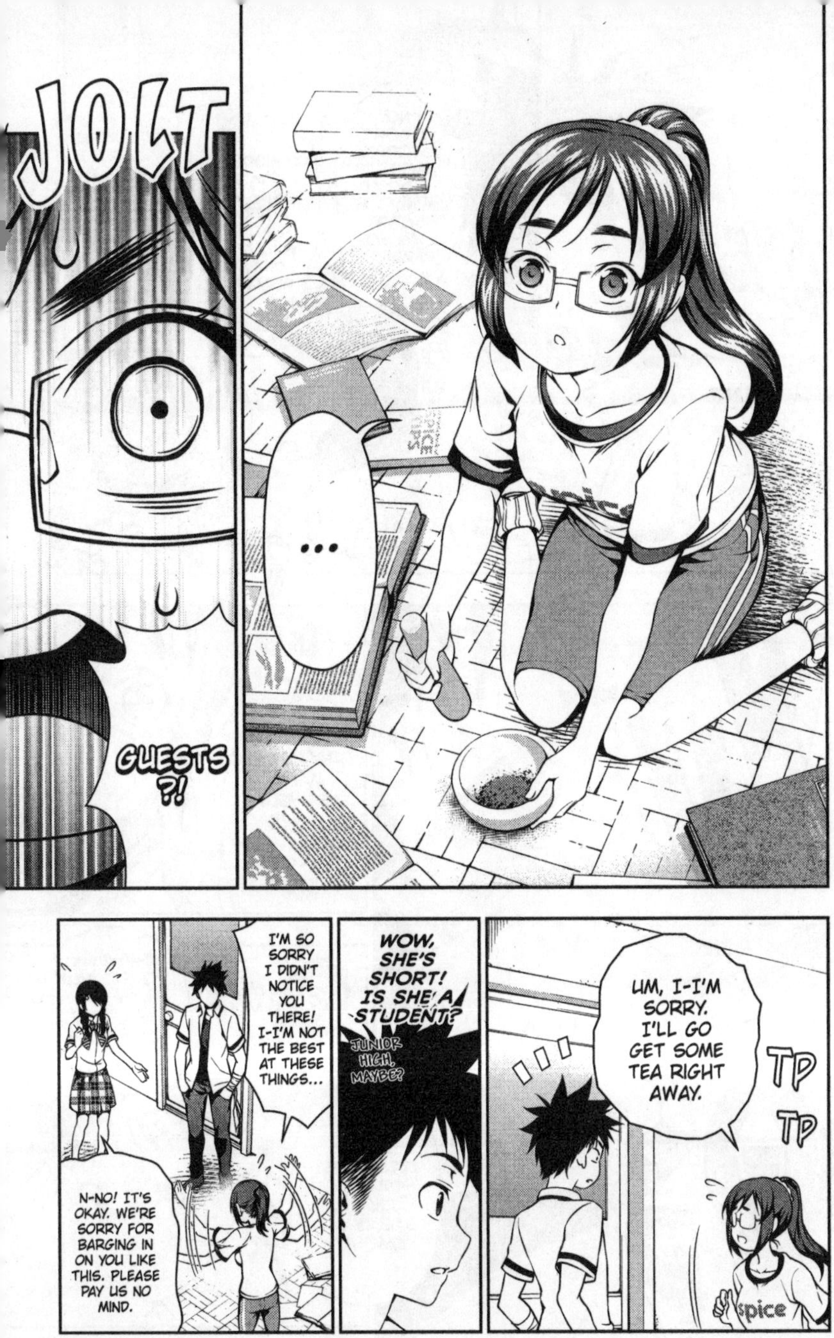
...
JOLT
GUESTS?!
UM, I-I'M SORRY. I'LL GO GET SOME TEA RIGHT AWAY.
TP
TP
...
WOW, SHE'S SHORT! IS SHE A STUDENT?
JUNIOR HIGH, MAYBE?
I'M SO SORRY I DIDN'T NOTICE YOU THERE! I-I'M NOT THE BEST AT THESE THINGS...
N-NO! IT'S OKAY. WE'RE SORRY FOR BARGING IN ON YOU LIKE THIS. PLEASE PAY US NO MIND.

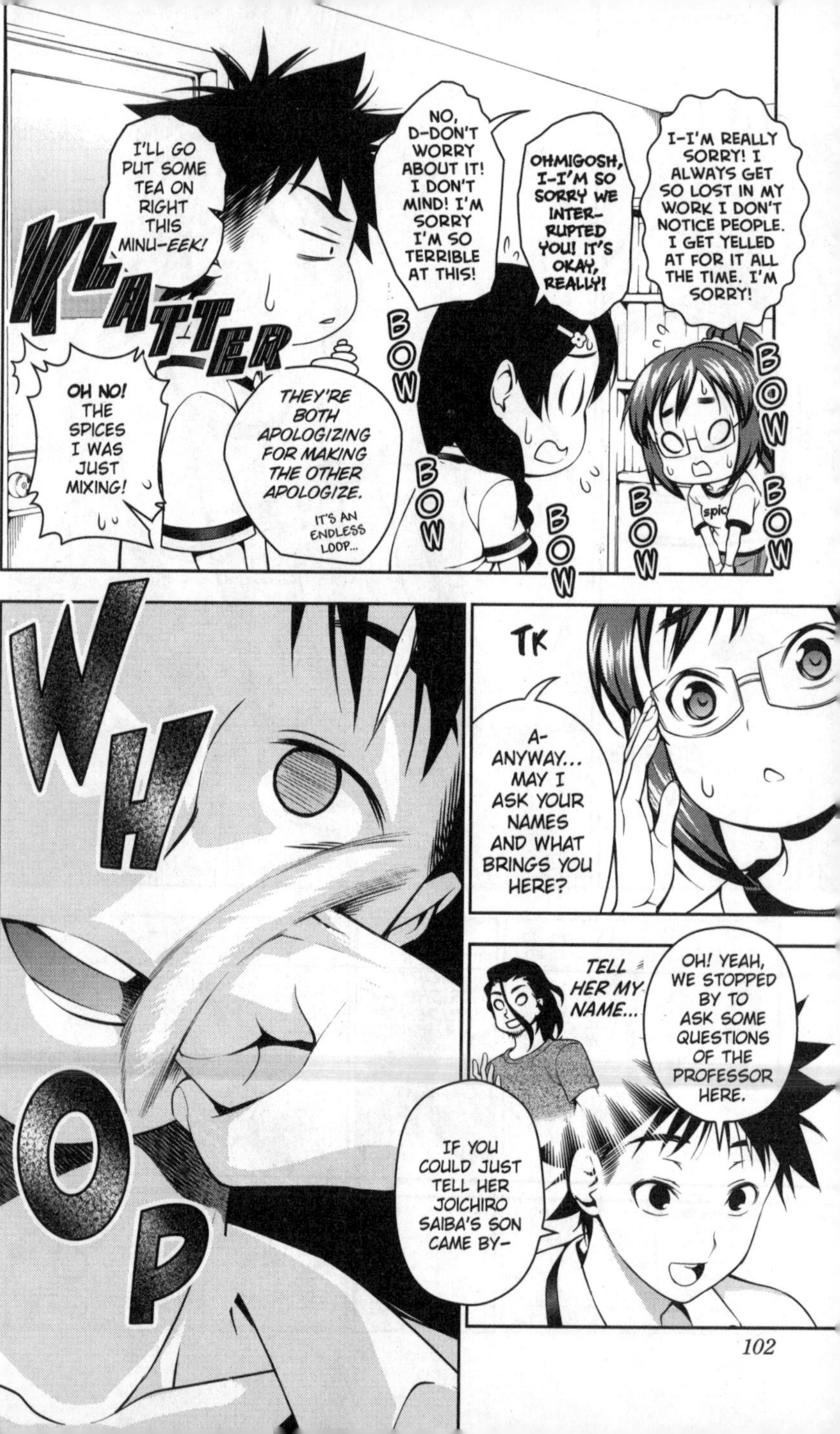
I-I'M REALLY SORRY! I ALWAYS GET SO LOST IN MY WORK I DON'T NOTICE PEOPLE. I GET YELLED AT FOR IT ALL THE TIME. I'M SORRY!
OHMIGOSH, I-I'M SO SORRY WE INTER-RUPTED YOU! IT'S OKAY, REALLY!
NO, D-DON'T WORRY ABOUT IT! I DON'T MIND! I'M SORRY I'M SO TERRIBLE AT THIS!
I'LL GO PUT SOME TEA ON RIGHT THIS MINU-EEK!
KLATTER
OH NO! THE SPICES I WAS JUST MIXING!
THEY'RE BOTH APOLOGIZING FOR MAKING THE OTHER APOLOGIZE.
IT'S AN ENDLESS LOOP...
BOW BOW
BOW BOW
BOW BOW
BOW BOW
TK
A-ANYWAY... MAY I ASK YOUR NAMES AND WHAT BRINGS YOU HERE?
OH! YEAH, WE STOPPED BY TO ASK SOME QUESTIONS OF THE PROFESSOR HERE.
TELL HER MY NAME...
IF YOU COULD JUST TELL HER JOICHIRO SAIBA'S SON CAME BY-
WHOOP

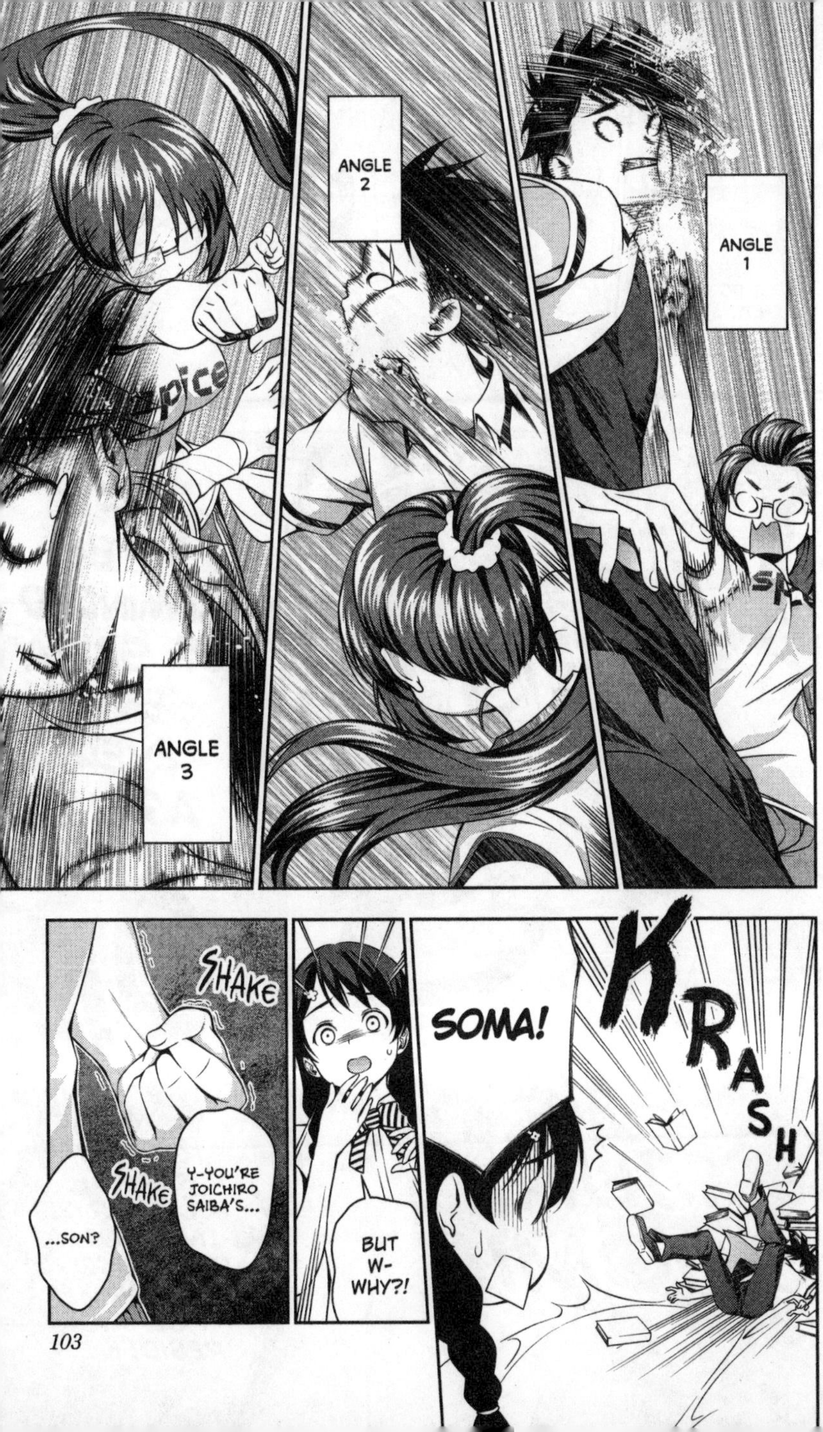
ANGLE 1
ANGLE 2
ANGLE 3
KRASH
SOMA!
BUT W-WHY?!
SHAKE
SHAKE
Y-YOU'RE JOICHIRO SAIBA'S...
...SON?

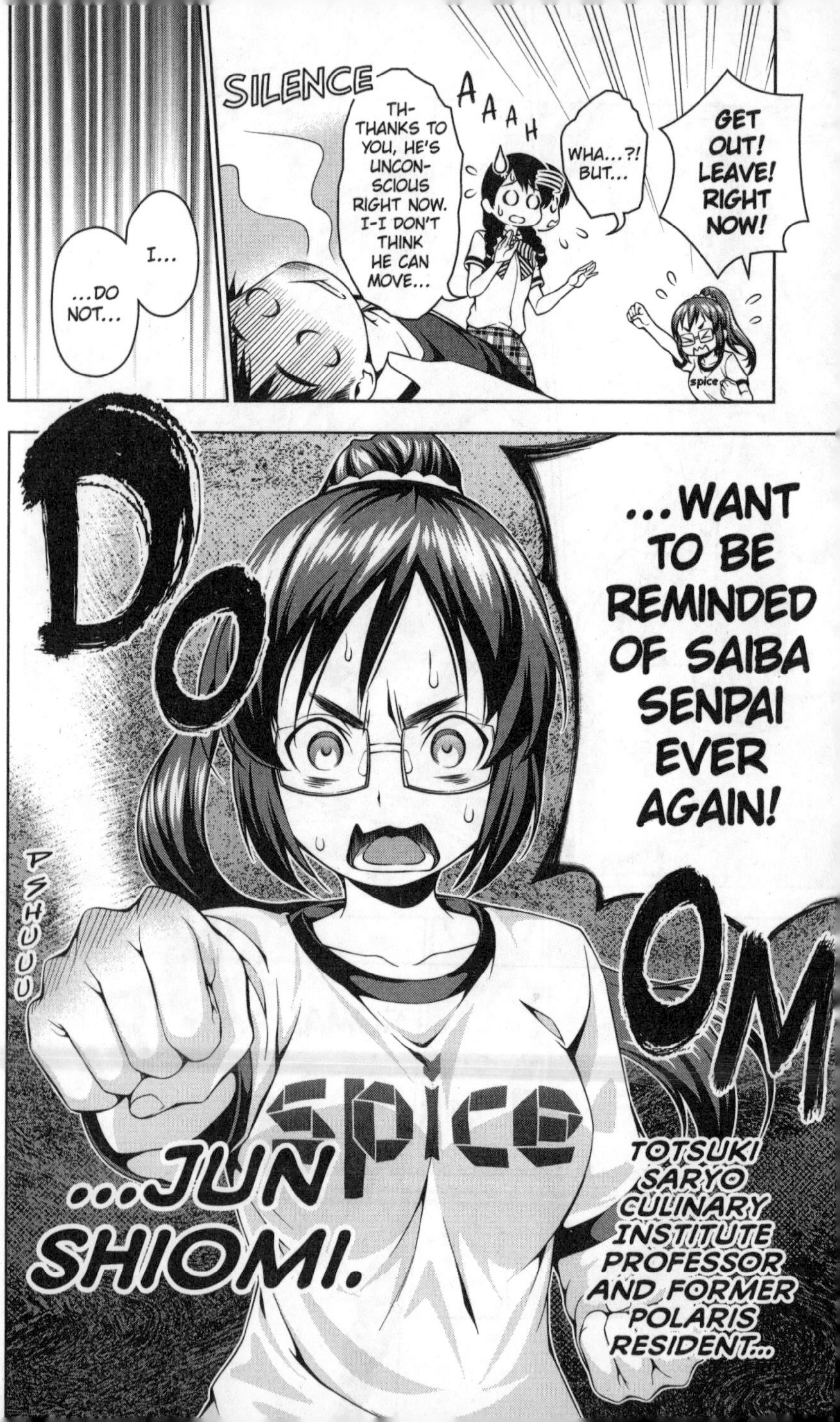
GET OUT! LEAVE! RIGHT NOW!
WHA...?! BUT...
AAAH
TH- THANKS TO YOU, HE'S UNCONSCIOUS RIGHT NOW. I-I DON'T THINK HE CAN MOVE...
SILENCE
I...
...DO NOT...
spice
DOOOM
...WANT TO BE REMINDED OF SAIBA SENPAI EVER AGAIN!
PSHUUU
TOTSUKI SARYO CULINARY INSTITUTE PROFESSOR AND FORMER POLARIS RESIDENT...
...JUN SHIOMI.
spice

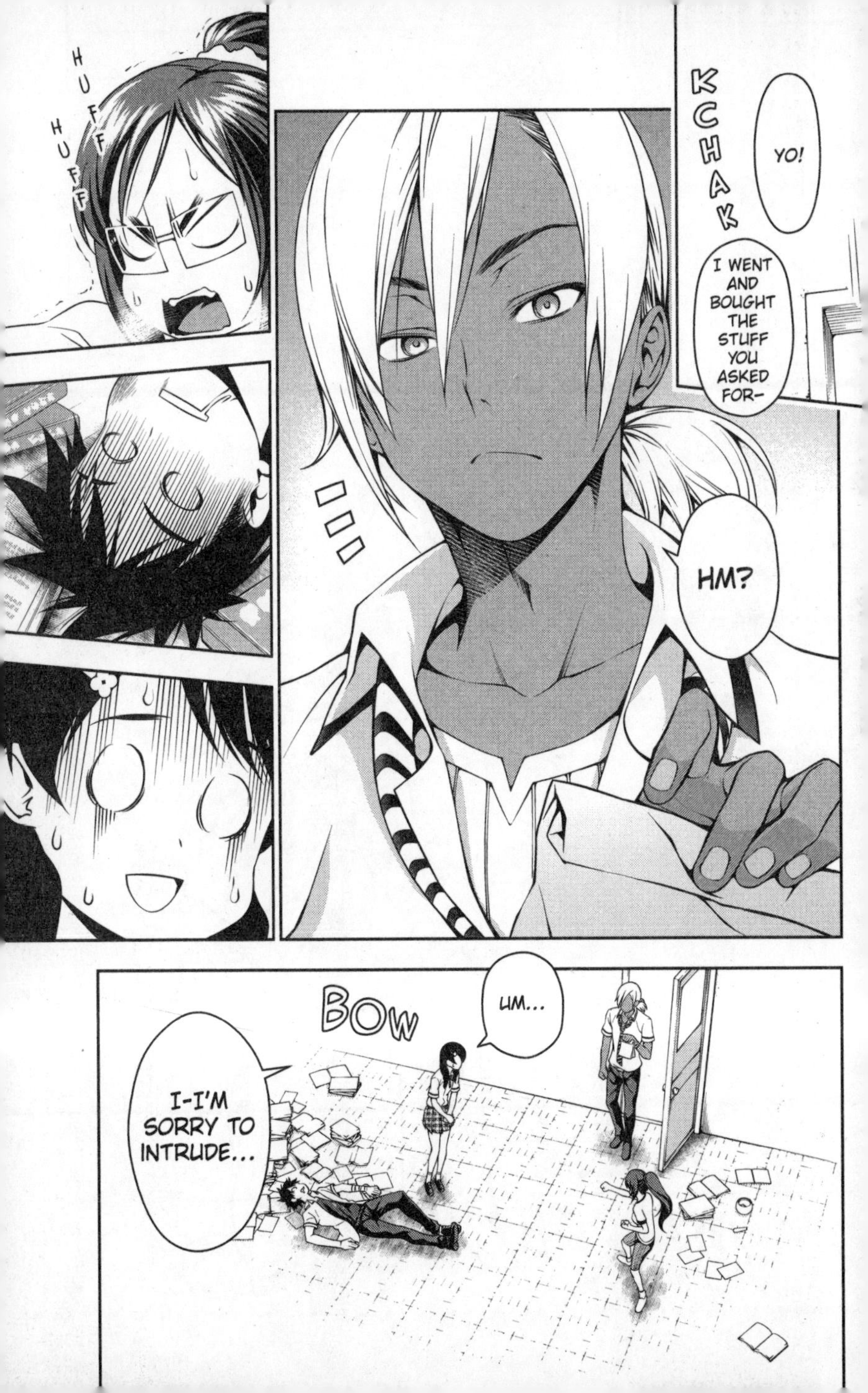
KCHAK
YO!
I WENT AND BOUGHT THE STUFF YOU ASKED FOR-
HM?
HUFF
HUFF
UM...
BOW
I-I'M SORRY TO INTRUDE...

145 THE ACCOMPANIST TO FRAGRANCE AND SPICE

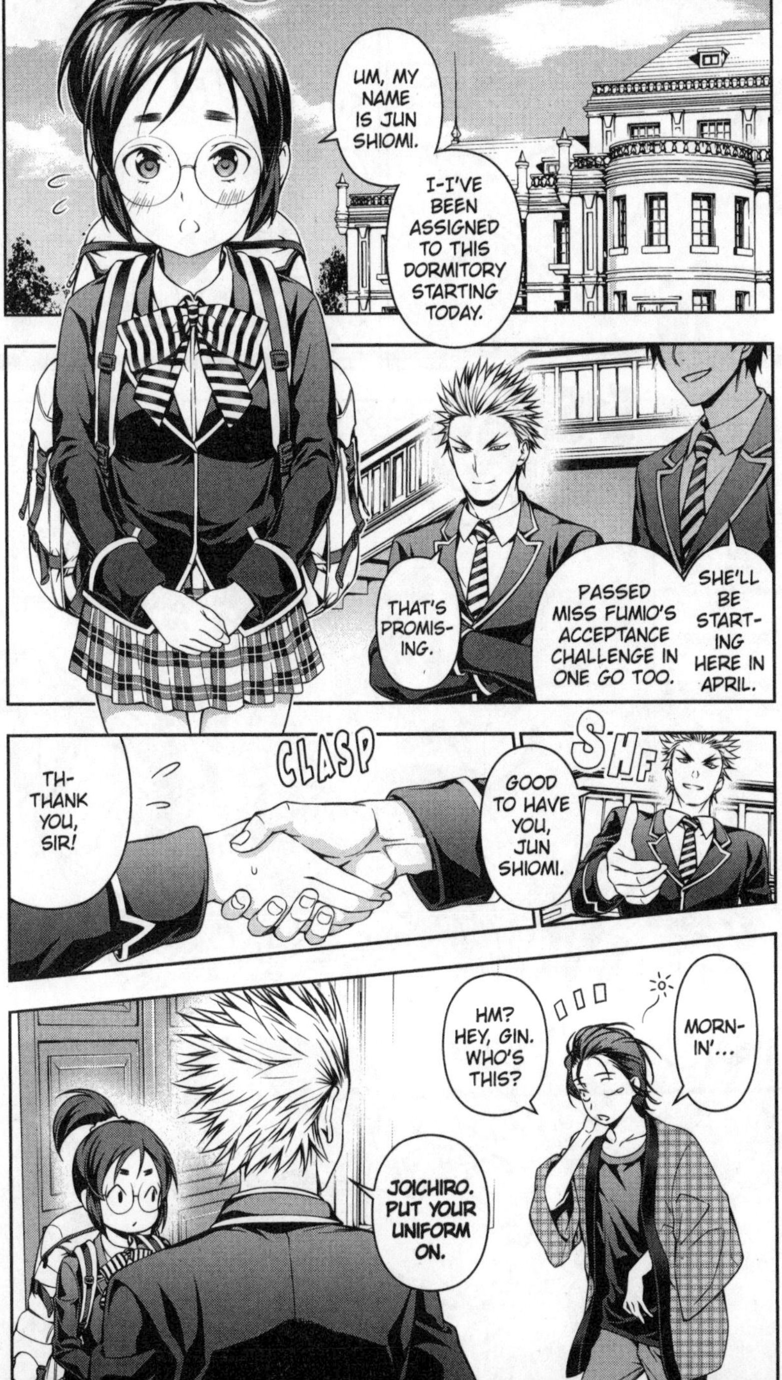
UM, MY NAME IS JUN SHIOMI.
I-I'VE BEEN ASSIGNED TO THIS DORMITORY STARTING TODAY.
SHE'LL BE STARTING HERE IN APRIL.
PASSED MISS FUMIO'S ACCEPTANCE CHALLENGE IN ONE GO TOO.
THAT'S PROMISING.
SHF
GOOD TO HAVE YOU, JUN SHIOMI.
CLASP
TH-THANK YOU, SIR!
MORN-IN'...
HM? HEY, GIN. WHO'S THIS?
JOICHIRO. PUT YOUR UNIFORM ON.

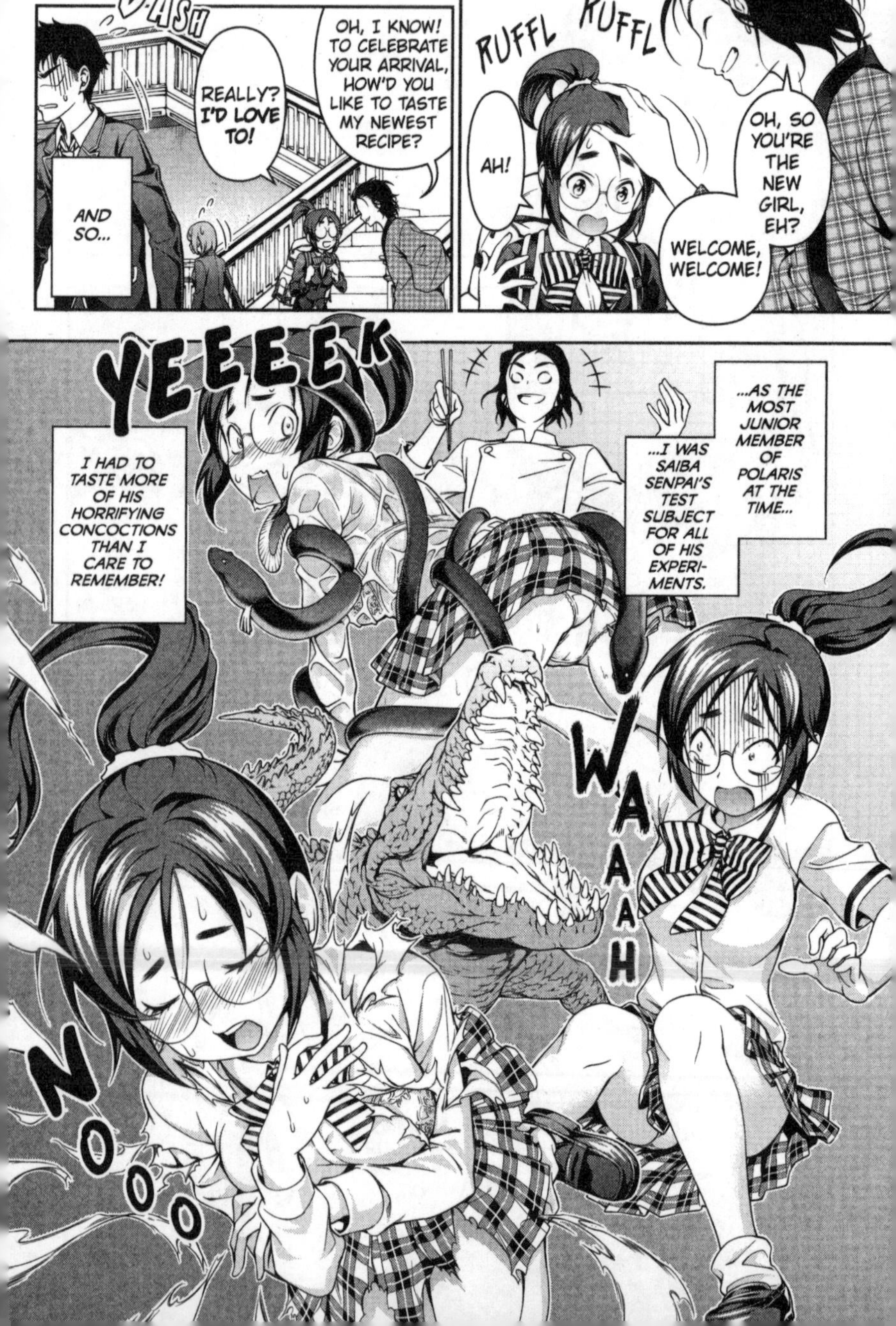
RUFFL RUFFL
OH, SO YOU'RE THE NEW GIRL, EH?
WELCOME, WELCOME!
AH!
DASH
OH, I KNOW! TO CELEBRATE YOUR ARRIVAL, HOW'D YOU LIKE TO TASTE MY NEWEST RECIPE?
REALLY? I'D LOVE TO!
AND SO...
...AS THE MOST JUNIOR MEMBER OF POLARIS AT THE TIME...
...I WAS SAIBA SENPAI'S TEST SUBJECT FOR ALL OF HIS EXPERI-MENTS.
YEEEEK
I HAD TO TASTE MORE OF HIS HORRIFYING CONCOCTIONS THAN I CARE TO REMEMBER!
WAAAAH
NOOOO

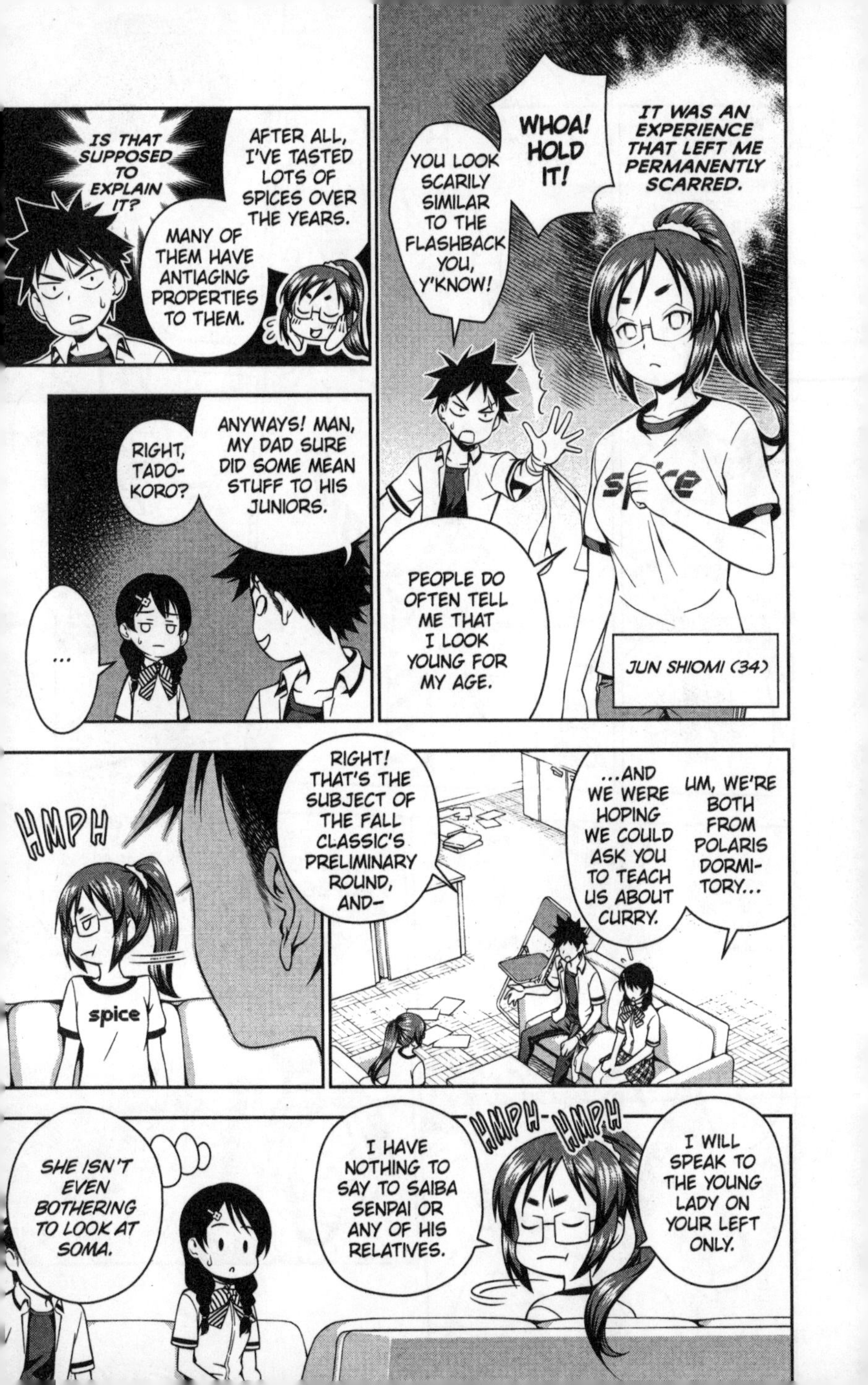
IT WAS AN EXPERIENCE THAT LEFT ME PERMANENTLY SCARRED.
WHOA! HOLD IT!
YOU LOOK SCARILY SIMILAR TO THE FLASHBACK YOU, Y'KNOW!
PEOPLE DO OFTEN TELL ME THAT I LOOK YOUNG FOR MY AGE.
JUN SHIOMI (34)
AFTER ALL, I'VE TASTED LOTS OF SPICES OVER THE YEARS.
MANY OF THEM HAVE ANTIAGING PROPERTIES TO THEM.
IS THAT SUPPOSED TO EXPLAIN IT?
ANYWAYS! MAN, MY DAD SURE DID SOME MEAN STUFF TO HIS JUNIORS.
RIGHT, TADO-KORO?
...
UM, WE'RE BOTH FROM POLARIS DORMI-TORY...
...AND WE WERE HOPING WE COULD ASK YOU TO TEACH US ABOUT CURRY.
RIGHT! THAT'S THE SUBJECT OF THE FALL CLASSIC'S PRELIMINARY ROUND, AND—
HMPH
I WILL SPEAK TO THE YOUNG LADY ON YOUR LEFT ONLY.
HMPH-HMPH
I HAVE NOTHING TO SAY TO SAIBA SENPAI OR ANY OF HIS RELATIVES.
SHE ISN'T EVEN BOTHERING TO LOOK AT SOMA.

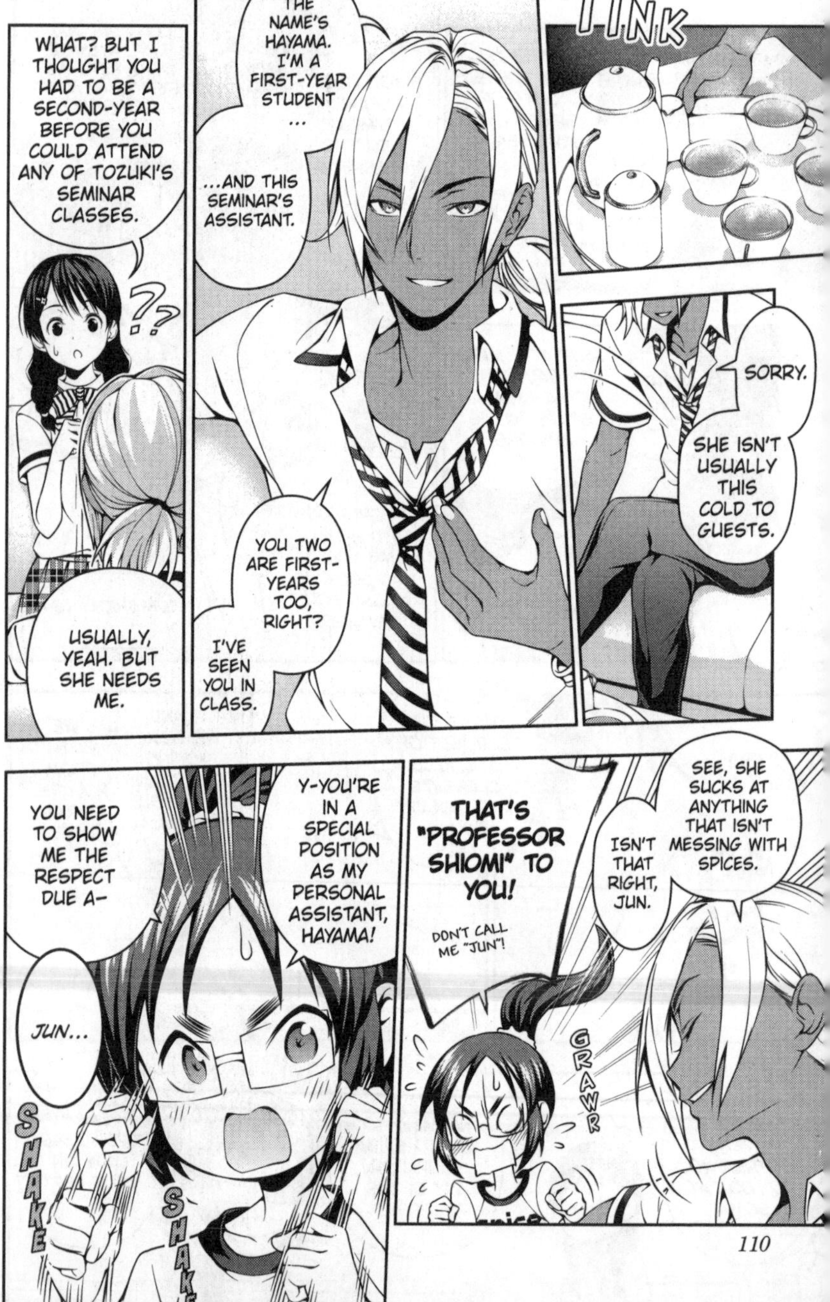

TINK
SORRY.
SHE ISN'T USUALLY THIS COLD TO GUESTS.
THE NAME'S HAYAMA. I'M A FIRST-YEAR STUDENT ...
...AND THIS SEMINAR'S ASSISTANT.
YOU TWO ARE FIRST-YEARS TOO, RIGHT?
I'VE SEEN YOU IN CLASS.
WHAT? BUT I THOUGHT YOU HAD TO BE A SECOND-YEAR BEFORE YOU COULD ATTEND ANY OF TOZUKI'S SEMINAR CLASSES.
??
USUALLY, YEAH. BUT SHE NEEDS ME.
SEE, SHE SUCKS AT ANYTHING THAT ISN'T MESSING WITH SPICES.
ISN'T THAT RIGHT, JUN.
THAT'S "PROFESSOR SHIOMI" TO YOU!
DON'T CALL ME "JUN"!
GRAWR
Y-YOU'RE IN A SPECIAL POSITION AS MY PERSONAL ASSISTANT, HAYAMA!
YOU NEED TO SHOW ME THE RESPECT DUE A-
JUN...
SHAKE
SHAKE

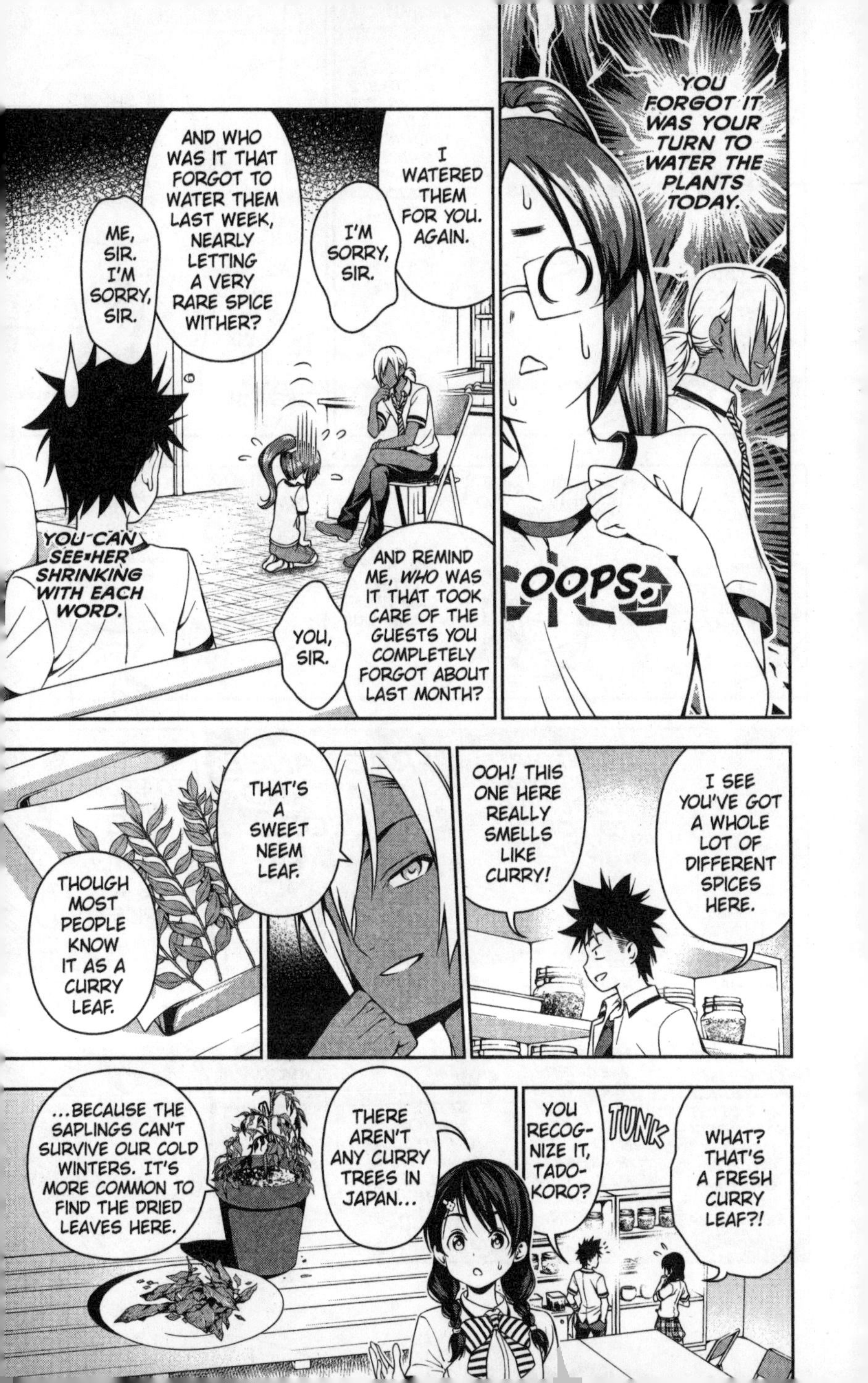
YOU FORGOT IT WAS YOUR TURN TO WATER THE PLANTS TODAY.
OOPS.
I WATERED THEM FOR YOU. AGAIN.
I'M SORRY, SIR.
AND WHO WAS IT THAT FORGOT TO WATER THEM LAST WEEK, NEARLY LETTING A VERY RARE SPICE WITHER?
ME, SIR. I'M SORRY, SIR.
AND REMIND ME, *WHO* WAS IT THAT TOOK CARE OF THE GUESTS YOU COMPLETELY FORGOT ABOUT LAST MONTH?
YOU, SIR.
YOU CAN SEE HER SHRINKING WITH EACH WORD.
I SEE YOU'VE GOT A WHOLE LOT OF DIFFERENT SPICES HERE.
OOH! THIS ONE HERE REALLY SMELLS LIKE CURRY!
THAT'S A SWEET NEEM LEAF.
THOUGH MOST PEOPLE KNOW IT AS A CURRY LEAF.
WHAT? THAT'S A FRESH CURRY LEAF?!
TUNK
YOU RECOG-NIZE IT, TADO-KORO?
THERE AREN'T ANY CURRY TREES IN JAPAN...
...BECAUSE THE SAPLINGS CAN'T SURVIVE OUR COLD WINTERS. IT'S MORE COMMON TO FIND THE DRIED LEAVES HERE.

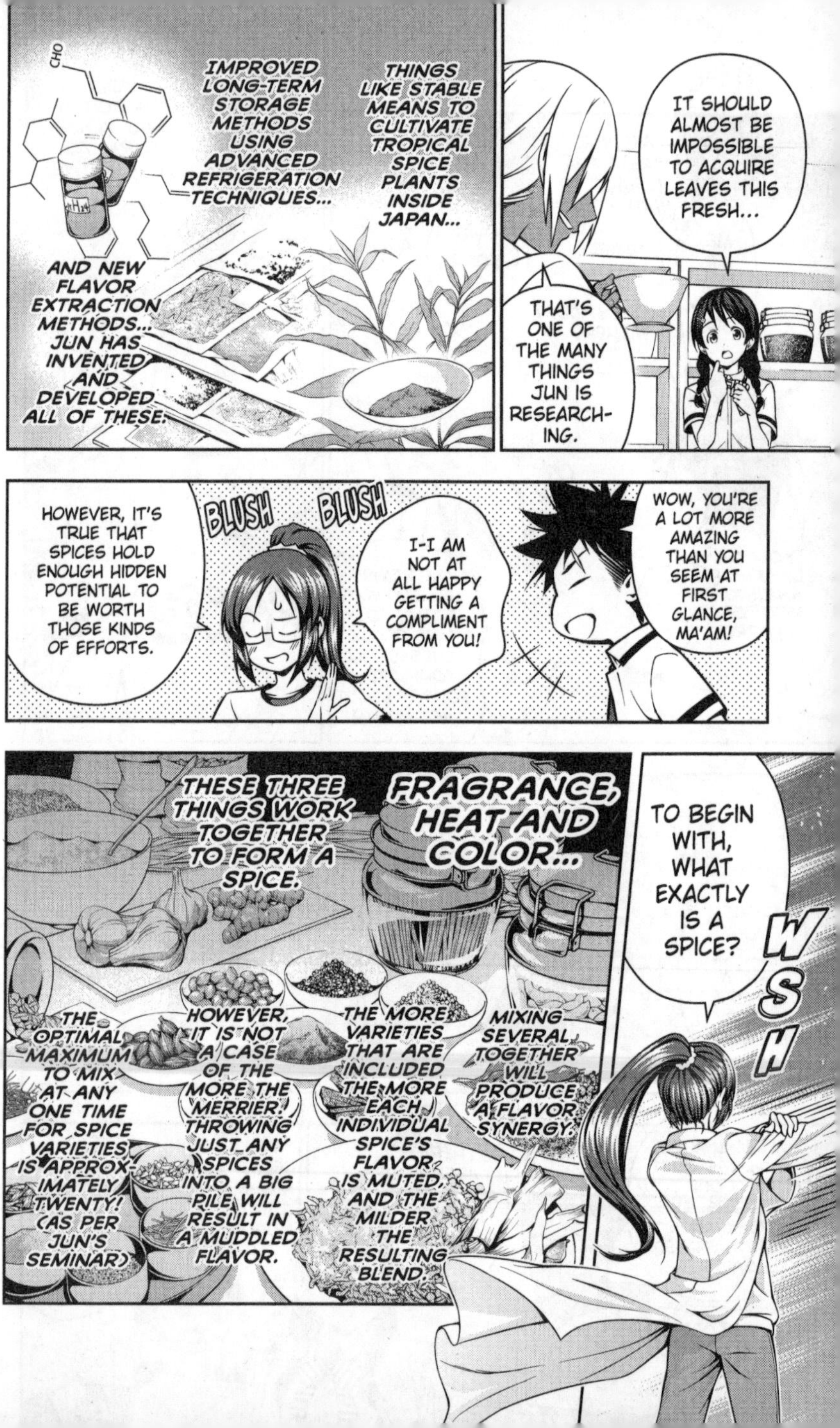
IT SHOULD ALMOST BE IMPOSSIBLE TO ACQUIRE LEAVES THIS FRESH...
THAT'S ONE OF THE MANY THINGS JUN IS RESEARCH-ING.
THINGS LIKE STABLE MEANS TO CULTIVATE TROPICAL SPICE PLANTS INSIDE JAPAN...
IMPROVED LONG-TERM STORAGE METHODS USING ADVANCED REFRIGERATION TECHNIQUES...
AND NEW FLAVOR EXTRACTION METHODS... JUN HAS INVENTED AND DEVELOPED ALL OF THESE.
WOW, YOU'RE A LOT MORE AMAZING THAN YOU SEEM AT FIRST GLANCE, MA'AM!
BLUSH BLUSH
I-I AM NOT AT ALL HAPPY GETTING A COMPLIMENT FROM YOU!
HOWEVER, IT'S TRUE THAT SPICES HOLD ENOUGH HIDDEN POTENTIAL TO BE WORTH THOSE KINDS OF EFFORTS.
TO BEGIN WITH, WHAT EXACTLY IS A SPICE?
WSH
FRAGRANCE, HEAT AND COLOR...
THESE THREE THINGS WORK TOGETHER TO FORM A SPICE.
MIXING SEVERAL TOGETHER WILL PRODUCE A FLAVOR SYNERGY.
THE MORE VARIETIES THAT ARE INCLUDED THE MORE EACH INDIVIDUAL SPICE'S FLAVOR IS MUTED, AND THE MILDER THE RESULTING BLEND.
HOWEVER, IT IS NOT A CASE OF THE MORE THE MERRIER. THROWING JUST ANY SPICES INTO A BIG PILE WILL RESULT IN A MUDDLED FLAVOR.
THE OPTIMAL MAXIMUM TO MIX AT ANY ONE TIME FOR SPICE VARIETIES IS APPROX-IMATELY TWENTY! (AS PER JUN'S SEMINAR)

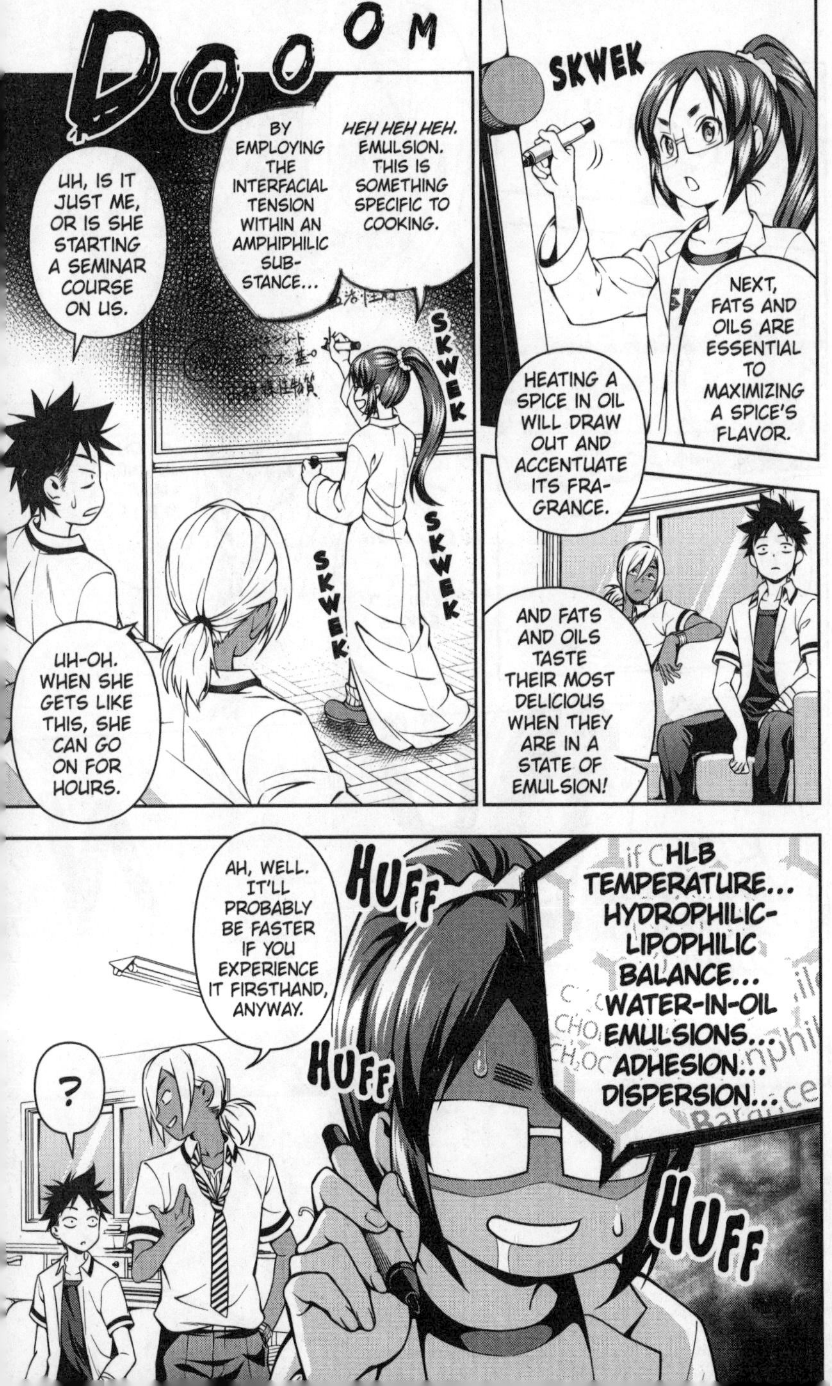
SKWEK
NEXT, FATS AND OILS ARE ESSENTIAL TO MAXIMIZING A SPICE'S FLAVOR.
HEATING A SPICE IN OIL WILL DRAW OUT AND ACCENTUATE ITS FRA-GRANCE.
AND FATS AND OILS TASTE THEIR MOST DELICIOUS WHEN THEY ARE IN A STATE OF EMULSION!
DOOOOM
HEH HEH HEH. EMULSION. THIS IS SOMETHING SPECIFIC TO COOKING.
BY EMPLOYING THE INTERFACIAL TENSION WITHIN AN AMPHIPHILIC SUB-STANCE...
UH, IS IT JUST ME, OR IS SHE STARTING A SEMINAR COURSE ON US.
SKWEK
SKWEK
SKWEK
UH-OH. WHEN SHE GETS LIKE THIS, SHE CAN GO ON FOR HOURS.
HLB TEMPERATURE... HYDROPHILIC-LIPOPHILIC BALANCE... WATER-IN-OIL EMULSIONS... ADHESION... DISPERSION...
HUFF
AH, WELL. IT'LL PROBABLY BE FASTER IF YOU EXPERIENCE IT FIRSTHAND, ANYWAY.
HUFF
?
HUFF

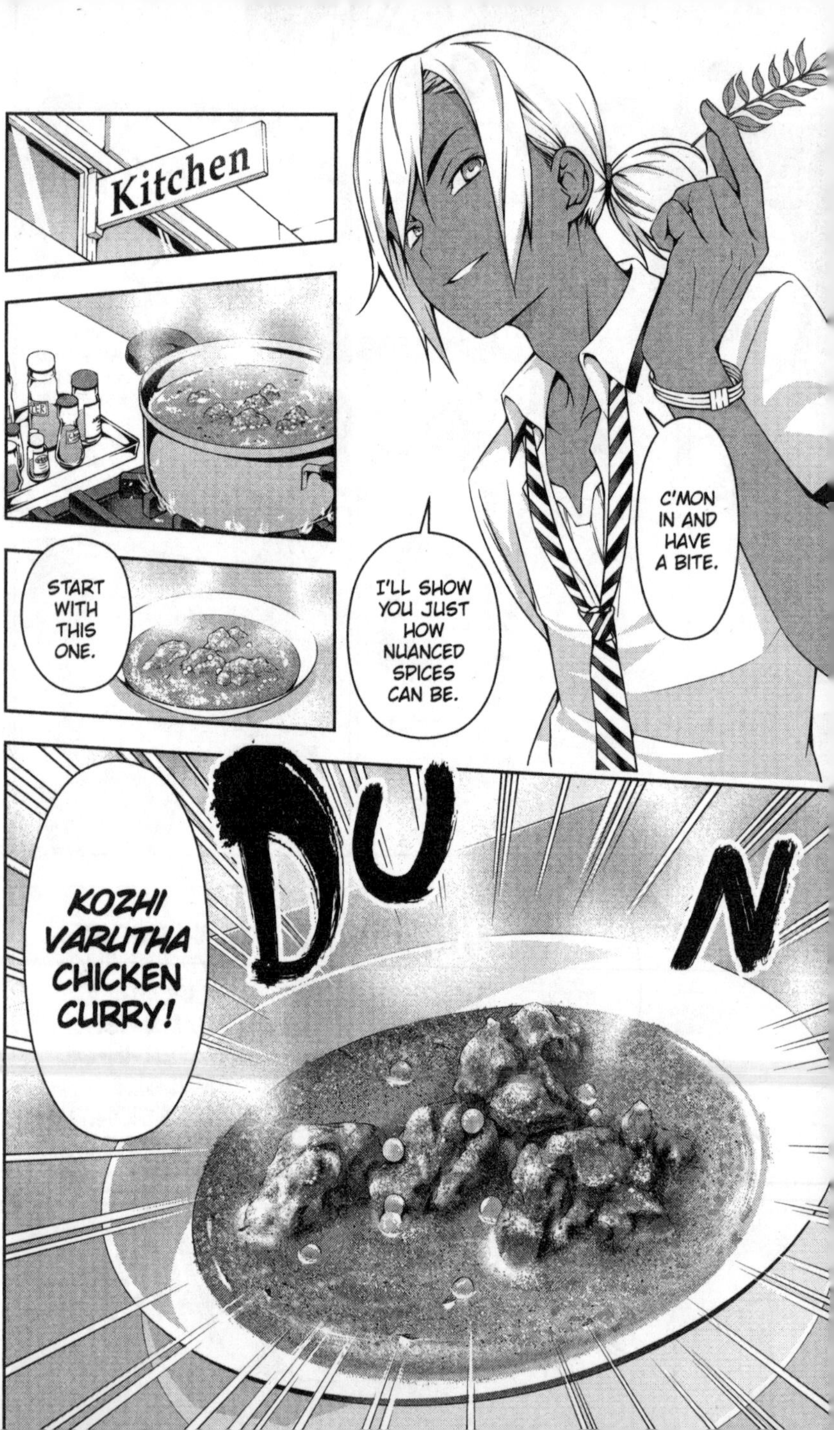
C'MON IN AND HAVE A BITE.
I'LL SHOW YOU JUST HOW NUANCED SPICES CAN BE.
Kitchen
START WITH THIS ONE.
DUN
KOZHI VARUTHA CHICKEN CURRY!

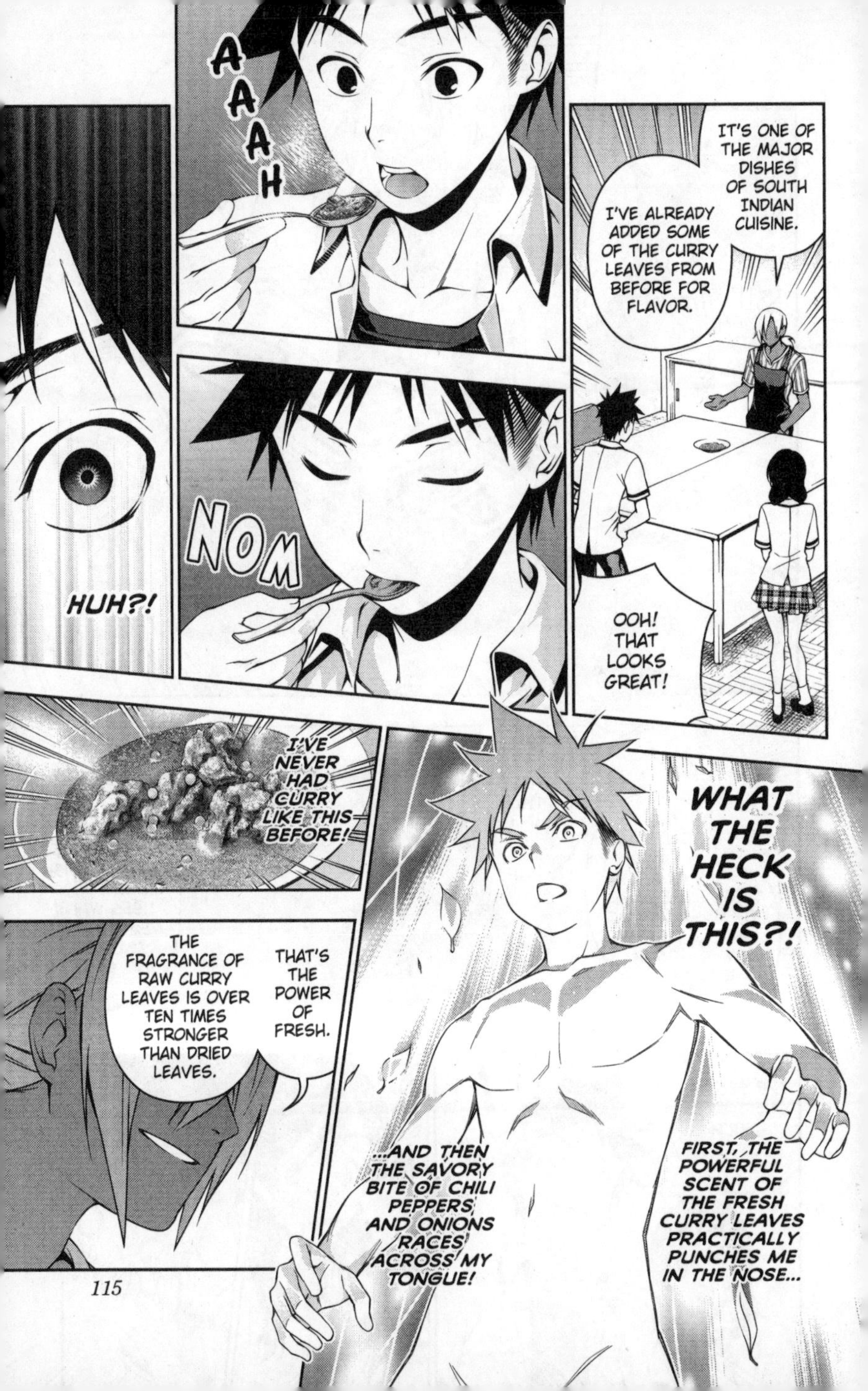
IT'S ONE OF THE MAJOR DISHES OF SOUTH INDIAN CUISINE.
I'VE ALREADY ADDED SOME OF THE CURRY LEAVES FROM BEFORE FOR FLAVOR.
OOH! THAT LOOKS GREAT!
AAAH
NOM
HUH?!
WHAT THE HECK IS THIS?!
FIRST, THE POWERFUL SCENT OF THE FRESH CURRY LEAVES PRACTICALLY PUNCHES ME IN THE NOSE...
...AND THEN THE SAVORY BITE OF CHILI PEPPERS AND ONIONS RACES ACROSS MY TONGUE!
I'VE NEVER HAD CURRY LIKE THIS BEFORE!
THAT'S THE POWER OF FRESH.
THE FRAGRANCE OF RAW CURRY LEAVES IS OVER TEN TIMES STRONGER THAN DRIED LEAVES.

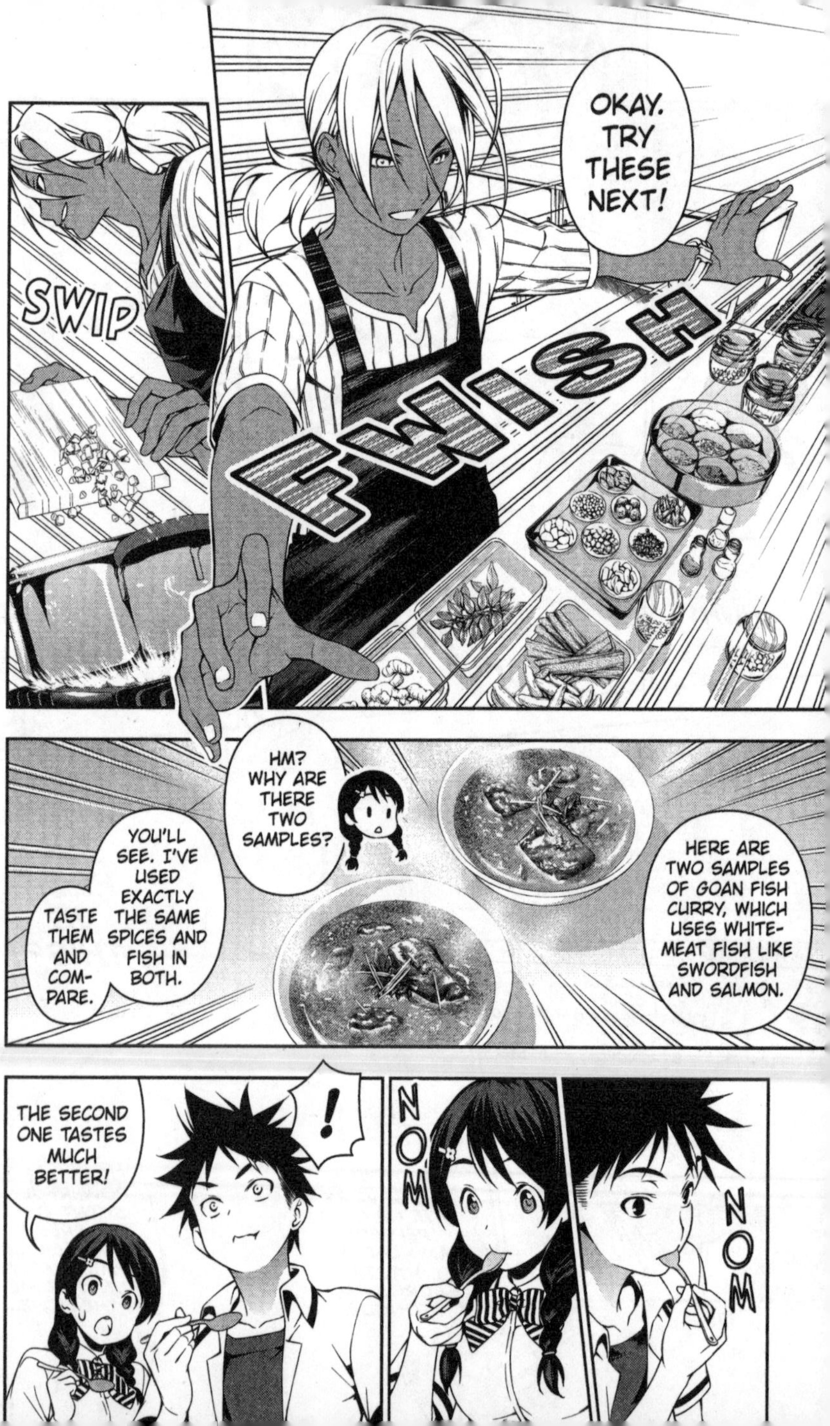

OKAY. TRY THESE NEXT!
FWISH
SWIP
HERE ARE TWO SAMPLES OF GOAN FISH CURRY, WHICH USES WHITE-MEAT FISH LIKE SWORDFISH AND SALMON.
HM? WHY ARE THERE TWO SAMPLES?
YOU'LL SEE. I'VE USED EXACTLY THE SAME SPICES AND FISH IN BOTH.
TASTE THEM AND COM-PARE.
NOM
NOM
!
THE SECOND ONE TASTES MUCH BETTER!

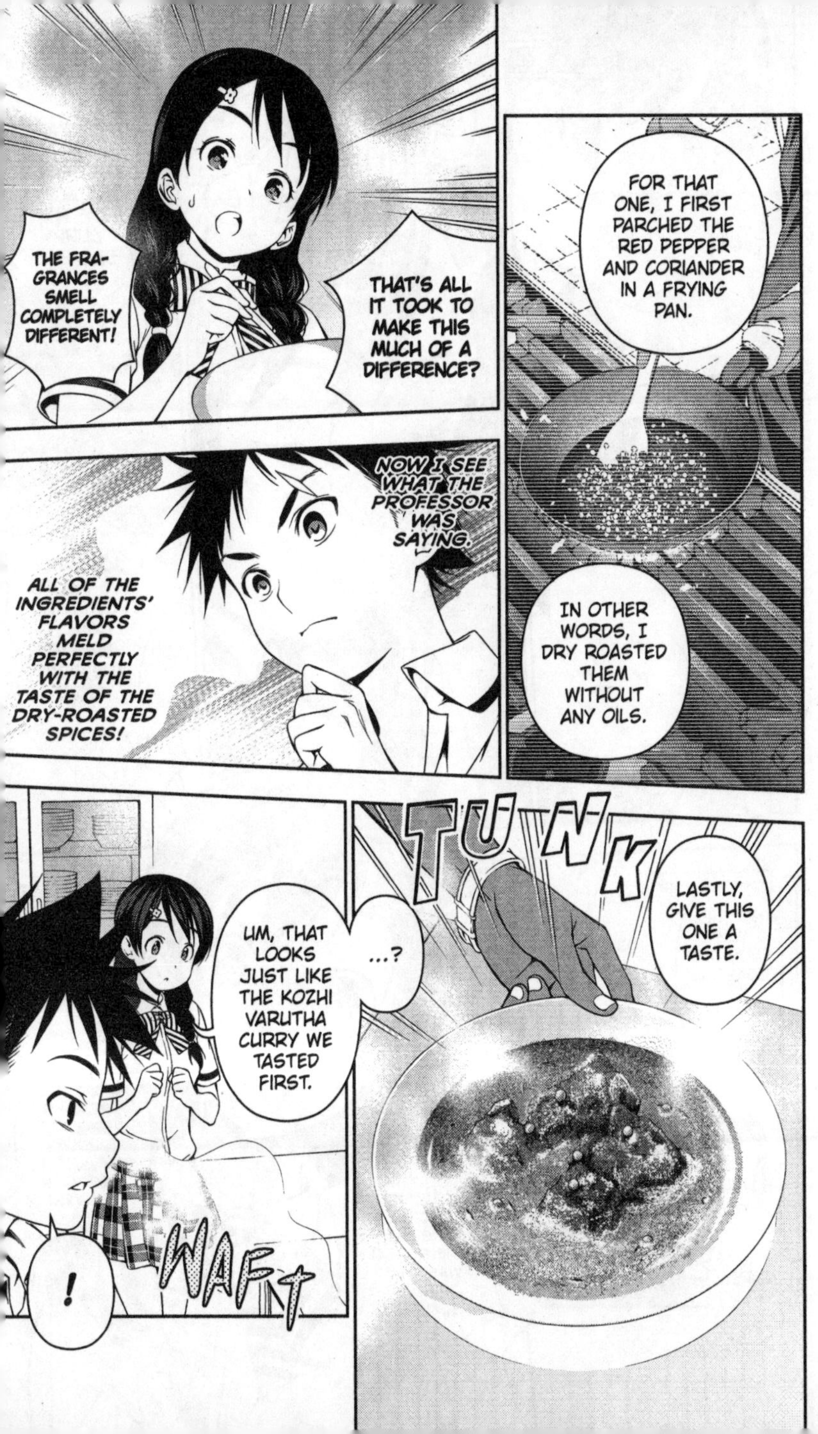
FOR THAT ONE, I FIRST PARCHED THE RED PEPPER AND CORIANDER IN A FRYING PAN.
IN OTHER WORDS, I DRY ROASTED THEM WITHOUT ANY OILS.
THAT'S ALL IT TOOK TO MAKE THIS MUCH OF A DIFFERENCE?
THE FRA-GRANCES SMELL COMPLETELY DIFFERENT!
NOW I SEE WHAT THE PROFESSOR WAS SAYING.
ALL OF THE INGREDIENTS' FLAVORS MELD PERFECTLY WITH THE TASTE OF THE DRY-ROASTED SPICES!
TUNK
LASTLY, GIVE THIS ONE A TASTE.
...?
UM, THAT LOOKS JUST LIKE THE KOZHI VARUTHA CURRY WE TASTED FIRST.
WAFT
!

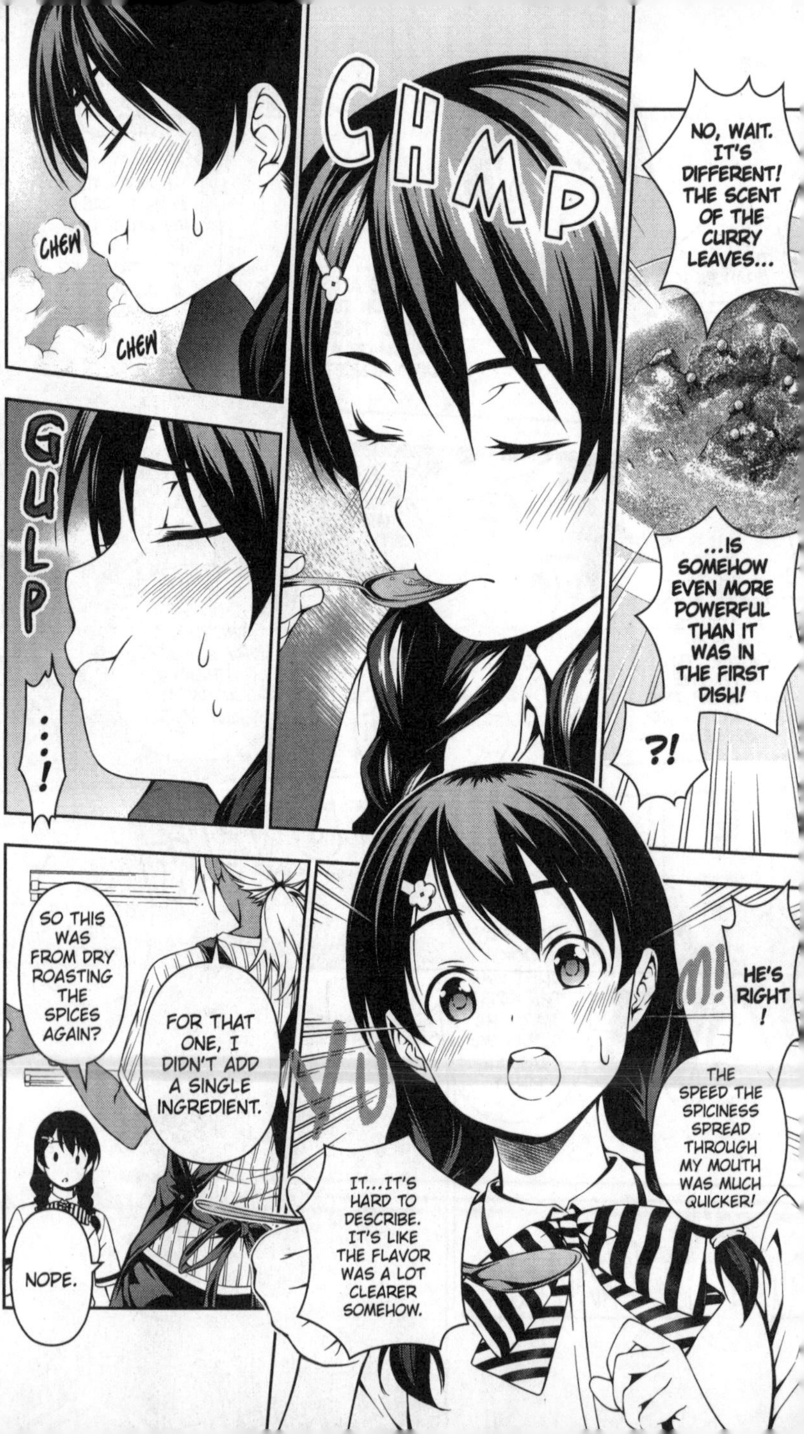
NO, WAIT. IT'S DIFFERENT! THE SCENT OF THE CURRY LEAVES...
...IS SOMEHOW EVEN MORE POWERFUL THAN IT WAS IN THE FIRST DISH!
?!
CHMP
CHEW
CHEW
GULP
...!
HE'S RIGHT!
THE SPEED THE SPICINESS SPREAD THROUGH MY MOUTH WAS MUCH QUICKER!
IT...IT'S HARD TO DESCRIBE. IT'S LIKE THE FLAVOR WAS A LOT CLEARER SOMEHOW.
SO THIS WAS FROM DRY ROASTING THE SPICES AGAIN?
NOPE.
FOR THAT ONE, I DIDN'T ADD A SINGLE INGREDIENT.

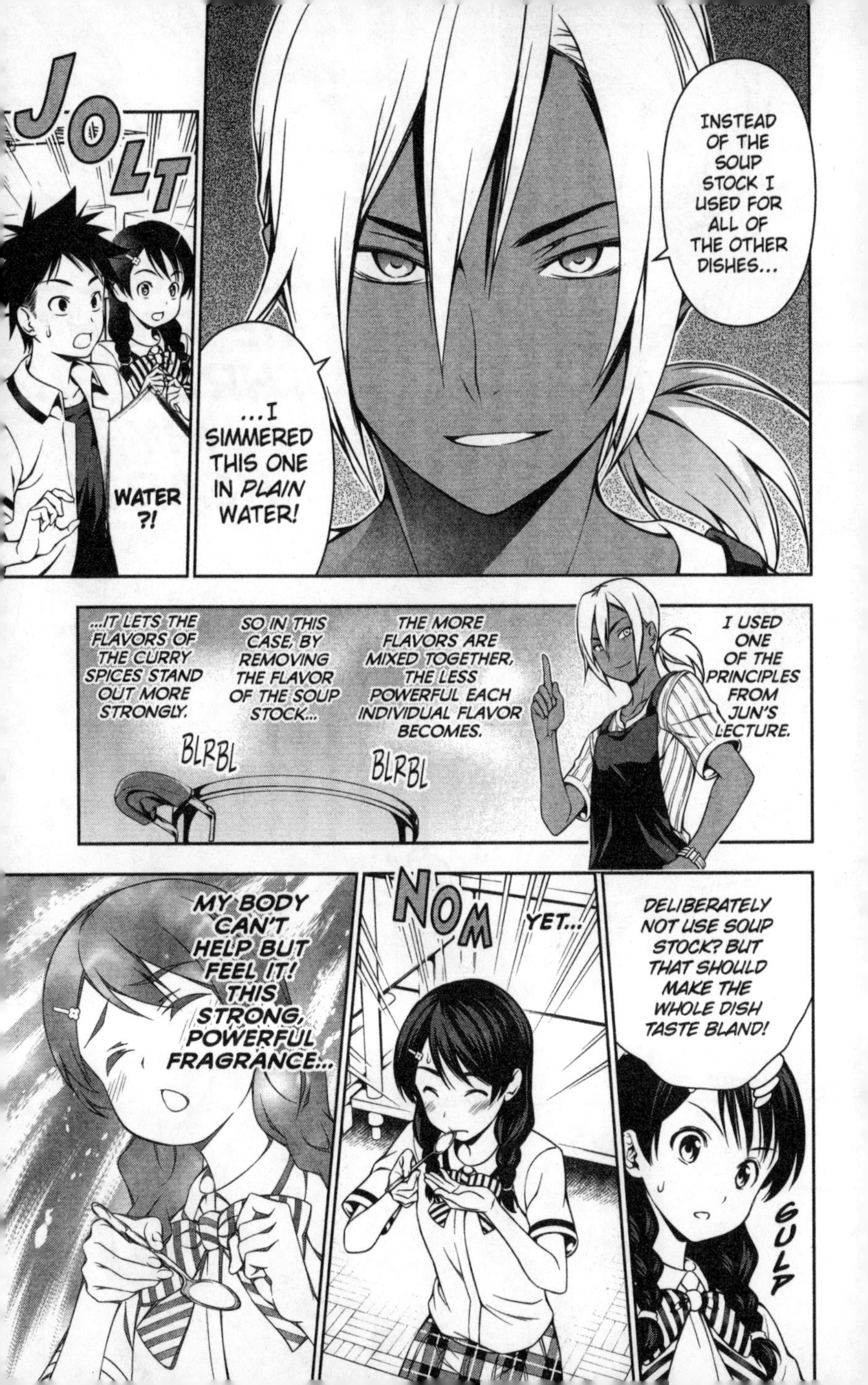
INSTEAD OF THE SOUP STOCK I USED FOR ALL OF THE OTHER DISHES...
...I SIMMERED THIS ONE IN *PLAIN* WATER!
JOLT
WATER ?!
I USED ONE OF THE PRINCIPLES FROM JUN'S LECTURE.
THE MORE FLAVORS ARE MIXED TOGETHER, THE LESS POWERFUL EACH INDIVIDUAL FLAVOR BECOMES.
SO IN THIS CASE, BY REMOVING THE FLAVOR OF THE SOUP STOCK...
...IT LETS THE FLAVORS OF THE CURRY SPICES STAND OUT MORE STRONGLY.
BLRBL
BLRBL
DELIBERATELY NOT USE SOUP STOCK? BUT THAT SHOULD MAKE THE WHOLE DISH TASTE BLAND!
GULP
YET...
NOM
MY BODY CAN'T HELP BUT FEEL IT! THIS STRONG, POWERFUL FRAGRANCE...

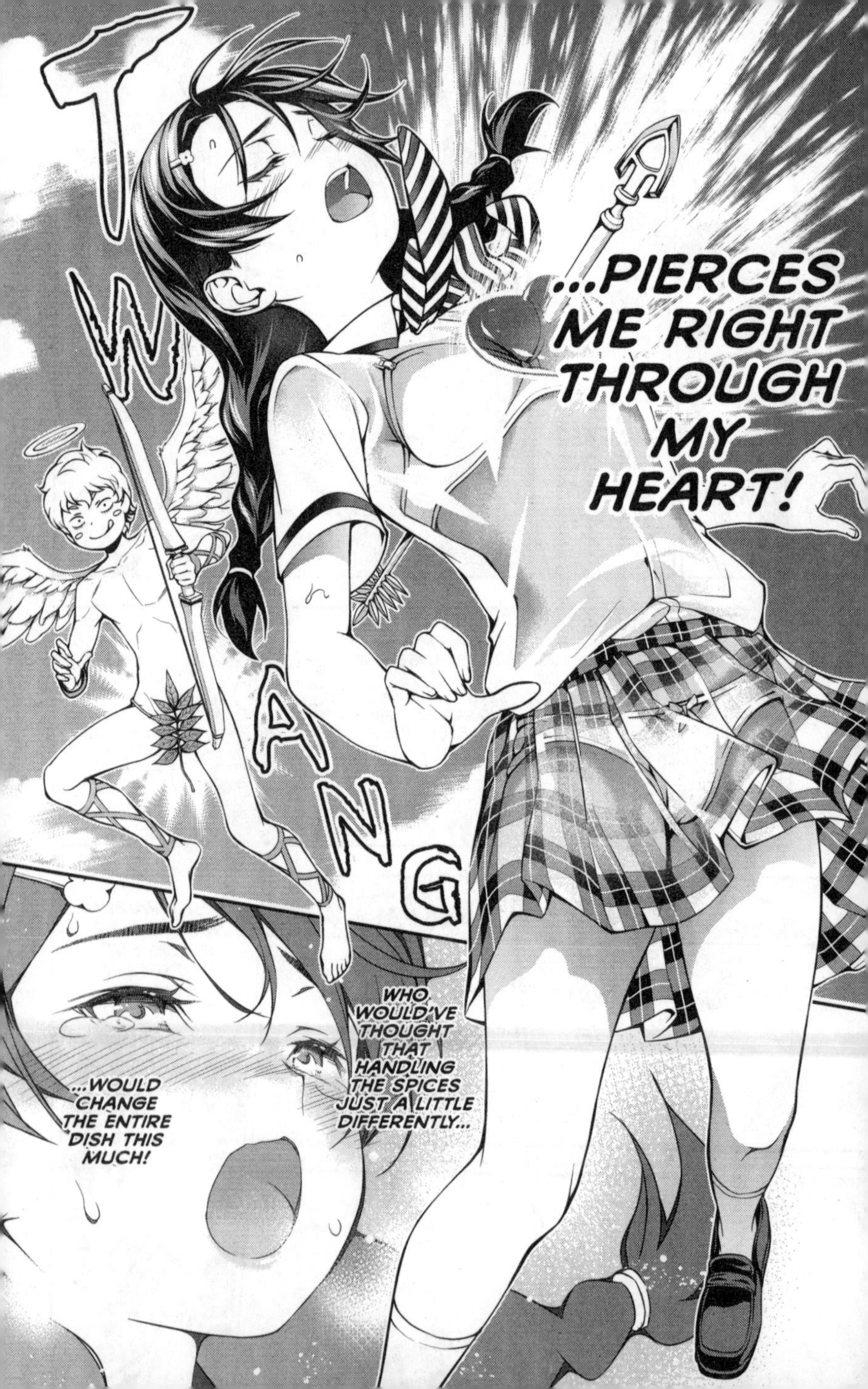
...PIERCES ME RIGHT THROUGH MY HEART!
TWANG
WHO WOULD'VE THOUGHT THAT HANDLING THE SPICES JUST A LITTLE DIFFERENTLY...
...WOULD CHANGE THE ENTIRE DISH THIS MUCH!

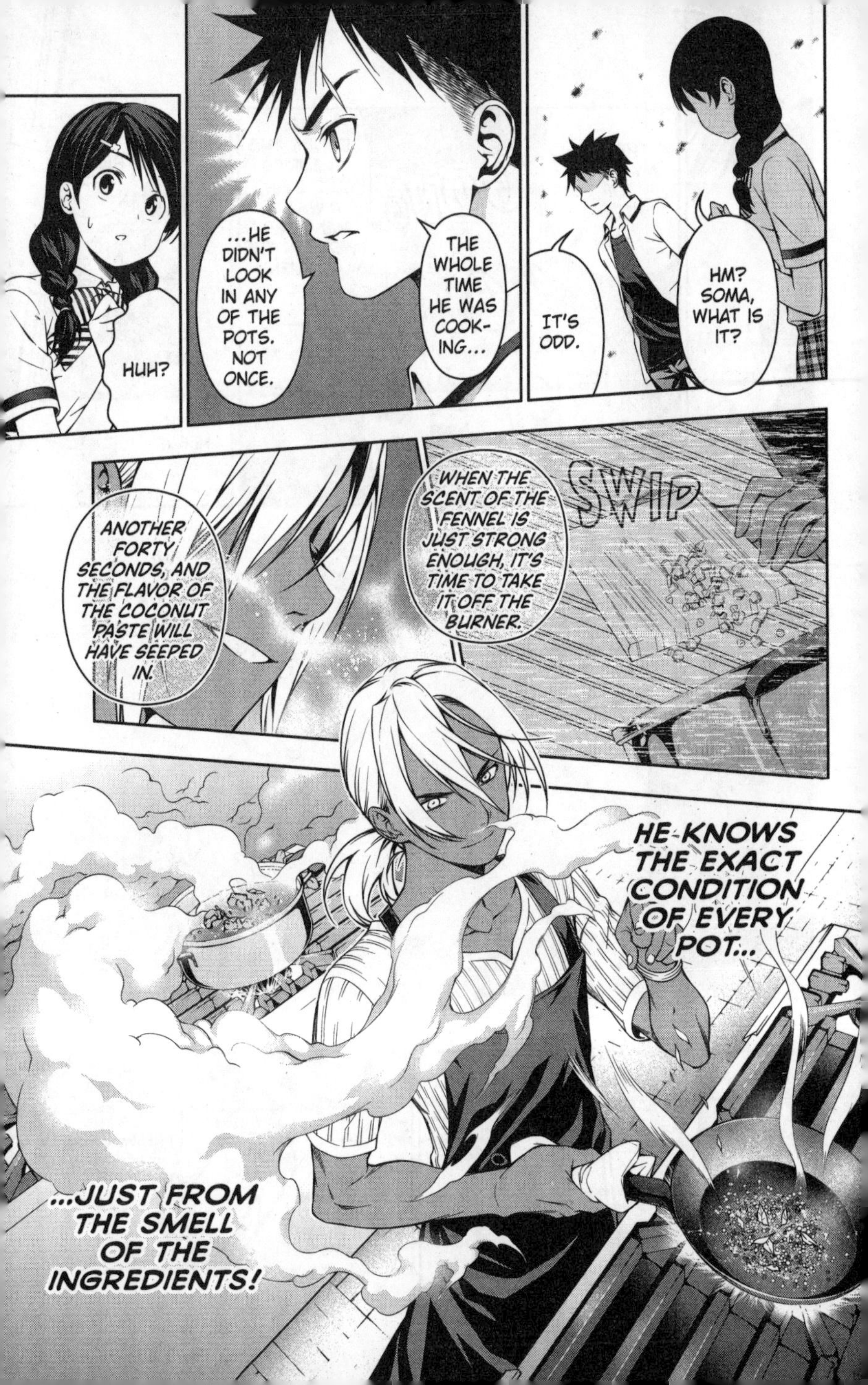
HM? SOMA, WHAT IS IT?
IT'S ODD.
THE WHOLE TIME HE WAS COOK-ING...
...HE DIDN'T LOOK IN ANY OF THE POTS. NOT ONCE.
HUH?
SWIP
WHEN THE SCENT OF THE FENNEL IS JUST STRONG ENOUGH, IT'S TIME TO TAKE IT OFF THE BURNER.
ANOTHER FORTY SECONDS, AND THE FLAVOR OF THE COCONUT PASTE WILL HAVE SEEPED IN.
HE KNOWS THE EXACT CONDITION OF EVERY POT...
...JUST FROM THE SMELL OF THE INGREDIENTS!

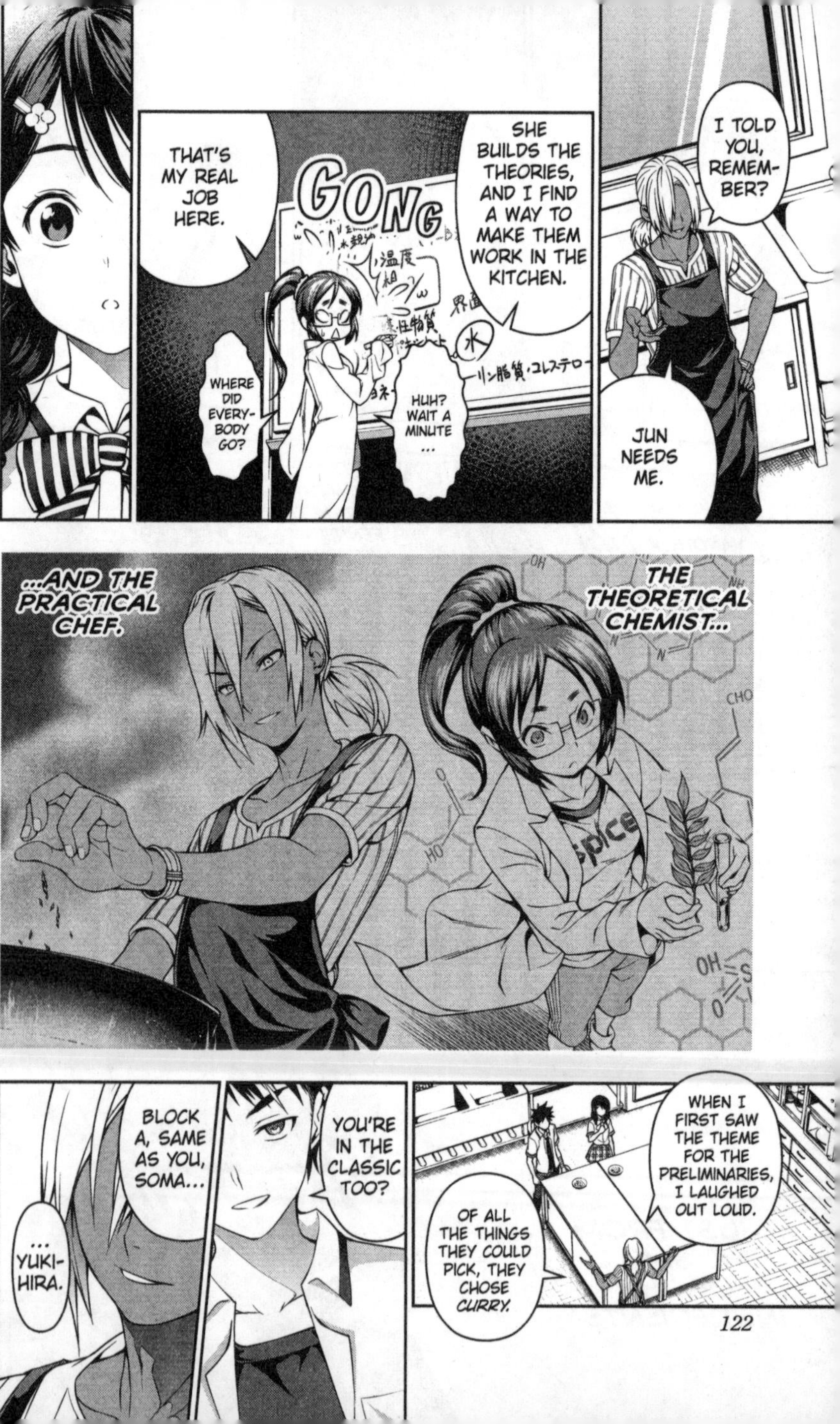

I TOLD YOU, REMEMBER?
JUN NEEDS ME.
SHE BUILDS THE THEORIES, AND I FIND A WAY TO MAKE THEM WORK IN THE KITCHEN.
THAT'S MY REAL JOB HERE.
GONG
HUH? WAIT A MINUTE ...
WHERE DID EVERYBODY GO?
THE THEORETICAL CHEMIST...
...AND THE PRACTICAL CHEF.
spice
WHEN I FIRST SAW THE THEME FOR THE PRELIMINARIES, I LAUGHED OUT LOUD.
OF ALL THE THINGS THEY COULD PICK, THEY CHOSE CURRY.
YOU'RE IN THE CLASSIC TOO?
BLOCK A, SAME AS YOU, SOMA...
... YUKIHIRA.

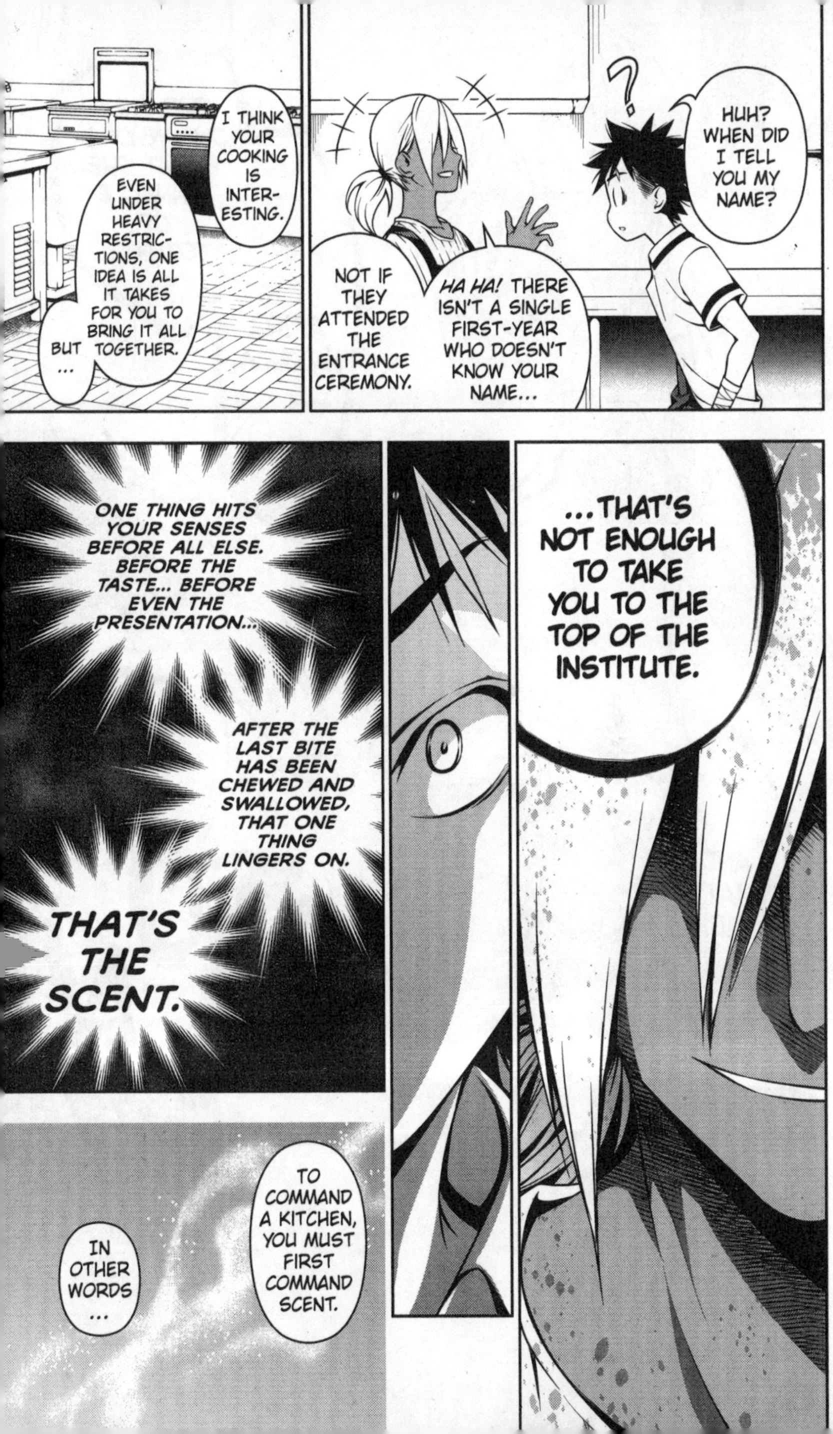
HUH? WHEN DID I TELL YOU MY NAME?
HA HA! THERE ISN'T A SINGLE FIRST-YEAR WHO DOESN'T KNOW YOUR NAME...
NOT IF THEY ATTENDED THE ENTRANCE CEREMONY.
I THINK YOUR COOKING IS INTERESTING.
EVEN UNDER HEAVY RESTRICTIONS, ONE IDEA IS ALL IT TAKES FOR YOU TO BRING IT ALL TOGETHER.
BUT ...
...THAT'S NOT ENOUGH TO TAKE YOU TO THE TOP OF THE INSTITUTE.
ONE THING HITS YOUR SENSES BEFORE ALL ELSE. BEFORE THE TASTE... BEFORE EVEN THE PRESENTATION...
AFTER THE LAST BITE HAS BEEN CHEWED AND SWALLOWED, THAT ONE THING LINGERS ON.
THAT'S THE SCENT.
TO COMMAND A KITCHEN, YOU MUST FIRST COMMAND SCENT.
IN OTHER WORDS ...

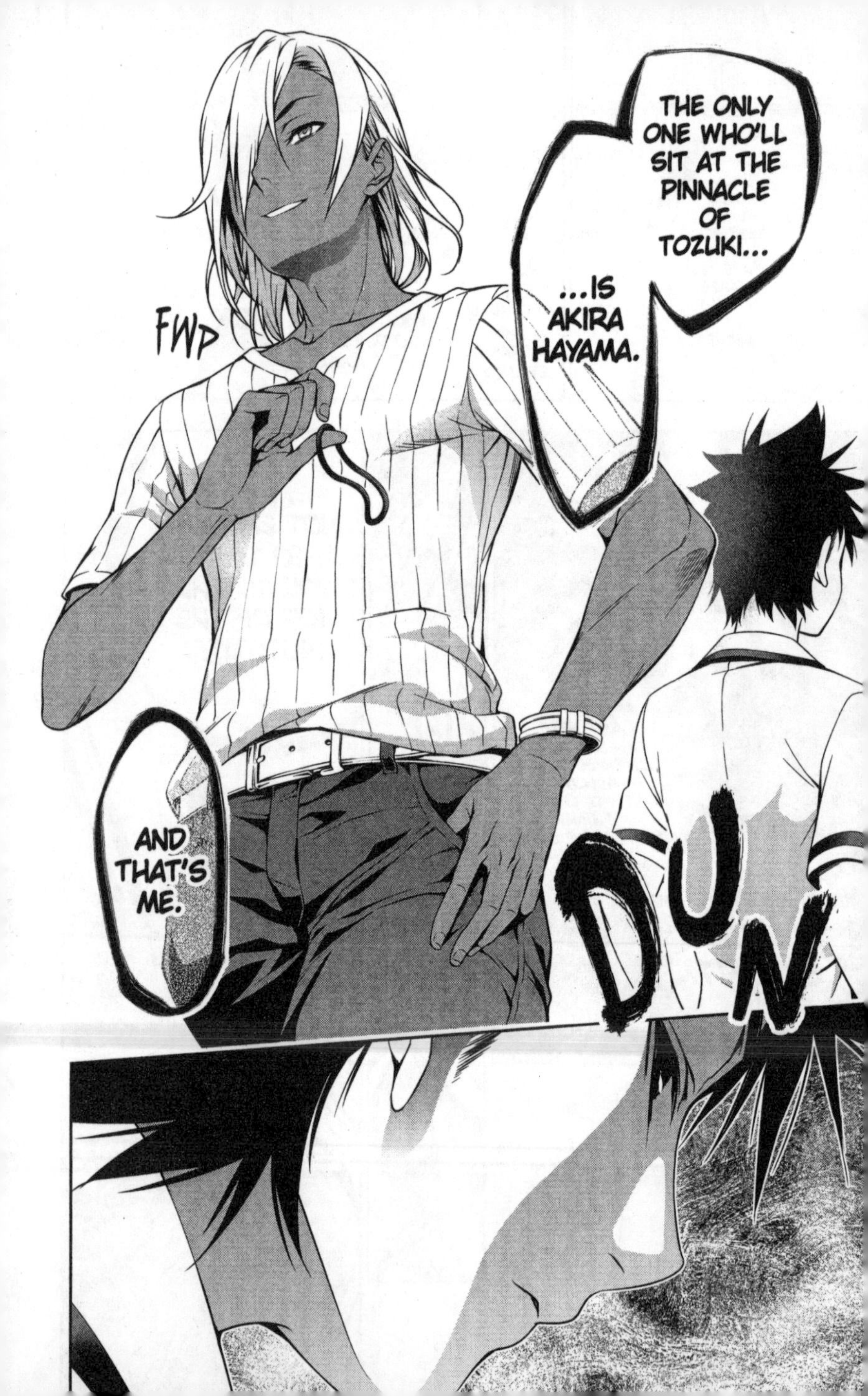
THE ONLY ONE WHO'LL SIT AT THE PINNACLE OF TOZUKI...
...IS AKIRA HAYAMA.
FWP
AND THAT'S ME.
DUN

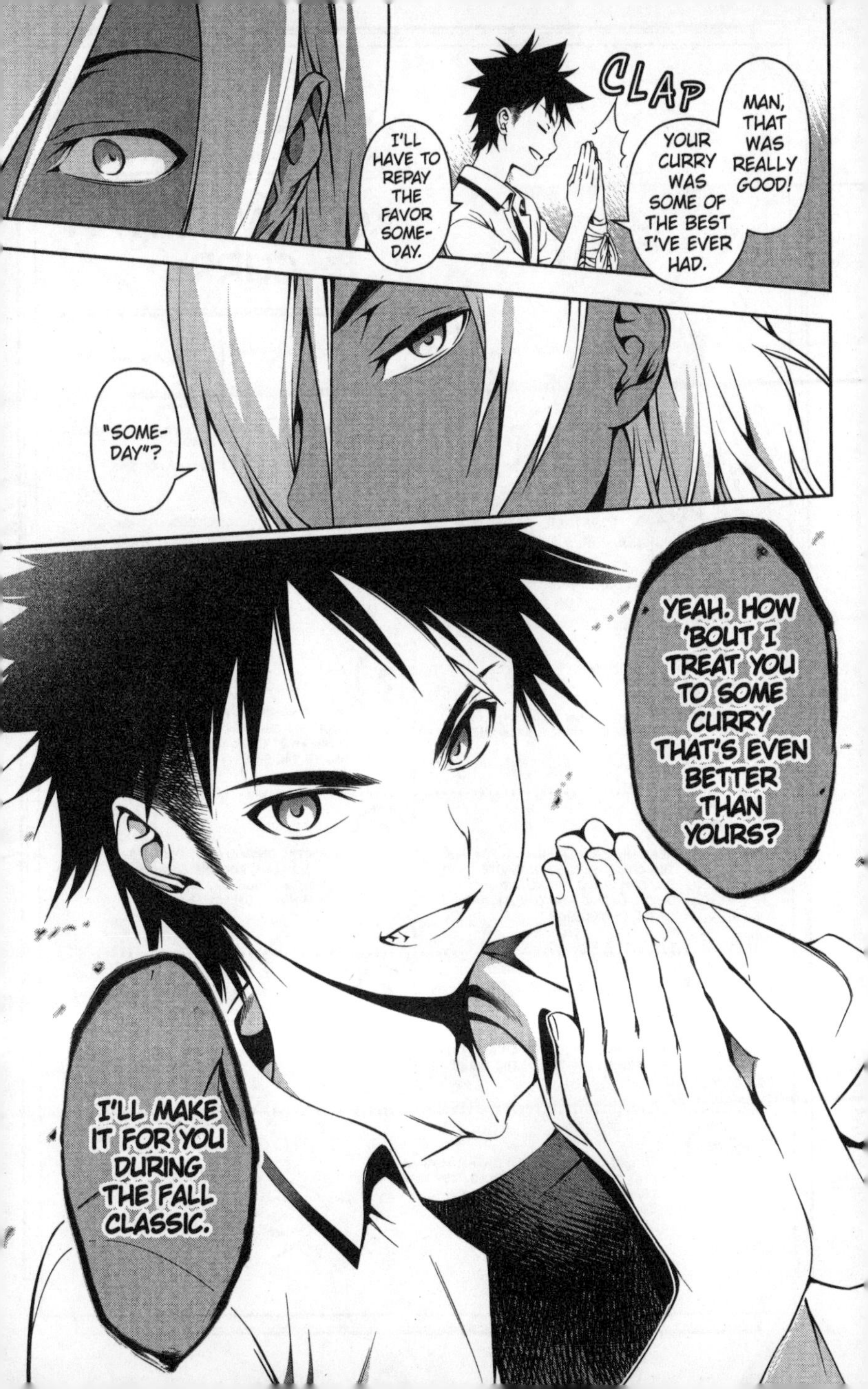

MAN, THAT WAS REALLY GOOD!
CLAP
YOUR CURRY WAS SOME OF THE BEST I'VE EVER HAD.
I'LL HAVE TO REPAY THE FAVOR SOME-DAY.
"SOME-DAY"?
YEAH. HOW 'BOUT I TREAT YOU TO SOME CURRY THAT'S EVEN BETTER THAN YOURS?
I'LL MAKE IT FOR YOU DURING THE FALL CLASSIC.

PRACTICAL RECIPE #3

VOLUME 6 SPECIAL SUPPLEMENT!

KOZHI VARUTHA CURRY

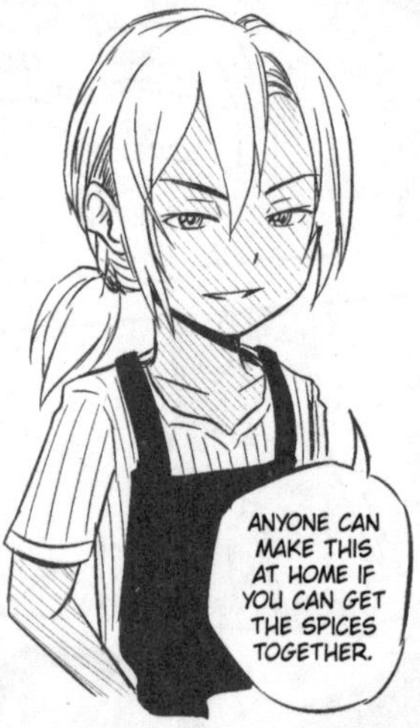
ANYONE CAN MAKE THIS AT HOME IF YOU CAN GET THE SPICES TOGETHER.

ARTIST: YUTO TSUKUDA

INGREDIENTS

SERVES 2

- 1 CHICKEN THIGH
- 1 ONION
- 100 GRAMS CANNED DICED TOMATOES
- 1 TEASPOON EACH GRATED GARLIC AND GINGER
- 1/3 TEASPOON EACH CUMIN SEEDS AND GARAM MASALA

A
- 1/4 TEASPOON RED PEPPER
- 1/2 TABLESPOON CORIANDER POWDER
- 1/3 TEASPOON TURMERIC POWDER
- 1/2 TEASPOON SALT

- 200 CC COCONUT MILK
- 100 CC WATER
- 3 TABLESPOONS CANOLA OIL
- CILANTRO LEAVES, COCONUT MILK

1. CUT THE CHICKEN THIGH INTO BITE-SIZED PIECES. THINLY SLICE THE ONION.
2. HEAT A NONSTICK FRYING PAN, AND COOK THE CHICKEN THIGH, SKIN SIDE DOWN FIRST UNTIL GOLDEN BROWN. SET TO THE SIDE.
3. HEAT THE CANOLA OIL IN A POT. ADD THE CUMIN SEEDS AND SAUTÉ UNTIL YOU CAN SMELL THEM. ADD THE ONION, GARLIC AND GINGER AND SAUTÉ THOROUGHLY.
4. WHEN THE ONIONS ARE GOLDEN AND TRANSLUCENT, ADD THE CANNED DICED TOMATOES AND SIMMER FOR FIVE MINUTES ON LOW.
5. MIX (A) TOGETHER AND ADD TO (4). STIR UNTIL BLENDED, AND THEN ADD (2). STIR UNTIL THE CHICKEN IS THOROUGHLY COATED IN THE SAUCE.
6. POUR THE WATER AND COCONUT MILK INTO (5) AND LET SIMMER FOR TEN MINUTES.
7. SEASON TO TASTE WITH GARAM MASALA AND SALT. POUR INTO A BOWL, TOP WITH CILANTRO LEAVES AND A SPLASH OF COCONUT MILK AND DONE!

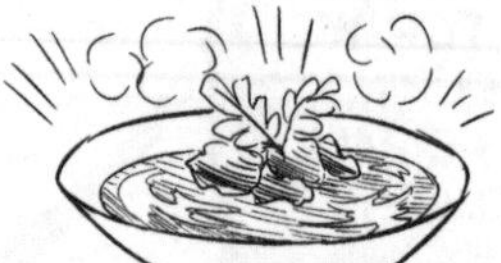

46 CROUCHING DRAGON ASCENDS

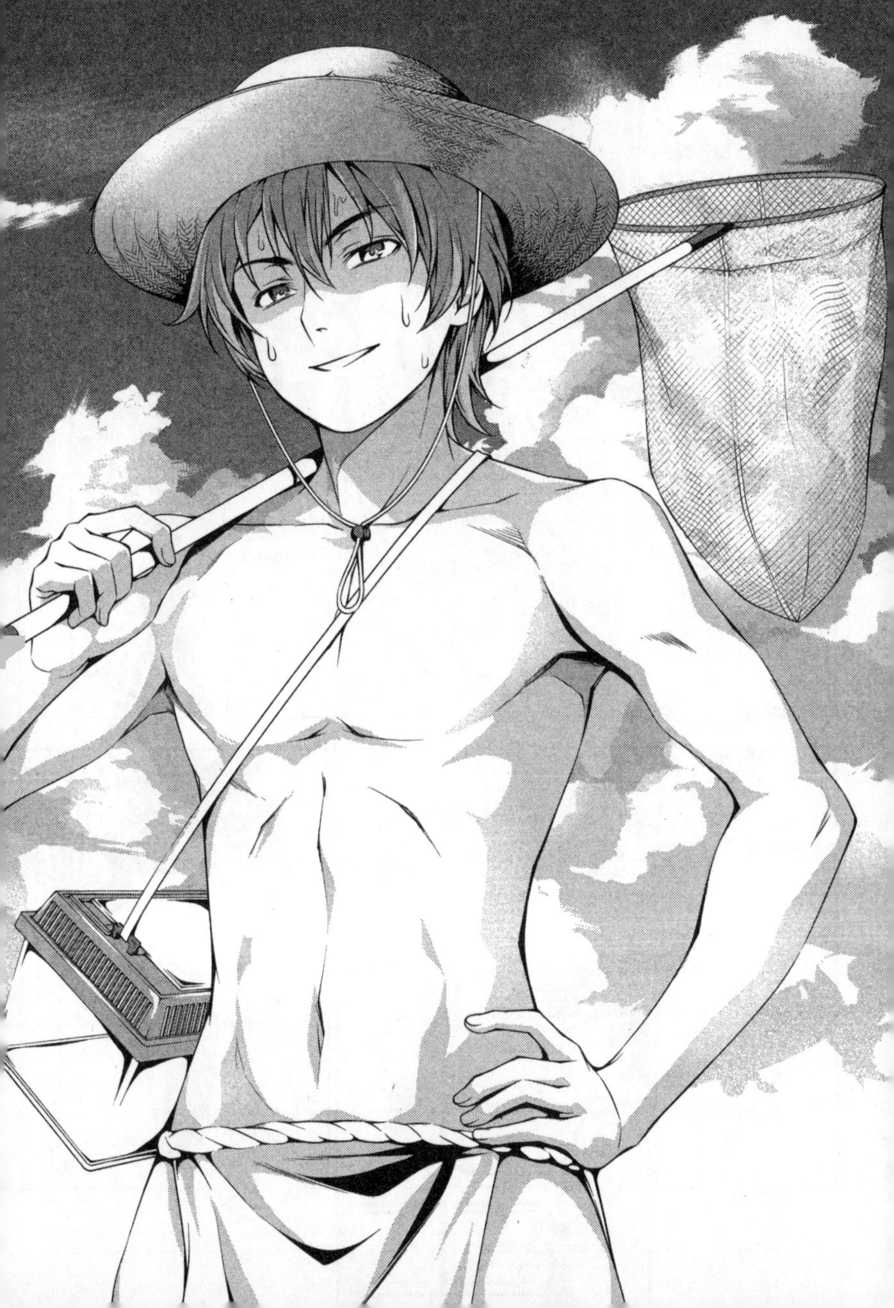

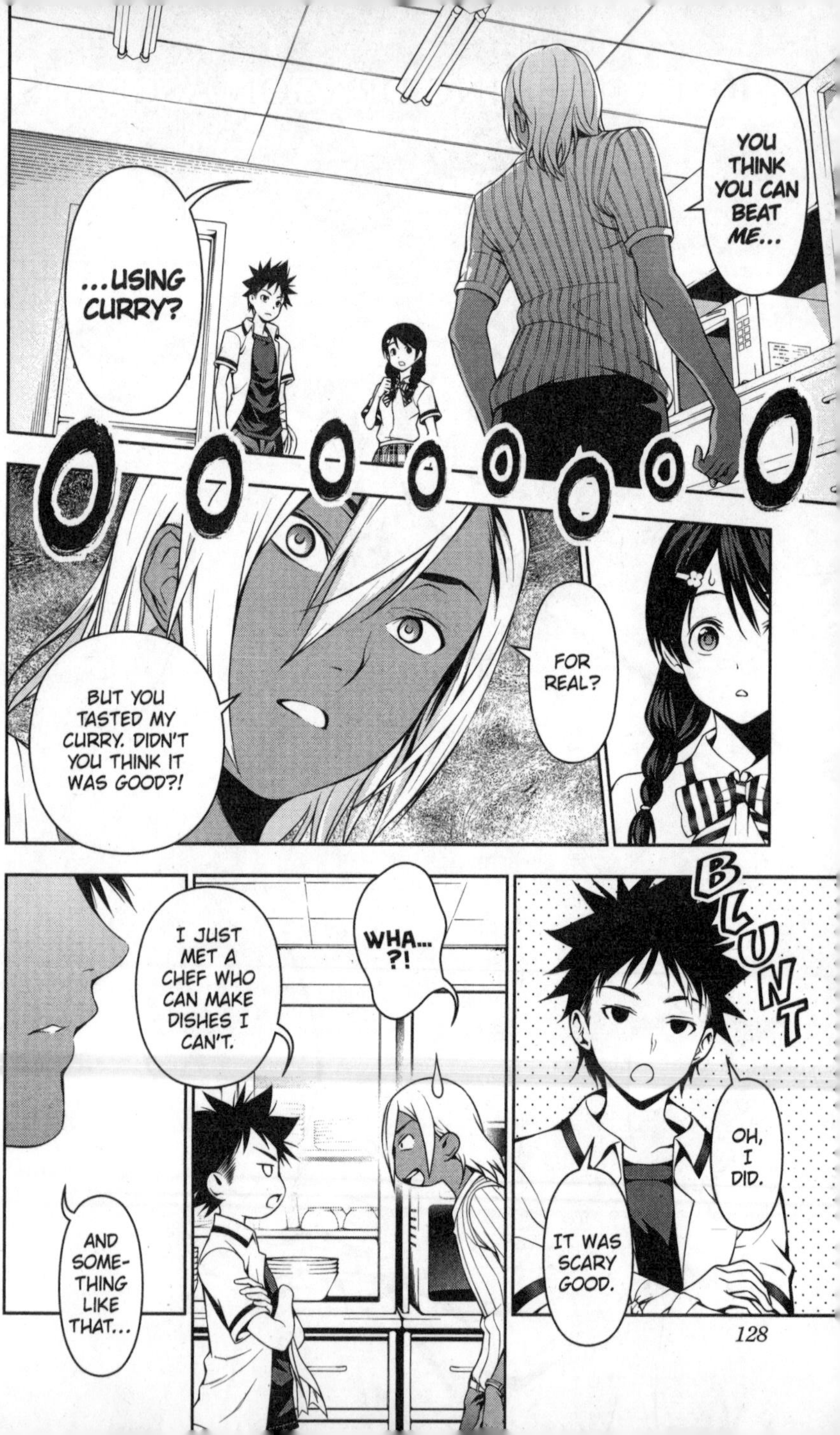
YOU THINK YOU CAN BEAT ME...
...USING CURRY?
FOR REAL?
BUT YOU TASTED MY CURRY. DIDN'T YOU THINK IT WAS GOOD?!
BLUNT
OH, I DID.
IT WAS SCARY GOOD.
WHA... ?!
I JUST MET A CHEF WHO CAN MAKE DISHES I CAN'T.
AND SOME-THING LIKE THAT...

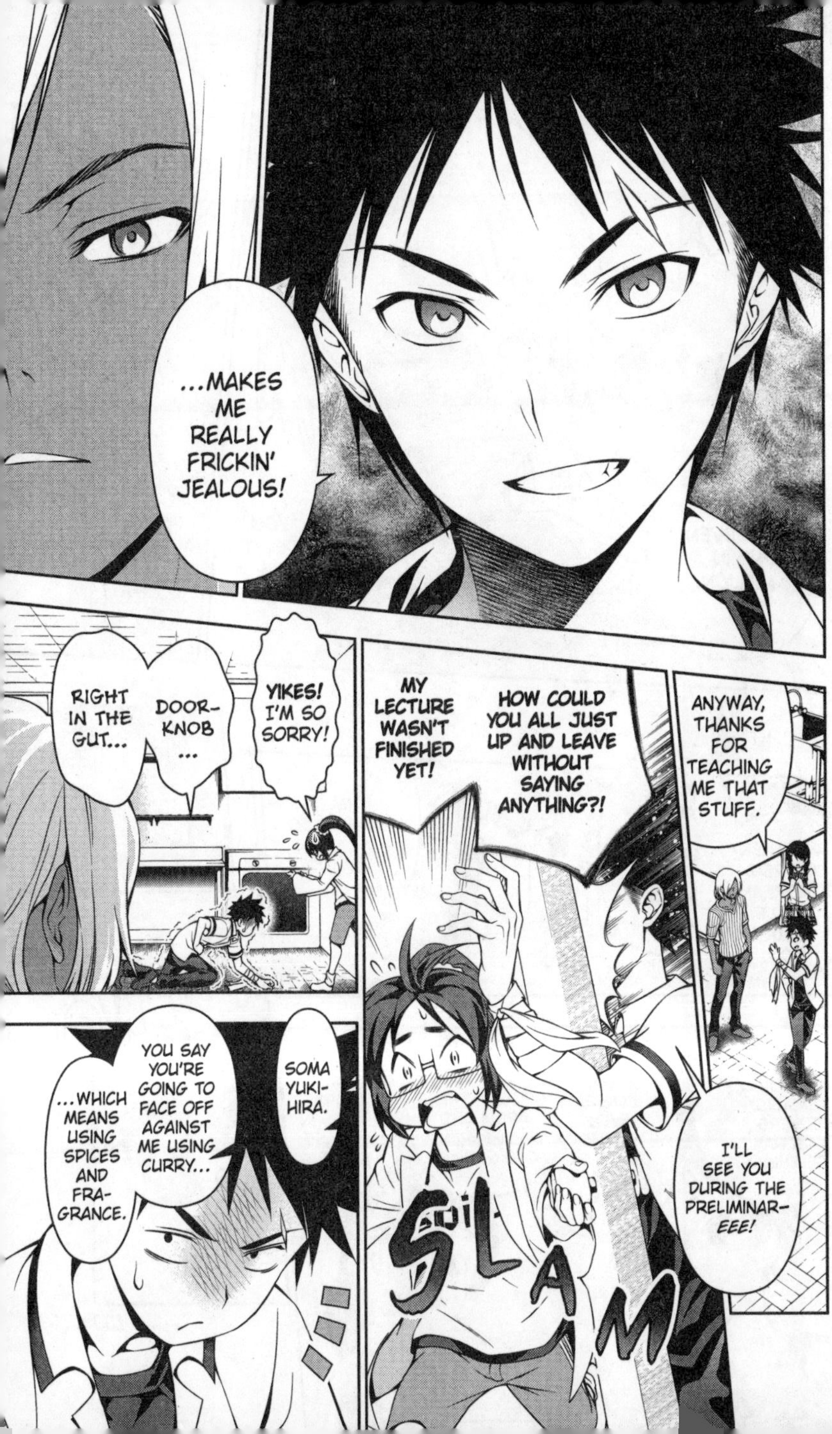
...MAKES ME REALLY FRICKIN' JEALOUS!
ANYWAY, THANKS FOR TEACHING ME THAT STUFF.
I'LL SEE YOU DURING THE PRELIMINAR-EEE!
HOW COULD YOU ALL JUST UP AND LEAVE WITHOUT SAYING ANYTHING?!
MY LECTURE WASN'T FINISHED YET!
SLAM
YIKES! I'M SO SORRY!
DOOR-KNOB...
RIGHT IN THE GUT...
SOMA YUKI-HIRA.
YOU SAY YOU'RE GOING TO FACE OFF AGAINST ME USING CURRY...
...WHICH MEANS USING SPICES AND FRA-GRANCE.

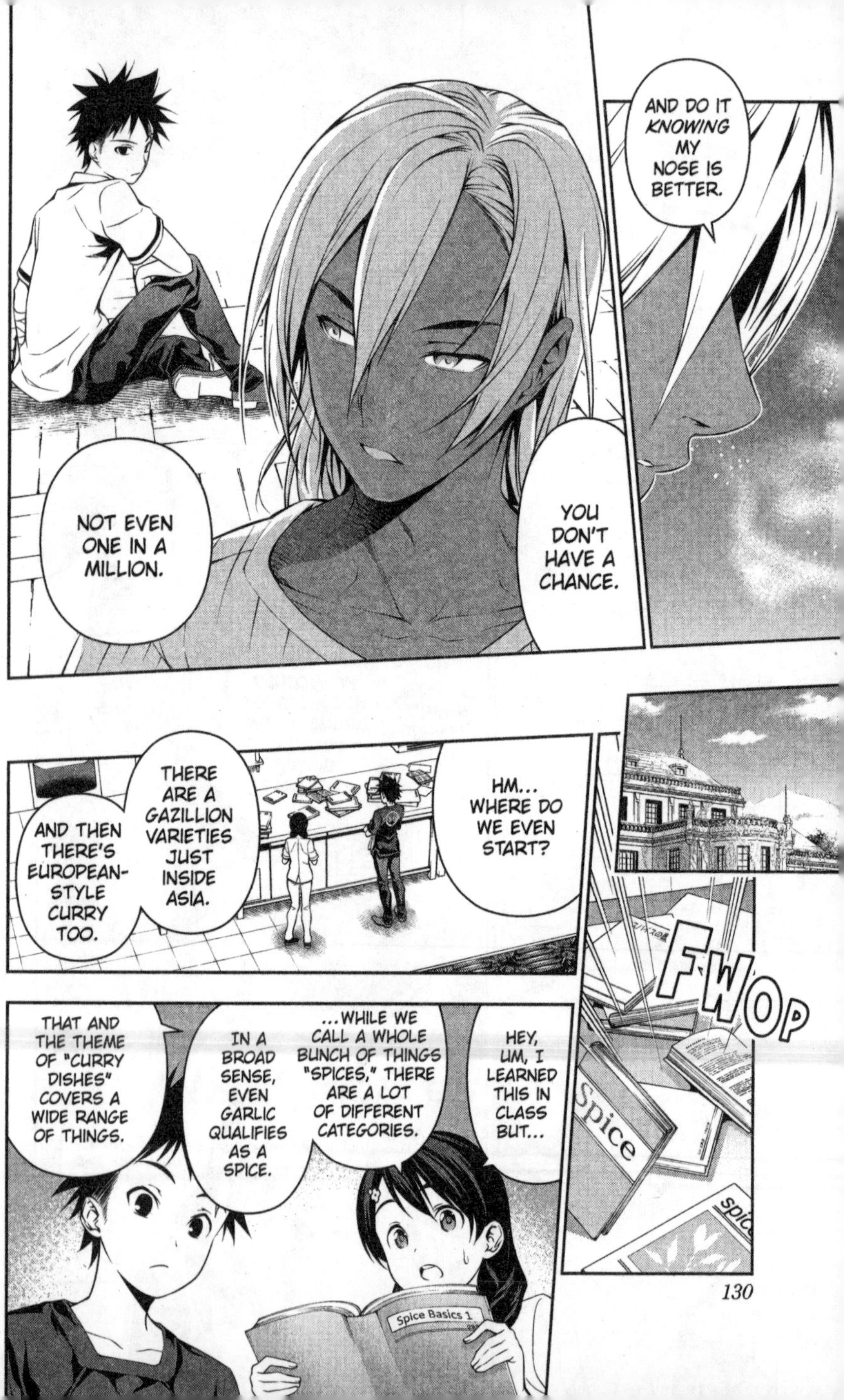
AND DO IT *KNOWING* MY NOSE IS BETTER.
YOU DON'T HAVE A CHANCE.
NOT EVEN ONE IN A MILLION.
FWOP
Spice
spice
HM... WHERE DO WE EVEN START?
THERE ARE A GAZILLION VARIETIES JUST INSIDE ASIA.
AND THEN THERE'S EUROPEAN-STYLE CURRY TOO.
HEY, UM, I LEARNED THIS IN CLASS BUT...
...WHILE WE CALL A WHOLE BUNCH OF THINGS "SPICES," THERE ARE A LOT OF DIFFERENT CATEGORIES.
IN A BROAD SENSE, EVEN GARLIC QUALIFIES AS A SPICE.
THAT AND THE THEME OF "CURRY DISHES" COVERS A WIDE RANGE OF THINGS.
Spice Basics 1

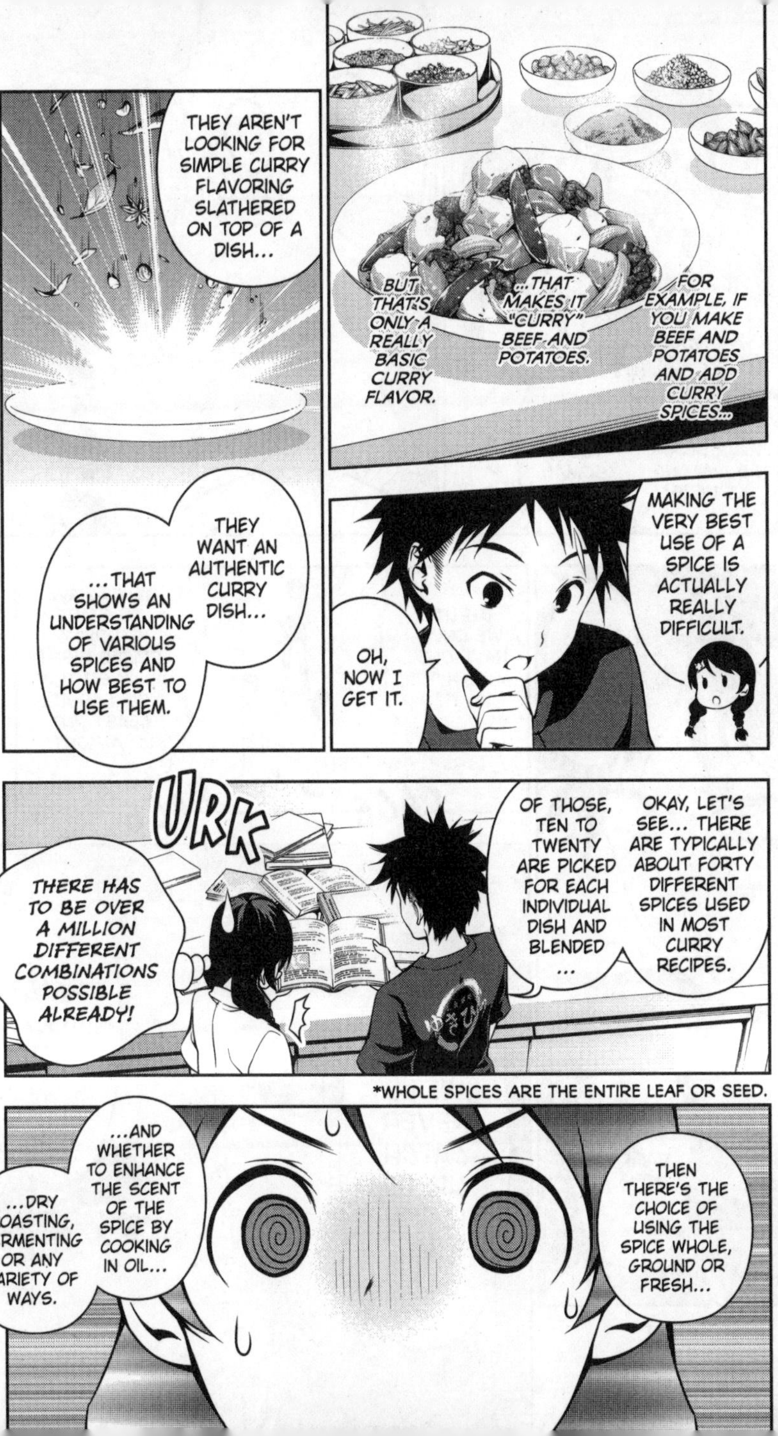
FOR EXAMPLE, IF YOU MAKE BEEF AND POTATOES AND ADD CURRY SPICES...
...THAT MAKES IT "CURRY" BEEF AND POTATOES.
BUT THAT'S ONLY A REALLY BASIC CURRY FLAVOR.
THEY AREN'T LOOKING FOR SIMPLE CURRY FLAVORING SLATHERED ON TOP OF A DISH...
MAKING THE VERY BEST USE OF A SPICE IS ACTUALLY REALLY DIFFICULT.
OH, NOW I GET IT.
THEY WANT AN AUTHENTIC CURRY DISH...
...THAT SHOWS AN UNDERSTANDING OF VARIOUS SPICES AND HOW BEST TO USE THEM.
OKAY, LET'S SEE... THERE ARE TYPICALLY ABOUT FORTY DIFFERENT SPICES USED IN MOST CURRY RECIPES.
OF THOSE, TEN TO TWENTY ARE PICKED FOR EACH INDIVIDUAL DISH AND BLENDED...
URK
THERE HAS TO BE OVER A MILLION DIFFERENT COMBINATIONS POSSIBLE ALREADY!
THEN THERE'S THE CHOICE OF USING THE SPICE WHOLE, GROUND OR FRESH...
...AND WHETHER TO ENHANCE THE SCENT OF THE SPICE BY COOKING IN OIL...
...DRY ROASTING, FERMENTING OR ANY VARIETY OF WAYS.

*WHOLE SPICES ARE THE ENTIRE LEAF OR SEED.

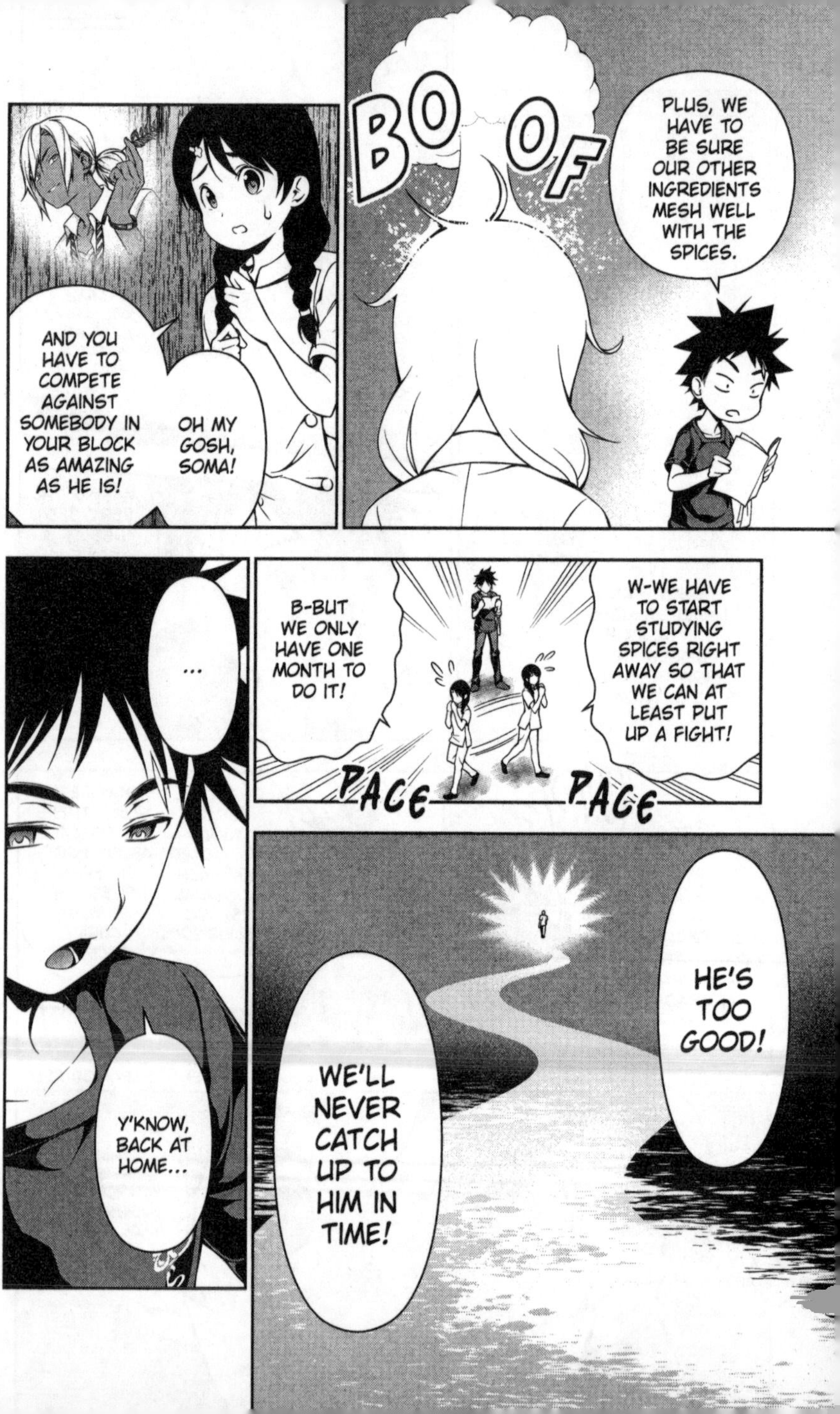
PLUS, WE HAVE TO BE SURE OUR OTHER INGREDIENTS MESH WELL WITH THE SPICES.
BOOF
OH MY GOSH, SOMA!
AND YOU HAVE TO COMPETE AGAINST SOMEBODY IN YOUR BLOCK AS AMAZING AS HE IS!
W-WE HAVE TO START STUDYING SPICES RIGHT AWAY SO THAT WE CAN AT LEAST PUT UP A FIGHT!
B-BUT WE ONLY HAVE ONE MONTH TO DO IT!
PACE PACE
HE'S TOO GOOD!
WE'LL NEVER CATCH UP TO HIM IN TIME!
...
Y'KNOW, BACK AT HOME...

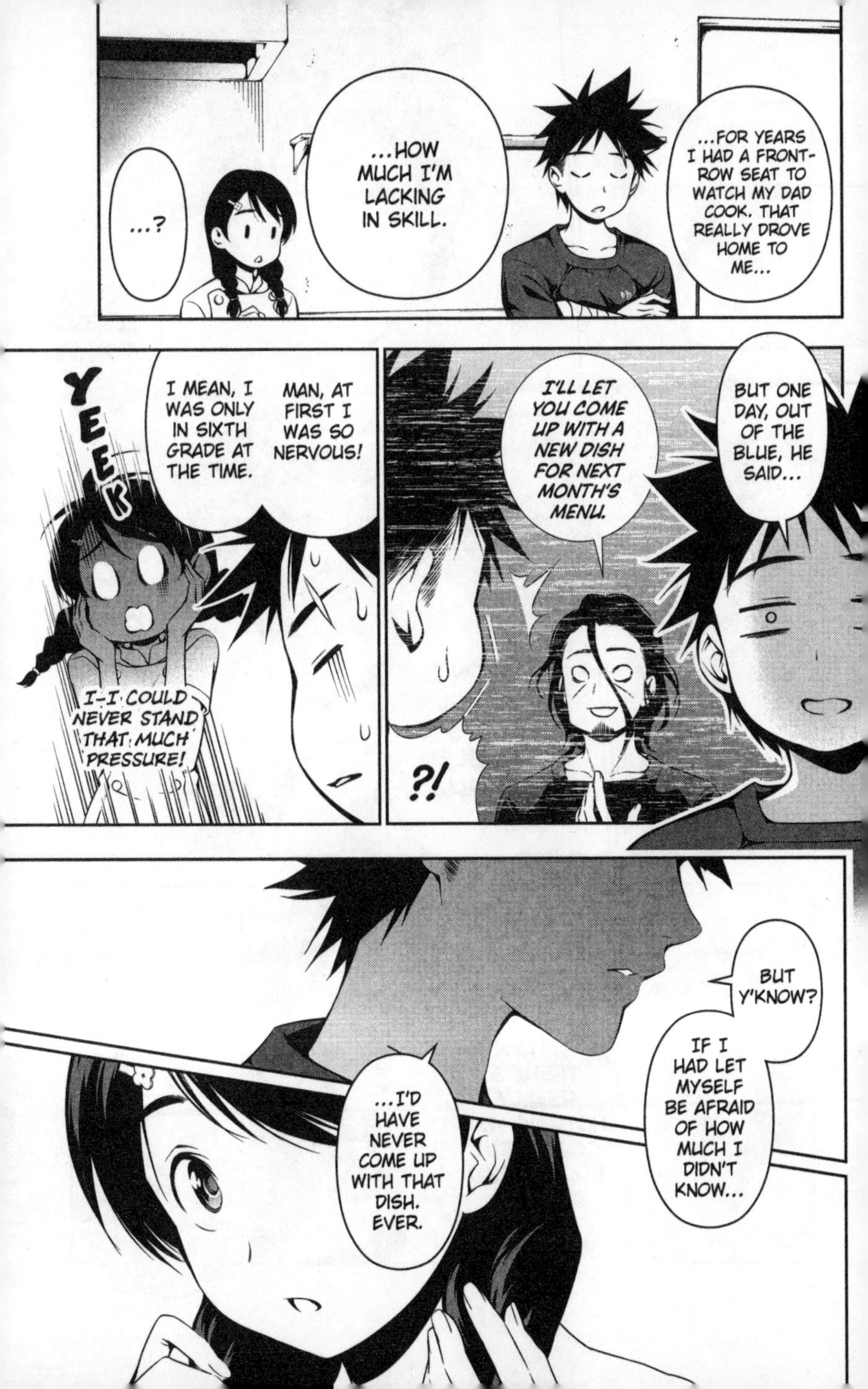
...FOR YEARS I HAD A FRONT-ROW SEAT TO WATCH MY DAD COOK. THAT REALLY DROVE HOME TO ME...
...HOW MUCH I'M LACKING IN SKILL.
...?
BUT ONE DAY, OUT OF THE BLUE, HE SAID...
I'LL LET YOU COME UP WITH A NEW DISH FOR NEXT MONTH'S MENU.
?!
MAN, AT FIRST I WAS SO NERVOUS!
I MEAN, I WAS ONLY IN SIXTH GRADE AT THE TIME.
YEEK
I-I COULD NEVER STAND THAT MUCH PRESSURE!
BUT Y'KNOW?
IF I HAD LET MYSELF BE AFRAID OF HOW MUCH I DIDN'T KNOW...
...I'D HAVE NEVER COME UP WITH THAT DISH. EVER.

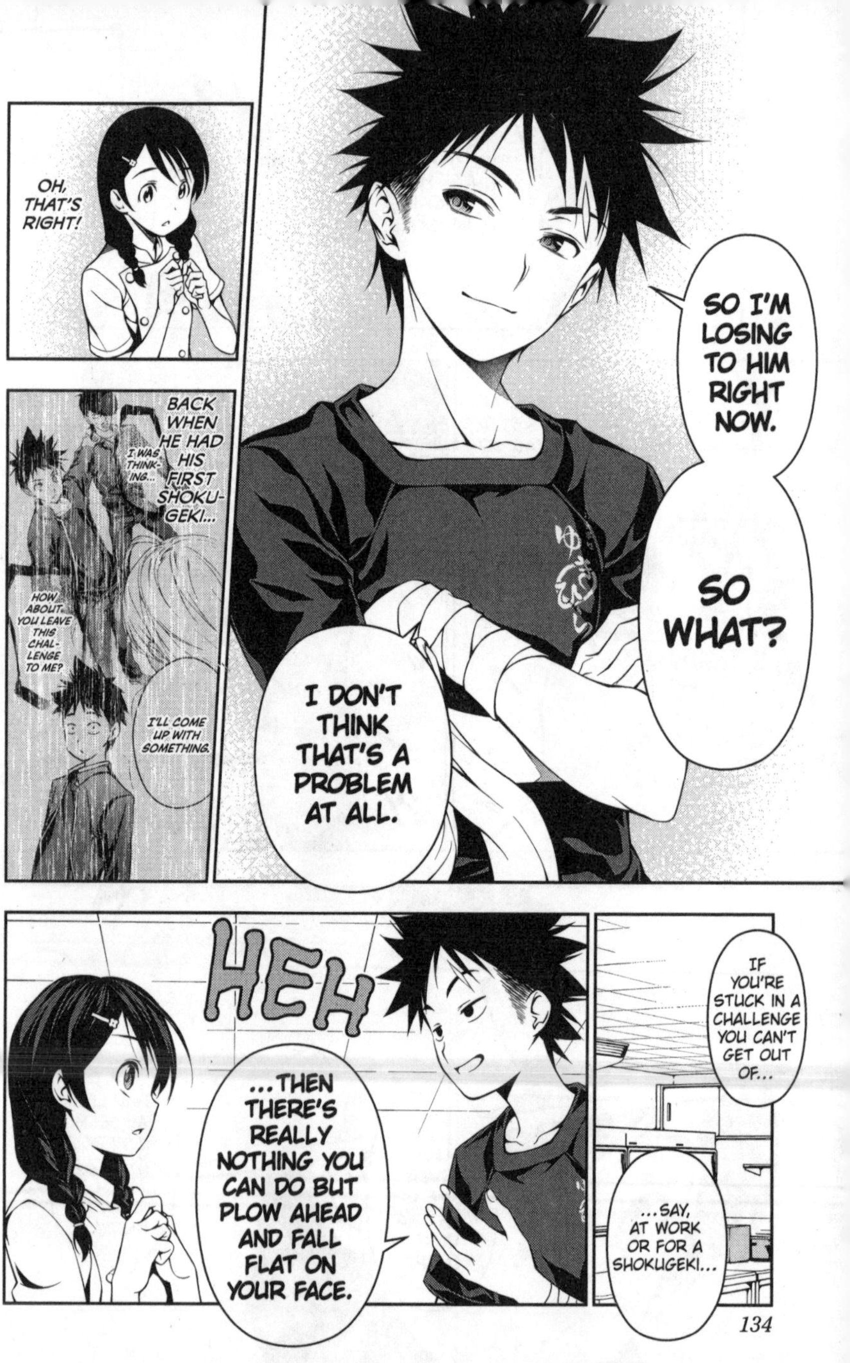
SO I'M LOSING TO HIM RIGHT NOW.
SO WHAT?
I DON'T THINK THAT'S A PROBLEM AT ALL.
OH, THAT'S RIGHT!
BACK WHEN HE HAD HIS FIRST SHOKUGEKI...
I WAS THINKING...
HOW ABOUT YOU LEAVE THIS CHALLENGE TO ME?
I'LL COME UP WITH SOMETHING.
IF YOU'RE STUCK IN A CHALLENGE YOU CAN'T GET OUT OF...
...SAY, AT WORK OR FOR A SHOKUGEKI...
HEH
...THEN THERE'S REALLY NOTHING YOU CAN DO BUT PLOW AHEAD AND FALL FLAT ON YOUR FACE.

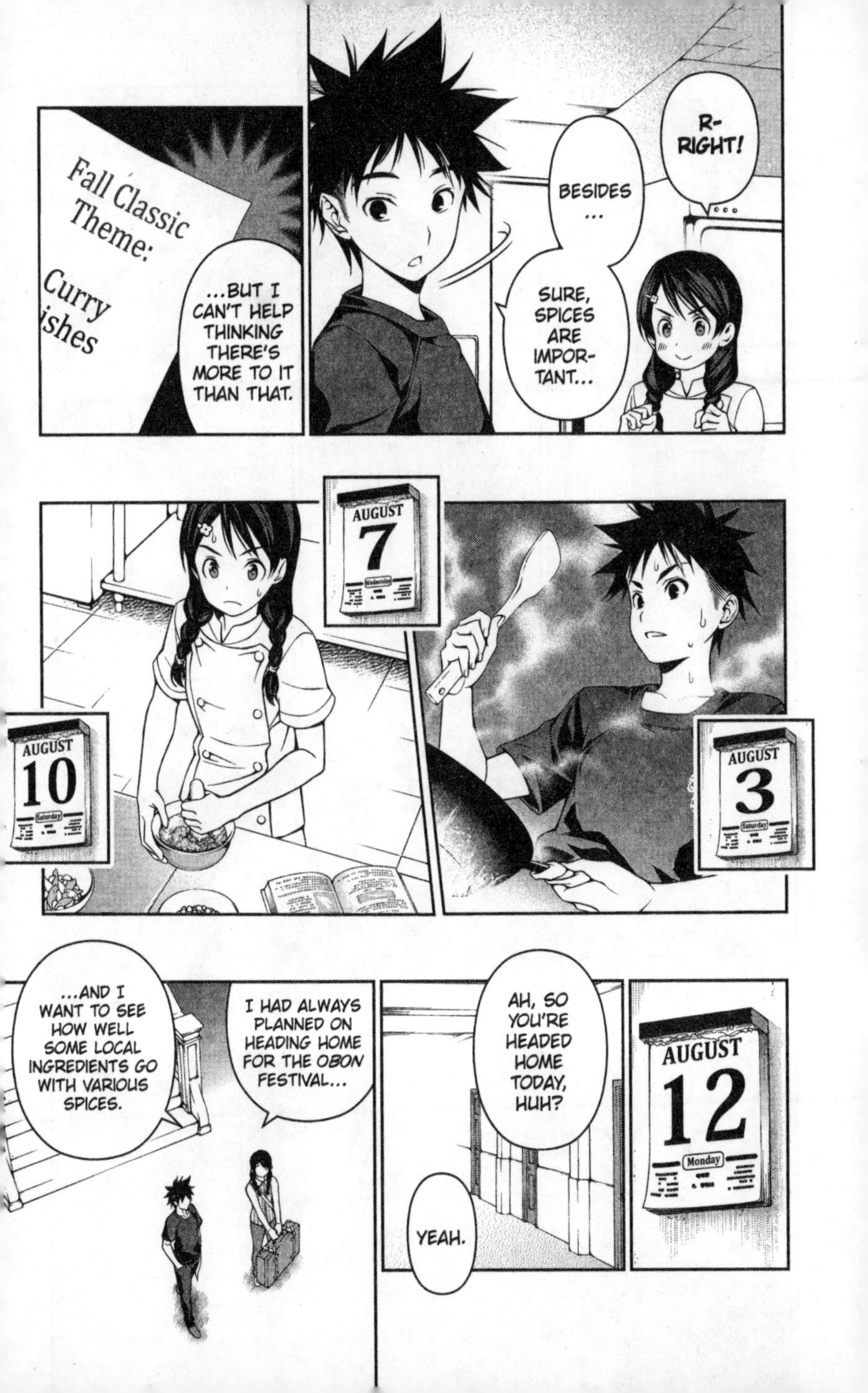
R-RIGHT!
BESIDES...
SURE, SPICES ARE IMPORTANT...
...BUT I CAN'T HELP THINKING THERE'S MORE TO IT THAN THAT.
Fall Classic Theme: Curry ishes
AUGUST 3 Saturday
AUGUST 7 Wednesday
AUGUST 10 Saturday
AUGUST 12 Monday
AH, SO YOU'RE HEADED HOME TODAY, HUH?
YEAH.
I HAD ALWAYS PLANNED ON HEADING HOME FOR THE *OBON* FESTIVAL...
...AND I WANT TO SEE HOW WELL SOME LOCAL INGREDIENTS GO WITH VARIOUS SPICES.

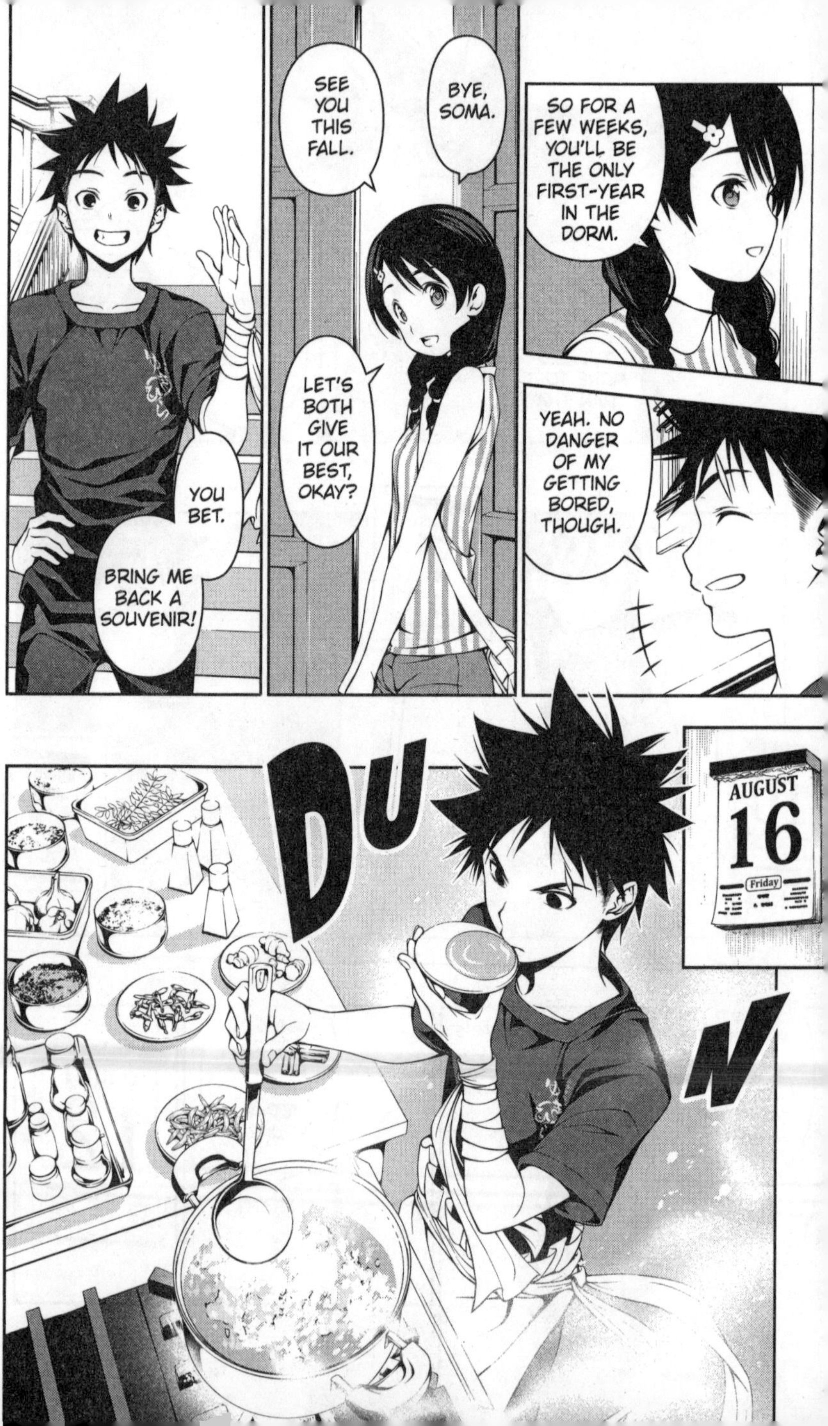
SO FOR A FEW WEEKS, YOU'LL BE THE ONLY FIRST-YEAR IN THE DORM.
YEAH. NO DANGER OF MY GETTING BORED, THOUGH.
BYE, SOMA.
SEE YOU THIS FALL.
LET'S BOTH GIVE IT OUR BEST, OKAY?
YOU BET.
BRING ME BACK A SOUVENIR!
AUGUST
16
Friday
DUN

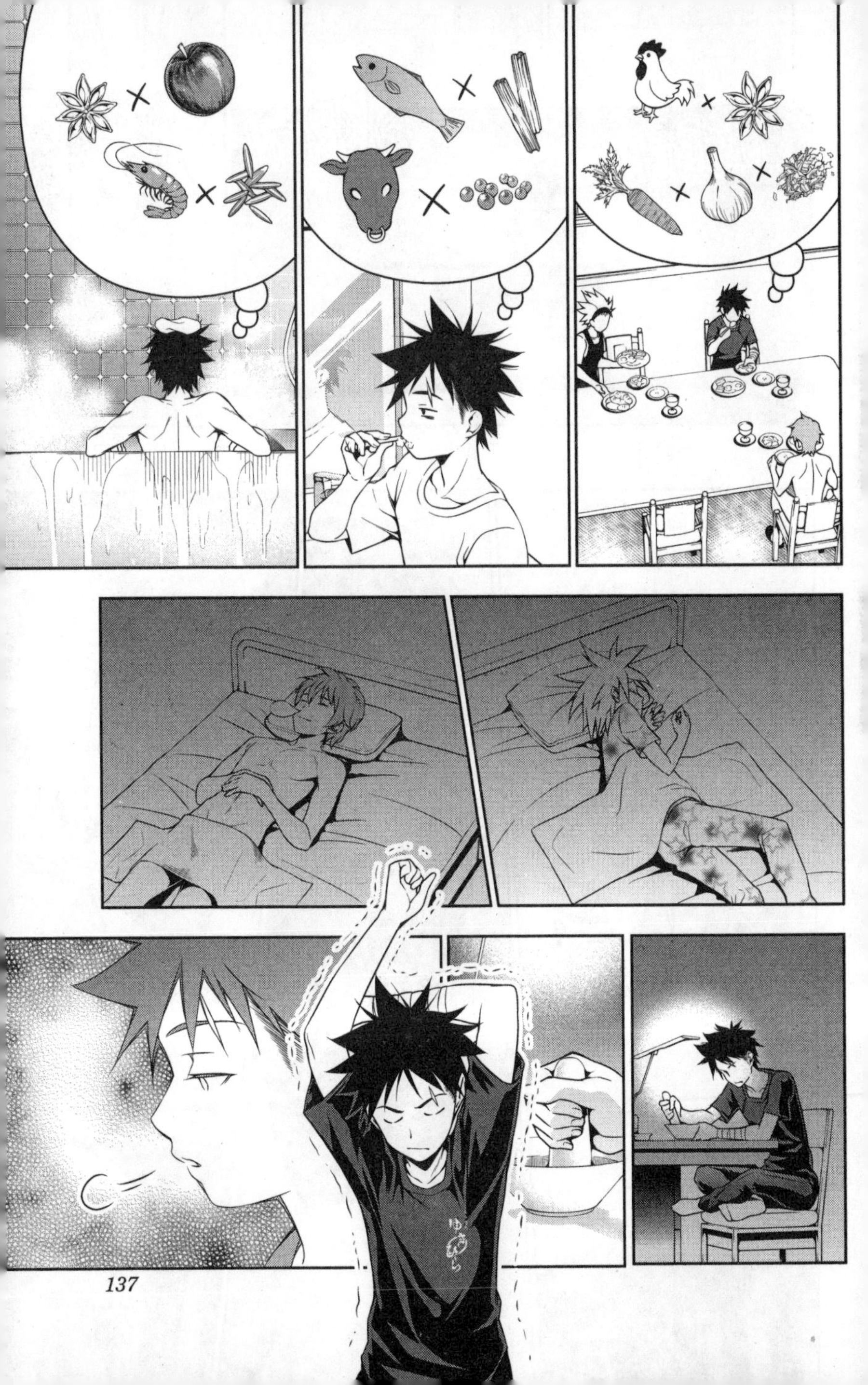

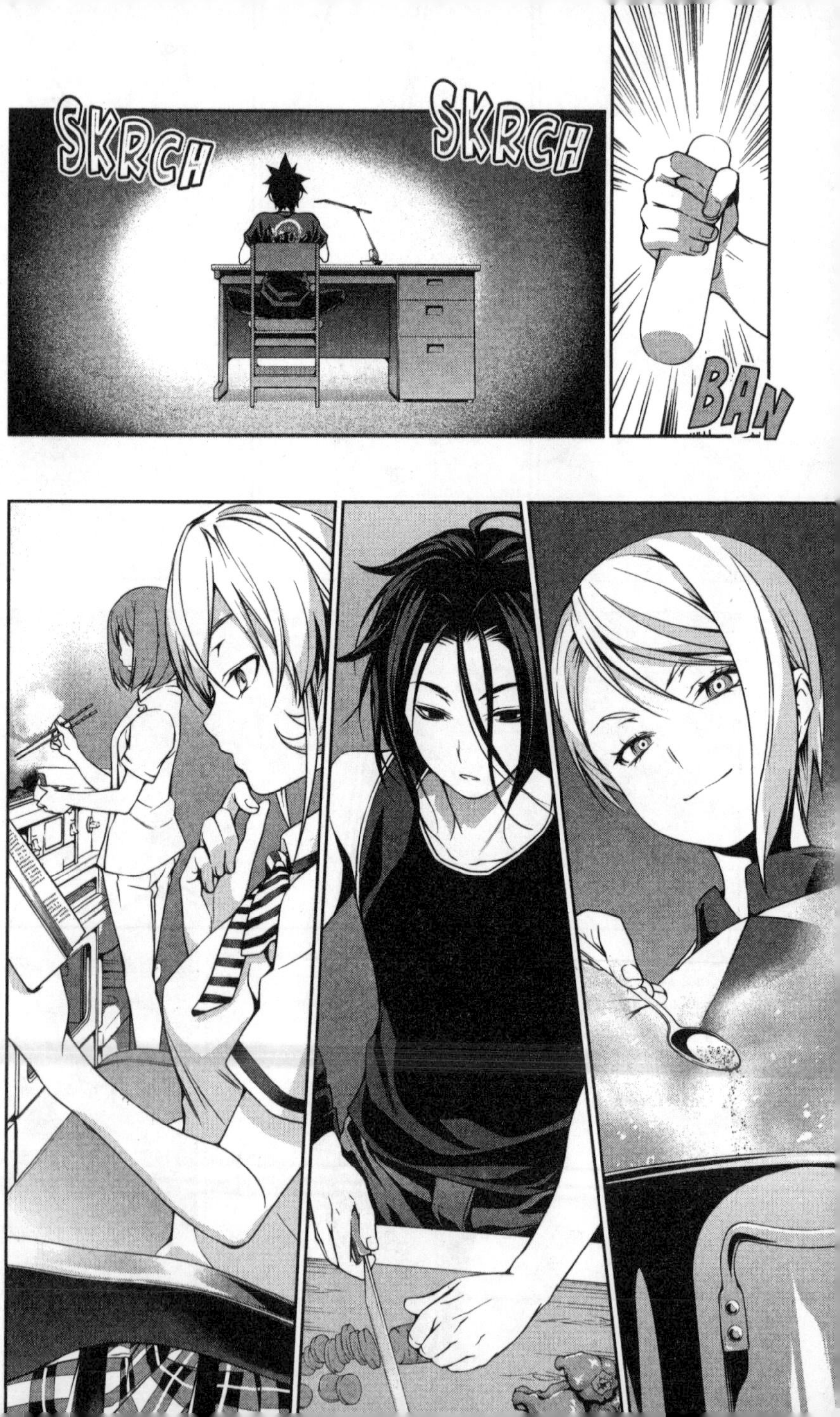
BAN
SKRCH
SKRCH

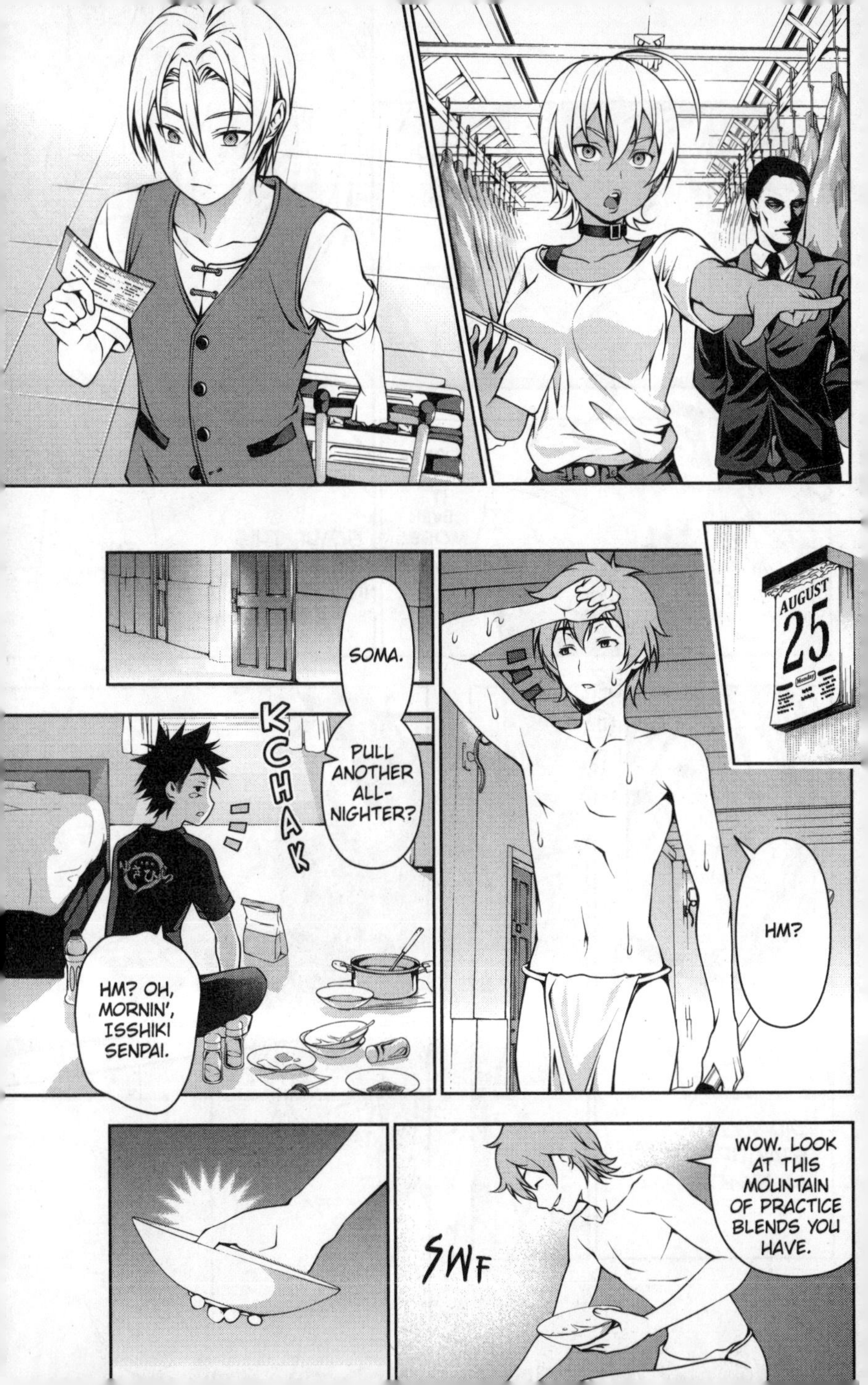
AUGUST
25
Monday
HM?
SOMA.
KCHAK
PULL ANOTHER ALL-NIGHTER?
HM? OH, MORNIN', ISSHIKI SENPAI.
WOW. LOOK AT THIS MOUNTAIN OF PRACTICE BLENDS YOU HAVE.
SWF

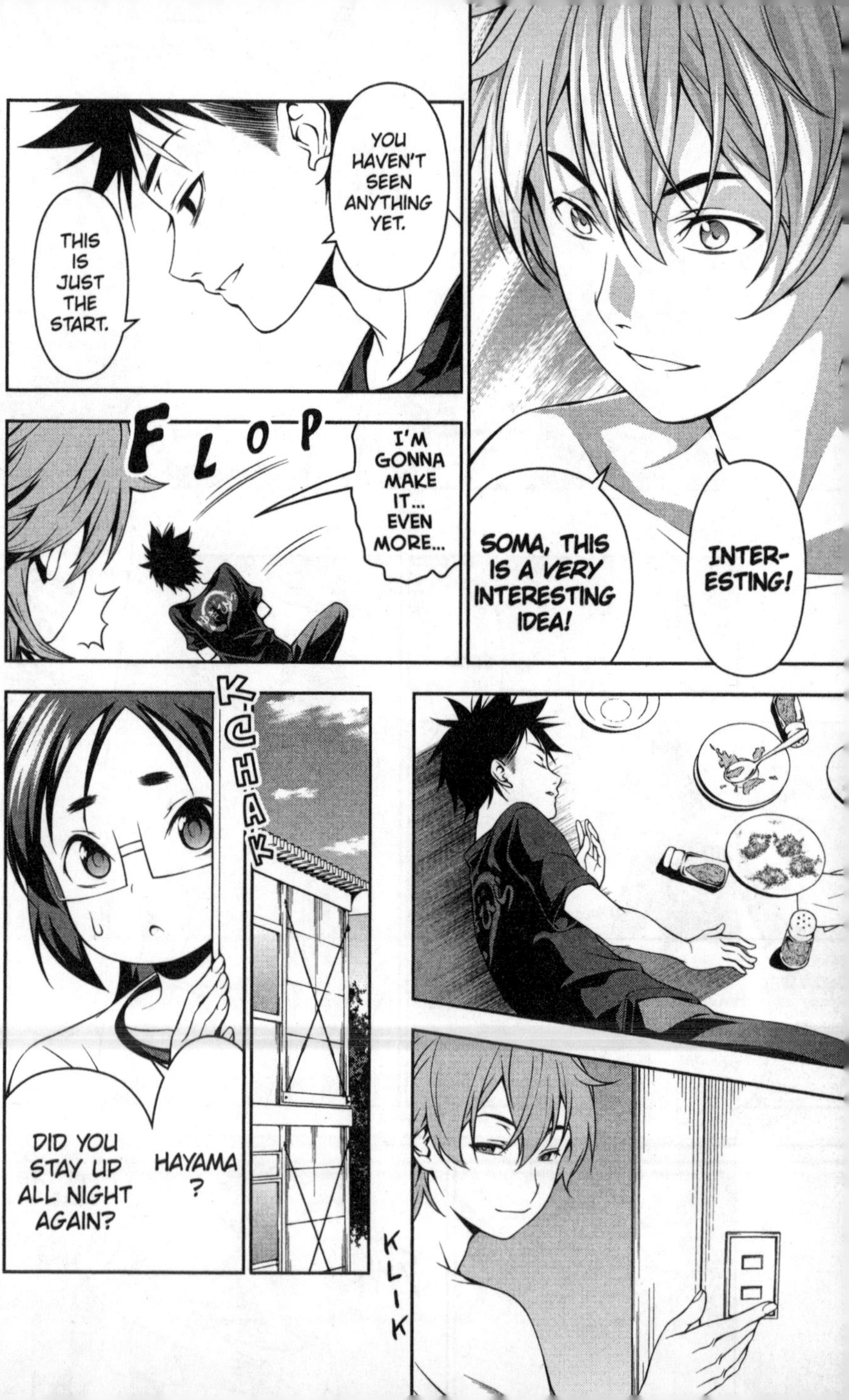
INTER-ESTING!
SOMA, THIS IS A *VERY* INTERESTING IDEA!
YOU HAVEN'T SEEN ANYTHING YET.
THIS IS JUST THE START.
I'M GONNA MAKE IT... EVEN MORE...
FLOP
KLIK
KCHAK
HAYAMA?
DID YOU STAY UP ALL NIGHT AGAIN?

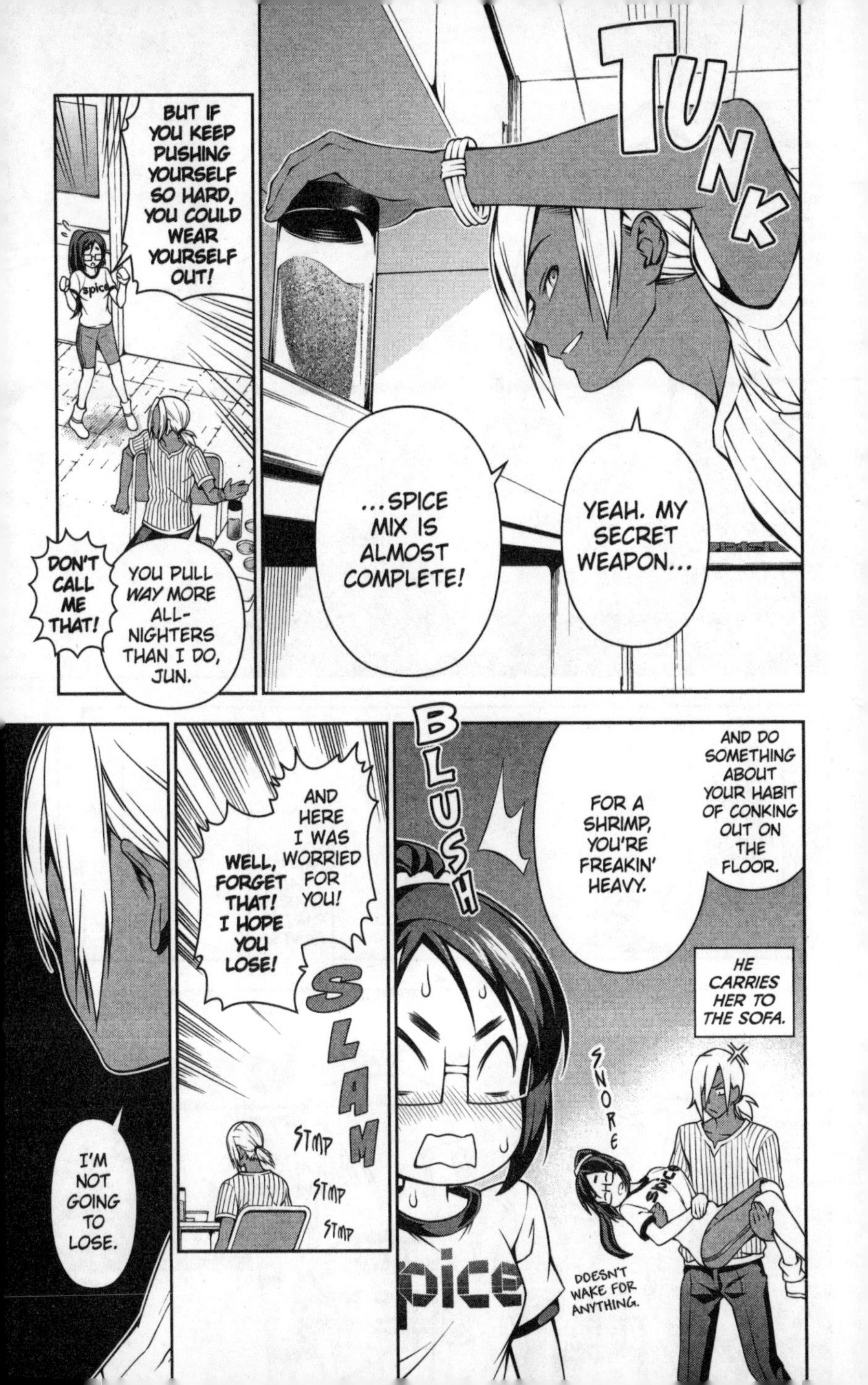
TUNK
YEAH. MY SECRET WEAPON...
...SPICE MIX IS ALMOST COMPLETE!
BUT IF YOU KEEP PUSHING YOURSELF SO HARD, YOU COULD WEAR YOURSELF OUT!
YOU PULL WAY MORE ALL-NIGHTERS THAN I DO, JUN.
DON'T CALL ME THAT!
FOR A SHRIMP, YOU'RE FREAKIN' HEAVY.
AND DO SOMETHING ABOUT YOUR HABIT OF CONKING OUT ON THE FLOOR.
HE CARRIES HER TO THE SOFA.
SNORE
DOESN'T WAKE FOR ANYTHING.
BLUSH
AND HERE I WAS WORRIED FOR YOU!
WELL, FORGET THAT! I HOPE YOU LOSE!
SLAM
STMP
STMP
STMP
I'M NOT GOING TO LOSE.

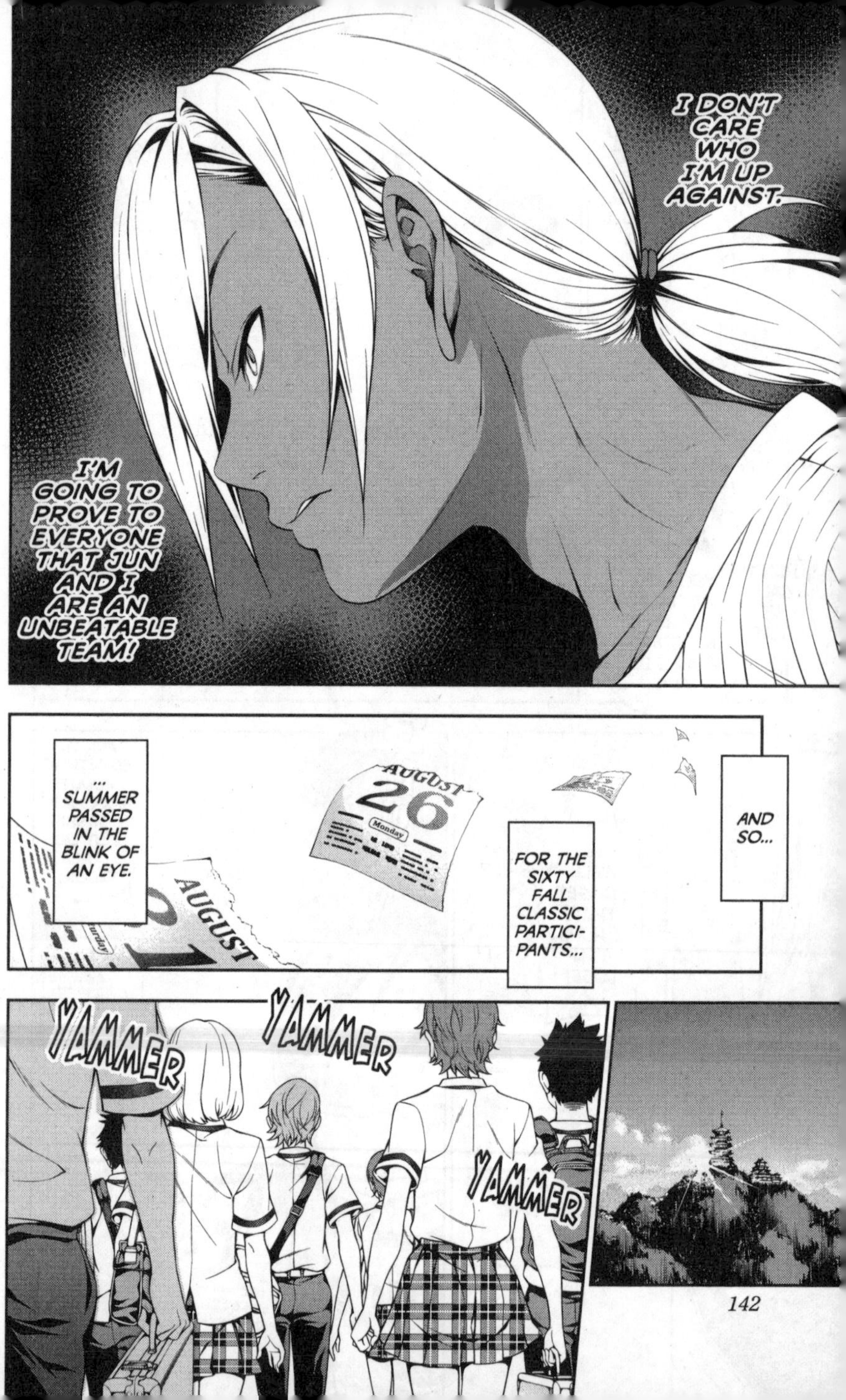
I DON'T CARE WHO I'M UP AGAINST.
I'M GOING TO PROVE TO EVERYONE THAT JUN AND I ARE AN UNBEATABLE TEAM!
AND SO...
FOR THE SIXTY FALL CLASSIC PARTICI-PANTS...
AUGUST 26 Monday
... SUMMER PASSED IN THE BLINK OF AN EYE.
AUGUST
YAMMER
YAMMER
YAMMER

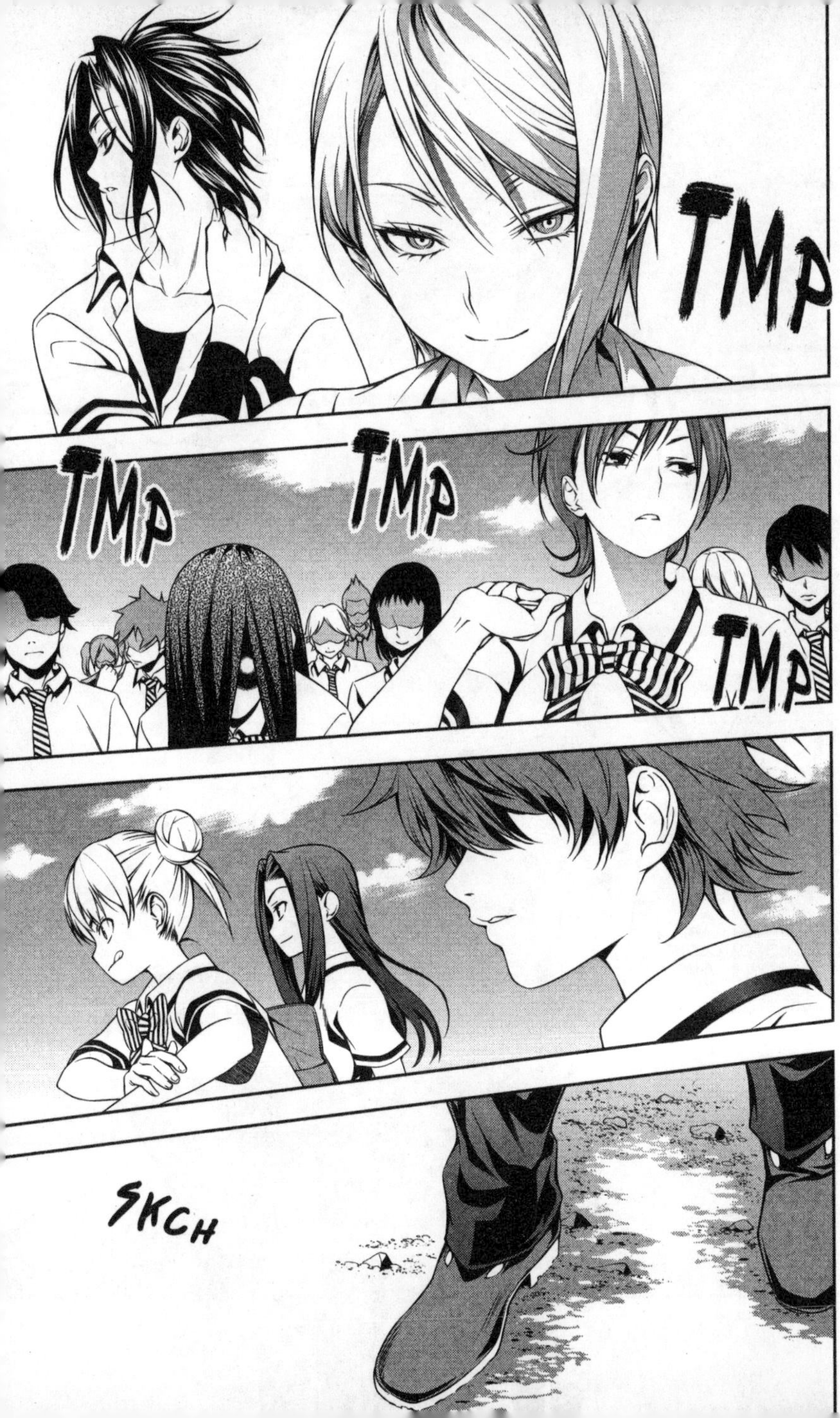
TMP
TMP
TMP
TMP
SKCH

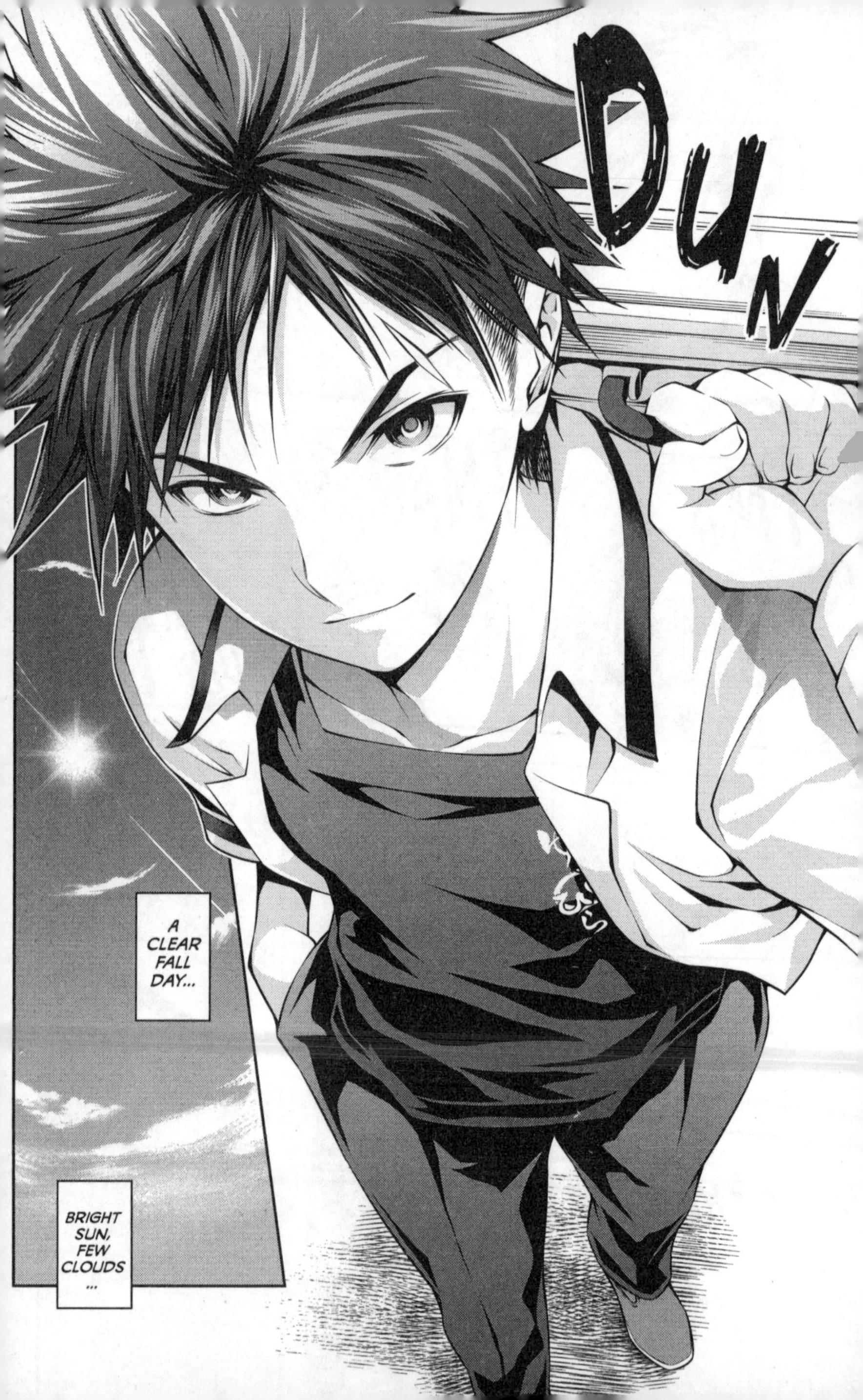
DUN
A CLEAR FALL DAY...
BRIGHT SUN, FEW CLOUDS ...

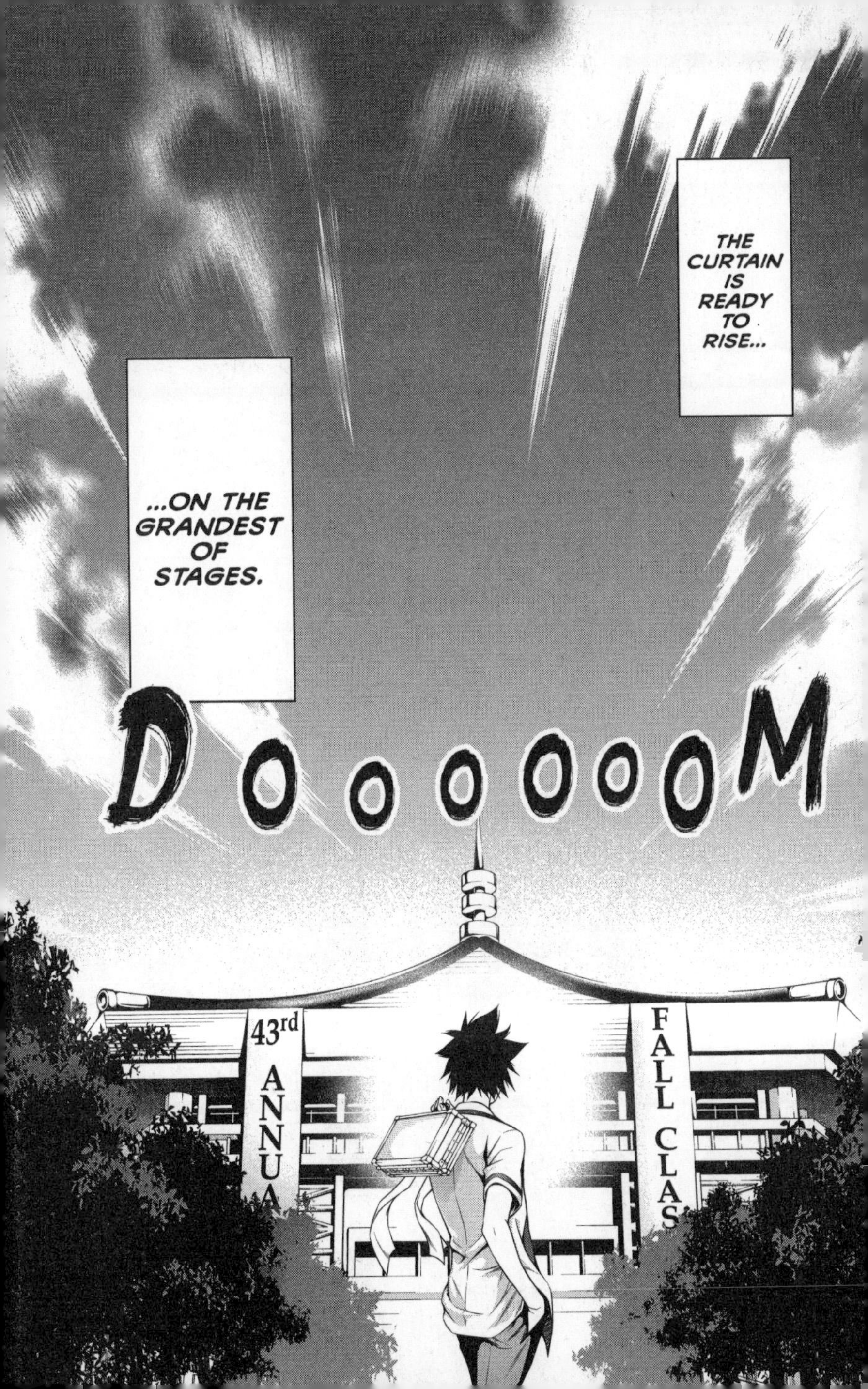
THE CURTAIN IS READY TO RISE...
...ON THE GRANDEST OF STAGES.
DOOOOOM
43rd ANNUA
FALL CLAS

SUMMER
OF
YOUTH

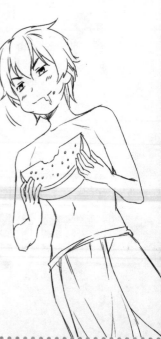

147 MEMORIES OF BATTLE

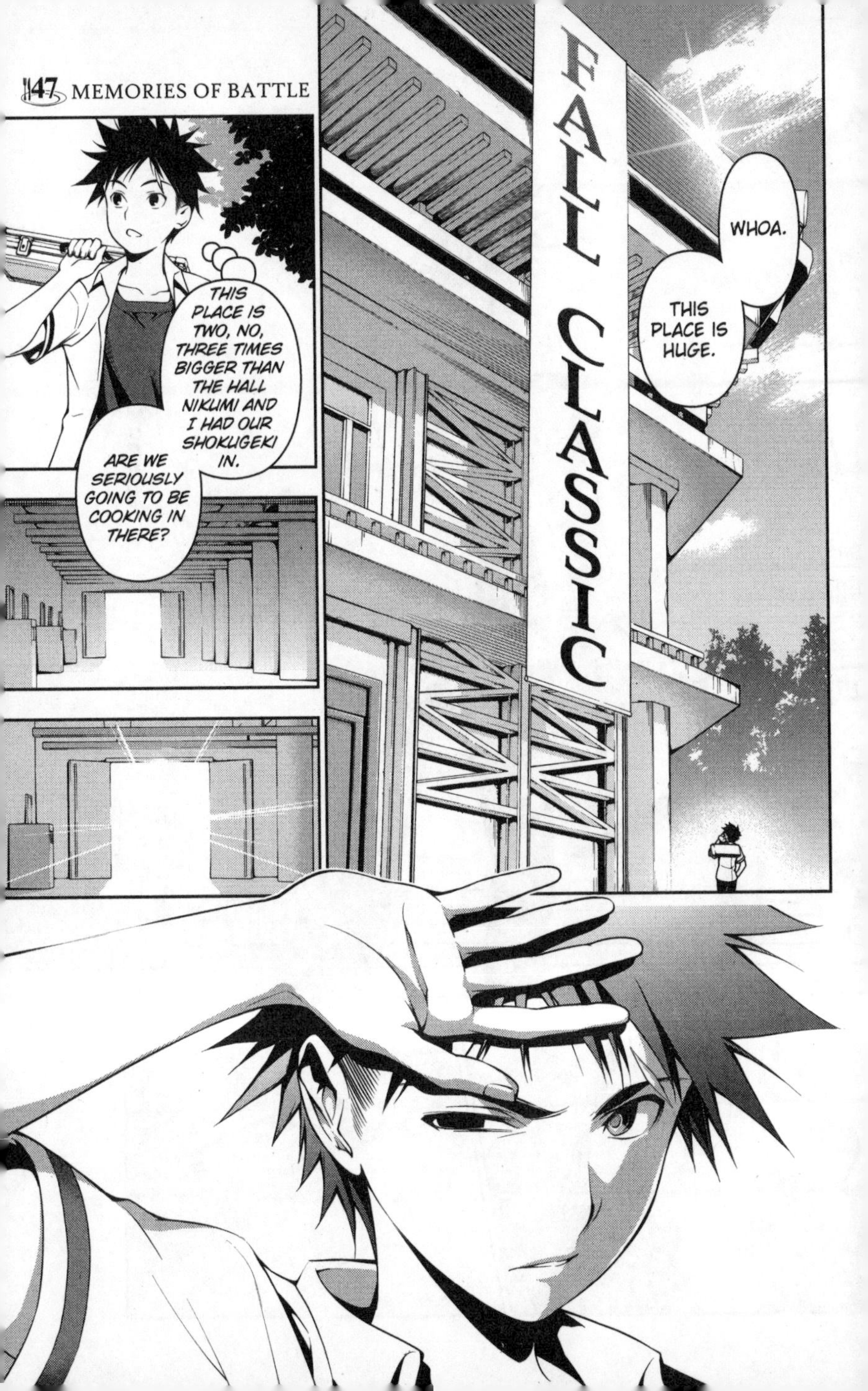
WHOA.
THIS PLACE IS HUGE.
FALL CLASSIC
THIS PLACE IS TWO, NO, THREE TIMES BIGGER THAN THE HALL NIKUMI AND I HAD OUR SHOKUGEKI IN.
ARE WE SERIOUSLY GOING TO BE COOKING IN THERE?

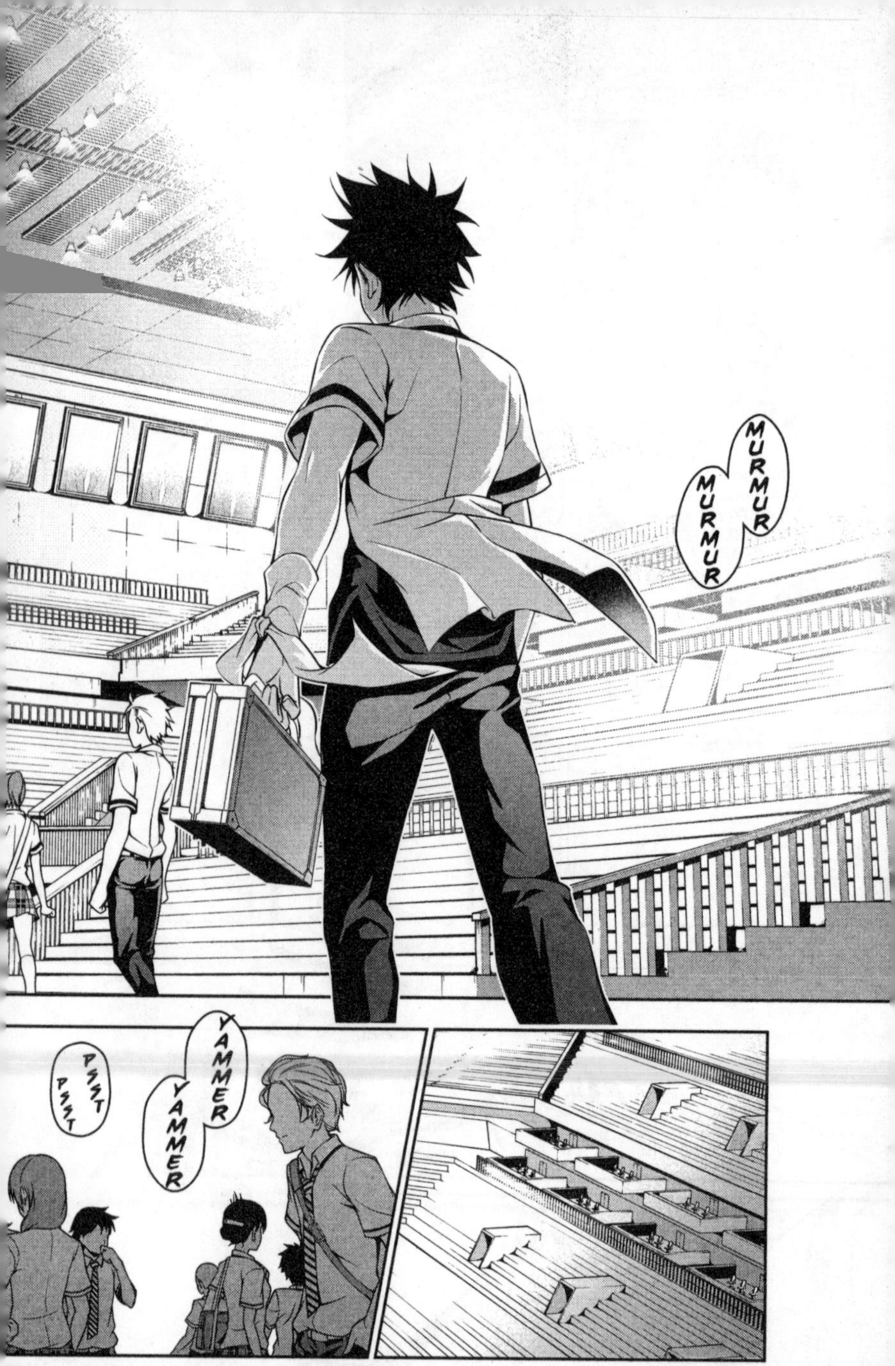
MURMUR
MURMUR
YAMMER
YAMMER
PSST
PSST

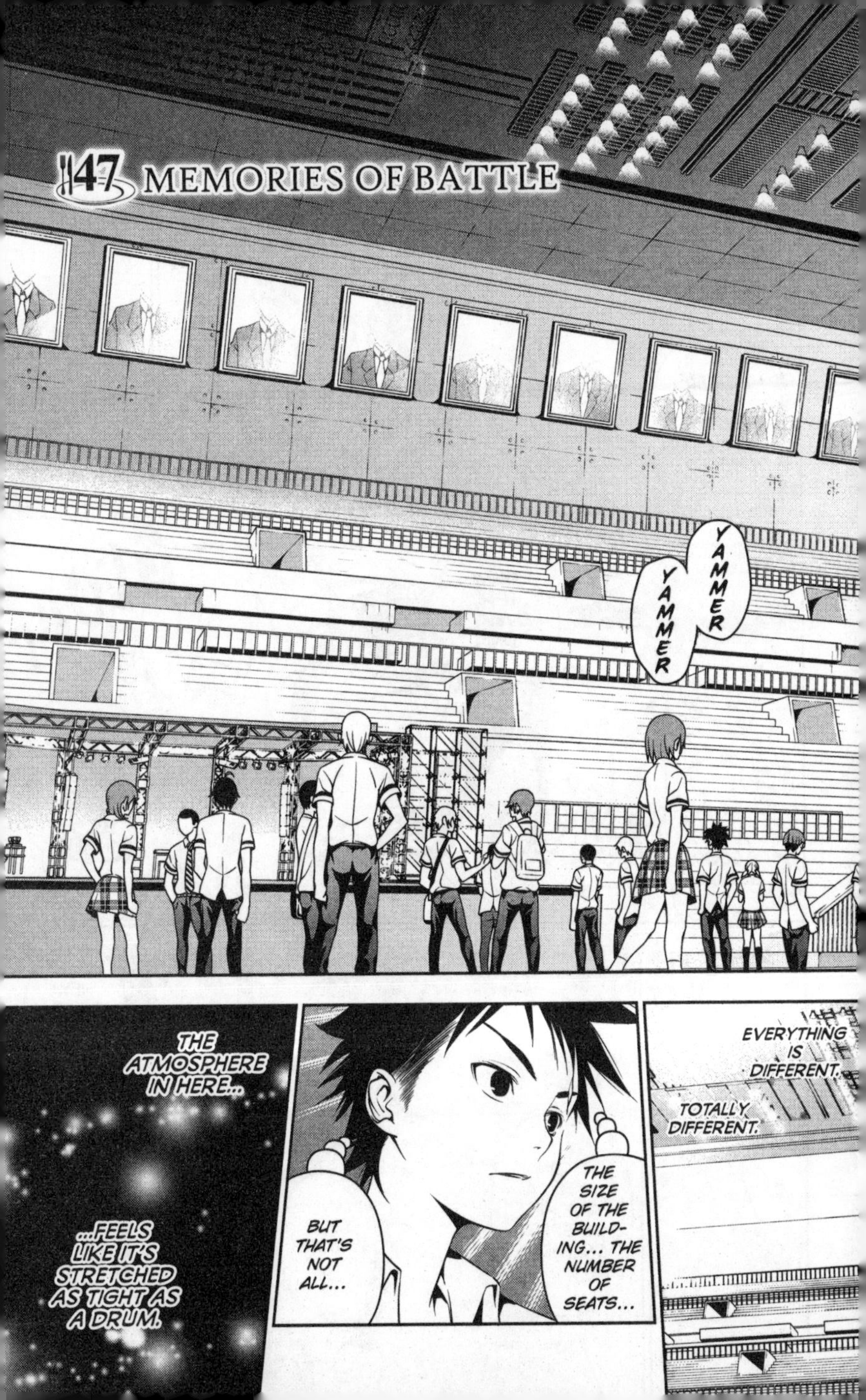
47 MEMORIES OF BATTLE
YAMMER YAMMER
EVERYTHING IS DIFFERENT.
TOTALLY DIFFERENT.
THE SIZE OF THE BUILDING... THE NUMBER OF SEATS...
BUT THAT'S NOT ALL...
THE ATMOSPHERE IN HERE...
...FEELS LIKE IT'S STRETCHED AS TIGHT AS A DRUM.

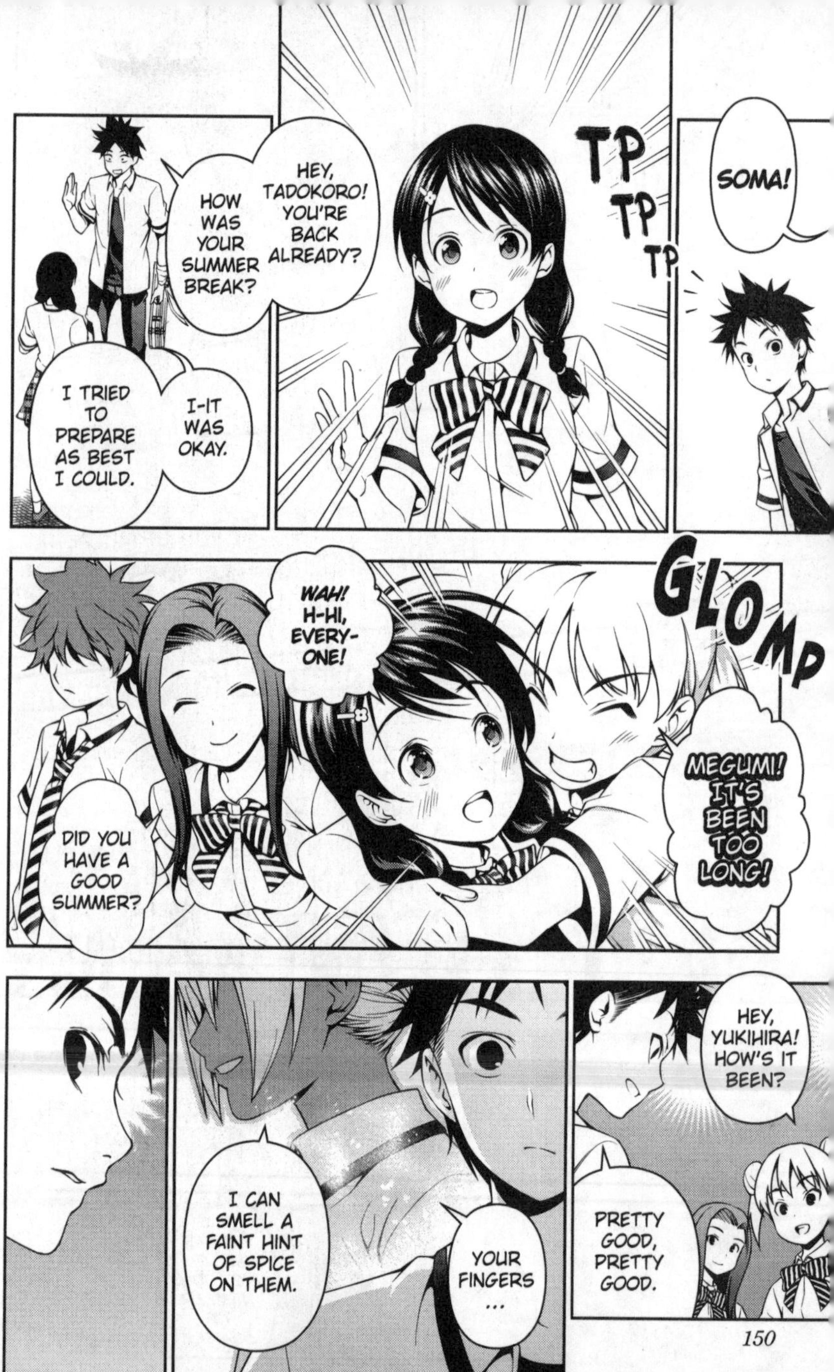
SOMA!
TP TP TP
HEY, TADOKORO! YOU'RE BACK ALREADY?
HOW WAS YOUR SUMMER BREAK?
I-IT WAS OKAY.
I TRIED TO PREPARE AS BEST I COULD.
GLOMP
MEGUMI! IT'S BEEN TOO LONG!
WAH! H-HI, EVERYONE!
DID YOU HAVE A GOOD SUMMER?
HEY, YUKIHIRA! HOW'S IT BEEN?
PRETTY GOOD, PRETTY GOOD.
YOUR FINGERS...
I CAN SMELL A FAINT HINT OF SPICE ON THEM.

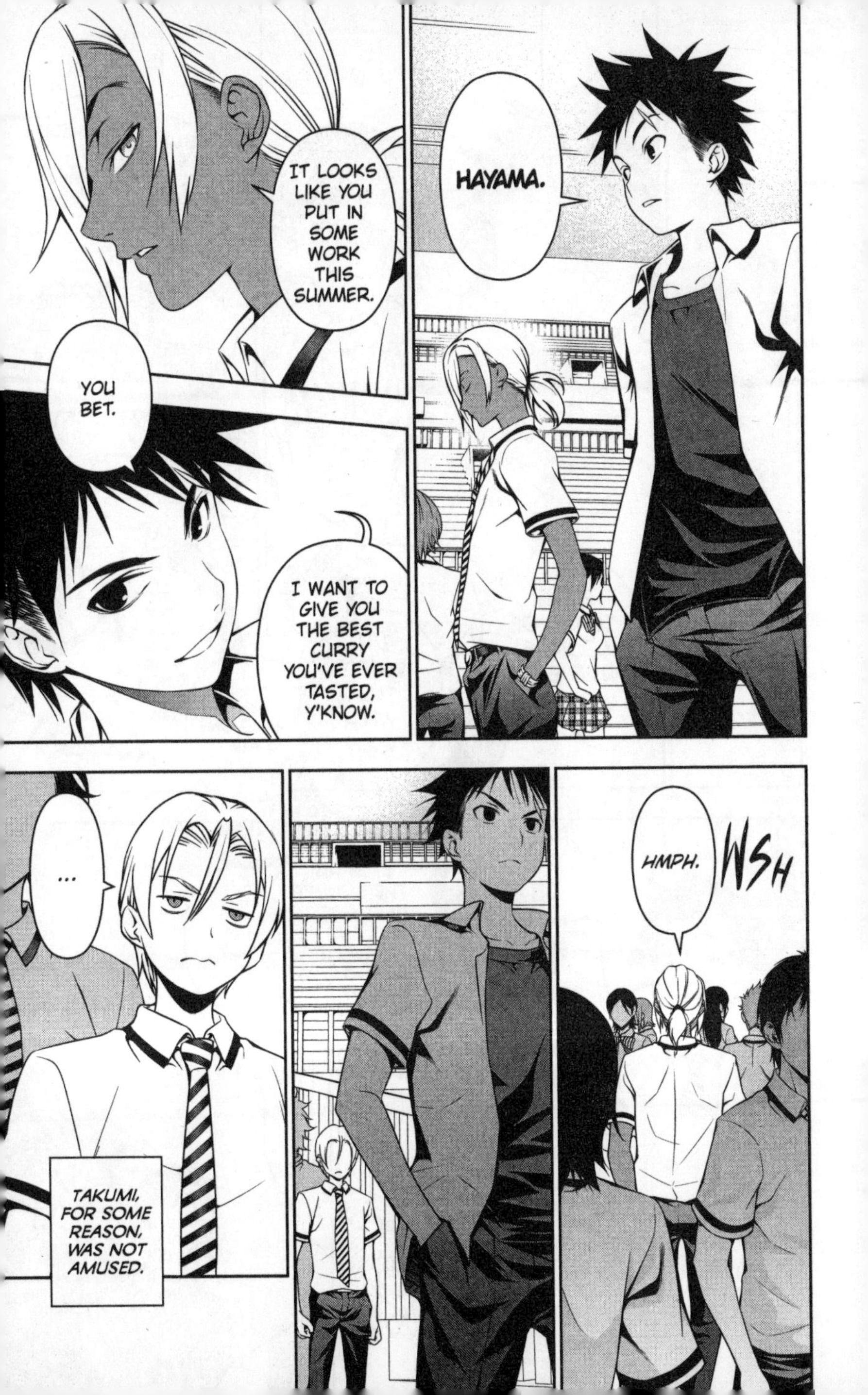
HAYAMA.
IT LOOKS LIKE YOU PUT IN SOME WORK THIS SUMMER.
YOU BET.
I WANT TO GIVE YOU THE BEST CURRY YOU'VE EVER TASTED, Y'KNOW.
HMPH.
WSH
...
TAKUMI, FOR SOME REASON, WAS NOT AMUSED.

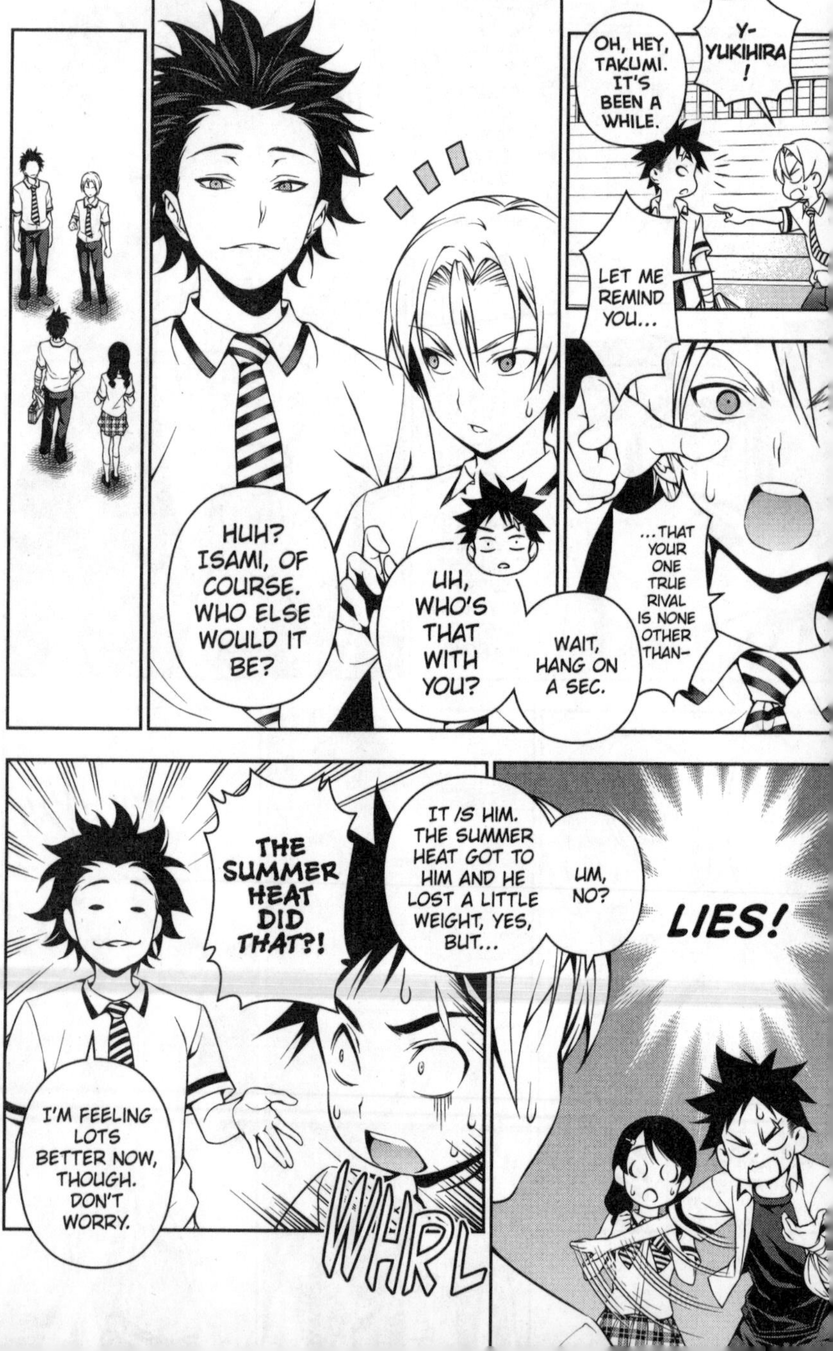
Y-YUKIHIRA!
OH, HEY, TAKUMI. IT'S BEEN A WHILE.
LET ME REMIND YOU...
...THAT YOUR ONE TRUE RIVAL IS NONE OTHER THAN-
UH, WHO'S THAT WITH YOU?
WAIT, HANG ON A SEC.
HUH? ISAMI, OF COURSE. WHO ELSE WOULD IT BE?
IT *IS* HIM. THE SUMMER HEAT GOT TO HIM AND HE LOST A LITTLE WEIGHT, YES, BUT...
UM, NO?
LIES!
THE SUMMER HEAT DID *THAT*?!
I'M FEELING LOTS BETTER NOW, THOUGH. DON'T WORRY.
WHRL

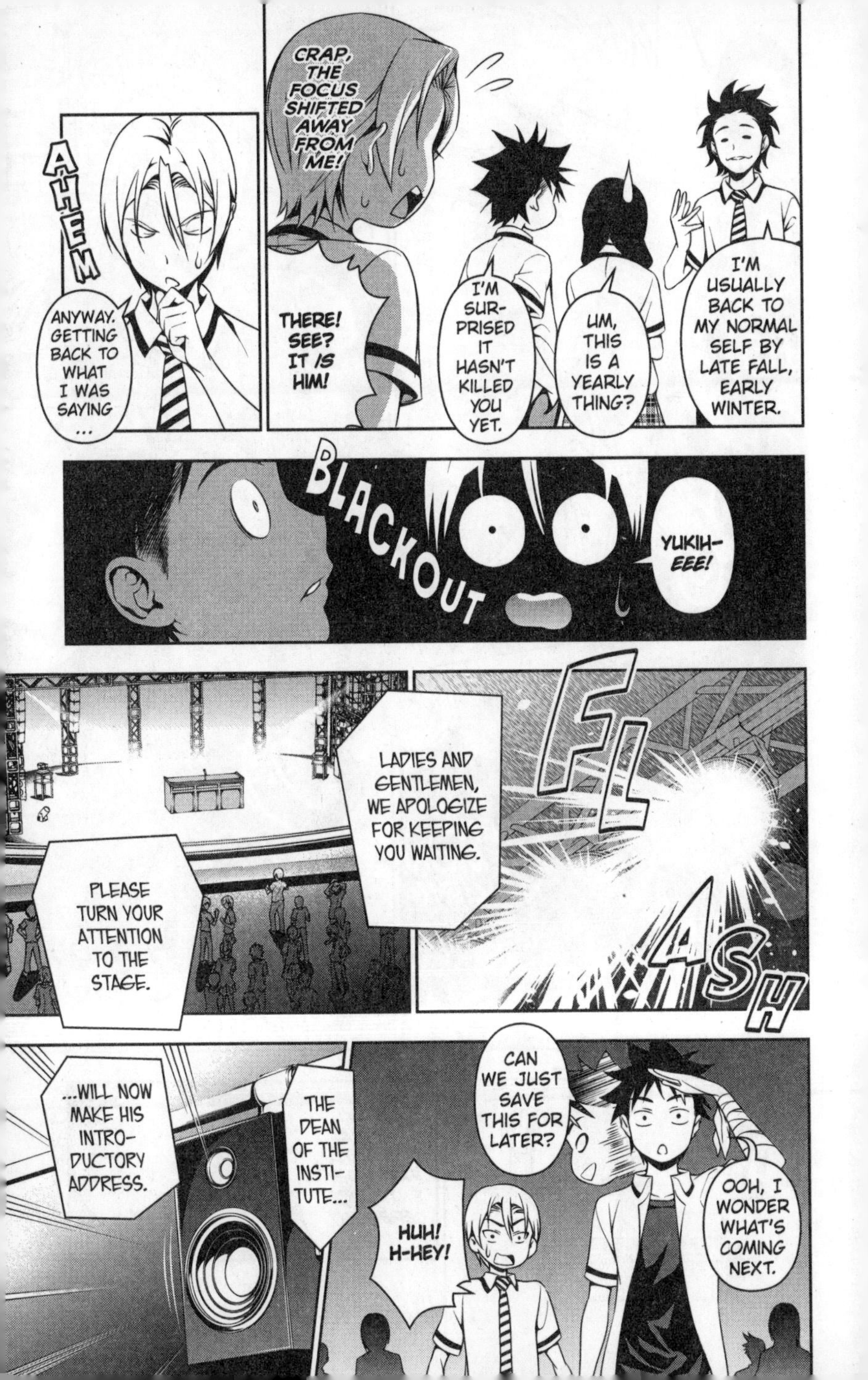
I'M USUALLY BACK TO MY NORMAL SELF BY LATE FALL, EARLY WINTER.
UM, THIS IS A YEARLY THING?
I'M SUR-PRISED IT HASN'T KILLED YOU YET.
THERE! SEE? IT *IS* HIM!
CRAP, THE FOCUS SHIFTED AWAY FROM ME!
AHEM
ANYWAY. GETTING BACK TO WHAT I WAS SAYING...
BLACKOUT
YUKIH-EEE!
FLASH
LADIES AND GENTLEMEN, WE APOLOGIZE FOR KEEPING YOU WAITING.
PLEASE TURN YOUR ATTENTION TO THE STAGE.
CAN WE JUST SAVE THIS FOR LATER?
OOH, I WONDER WHAT'S COMING NEXT.
HUH! H-HEY!
THE DEAN OF THE INSTI-TUTE...
...WILL NOW MAKE HIS INTRO-DUCTORY ADDRESS.

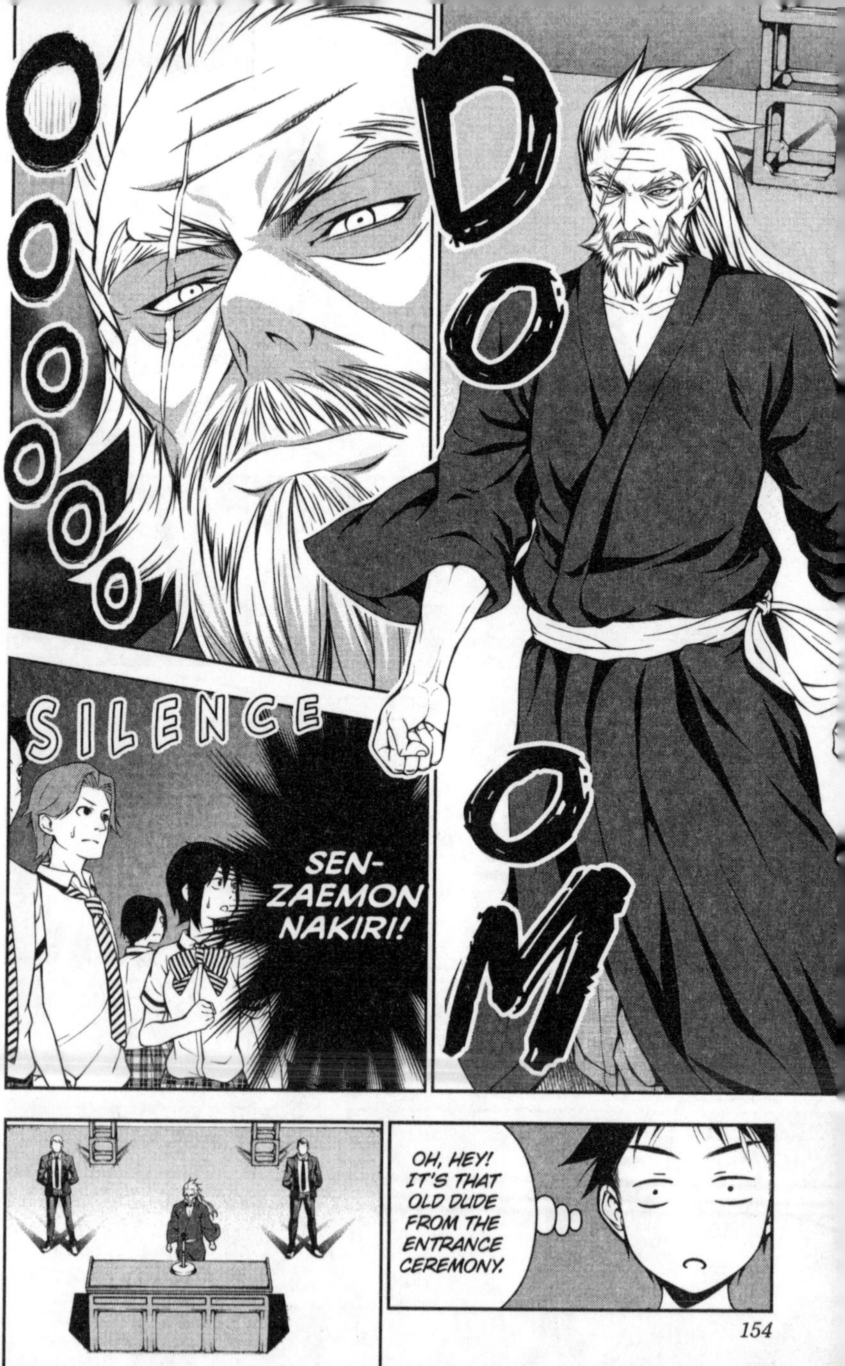
DOOM
OOOOOOO
SILENCE
SEN-ZAEMON NAKIRI!
OH, HEY! IT'S THAT OLD DUDE FROM THE ENTRANCE CEREMONY.

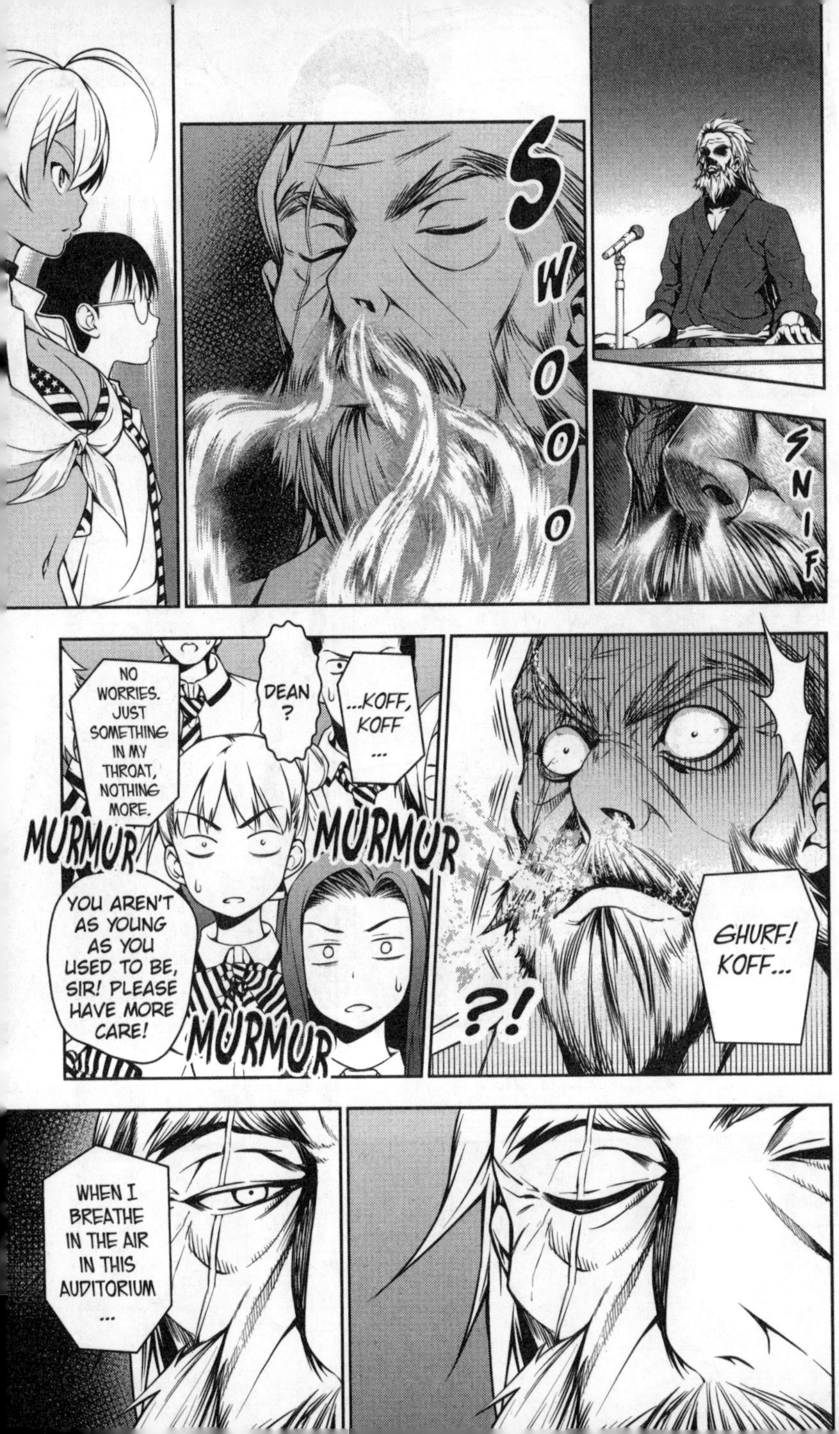
SNIF
SWOOOO
GHURF! KOFF...
?!
DEAN?
...KOFF, KOFF ...
NO WORRIES. JUST SOMETHING IN MY THROAT, NOTHING MORE.
MURMUR
MURMUR
YOU AREN'T AS YOUNG AS YOU USED TO BE, SIR! PLEASE HAVE MORE CARE!
MURMUR
WHEN I BREATHE IN THE AIR IN THIS AUDITORIUM ...

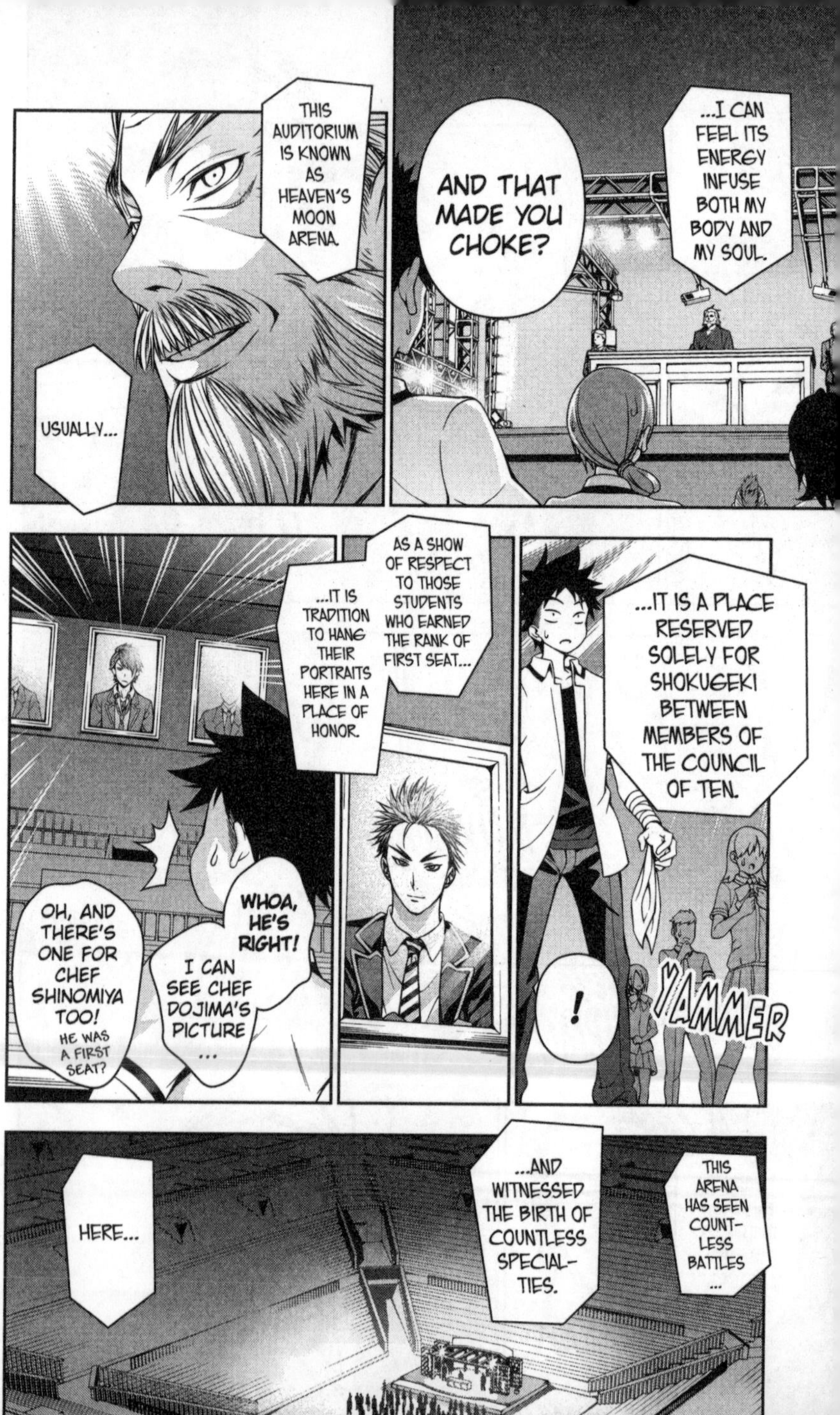
...I CAN FEEL ITS ENERGY INFUSE BOTH MY BODY AND MY SOUL.
AND THAT MADE YOU CHOKE?
THIS AUDITORIUM IS KNOWN AS HEAVEN'S MOON ARENA.
USUALLY...
...IT IS A PLACE RESERVED SOLELY FOR SHOKUGEKI BETWEEN MEMBERS OF THE COUNCIL OF TEN.
!
YAMMER
AS A SHOW OF RESPECT TO THOSE STUDENTS WHO EARNED THE RANK OF FIRST SEAT...
...IT IS TRADITION TO HANG THEIR PORTRAITS HERE IN A PLACE OF HONOR.
WHOA, HE'S RIGHT!
I CAN SEE CHEF DOJIMA'S PICTURE...
OH, AND THERE'S ONE FOR CHEF SHINOMIYA TOO!
HE WAS A FIRST SEAT?
THIS ARENA HAS SEEN COUNTLESS BATTLES...
...AND WITNESSED THE BIRTH OF COUNTLESS SPECIALTIES.
HERE...

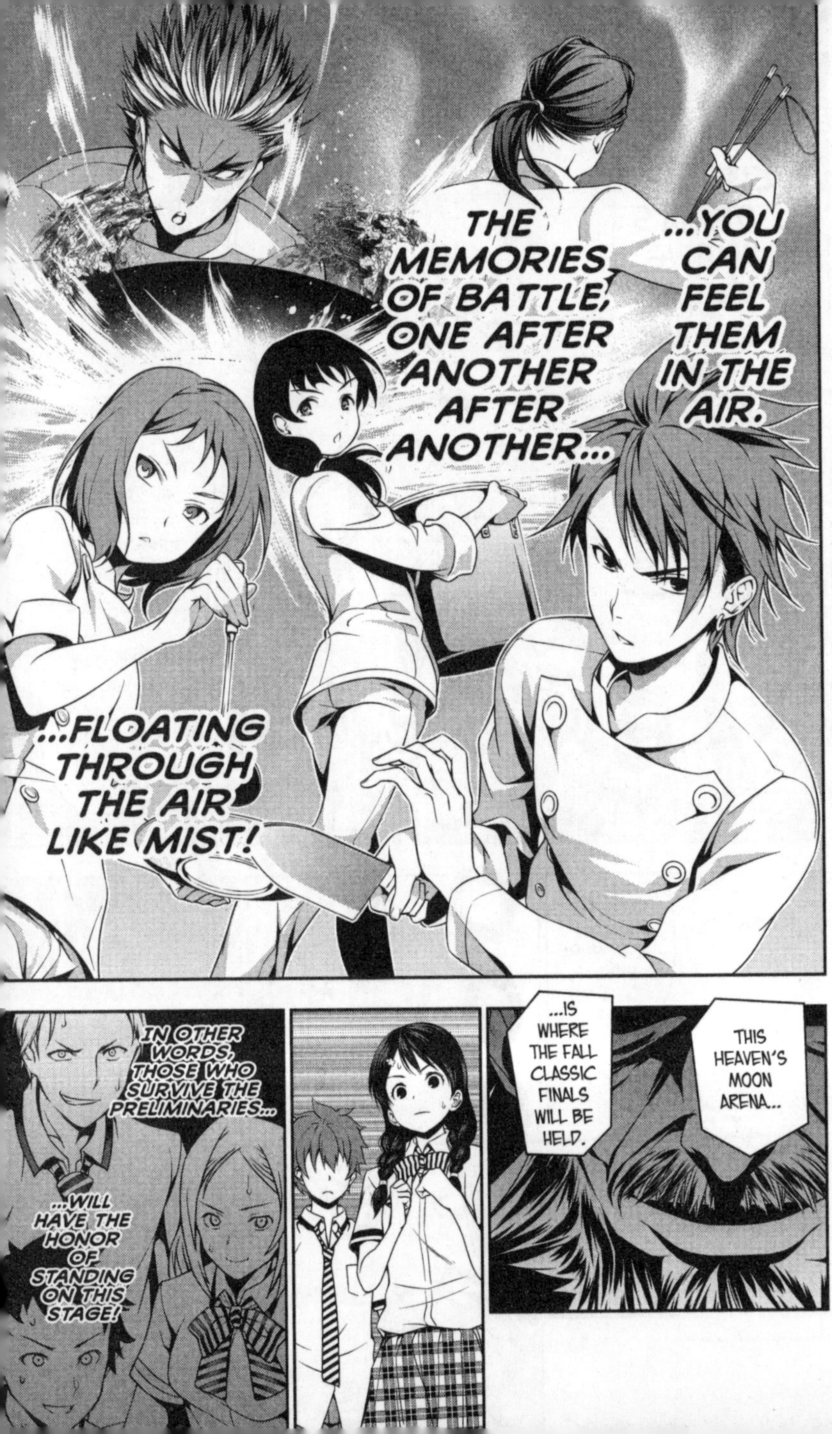
THE MEMORIES OF BATTLE, ONE AFTER ANOTHER AFTER ANOTHER...
...YOU CAN FEEL THEM IN THE AIR.
...FLOATING THROUGH THE AIR LIKE MIST!
THIS HEAVEN'S MOON ARENA...
...IS WHERE THE FALL CLASSIC FINALS WILL BE HELD.
IN OTHER WORDS, THOSE WHO SURVIVE THE PRELIMINARIES...
...WILL HAVE THE HONOR OF STANDING ON THIS STAGE!

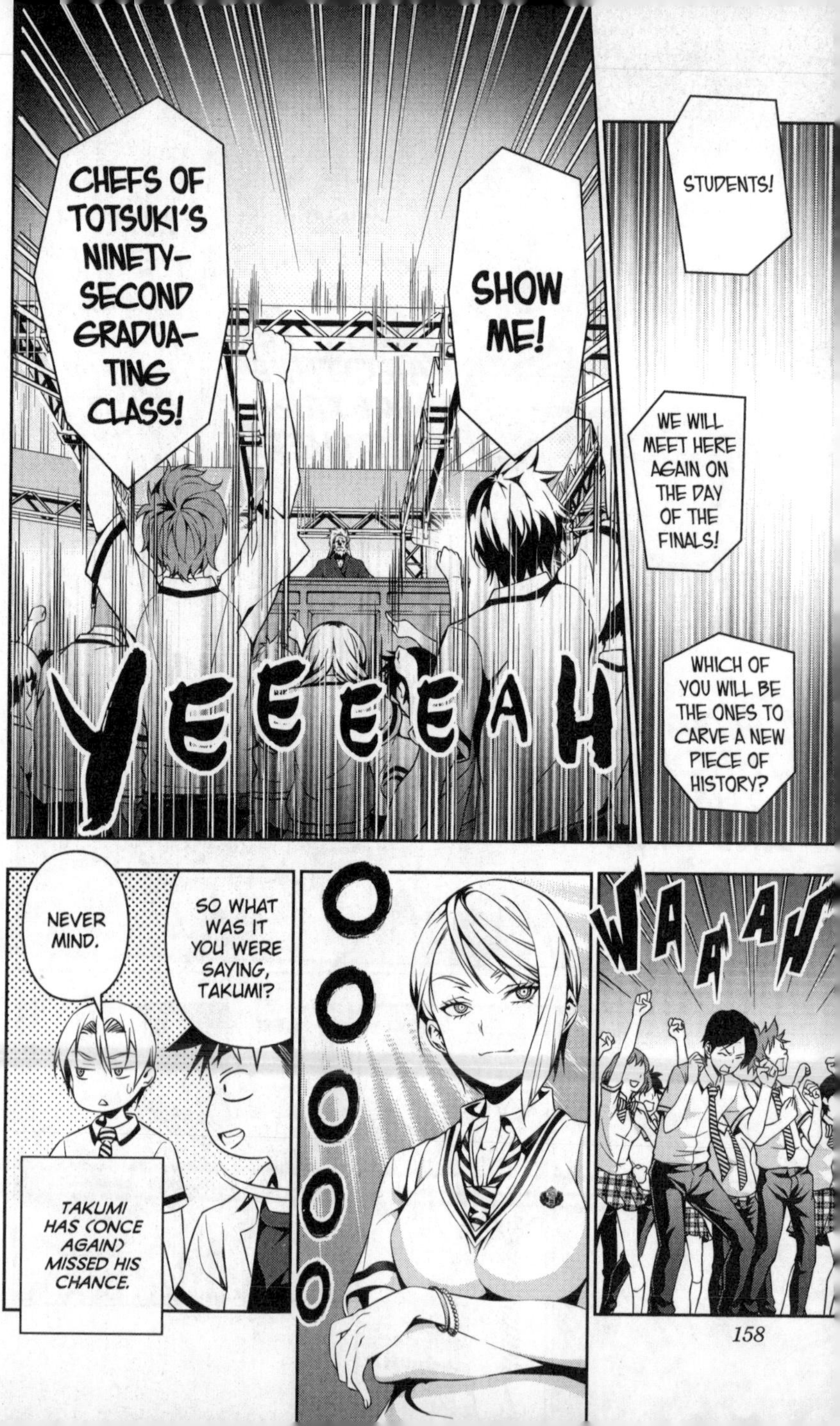
STUDENTS!
WE WILL MEET HERE AGAIN ON THE DAY OF THE FINALS!
WHICH OF YOU WILL BE THE ONES TO CARVE A NEW PIECE OF HISTORY?
CHEFS OF TOTSUKI'S NINETY-SECOND GRADUATING CLASS!
SHOW ME!
YEEEEAH
WAAAH
OOOOOO
SO WHAT WAS IT YOU WERE SAYING, TAKUMI?
NEVER MIND.
TAKUMI HAS (ONCE AGAIN) MISSED HIS CHANCE.

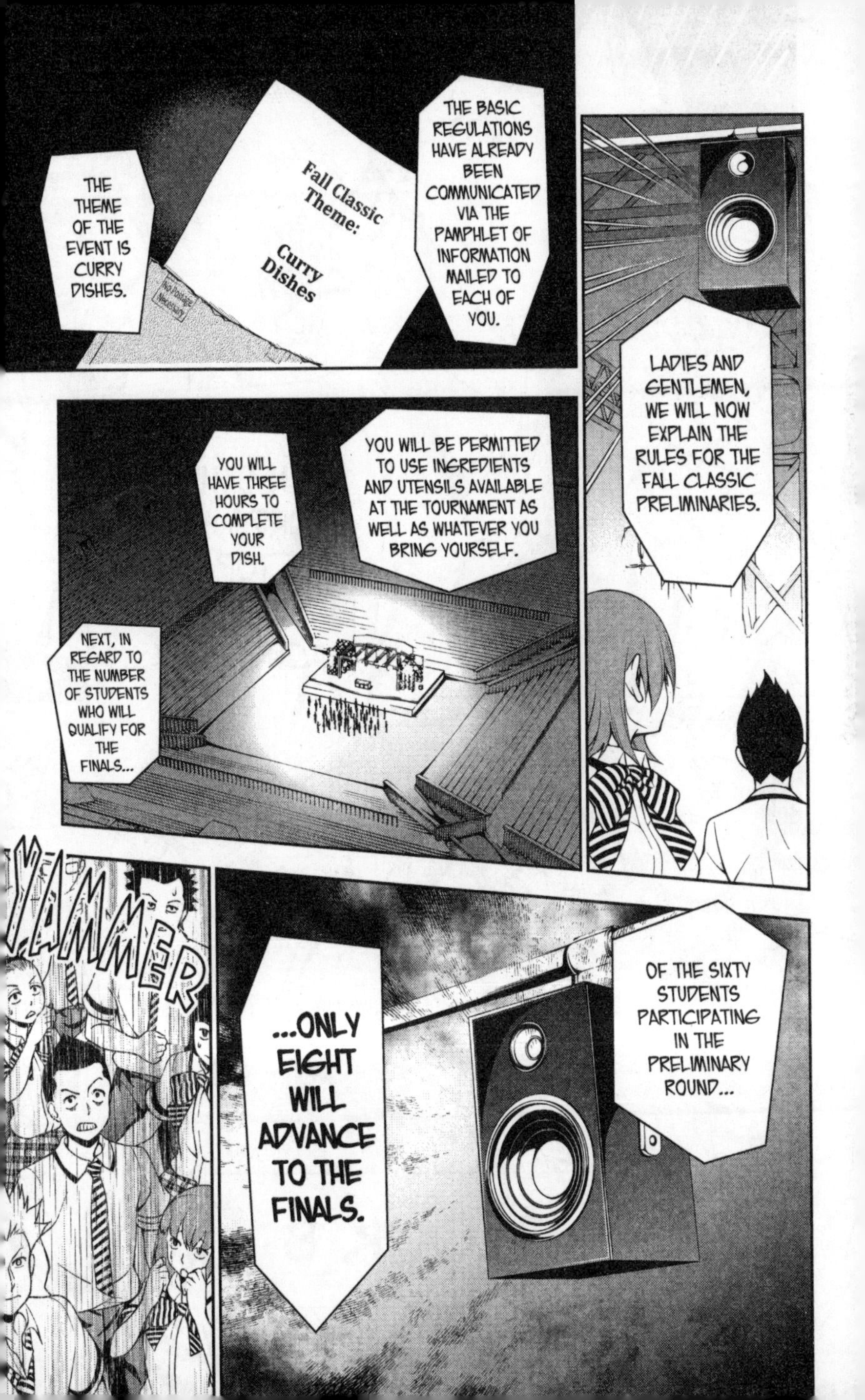
LADIES AND GENTLEMEN, WE WILL NOW EXPLAIN THE RULES FOR THE FALL CLASSIC PRELIMINARIES.
THE BASIC REGULATIONS HAVE ALREADY BEEN COMMUNICATED VIA THE PAMPHLET OF INFORMATION MAILED TO EACH OF YOU.
Fall Classic Theme:
Curry Dishes
THE THEME OF THE EVENT IS CURRY DISHES.
YOU WILL BE PERMITTED TO USE INGREDIENTS AND UTENSILS AVAILABLE AT THE TOURNAMENT AS WELL AS WHATEVER YOU BRING YOURSELF.
YOU WILL HAVE THREE HOURS TO COMPLETE YOUR DISH.
NEXT, IN REGARD TO THE NUMBER OF STUDENTS WHO WILL QUALIFY FOR THE FINALS...
OF THE SIXTY STUDENTS PARTICIPATING IN THE PRELIMINARY ROUND...
...ONLY EIGHT WILL ADVANCE TO THE FINALS.
YAMMER

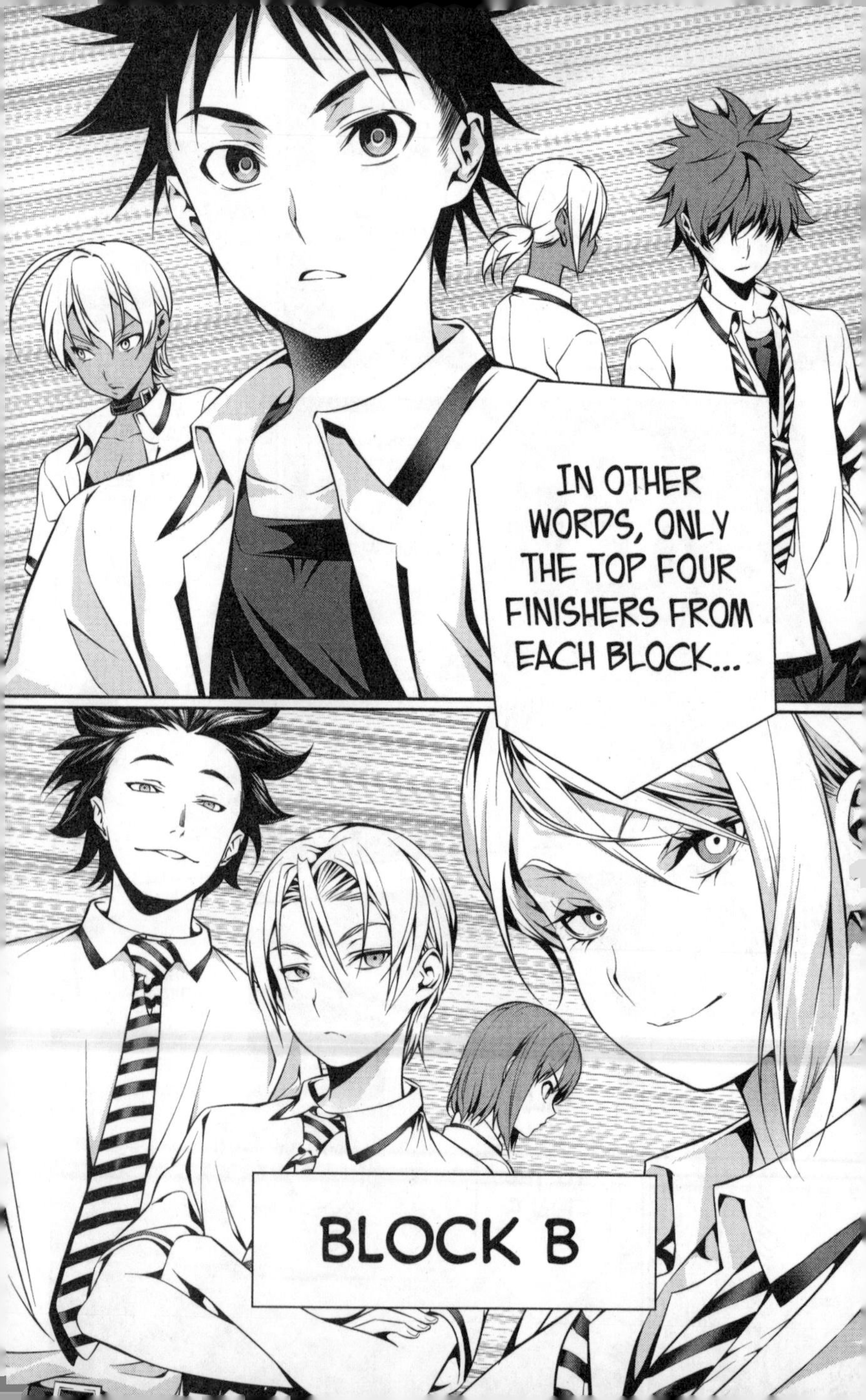
IN OTHER WORDS, ONLY THE TOP FOUR FINISHERS FROM EACH BLOCK...
BLOCK B

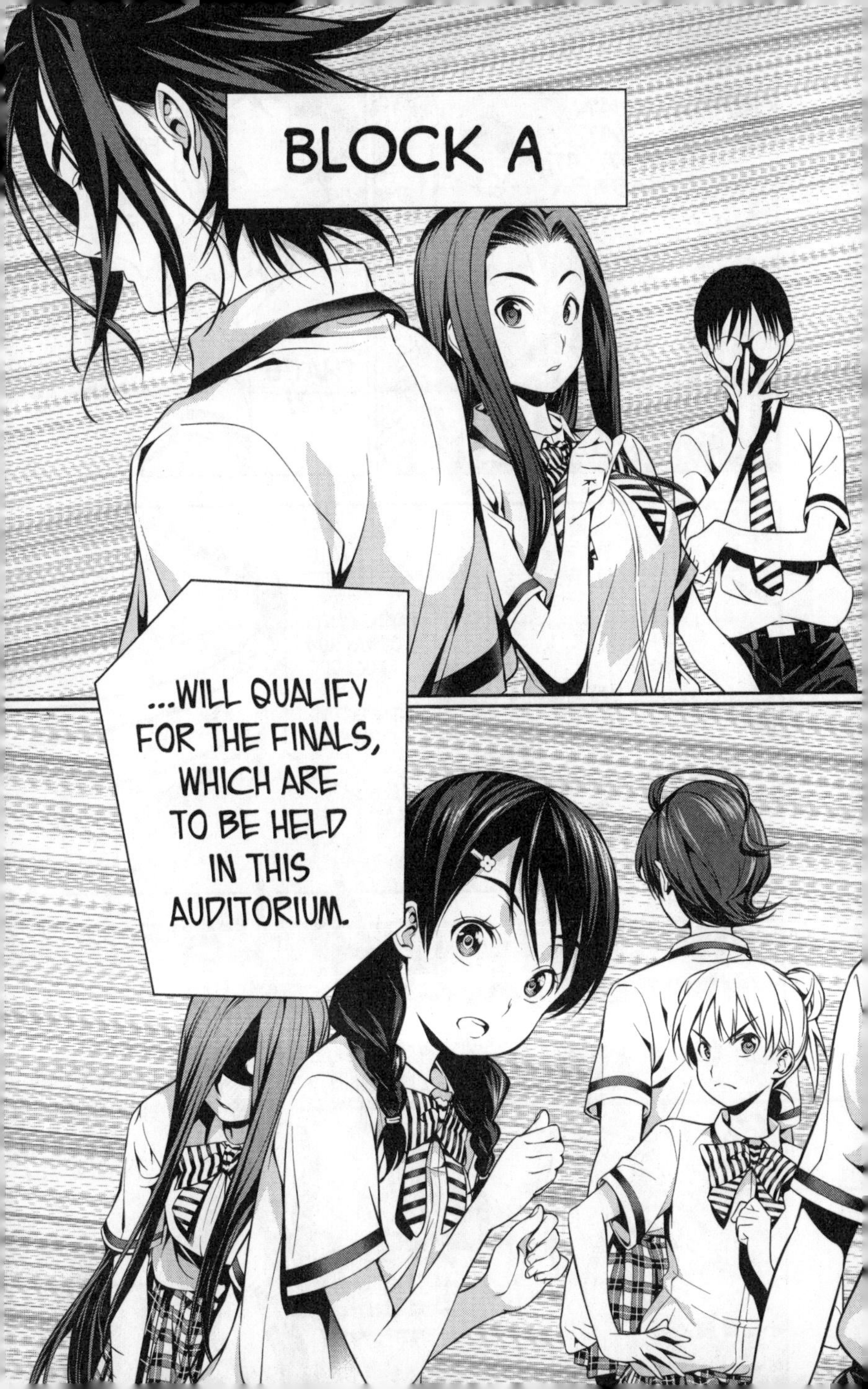
BLOCK A
...WILL QUALIFY FOR THE FINALS, WHICH ARE TO BE HELD IN THIS AUDITORIUM.

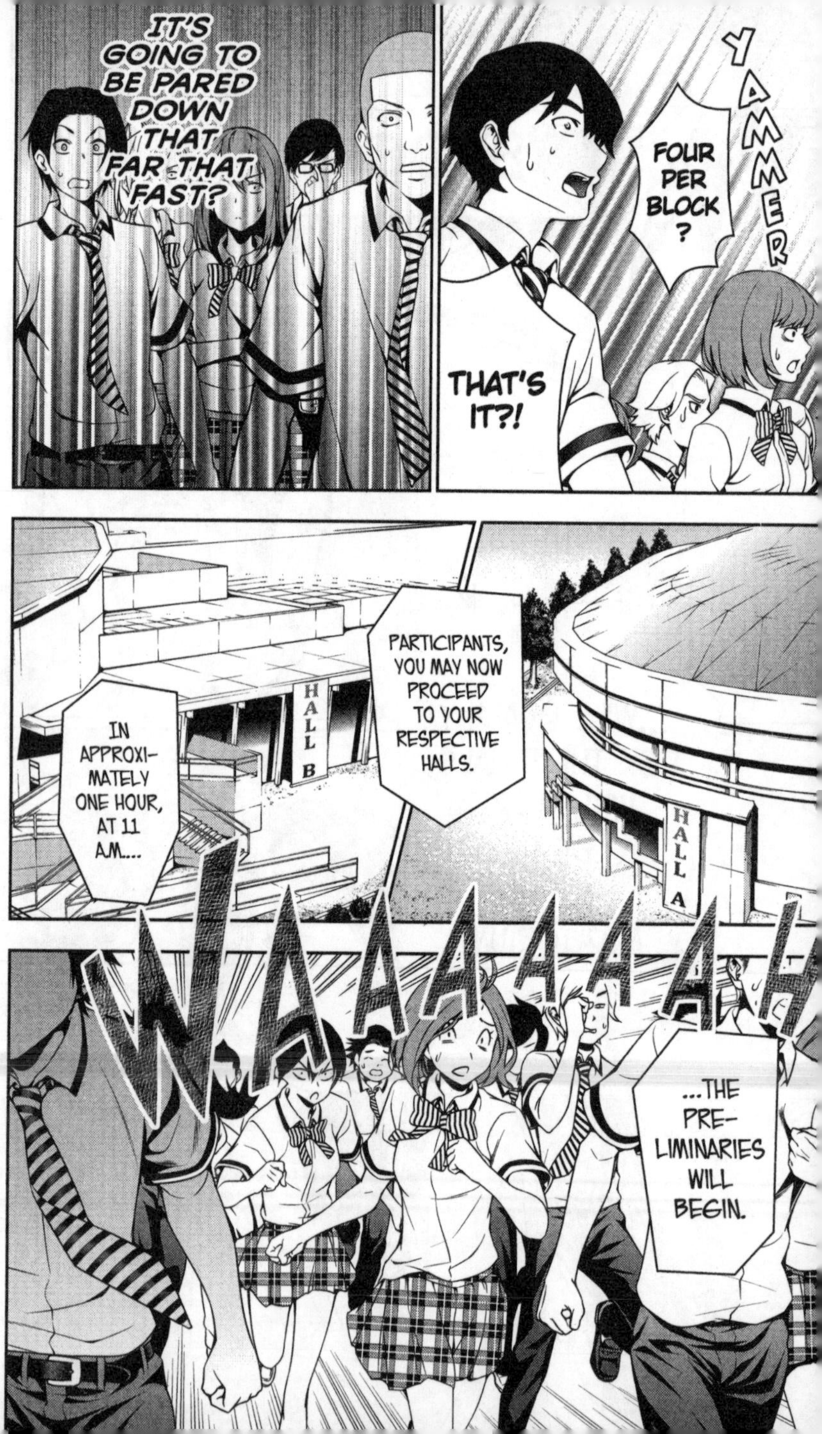
YAMMER
FOUR PER BLOCK?
THAT'S IT?!
IT'S GOING TO BE PARED DOWN THAT FAR THAT FAST?
HALL A
PARTICIPANTS, YOU MAY NOW PROCEED TO YOUR RESPECTIVE HALLS.
HALL B
IN APPROXI-MATELY ONE HOUR, AT 11 A.M....
WAAAAAAH
...THE PRE-LIMINARIES WILL BEGIN.

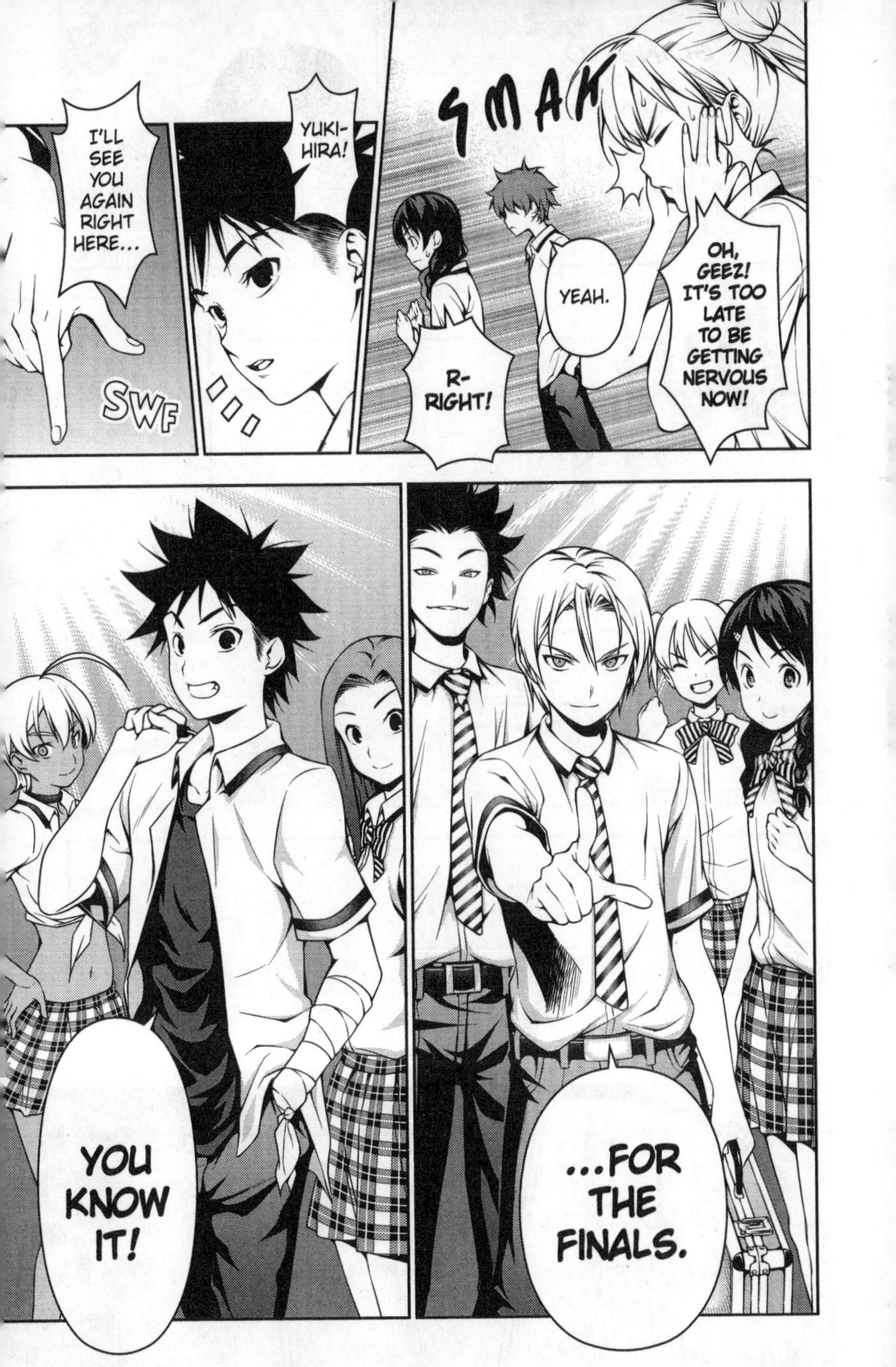
SMAK
OH, GEEZ! IT'S TOO LATE TO BE GETTING NERVOUS NOW!
YEAH.
R-RIGHT!
YUKI-HIRA!
...
I'LL SEE YOU AGAIN RIGHT HERE...
SWF
...FOR THE FINALS.
YOU KNOW IT!

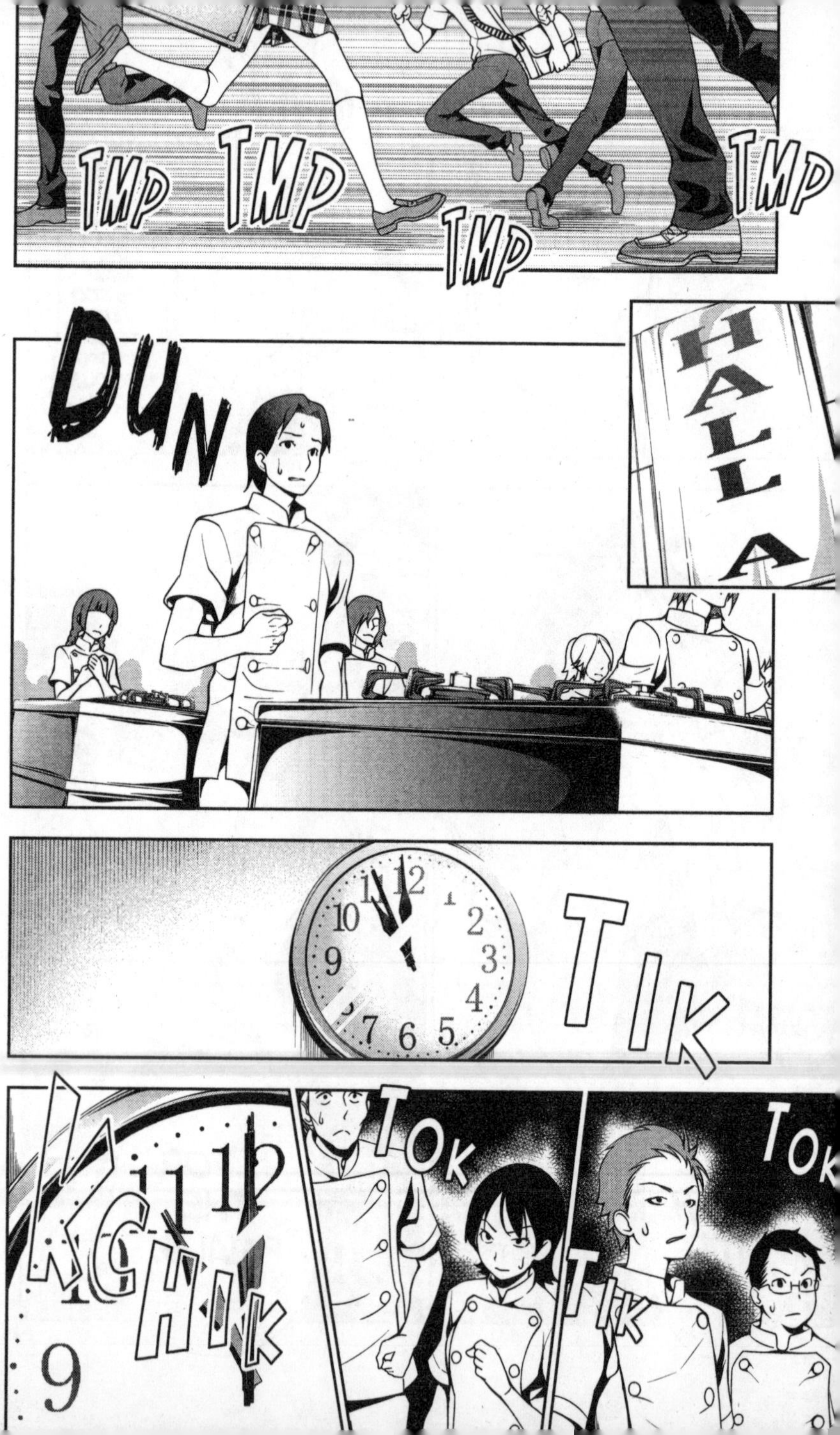
TMP TMP TMP TMP
TMP
HALLA
DUN
TIK
TOK
TIK
TOK
KCHIK

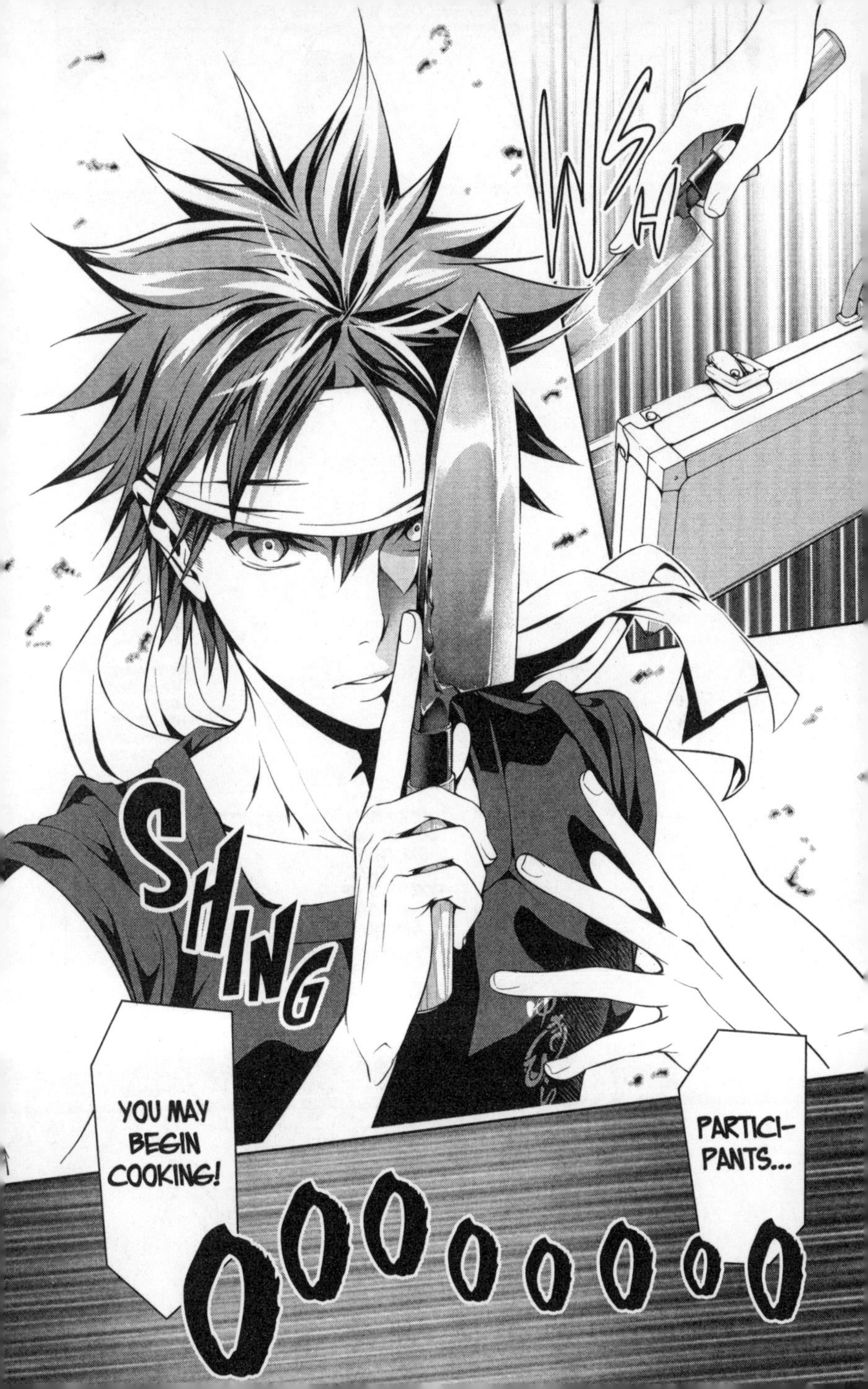
WSH
SHING
PARTICI-PANTS...
YOU MAY BEGIN COOKING!
OOOOOOOOO

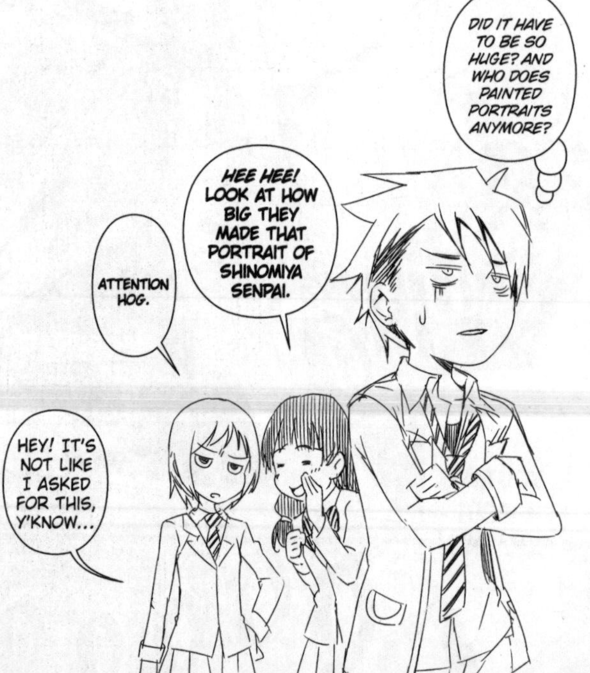
DID IT HAVE TO BE SO HUGE? AND WHO DOES PAINTED PORTRAITS ANYMORE?
HEE HEE! LOOK AT HOW BIG THEY MADE THAT PORTRAIT OF SHINOMIYA SENPAI.
ATTENTION HOG.
HEY! IT'S NOT LIKE I ASKED FOR THIS, Y'KNOW...

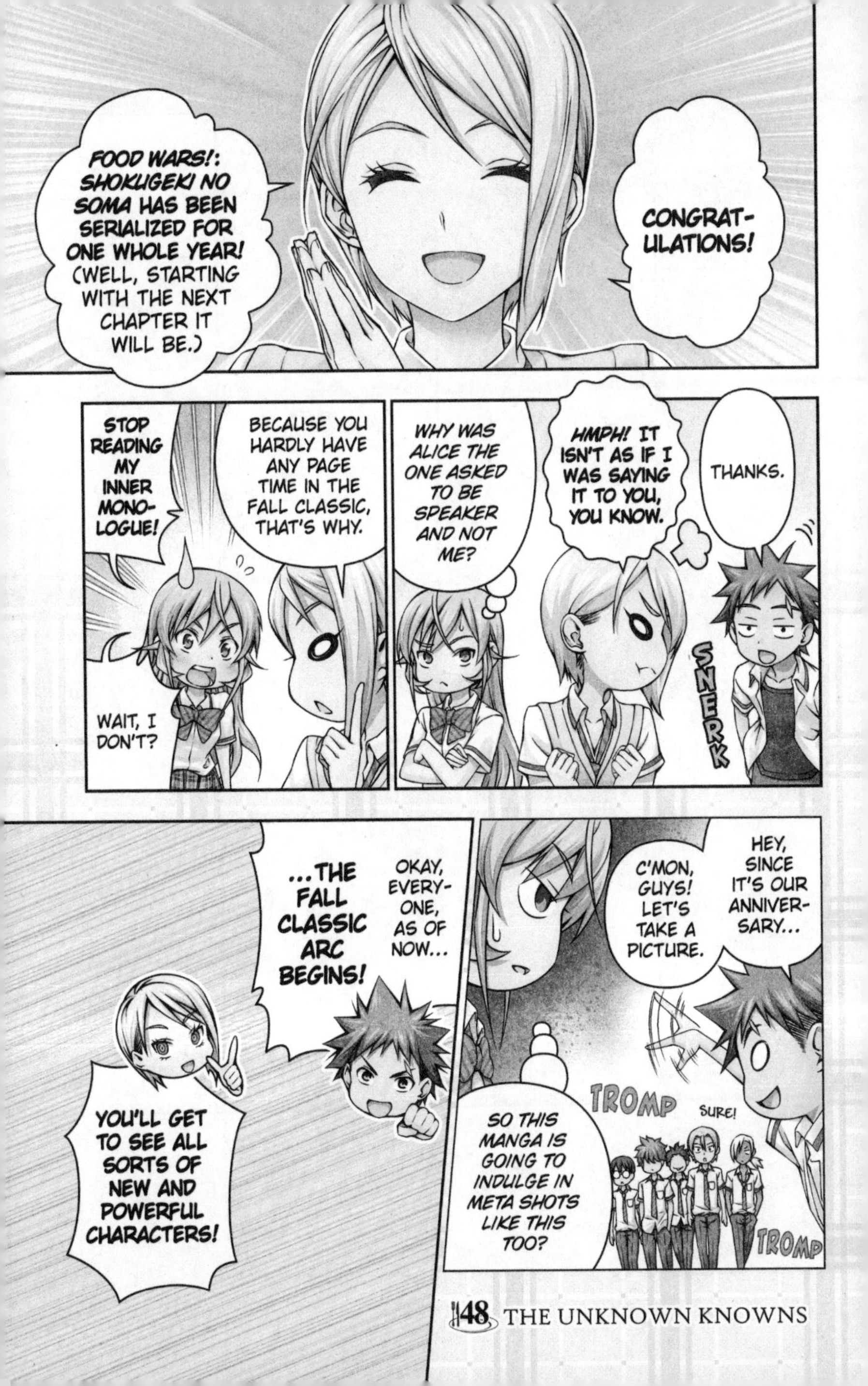
FOOD WARS!: SHOKUGEKI NO SOMA HAS BEEN SERIALIZED FOR ONE WHOLE YEAR! (WELL, STARTING WITH THE NEXT CHAPTER IT WILL BE.)
CONGRAT-ULATIONS!
THANKS.
HMPH! IT ISN'T AS IF I WAS SAYING IT TO YOU, YOU KNOW.
SNERK
WHY WAS ALICE THE ONE ASKED TO BE SPEAKER AND NOT ME?
BECAUSE YOU HARDLY HAVE ANY PAGE TIME IN THE FALL CLASSIC, THAT'S WHY.
STOP READING MY INNER MONO-LOGUE!
WAIT, I DON'T?
HEY, SINCE IT'S OUR ANNIVER-SARY...
C'MON, GUYS! LET'S TAKE A PICTURE.
SURE!
TROMP
TROMP
SO THIS MANGA IS GOING TO INDULGE IN META SHOTS LIKE THIS TOO?
OKAY, EVERY-ONE, AS OF NOW...
...THE FALL CLASSIC ARC BEGINS!
YOU'LL GET TO SEE ALL SORTS OF NEW AND POWERFUL CHARACTERS!

48 THE UNKNOWN KNOWNS

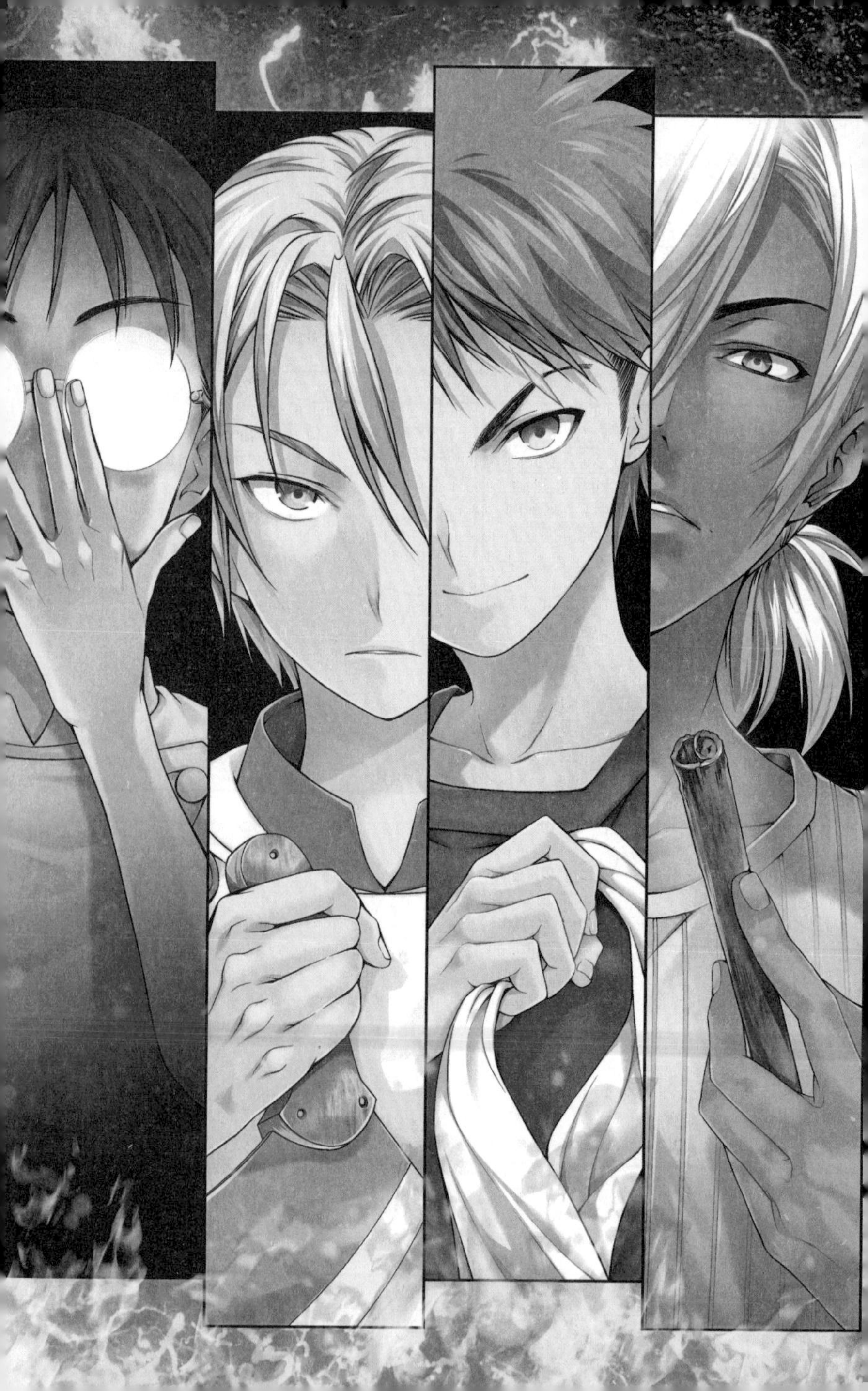

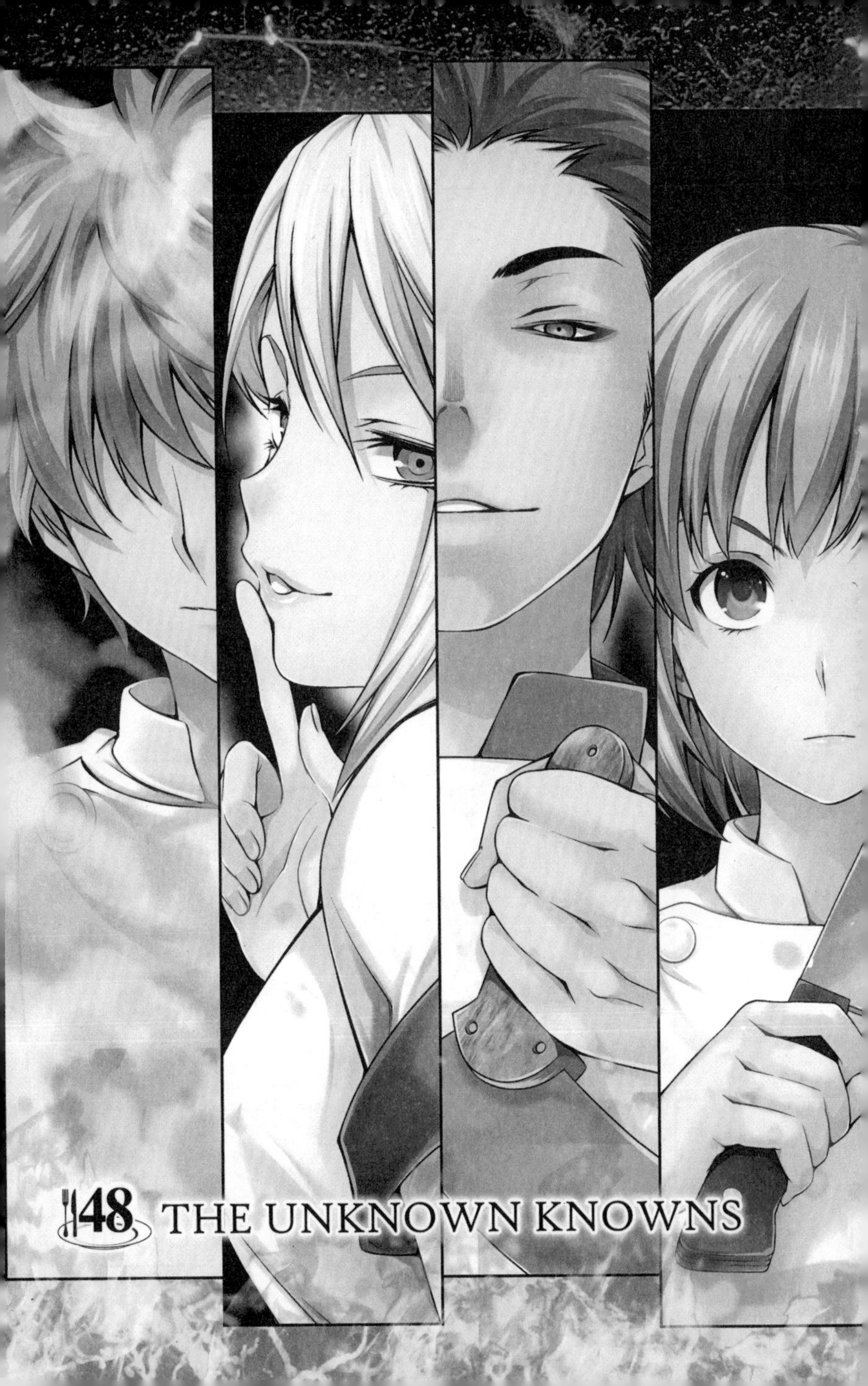
48 THE UNKNOWN KNOWNS

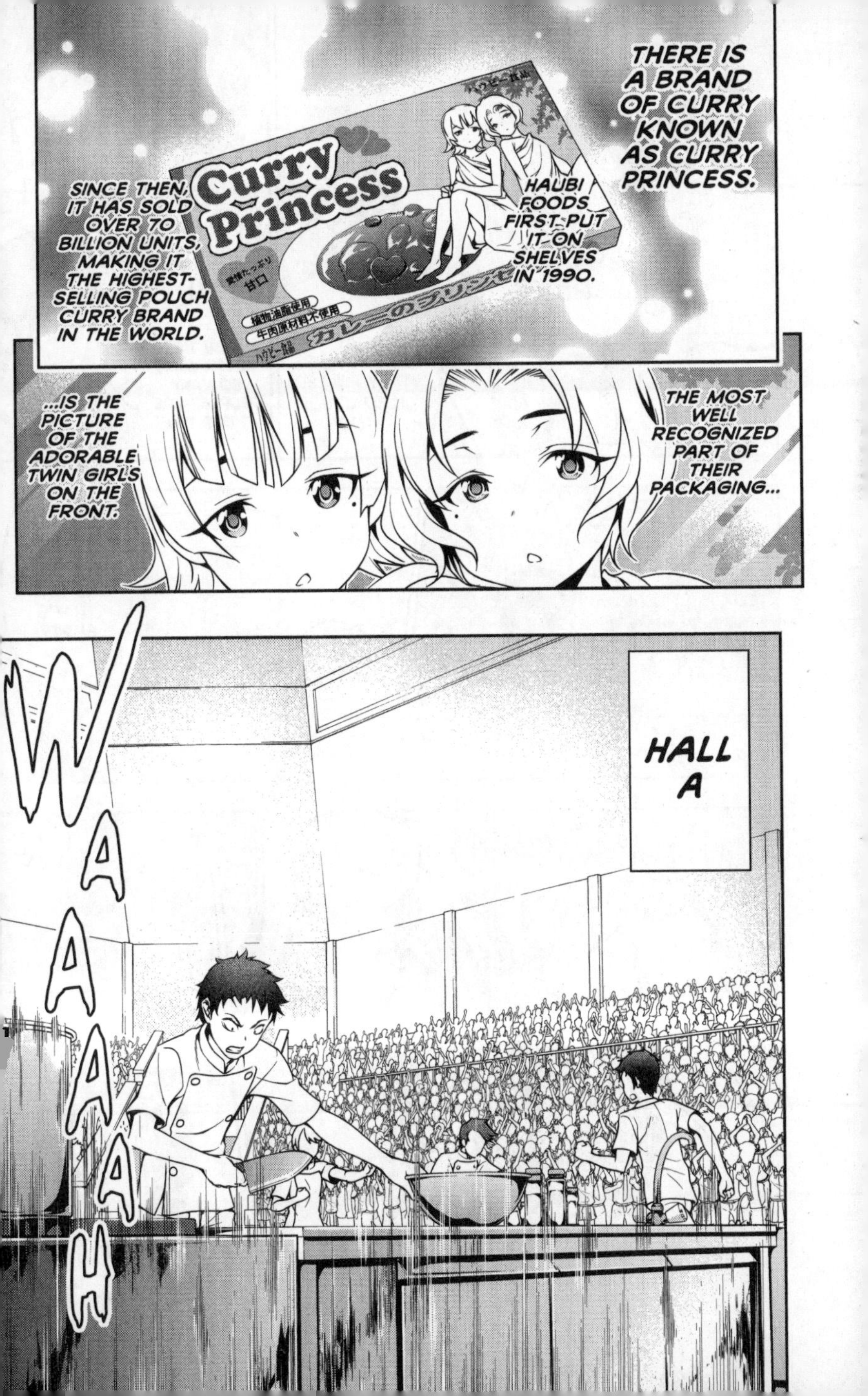
THERE IS A BRAND OF CURRY KNOWN AS CURRY PRINCESS.
HAUBI FOODS FIRST PUT IT ON SHELVES IN 1990.
Curry Princess
甘口
植物油脂使用
牛肉原材料不使用
SINCE THEN, IT HAS SOLD OVER 70 BILLION UNITS, MAKING IT THE HIGHEST-SELLING POUCH CURRY BRAND IN THE WORLD.
THE MOST WELL RECOGNIZED PART OF THEIR PACKAGING...
...IS THE PICTURE OF THE ADORABLE TWIN GIRLS ON THE FRONT.
HALL A
WAAAAAH

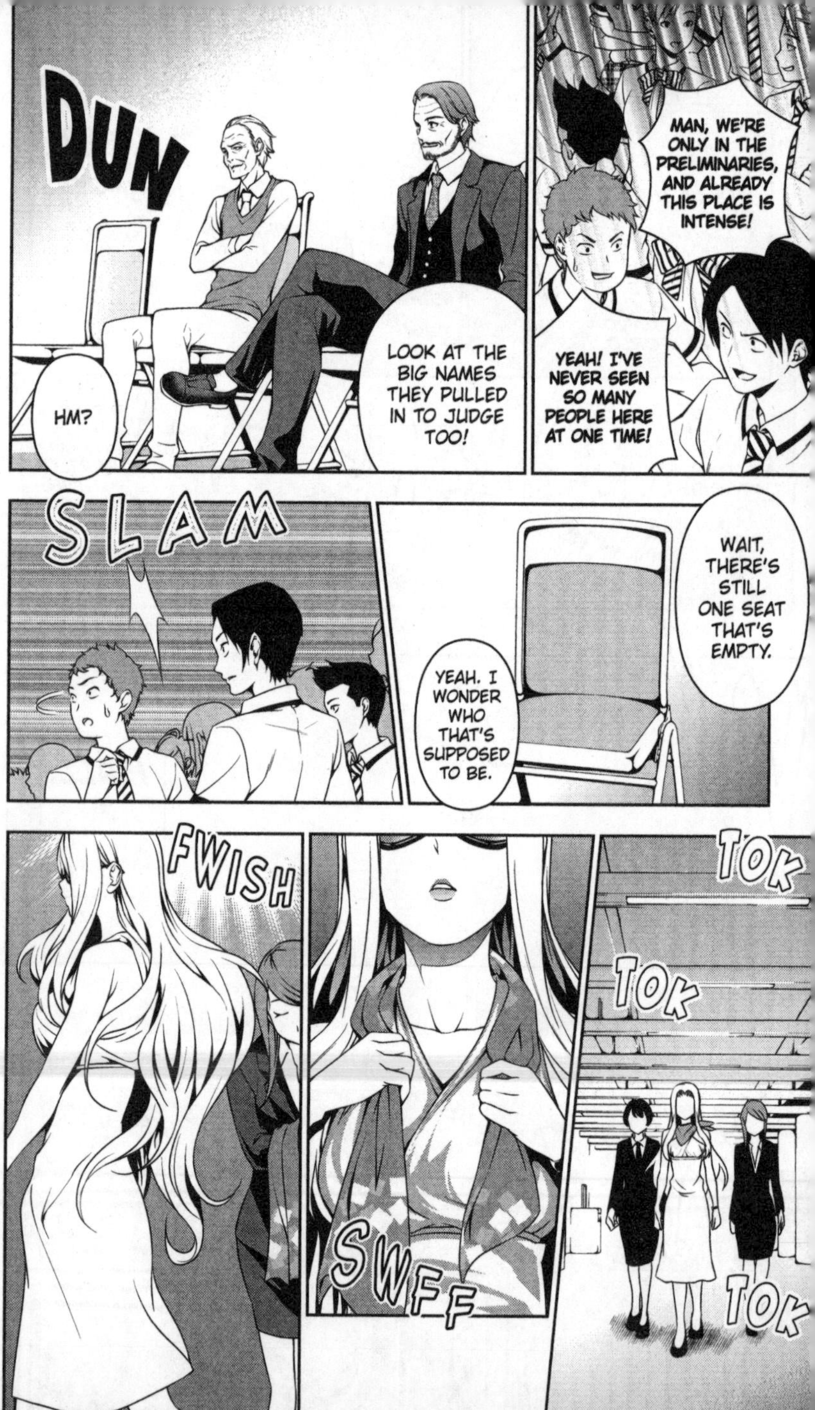
MAN, WE'RE ONLY IN THE PRELIMINARIES, AND ALREADY THIS PLACE IS INTENSE!
YEAH! I'VE NEVER SEEN SO MANY PEOPLE HERE AT ONE TIME!
DUN
LOOK AT THE BIG NAMES THEY PULLED IN TO JUDGE TOO!
HM?
WAIT, THERE'S STILL ONE SEAT THAT'S EMPTY.
YEAH. I WONDER WHO THAT'S SUPPOSED TO BE.
SLAM
TOK
TOK
TOK
SWFF
FWISH

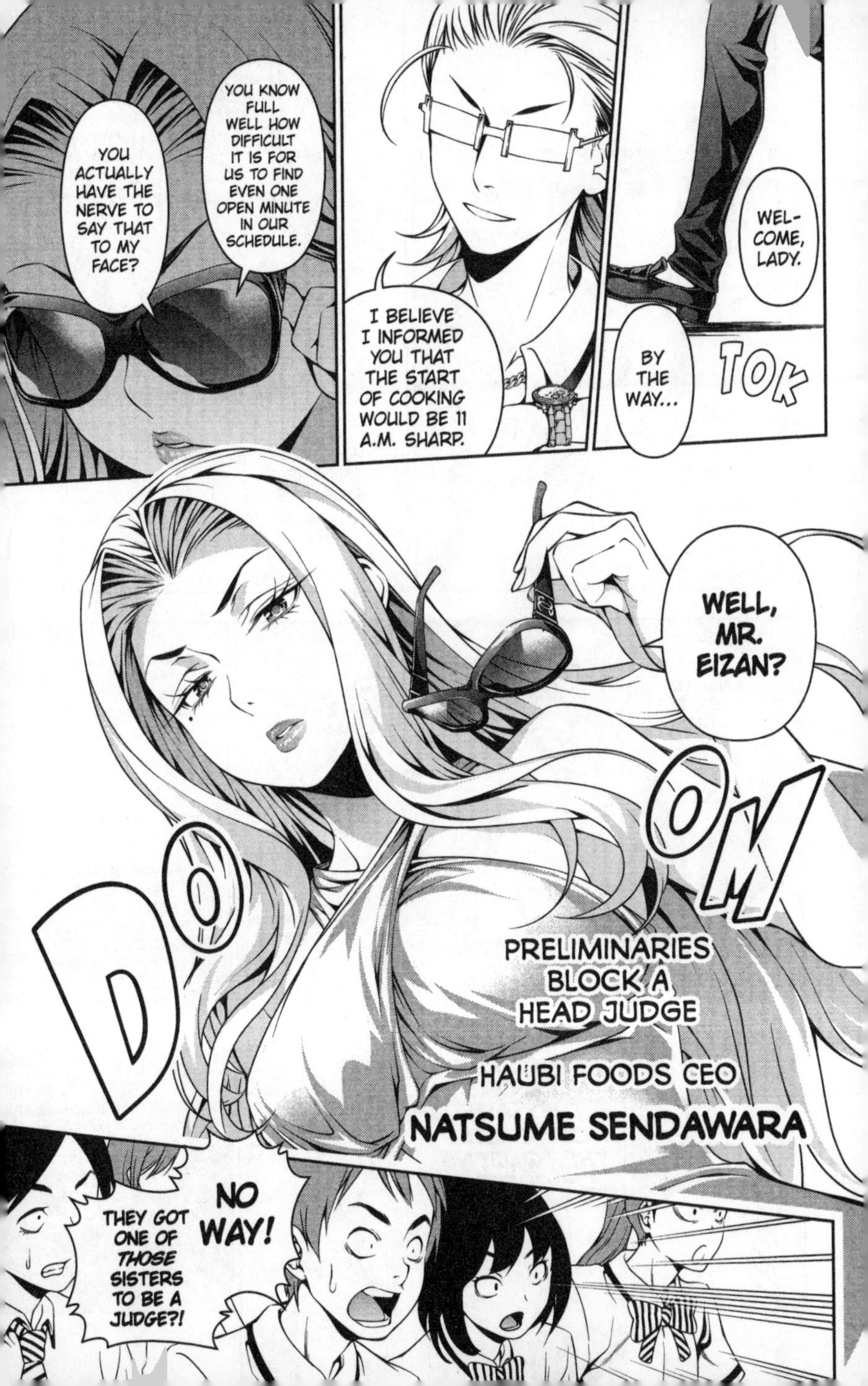
WELCOME, LADY.
BY THE WAY...
TOK
I BELIEVE I INFORMED YOU THAT THE START OF COOKING WOULD BE 11 A.M. SHARP.
YOU KNOW FULL WELL HOW DIFFICULT IT IS FOR US TO FIND EVEN ONE OPEN MINUTE IN OUR SCHEDULE.
YOU ACTUALLY HAVE THE NERVE TO SAY THAT TO MY FACE?
WELL, MR. EIZAN?
DOOM
PRELIMINARIES BLOCK A HEAD JUDGE
HAUBI FOODS CEO
NATSUME SENDAWARA
NO WAY!
THEY GOT ONE OF *THOSE* SISTERS TO BE A JUDGE?!

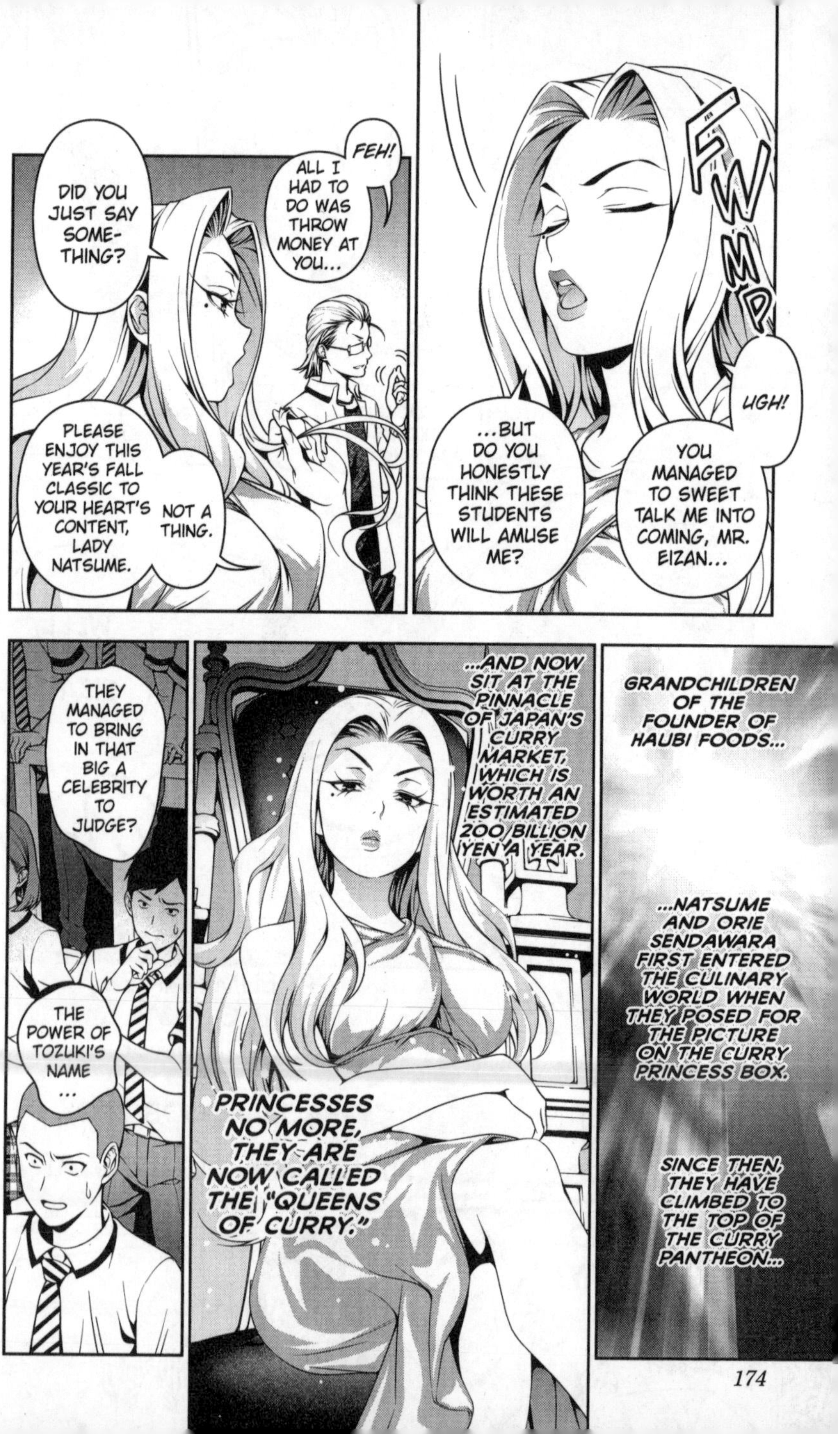
FWMP
UGH!
YOU MANAGED TO SWEET TALK ME INTO COMING, MR. EIZAN...
...BUT DO YOU HONESTLY THINK THESE STUDENTS WILL AMUSE ME?
FEH!
ALL I HAD TO DO WAS THROW MONEY AT YOU...
DID YOU JUST SAY SOME-THING?
PLEASE ENJOY THIS YEAR'S FALL CLASSIC TO YOUR HEART'S CONTENT, LADY NATSUME.
NOT A THING.
GRANDCHILDREN OF THE FOUNDER OF HAUBI FOODS...
...NATSUME AND ORIE SENDAWARA FIRST ENTERED THE CULINARY WORLD WHEN THEY POSED FOR THE PICTURE ON THE CURRY PRINCESS BOX.
SINCE THEN, THEY HAVE CLIMBED TO THE TOP OF THE CURRY PANTHEON...
...AND NOW SIT AT THE PINNACLE OF JAPAN'S CURRY MARKET, WHICH IS WORTH AN ESTIMATED 200 BILLION YEN A YEAR.
PRINCESSES NO MORE, THEY ARE NOW CALLED THE "QUEENS OF CURRY."
THEY MANAGED TO BRING IN THAT BIG A CELEBRITY TO JUDGE?
THE POWER OF TOZUKI'S NAME ...

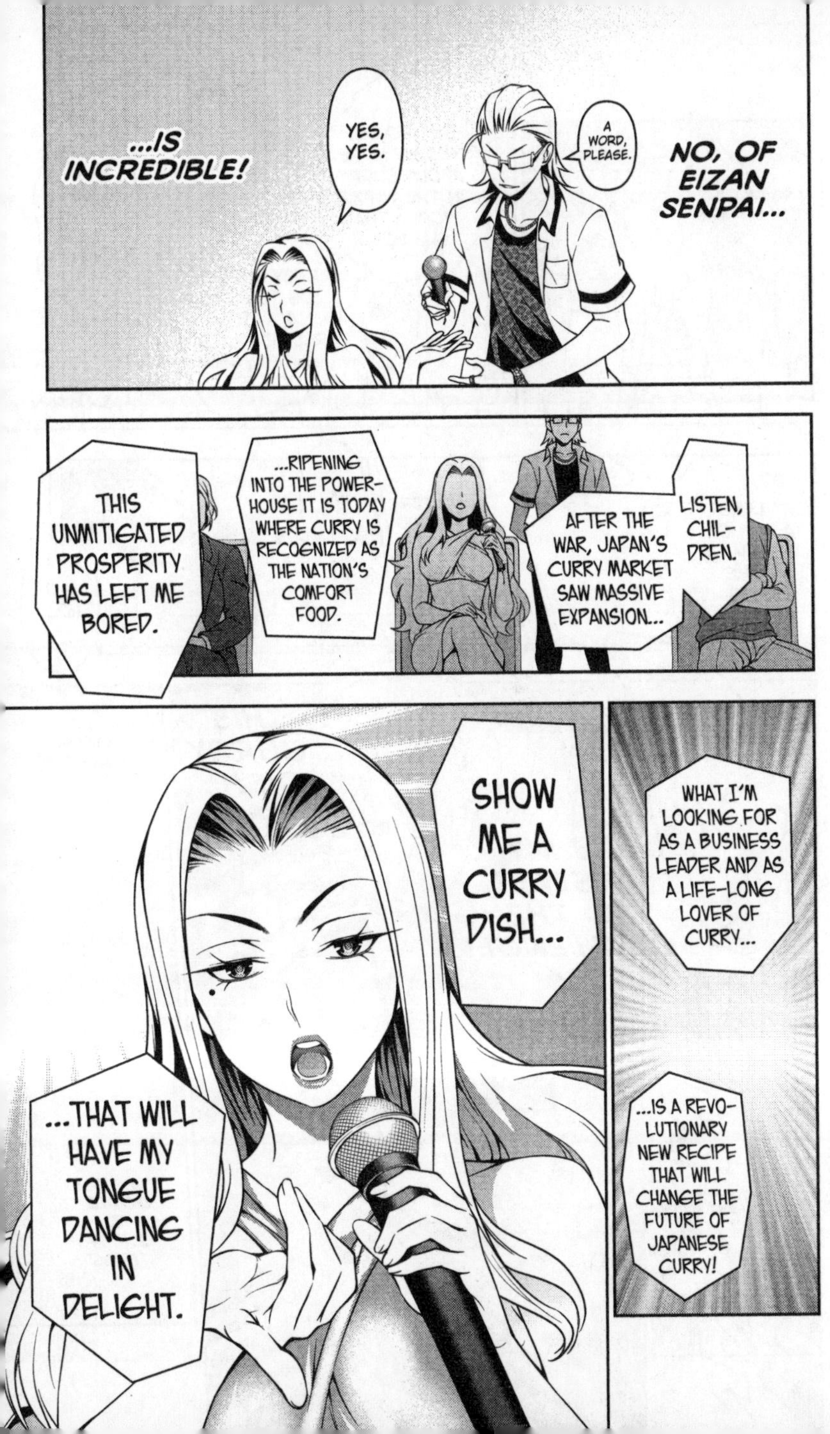
NO, OF EIZAN SENPAI...
A WORD, PLEASE.
YES, YES.
...IS INCREDIBLE!
LISTEN, CHILDREN.
AFTER THE WAR, JAPAN'S CURRY MARKET SAW MASSIVE EXPANSION...
...RIPENING INTO THE POWERHOUSE IT IS TODAY WHERE CURRY IS RECOGNIZED AS THE NATION'S COMFORT FOOD.
THIS UNMITIGATED PROSPERITY HAS LEFT ME BORED.
WHAT I'M LOOKING FOR AS A BUSINESS LEADER AND AS A LIFE-LONG LOVER OF CURRY...
...IS A REVOLUTIONARY NEW RECIPE THAT WILL CHANGE THE FUTURE OF JAPANESE CURRY!
SHOW ME A CURRY DISH...
...THAT WILL HAVE MY TONGUE DANCING IN DELIGHT.

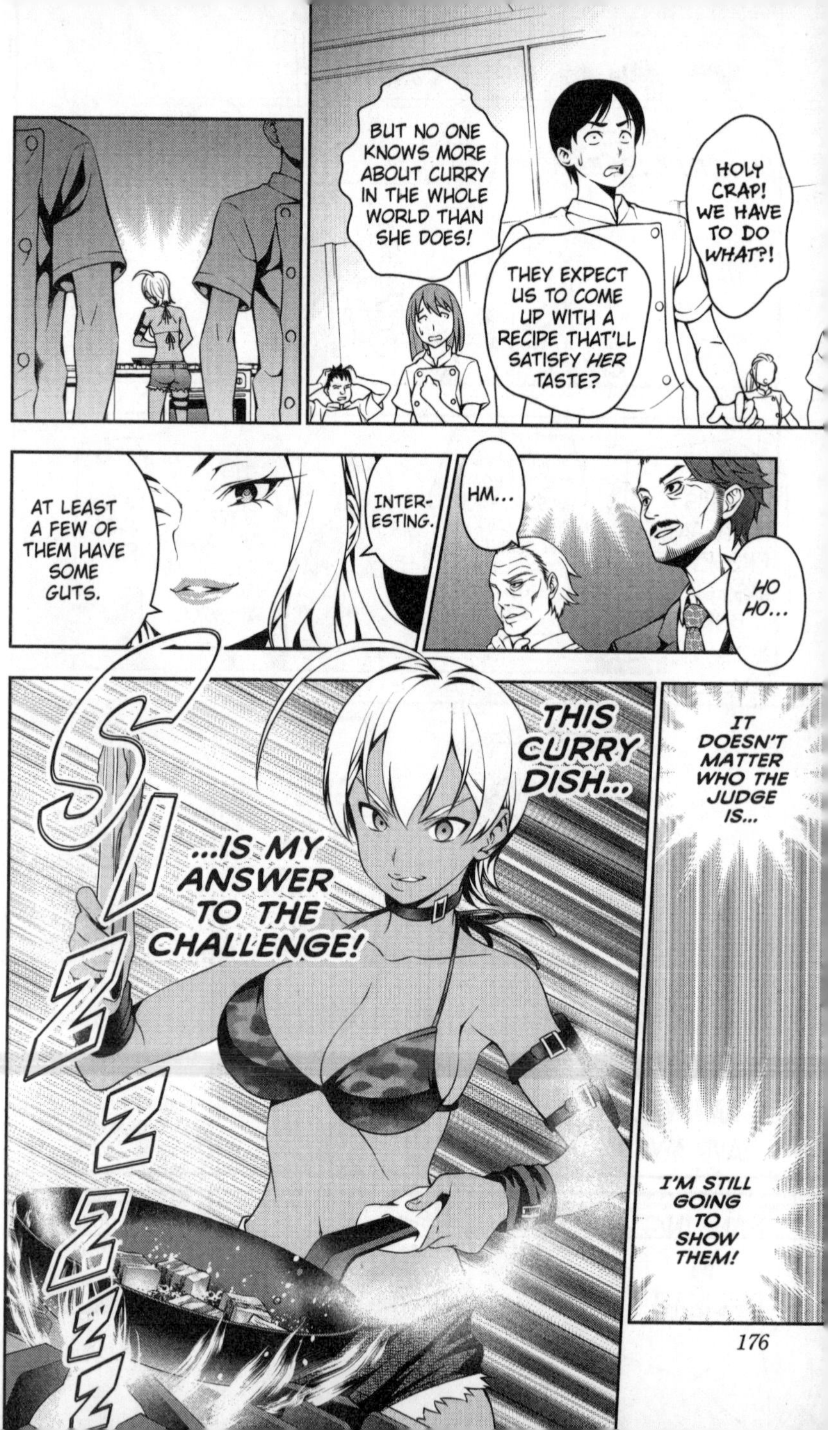
HOLY CRAP! WE HAVE TO DO WHAT?!
THEY EXPECT US TO COME UP WITH A RECIPE THAT'LL SATISFY HER TASTE?
BUT NO ONE KNOWS MORE ABOUT CURRY IN THE WHOLE WORLD THAN SHE DOES!
HO HO...
HM...
INTER-ESTING.
AT LEAST A FEW OF THEM HAVE SOME GUTS.
IT DOESN'T MATTER WHO THE JUDGE IS...
I'M STILL GOING TO SHOW THEM!
THIS CURRY DISH...
...IS MY ANSWER TO THE CHALLENGE!
SIZZZZZ

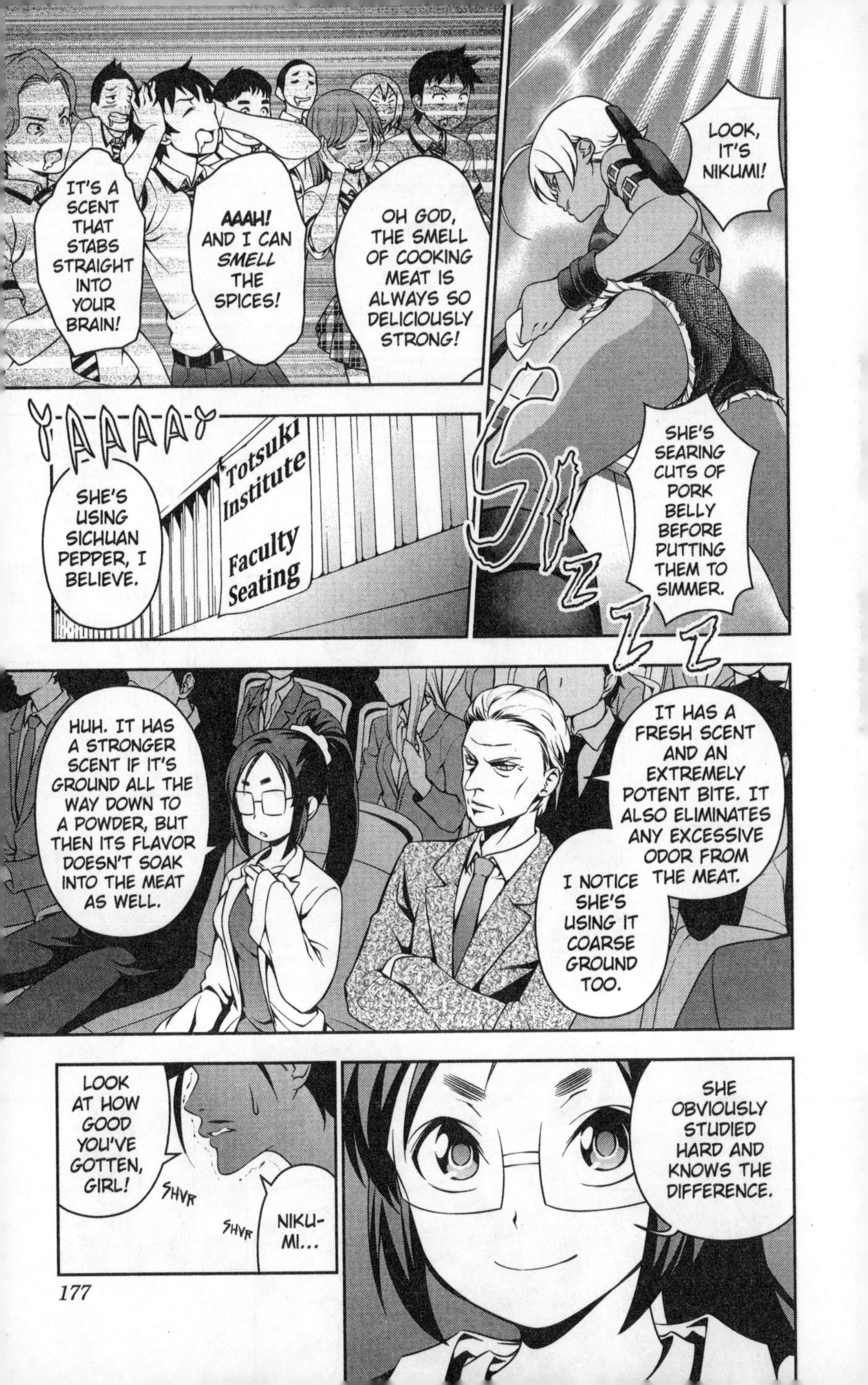
LOOK, IT'S NIKUMI!
SIZZZZ
SHE'S SEARING CUTS OF PORK BELLY BEFORE PUTTING THEM TO SIMMER.
OH GOD, THE SMELL OF COOKING MEAT IS ALWAYS SO DELICIOUSLY STRONG!
AAAH! AND I CAN SMELL THE SPICES!
IT'S A SCENT THAT STABS STRAIGHT INTO YOUR BRAIN!
YAAAAY
Totsuki Institute Faculty Seating
SHE'S USING SICHUAN PEPPER, I BELIEVE.
IT HAS A FRESH SCENT AND AN EXTREMELY POTENT BITE. IT ALSO ELIMINATES ANY EXCESSIVE ODOR FROM THE MEAT.
I NOTICE SHE'S USING IT COARSE GROUND TOO.
HUH. IT HAS A STRONGER SCENT IF IT'S GROUND ALL THE WAY DOWN TO A POWDER, BUT THEN ITS FLAVOR DOESN'T SOAK INTO THE MEAT AS WELL.
SHE OBVIOUSLY STUDIED HARD AND KNOWS THE DIFFERENCE.
NIKU-MI...
SHVR
SHVR
LOOK AT HOW GOOD YOU'VE GOTTEN, GIRL!

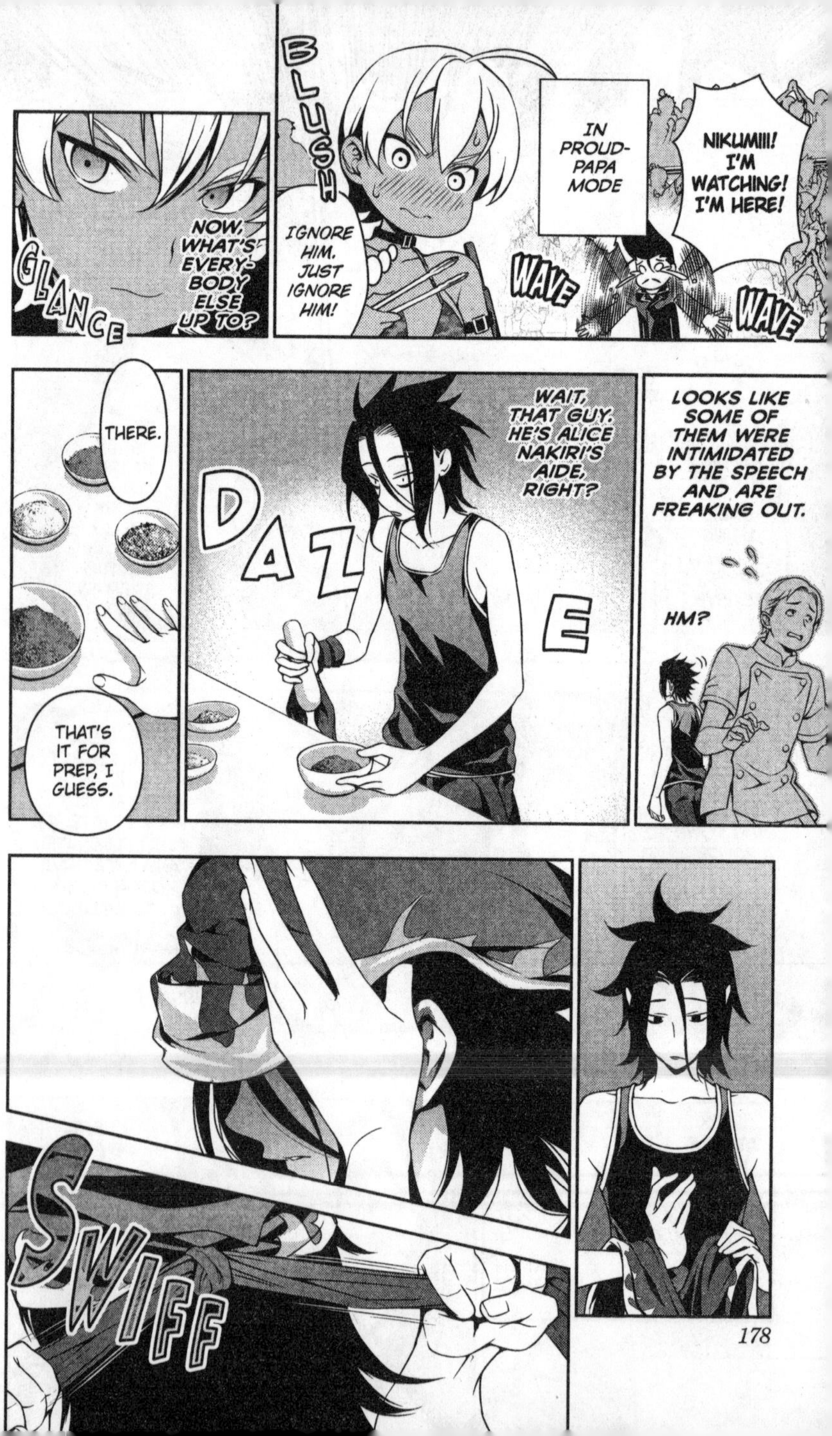

NIKUMIII! I'M WATCHING! I'M HERE!
IN PROUD-PAPA MODE
WAVE
WAVE
BLUSH
IGNORE HIM. JUST IGNORE HIM!
NOW, WHAT'S EVERYBODY ELSE UP TO?
GLANCE
LOOKS LIKE SOME OF THEM WERE INTIMIDATED BY THE SPEECH AND ARE FREAKING OUT.
HM?
WAIT, THAT GUY. HE'S ALICE NAKIRI'S AIDE, RIGHT?
DAZE
THERE.
THAT'S IT FOR PREP, I GUESS.
SWIFF

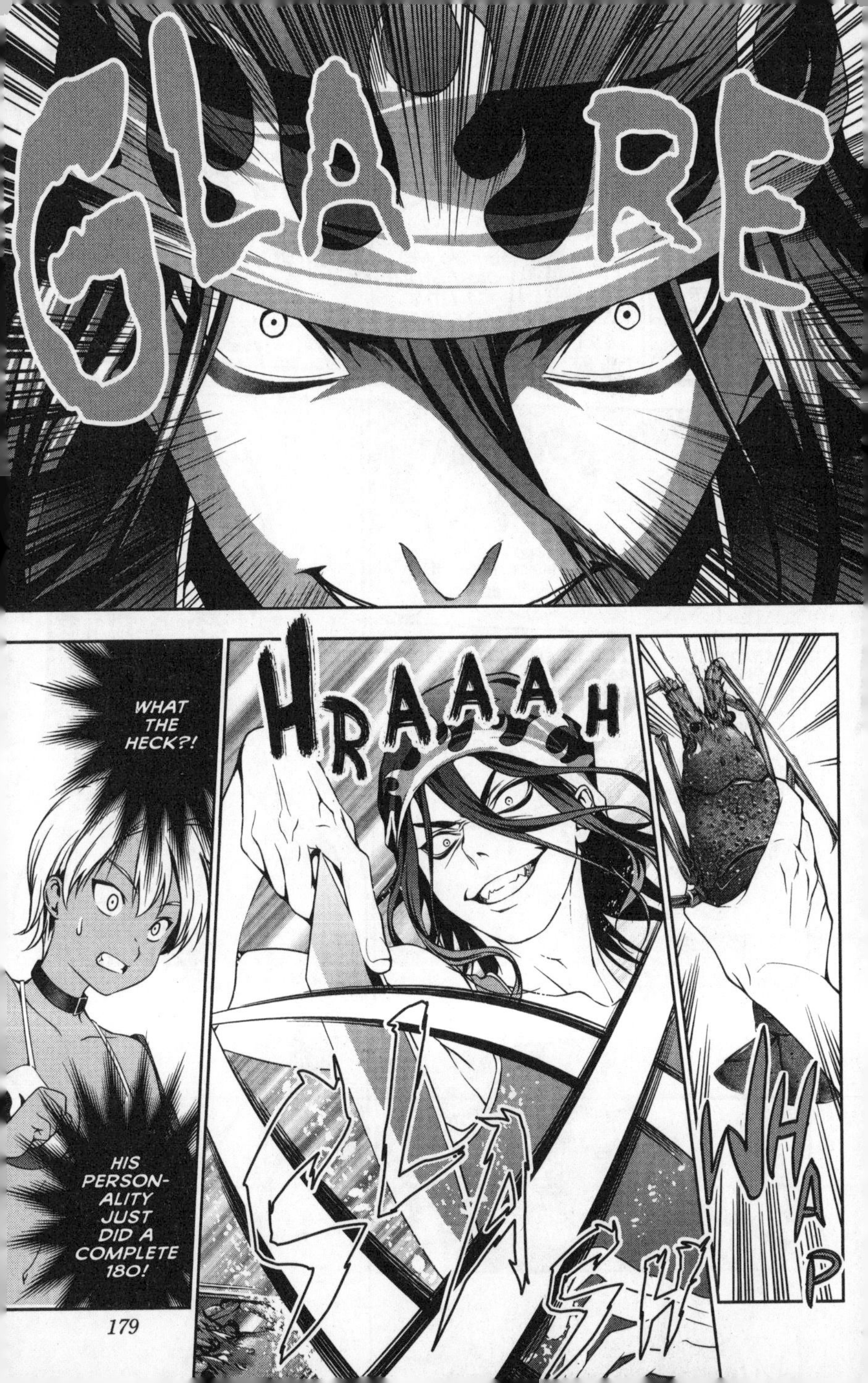
GLARE
WHAP
HRAAAAH
SLASH
WHAT THE HECK?!
HIS PERSON-ALITY JUST DID A COMPLETE 180!

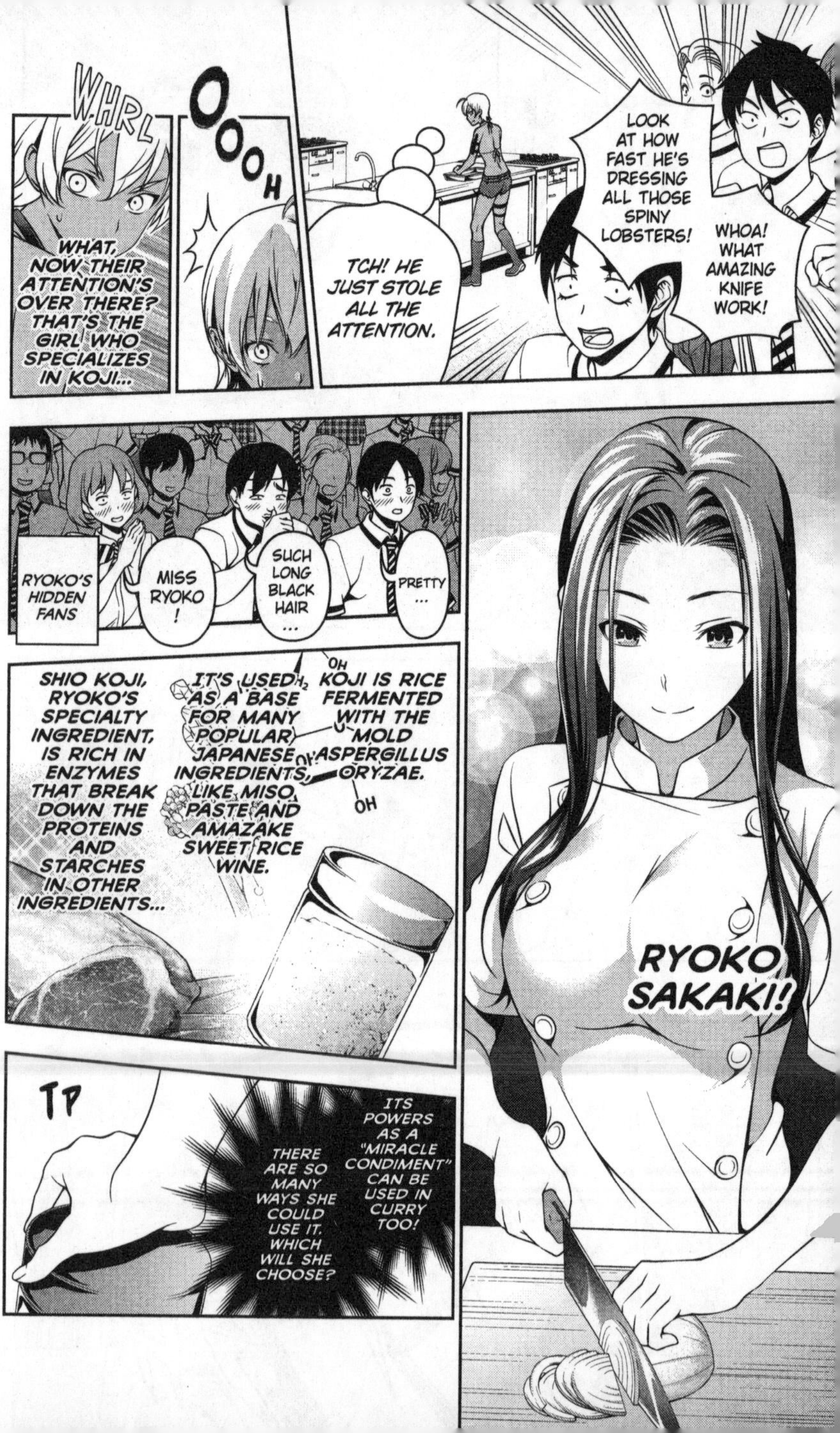
WHOA! WHAT AMAZING KNIFE WORK!
LOOK AT HOW FAST HE'S DRESSING ALL THOSE SPINY LOBSTERS!
OOOH
TCH! HE JUST STOLE ALL THE ATTENTION.
WHRL
WHAT, NOW THEIR ATTENTION'S OVER THERE? THAT'S THE GIRL WHO SPECIALIZES IN KOJI...
RYOKO SAKAKI!
PRETTY...
SUCH LONG BLACK HAIR...
MISS RYOKO!
RYOKO'S HIDDEN FANS
KOJI IS RICE FERMENTED WITH THE MOLD ASPERGILLUS ORYZAE.
IT'S USED AS A BASE FOR MANY POPULAR JAPANESE INGREDIENTS, LIKE MISO PASTE AND AMAZAKE SWEET RICE WINE.
SHIO KOJI, RYOKO'S SPECIALTY INGREDIENT, IS RICH IN ENZYMES THAT BREAK DOWN THE PROTEINS AND STARCHES IN OTHER INGREDIENTS...
ITS POWERS AS A "MIRACLE CONDIMENT" CAN BE USED IN CURRY TOO!
THERE ARE SO MANY WAYS SHE COULD USE IT. WHICH WILL SHE CHOOSE?
TP

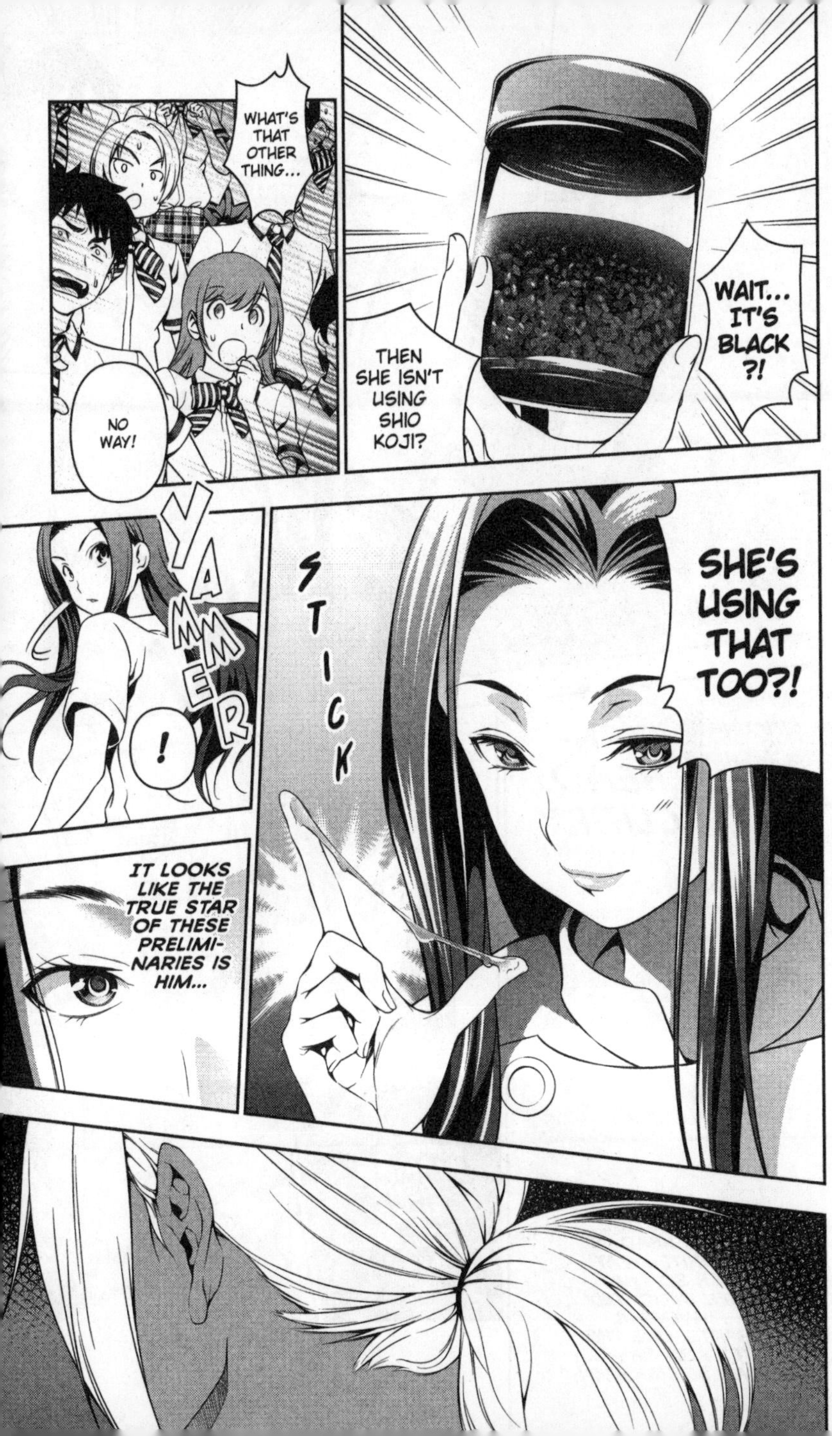
WAIT... IT'S BLACK?!
THEN SHE ISN'T USING SHIO KOJI?
WHAT'S THAT OTHER THING...
NO WAY!
SHE'S USING THAT TOO?!
STICK
YAMMMER
!
IT LOOKS LIKE THE TRUE STAR OF THESE PRELIMI-NARIES IS HIM...

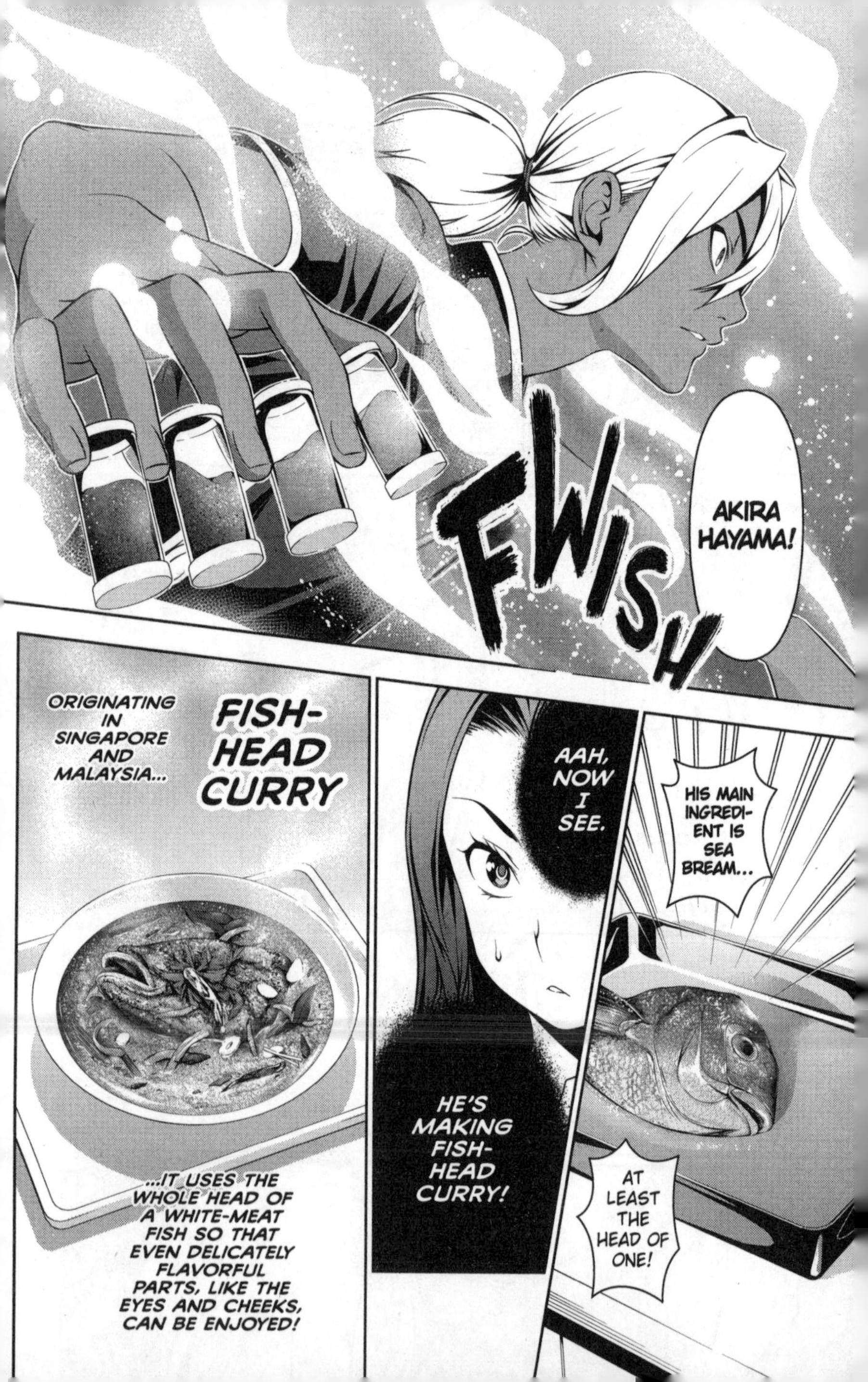
AKIRA HAYAMA!
FWISH
HIS MAIN INGREDIENT IS SEA BREAM...
AT LEAST THE HEAD OF ONE!
AAH, NOW I SEE.
HE'S MAKING FISH-HEAD CURRY!
FISH-HEAD CURRY
ORIGINATING IN SINGAPORE AND MALAYSIA...
...IT USES THE WHOLE HEAD OF A WHITE-MEAT FISH SO THAT EVEN DELICATELY FLAVORFUL PARTS, LIKE THE EYES AND CHEEKS, CAN BE ENJOYED!

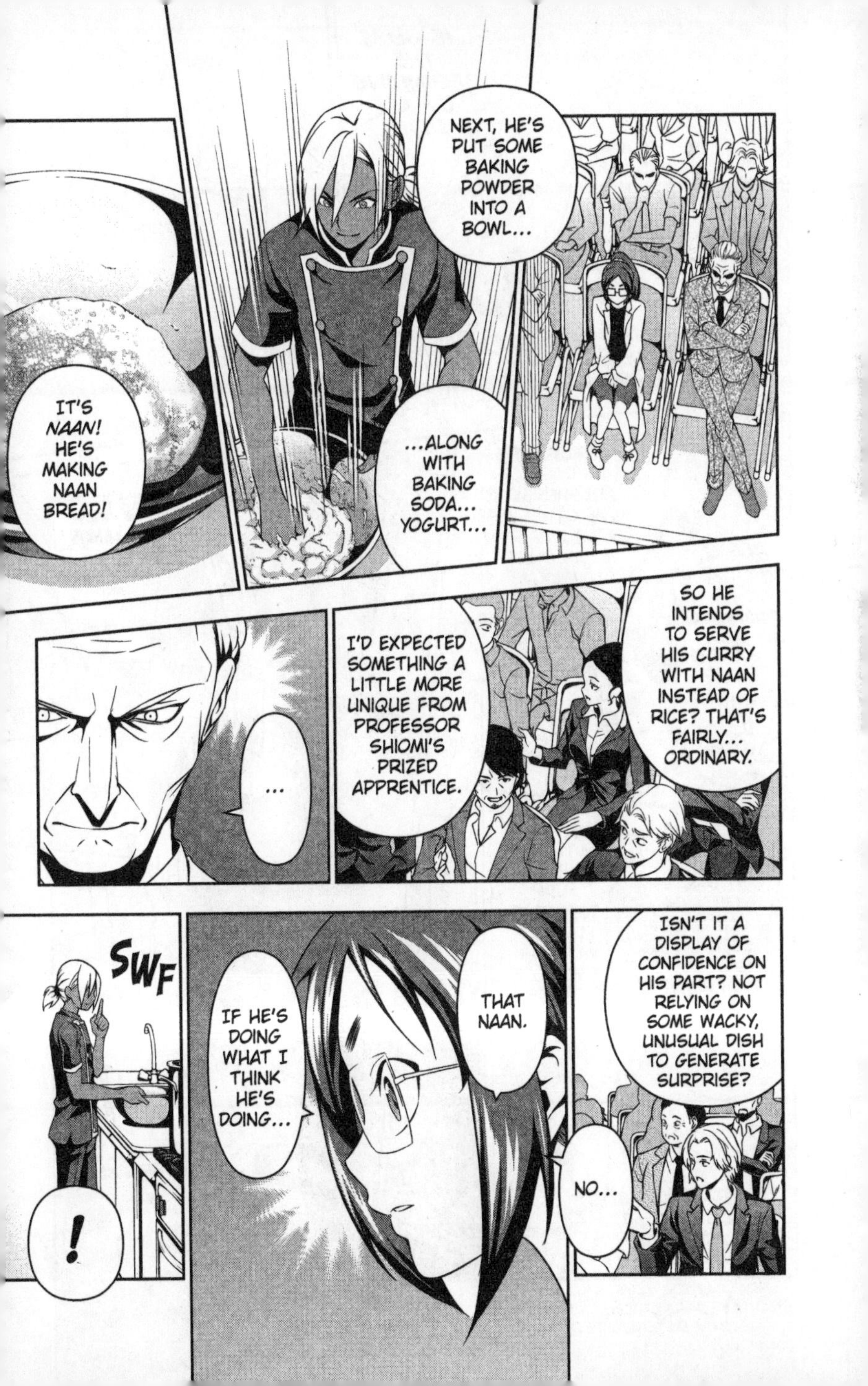
NEXT, HE'S PUT SOME BAKING POWDER INTO A BOWL...
...ALONG WITH BAKING SODA... YOGURT...
IT'S *NAAN*! HE'S MAKING NAAN BREAD!
SO HE INTENDS TO SERVE HIS CURRY WITH NAAN INSTEAD OF RICE? THAT'S FAIRLY... ORDINARY.
I'D EXPECTED SOMETHING A LITTLE MORE UNIQUE FROM PROFESSOR SHIOMI'S PRIZED APPRENTICE.
...
ISN'T IT A DISPLAY OF CONFIDENCE ON HIS PART? NOT RELYING ON SOME WACKY, UNUSUAL DISH TO GENERATE SURPRISE?
NO...
THAT NAAN.
IF HE'S DOING WHAT I THINK HE'S DOING...
SWF
!

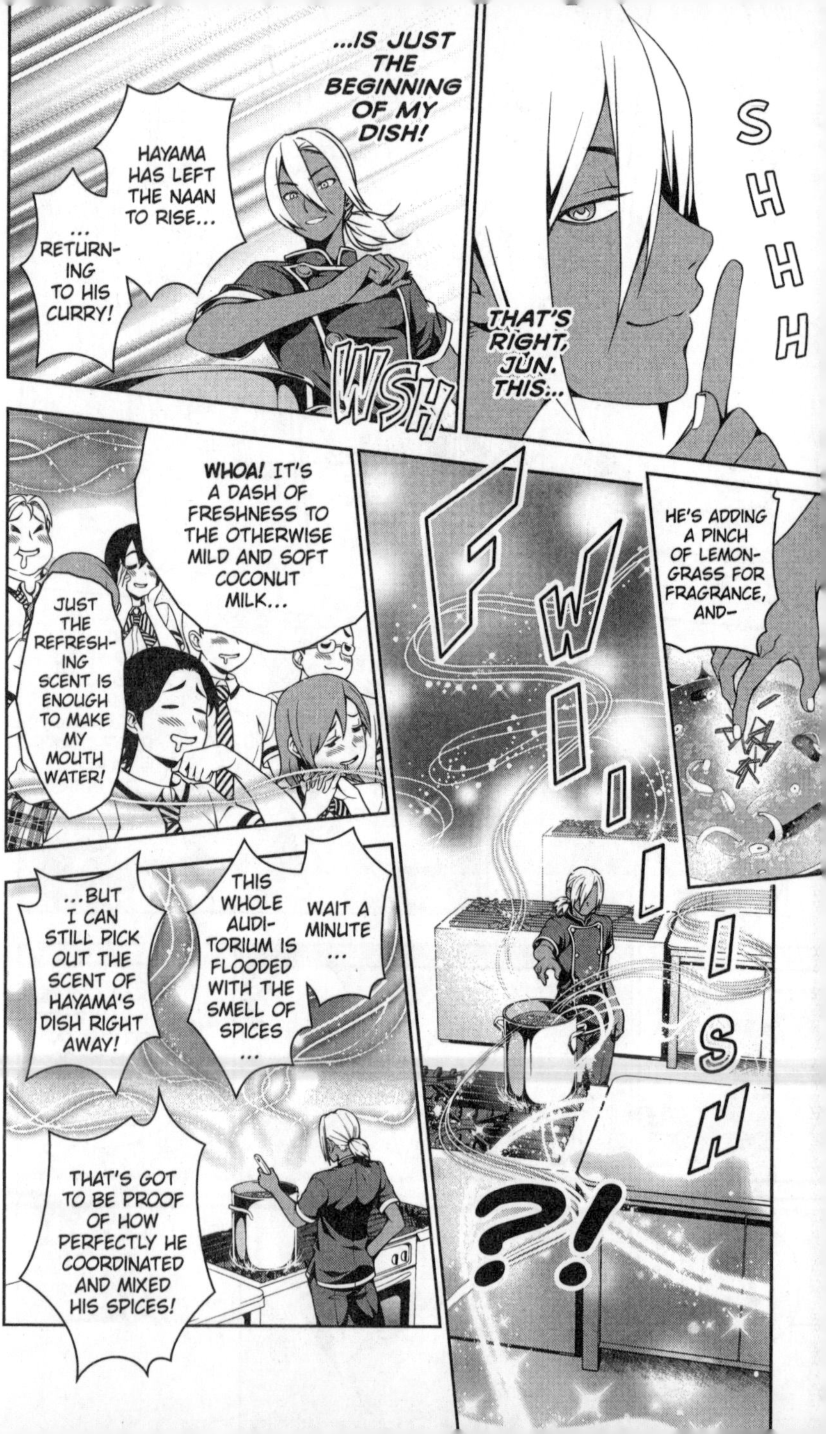
SHHHH
THAT'S RIGHT, JUN. THIS...
...IS JUST THE BEGINNING OF MY DISH!
HAYAMA HAS LEFT THE NAAN TO RISE...
...RETURNING TO HIS CURRY!
WSH
HE'S ADDING A PINCH OF LEMONGRASS FOR FRAGRANCE, AND-
FWIIIISH
?!
WHOA! IT'S A DASH OF FRESHNESS TO THE OTHERWISE MILD AND SOFT COCONUT MILK...
JUST THE REFRESHING SCENT IS ENOUGH TO MAKE MY MOUTH WATER!
WAIT A MINUTE...
THIS WHOLE AUDITORIUM IS FLOODED WITH THE SMELL OF SPICES...
...BUT I CAN STILL PICK OUT THE SCENT OF HAYAMA'S DISH RIGHT AWAY!
THAT'S GOT TO BE PROOF OF HOW PERFECTLY HE COORDINATED AND MIXED HIS SPICES!

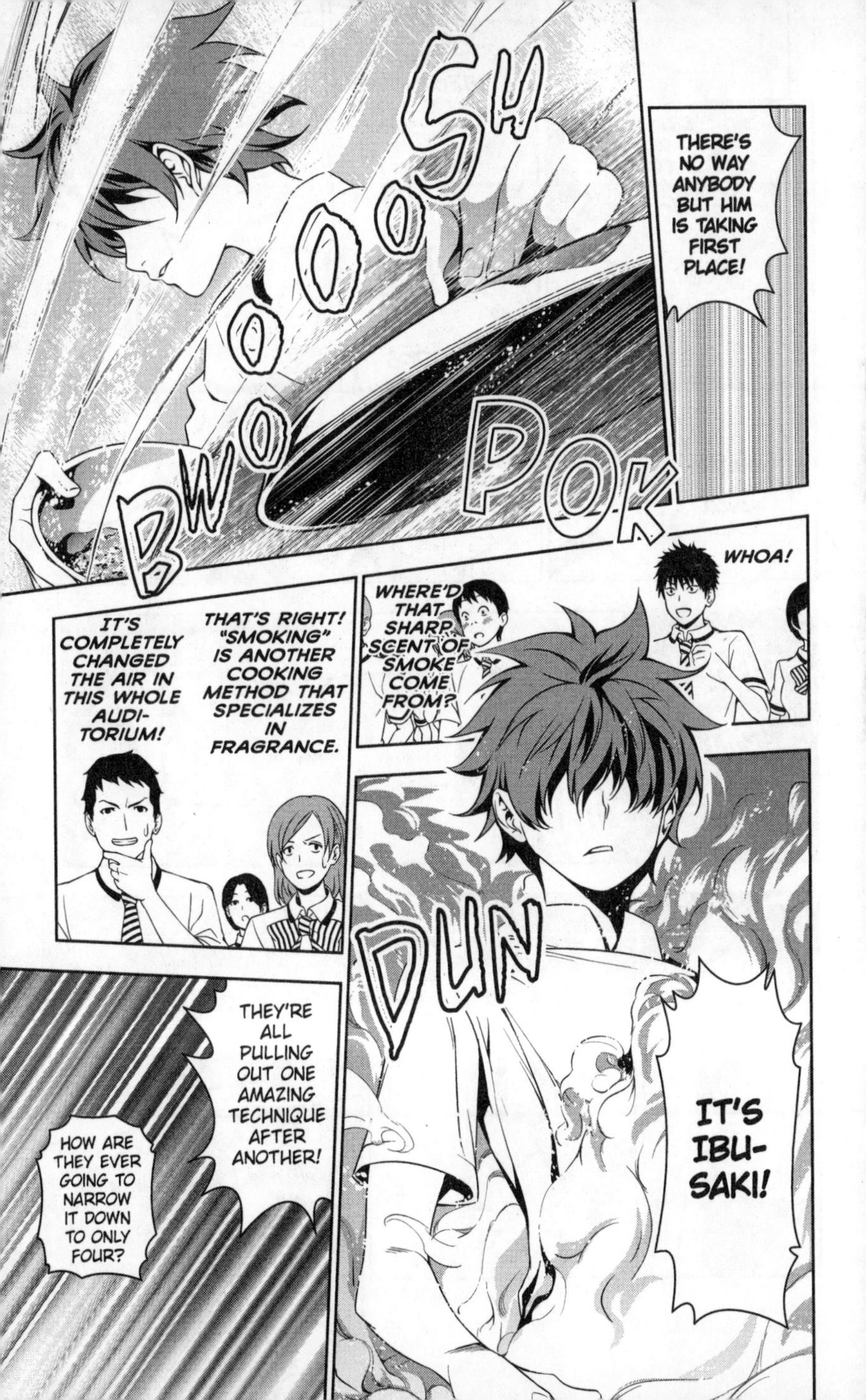
THERE'S NO WAY ANYBODY BUT HIM IS TAKING FIRST PLACE!
BWOOOOOSH
POK
WHOA!
WHERE'D THAT SHARP SCENT OF SMOKE COME FROM?
DUN
IT'S IBUSAKI!
THAT'S RIGHT! "SMOKING" IS ANOTHER COOKING METHOD THAT SPECIALIZES IN FRAGRANCE.
IT'S COMPLETELY CHANGED THE AIR IN THIS WHOLE AUDI-TORIUM!
THEY'RE ALL PULLING OUT ONE AMAZING TECHNIQUE AFTER ANOTHER!
HOW ARE THEY EVER GOING TO NARROW IT DOWN TO ONLY FOUR?

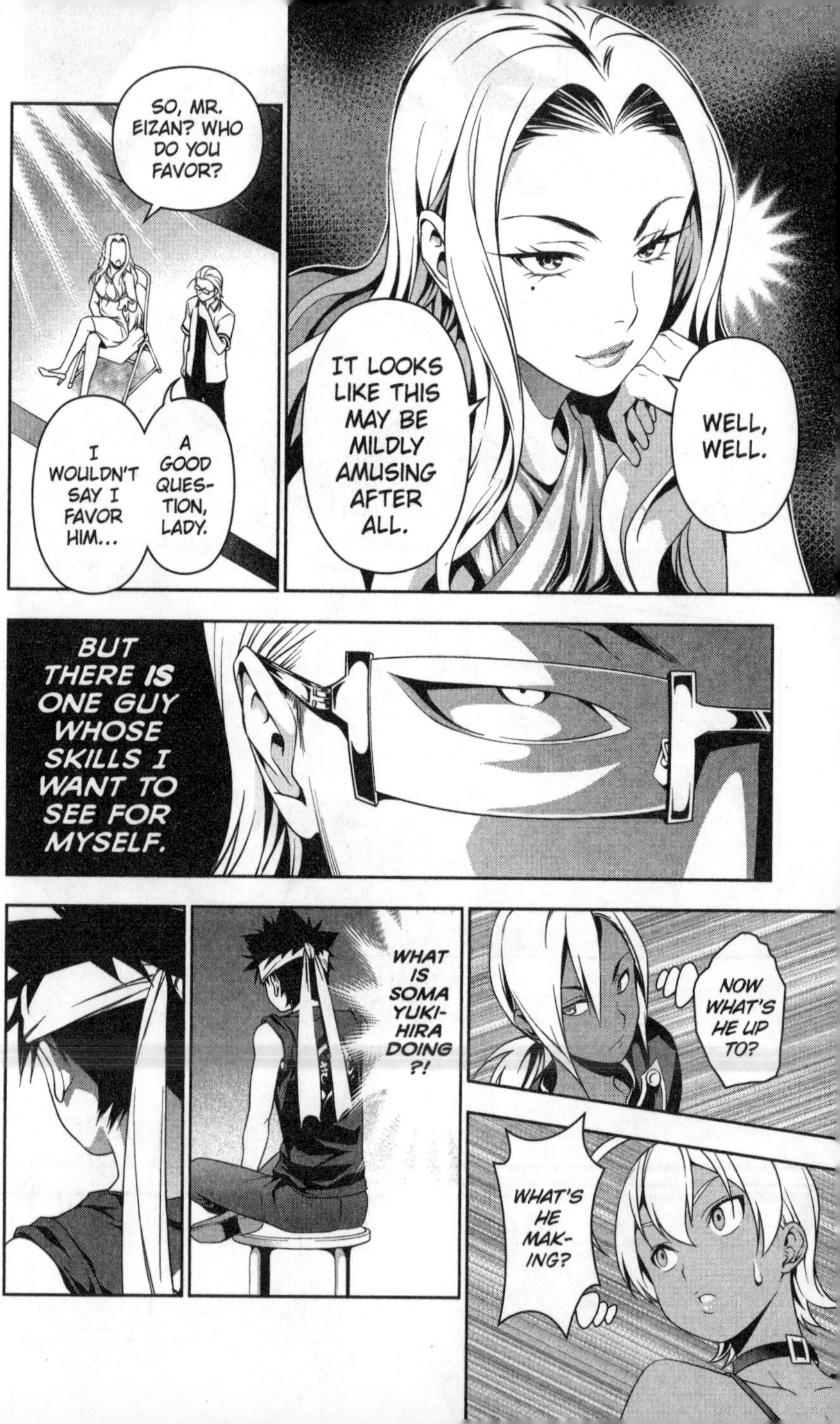
WELL, WELL.
IT LOOKS LIKE THIS MAY BE MILDLY AMUSING AFTER ALL.
SO, MR. EIZAN? WHO DO YOU FAVOR?
A GOOD QUES-TION, LADY.
I WOULDN'T SAY I FAVOR HIM...
BUT THERE IS ONE GUY WHOSE SKILLS I WANT TO SEE FOR MYSELF.
NOW WHAT'S HE UP TO?
WHAT'S HE MAK-ING?
WHAT IS SOMA YUKI-HIRA DOING ?!

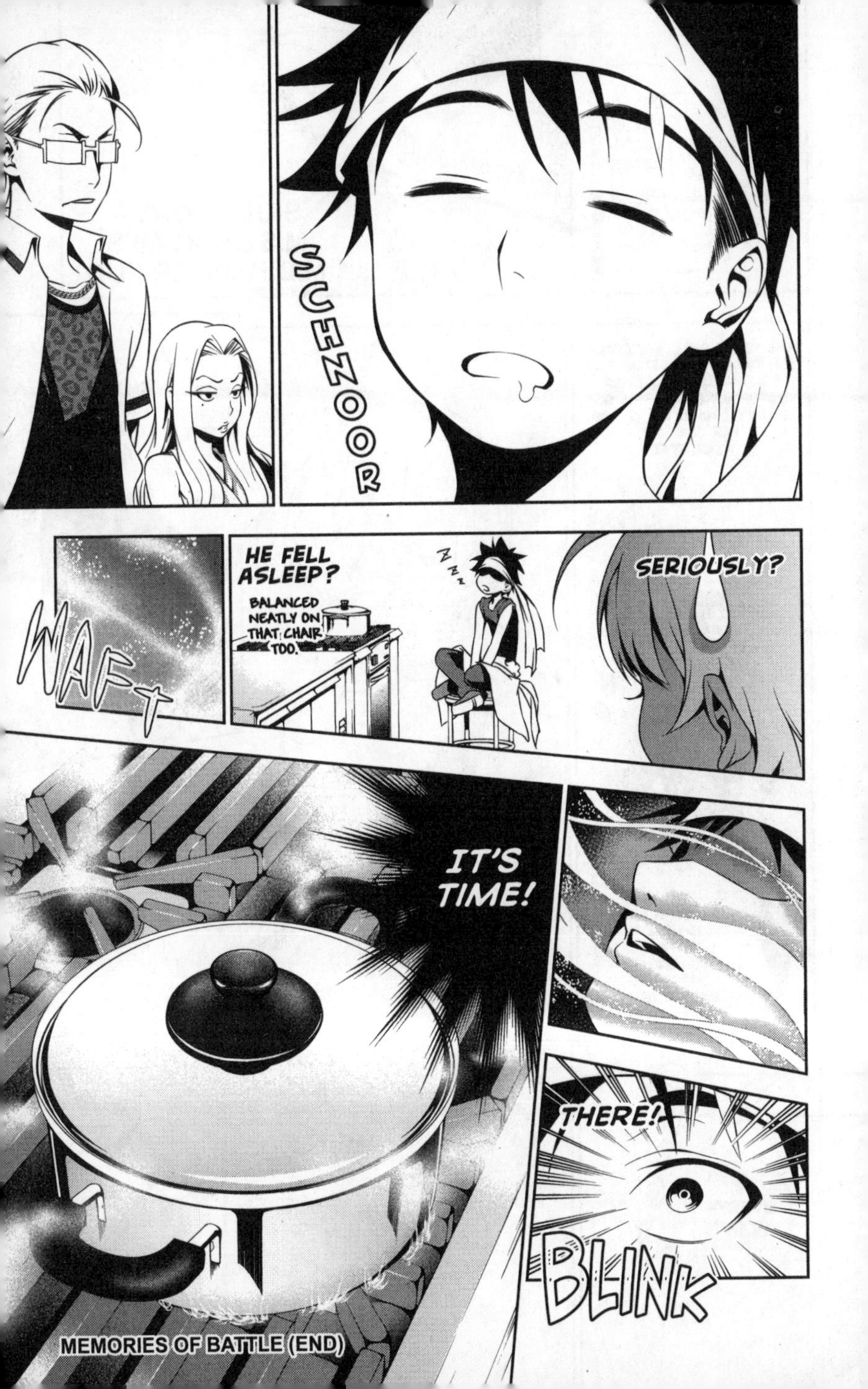
SCHNOOR
SERIOUSLY?
HE FELL ASLEEP?
BALANCED NEATLY ON THAT CHAIR TOO.
WAFT
THERE!
BLINK
IT'S TIME!

MEMORIES OF BATTLE (END)

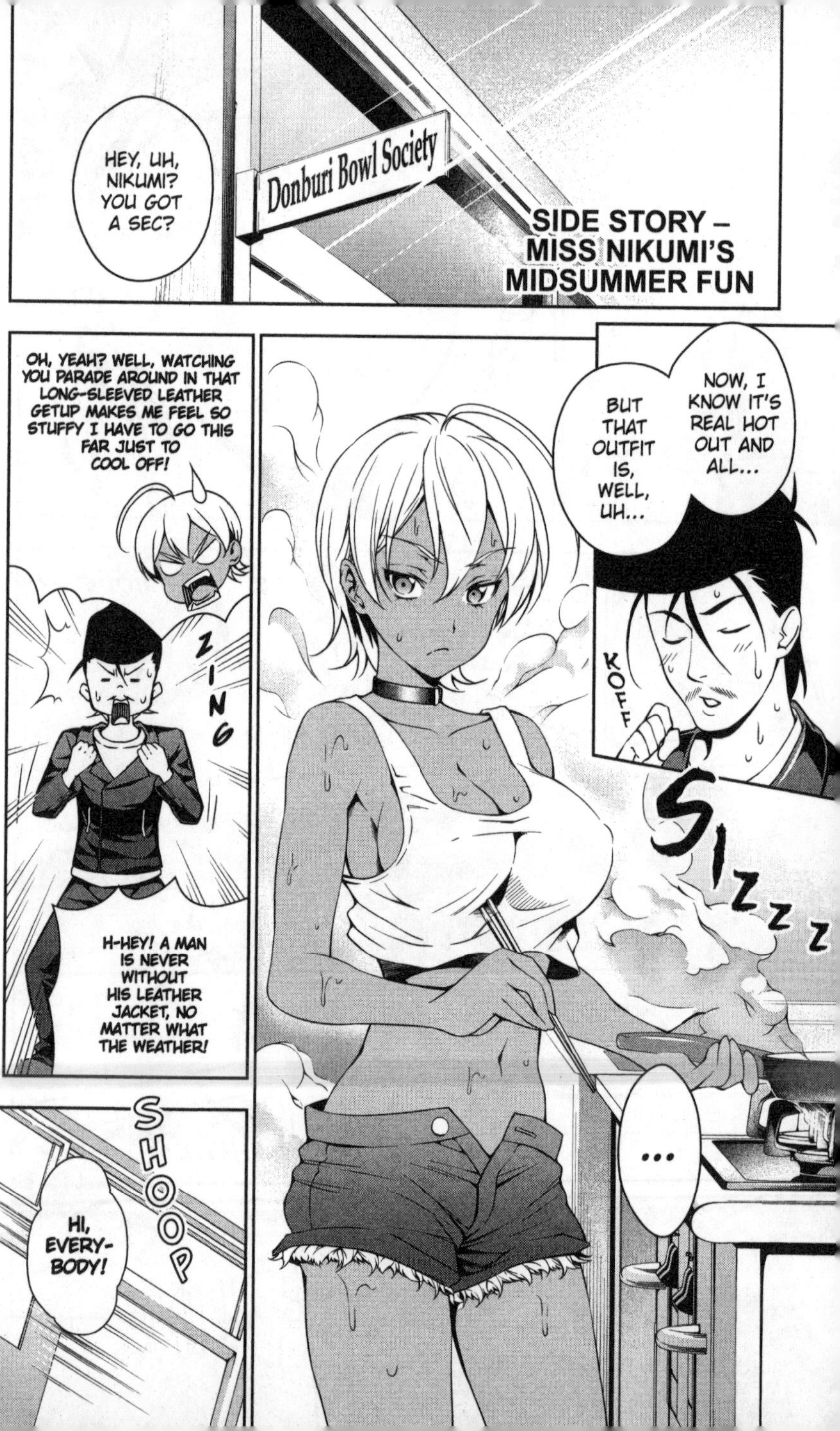
SIDE STORY – MISS NIKUMI'S MIDSUMMER FUN
Donburi Bowl Society
HEY, UH, NIKUMI? YOU GOT A SEC?
NOW, I KNOW IT'S REAL HOT OUT AND ALL...
BUT THAT OUTFIT IS, WELL, UH...
KOFF
SIZZZZ
...
OH, YEAH? WELL, WATCHING YOU PARADE AROUND IN THAT LONG-SLEEVED LEATHER GETUP MAKES ME FEEL SO STUFFY I HAVE TO GO THIS FAR JUST TO COOL OFF!
ZING
H-HEY! A MAN IS NEVER WITHOUT HIS LEATHER JACKET, NO MATTER WHAT THE WEATHER!
SHOOP
HI, EVERY-BODY!

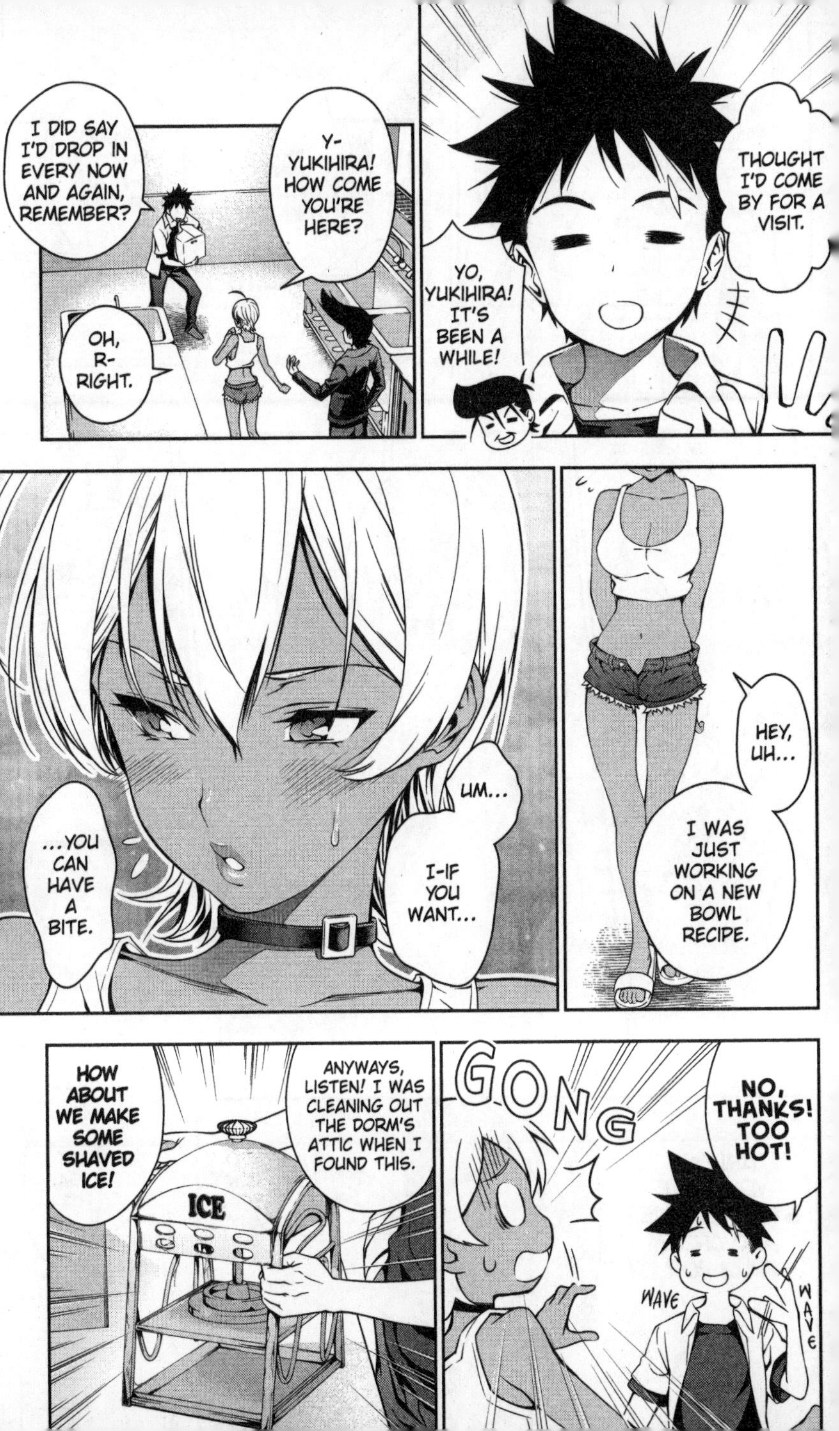
THOUGHT I'D COME BY FOR A VISIT.
YO, YUKIHIRA! IT'S BEEN A WHILE!
Y-YUKIHIRA! HOW COME YOU'RE HERE?
I DID SAY I'D DROP IN EVERY NOW AND AGAIN, REMEMBER?
OH, R-RIGHT.
HEY, UH...
I WAS JUST WORKING ON A NEW BOWL RECIPE.
UM...
I-IF YOU WANT...
...YOU CAN HAVE A BITE.
GONG
NO, THANKS! TOO HOT!
WAVE
WAVE
ANYWAYS, LISTEN! I WAS CLEANING OUT THE DORM'S ATTIC WHEN I FOUND THIS.
HOW ABOUT WE MAKE SOME SHAVED ICE!
ICE

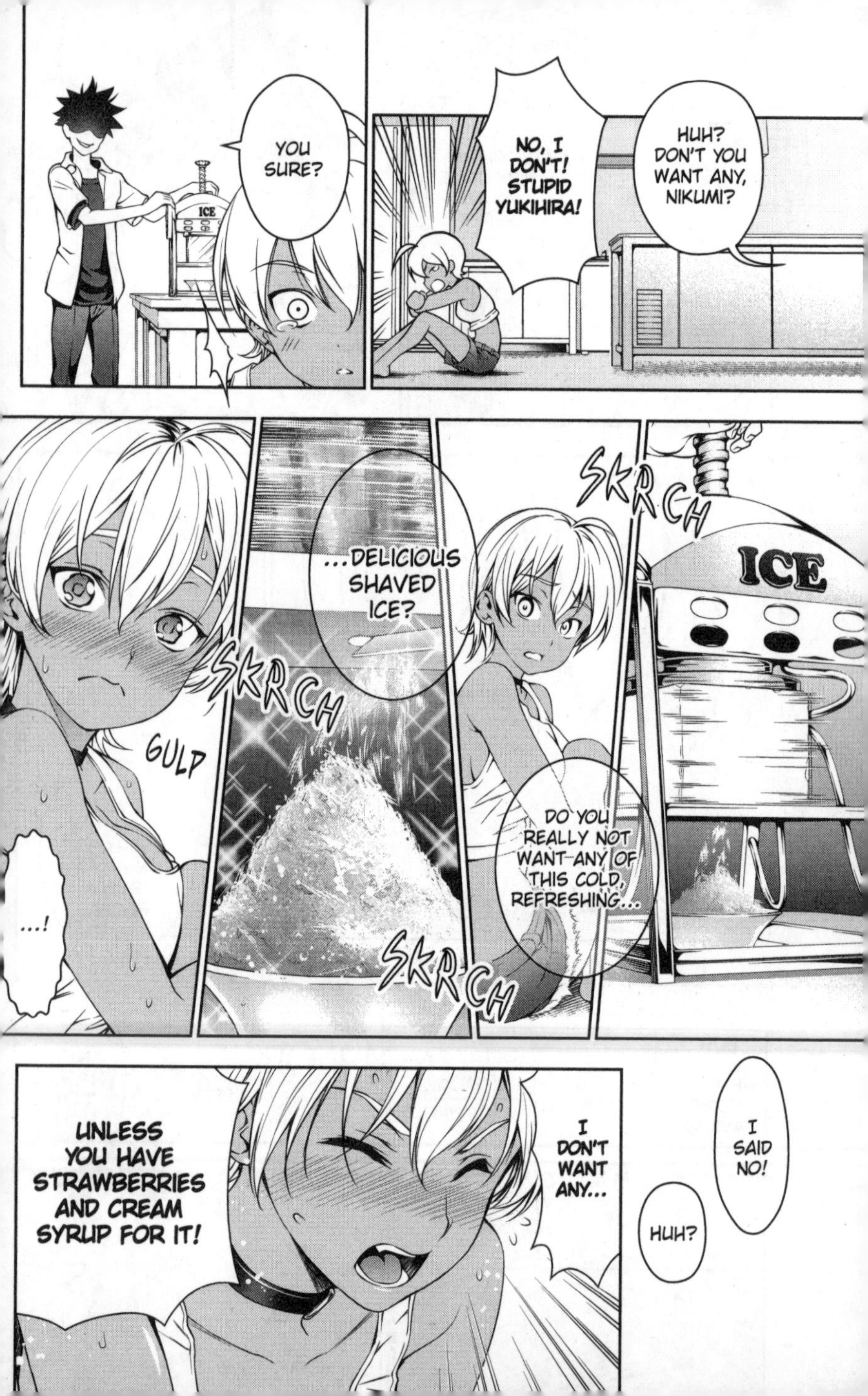
HUH? DON'T YOU WANT ANY, NIKUMI?
NO, I DON'T! STUPID YUKIHIRA!
ICE
YOU SURE?
SKRCH
ICE
DO YOU REALLY NOT WANT ANY OF THIS COLD, REFRESHING...
...DELICIOUS SHAVED ICE?
SKRCH
SKRCH
GULP
...!
I SAID NO!
HUH?
I DON'T WANT ANY...
UNLESS YOU HAVE STRAWBERRIES AND CREAM SYRUP FOR IT!

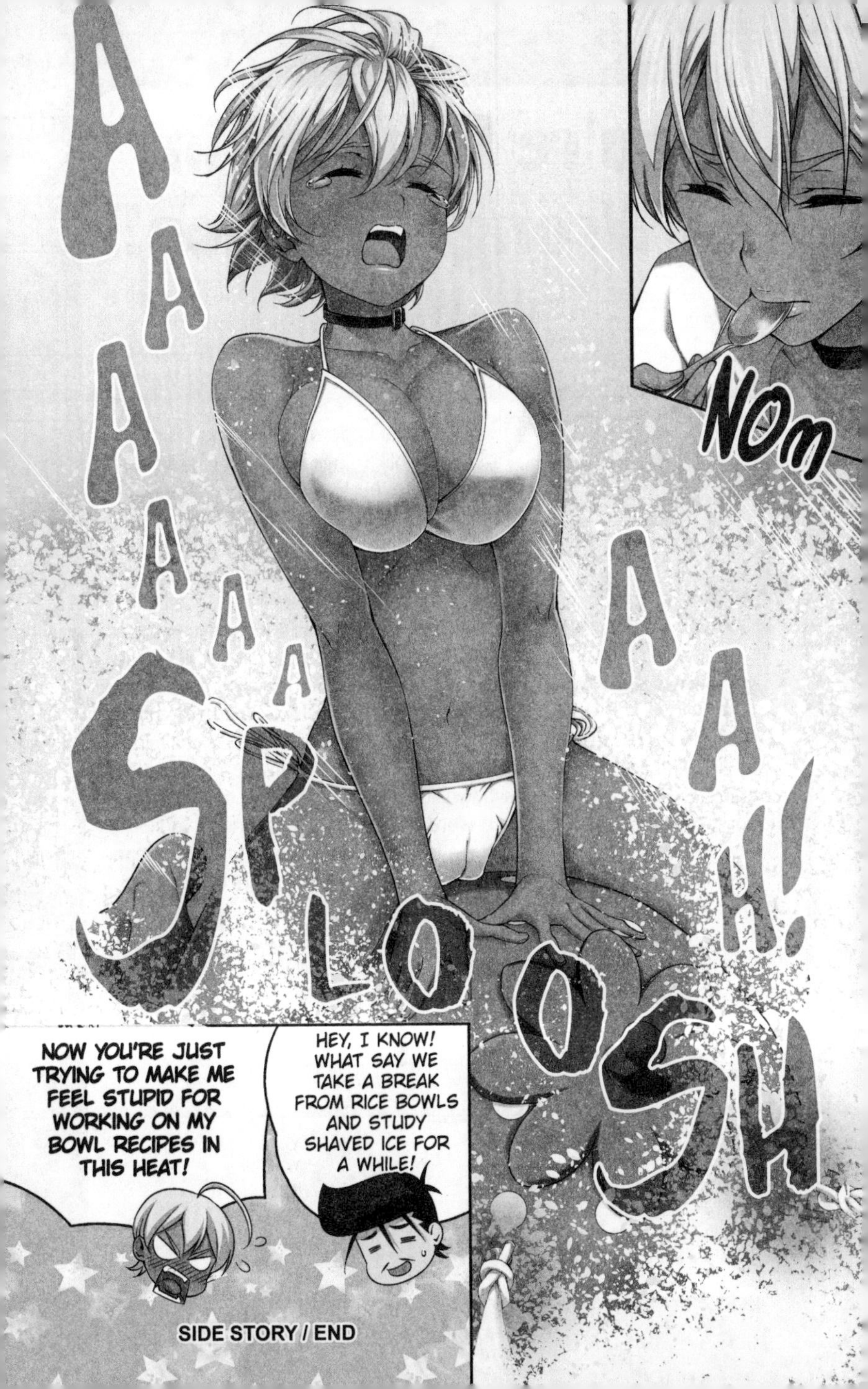
NOM
AAAAAAAAAH!
SPLOOOSH
HEY, I KNOW! WHAT SAY WE TAKE A BREAK FROM RICE BOWLS AND STUDY SHAVED ICE FOR A WHILE!
NOW YOU'RE JUST TRYING TO MAKE ME FEEL STUPID FOR WORKING ON MY BOWL RECIPES IN THIS HEAT!
SIDE STORY / END

You're Reading in the Wrong Direction!!

1
2
3
1
2
3
4
5
6

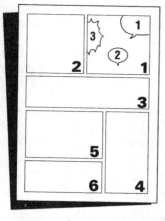

Whoops! Guess what? You're starting at the wrong end of the comic!

...It's true! In keeping with the original Japanese format, **Food Wars!** is meant to be read from right to left, starting in the upper-right corner.

Unlike English, which is read from left to right, Japanese is read from right to left, meaning that action, sound effects and word-balloon order are completely reversed... something which can make readers unfamiliar with Japanese feel pretty backwards themselves. For this reason, manga or Japanese comics published in the U.S. in English have sometimes been published "flopped"—that is, printed in exact reverse order, as though seen from the other side of a mirror.

By flopping pages, U.S. publishers can avoid confusing readers, but the compromise is not without its downside. For one thing, a character in a flopped manga series who once wore in the original Japanese version a T-shirt emblazoned with "M A Y" (as in "the merry month of") now wears one which reads "Y A M"! Additionally, many manga creators in Japan are themselves unhappy with the process, as some feel the mirror-imaging of their art skews their original intentions.

We are proud to bring you Yuto Tsukuda and Shun Saeki's **Food Wars!** in the original unflopped format.

For now, though, turn to the other side of the book and let the adventure begin...!

—Editor

HAYAMA, I'M SORRY. I FORGOT IT WAS MY TURN TO WATER AGAIN.
A-ARE YOU MAD?
NO, I'M NOT MAD.
PEEK
I-I'M SORRY!
SHHHH

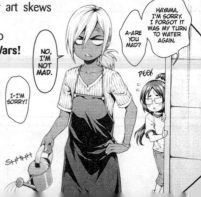